Captain Teach, commonly called Blackbeard

Captain Bartholomew Roberts

Pirates and Privateers
of the Caribbean

Pirates and Privateers of the Caribbean

By
Jenifer Marx

KRIEGER PUBLISHING COMPANY
MALABAR, FLORIDA
1992

Original Edition 1992

Printed and Published by
KRIEGER PUBLISHING COMPANY
KRIEGER DRIVE
MALABAR, FLORIDA 32950

Library of Congress Cataloging-in-Publication Data
Marx, Jenifer.
    Pirates and privateers of the Caribbean/by Jenifer Marx.
        p.   cm.
    Includes bibliographical references and index.
    ISBN 0-89464-483-1 (acid-free paper) (cloth)
    ISBN 0-89464-633-8 (paperback)
        1. Pirates—Caribbean Area—History.   2. Buccaneers—History.
    3. Spanish Main.   4. Caribbean Area—History—To 1810.   I. Title.
    F2161.M37   1992
    972.9—dc20   90-5095
                                                                       CIP

10 9 8 7 6 5 4 3 2

Contents

With gratitude and affection,
this book is dedicated
to
James Dawson

These men were of that breed of rovers
whose port lay always a little further on.
If they lived riotously, let it be argued
in their favor that at least they lived. . .
We think them terrible. Life itself is terrible.
But it was not so terrible to them; for they were comrades,
with the strength to live their own lives.
They may laugh at those who condemn
with the hate of impotence.

John Masefield
On the Spanish Main

Preface

I can't remember not being fascinated by pirates. One of my earliest memories is listening to my father reading Robert Louis Stevenson's *Treasure Island* to me and my brothers. He also read us Washington Irving's *The Guests from Gibbet Island* and a riveting book about Spanish treasure and pirates called *Pieces of Eight*. It was laid in the Bahamas where his mother's family was from and we felt a special connection with the story. My brothers and I were sure that somewhere among our ancestors on those palm-fringed islands there had been at least one swashbuckling pirate. Thanks to a volume of the dramatic pirate paintings of Howard Pyle, the American illustrator, we knew exactly what this archetypal forefather looked like.

Despite parental denials, we were convinced that a treasure he had buried awaited us on one of those tropic isles. However, as much as we longed to mount an expedition and sail over the bounding main, we had to be content with turning a curving staircase into a pirate ship. With sheets knotted to the banisters as slightly less than billowing sails and stuffed animals as pirate crew, our "ship" ventured far and wide on the sea of imagination.

Many years later I lived on Jamaica where I met my husband, Robert Marx, an underwater archaeologist who was excavating the pirate city of Port Royal which sunk in an earthquake and tidal wave in 1692. Bob has recovered sunken treasures from many shipwrecked Spanish galleons whose histories he has hunted down in government, ecclesiastical and private archives from Seville to the Vatican to Manila.

He introduced me to the addictive pleasures of archival sleuthing and together we have spent countless hours and contented days in archives around the world, poring over faded manuscripts which bring the past to vivid life.

My interest in pirates was renewed by the project at Port Royal and I decided to write a book about seaborne outlaws. As I researched the annals of piracy in the Caribbean, I discovered that historical fact is generally far more fascinating than the cliches of pirate lore perpetuated by most writers of fiction and Hollywood filmakers who ignore the complexities of historical context. For the record, however, I'd like to state that I relish pirate movies and never miss a rerun of *The Sea Hawk* or *A High Wind in Jamaica* on television.

I owe special thanks to my husband for his constant support. I appreciate the continuing encouragement of my editor and fellow pirate-movie fan, Elaine Rudd, whose devotion to clarity of expression is tempered with a delightful sense of humor.

In preparing this book, I researched material in the following archives and libraries whose staff members were unfailingly helpful. I am grateful also to the staffs of the Melbourne Library and the Satellite Beach Library in Brevard County, Florida for their assistance.

England

British Museum, London
National Maritime Museum, Greenwich
Public Records Office, London

France

Bibliothéque Nationale, Paris

Italy

Vatican Archives, Rome

Spain

Archivo Historico de la Marina, Viso del Marques
Archivo de las Indias, Seville.
Biblioteca Nacional, Madrid.
Museo Naval, Madrid

United States

Library of Congress, Washington D.C.
Clements Library, University of Michigan, Ann Arbor.
New York Public Library, New York City.
Huntington Library, San Marino, CA.

Introduction

"There was never a time," wrote Dio Cassius in the first century A.D., "when piracy was not practiced. Nor," he added, "may it cease to be so long as the nature of mankind remains the same." The Roman historian wrote during a period when shipping in the Mediterranean, the Red Sea and the Indian Ocean was plagued by bold pirates whose ancestors had preyed upon the earliest seaborne traffic. Time has supported Cassius's remark for sea robbers have been a universal menace of varying degree from ancient times until the present. Several eras stand out in the pirate annals of battles, boardings and booty. The history of piracy in the seas around Europe, Asia and Africa, which is beyond the scope of this book, is filled with intriguing tales. But the most spectacular pirate epoch of all dawned with the discovery of a rich New World the ancients never dreamed of.

From 1492 until the nineteenth century, the Caribbean was the focus of intense pirate activity. No ship was safe on the clear tropical sea. No settlement on the shores of the coral-girt islands or along the Spanish Main could relax its vigilance against the sea marauders who plundered at sea and on land with equal zeal. The Caribbean is studded with countless cays and islands whose nooks and crannies were breeding grounds for the sinister forces. Whether they were outlaw pirates, buccaneer "Brethren of the Coast" or privateers carrying letters of marque, which made them legitimate in the eyes of the issuing authority, mattered little to the Spaniards. They were all *piratas* and *diablos* to the Spanish Crown and the suffering colonists. The French, Dutch and English suffered too as they fought the Spaniards and each other in the scramble for a place in the golden sun.

Piracy was a significant factor in shaping the history of the Caribbean area and the stunning exploits of its practitioners make a fascinating study. Most of the pirates we are familiar with were members of an international fraternity which operated during the Golden Age of piracy between 1692 and 1725; however, pirate activity began far earlier. Columbus, sailing for the Spanish rulers Ferdinand and Isabella, encountered a French pirate ship on his first voyage of discovery. During his third voyage he changed course to avoid a fleet of French corsairs.

Pirate activity was sporadic and isolated until 1522 when Verrazano,

a Florentine privateer in the service of the King of France, seized three
Spanish ships. One was laden with hides, sugar and pearls from Hispaniola, and two were filled with Aztec treasure which Cortés and his conquistadores collected and were sending to the royal court of Spain. Instead
the Mexican treasures dazzled the French court. Francis I exclaimed:
"Why the Emperor Charles V can carry on the war against me by means
of the riches he draws from the Indies alone!" Benvenuto Cellini, the
greatest of Renaissance goldsmiths, was at the French court and marvelled
at the exquisite workmanship of the Aztec treasures, saying he had never
seen such genius. Soon, all of Europe coveted the riches that began to pour
into Spain from the New World which had been bestowed upon Spain
and Portugal by papal decree.

The Borgia Pope, Spanish-born Alexander VI, had been prevailed upon
by King Ferdinand to issue a papal decree in 1493, effectively dividing
the New World between Spain and Portugal. A year later the two nations
signed the Treaty of Tordesillas reaffirming the papal division but shifting
the line of demarcation which ran from Pole to Pole to 370 leagues west
of the Cape Verde Islands. Portugal, which had already claimed much of
the eastern trade in spices, was granted dominion over Brazil, while Spain
had the Pope's blessing for its claims to the rest of the New World.

France and England rejected the treaty and sent out their own expeditions to stake a claim in the world beyond the line. "The sun shines for
me as for others," said King Francis. "I should like to see the clause in
Adam's will that excludes me from a share in the world." The race was
on. During the centuries following Columbus, European maritime nations
vied for control of newly discovered lands and their riches. Sea raiders of
every nationality, color and creed infested the sea-lanes preying on shipping and sacking coastal settlements in the Caribbean and along the
coastal regions of Central America known as the Spanish Main. The pirates and privateers of the Spanish Main were far more than a thorn in
the side of Spain, which unwisely based its national economy on the plundered wealth of the New World. They jeopardized the economic security
of several European maritime nations and were a catalyst in the development of international trading and maritime law. They also stimulated
the transformation of national naval forces from small defense oriented
fleets to powerful navies capable of spearheading colonial expansion.
Ironically, with the development of effective navies, privateers were no
longer essential or even desirable.

Protestant Holland joined France and England in contesting the Iberian
New World monopoly. Foreign ambassadors and spies of the great merchant banking houses of Europe scrutinized and assessed the rivers of
gold, silver, pearls and emeralds unloaded from the treasure galleons at

Seville. The treasure was seen as fuel for Catholic military might which had to be crushed. The bitter European religious wars loomed and nationalism was on the rise. The Caribbean, often called the Spanish lake, became the watery arena in which the European powers pitted their expansionist forces against one another, spurred on by a mirage of gleaming treasure.

Today it is difficult to conceive of the importance of the Caribbean area during those centuries. Wars were waged throughout Europe over the islands of the West Indies and the Central American coast. Pirates and privateers played a leading role in the geopolitical drama that lasted for some three centuries. They prowled the seas preying on silver-laden galleons, merchantmen and slavers. They nibbled at Spanish claims and ravaged settlements along the Spanish Main and in the West Indies. Colonial cities were held for ransom or razed in orgies of looting. Sir Francis Drake, Elizabethan adventurer par excellence, is still recalled as "El Draque," the Dragon, on the coasts where he plundered in the name of his queen. A century later Henry Morgan's marauding inflicted such terror on Spain's dominions that even now island children shiver at his name.

The wars between Charles VI and Francis I gave French pirates from Dieppe and La Rochelle the impetus to be the first to poach on the Spanish preserve. Initially French corsairs, many of them Protestant Huguenots, predominated in the region. By 1550 they had pillaged every significant Spanish coastal settlement and found Havana so poorly defended that one pirate ship was able to ransom the city. In the 1560s they made ill-fated efforts to establish bases on the northern coast of Florida. Later French pirates were called *boucaniers* (buccaneers) after the semi-savage French hunters who roamed Hispaniola, smoking meat on wooden grills called *boucans*. Eventually pirates were interchangeably called buccaneers or freebooters without regard to nationality.

The New World's mineral wealth also attracted Dutch sea rovers (*Zee-Roovers*) whose prowess made up for their small numbers. They were called sea beggars for the "Beggars of the Sea," a guerrilla group of Protestant seamen from the Northern Provinces of Holland and Zeeland who were among the first to rise against Philip II at the outbreak of the Revolt of the Netherlands in 1568. The Dutch were also called freebooters by the English from the Dutch *vrijbuiter*, meaning plunderer or pirate from the two words for free and booty. In an interesting sequence the French corrupted the English freebooter into *flibustier* which came back into English as filibuster; that is, an adventurer who wages war on a country his own country is at peace with. An alternative derivation for *flibustier* traces the word to the Dutch *vlieboot*, or fly boat, a fast shallow-bottomed boat.

Shifting national alliances fostered opportunities for armed merchant ships operating under privateering contracts from the maritime countries. Even when there was official peace in Europe, Protestant governments winked an eye at attacks beyond the line. During the Counter-Reformation religious fervor coupled with nationalistic sentiment unleashed a horde of marauding privateers into the Spanish lake. During the course of the sixteenth century English pirates flocked to the region in increasing numbers. Spain's refusal to allow outside participation in New World opportunities came at a time of burgeoning commercial activity in Europe. England's Queen Elizabeth lent royal patronage to plundering expeditions against the ships and settlements of her arch-enemy Philip II. Sir Francis Drake, one of the first and one of the greatest of the English plunderers, was dubbed by Elizabeth, "mine own pyrate," and sailed with her sanction. Drake had her financial backing too. Elizabeth furnished cash and vessels for his 1585–6 Caribbean expedition. Drake's sack of Cartagena and Santo Domingo, which were regarded as acts of war by Spain, precipitated the Spanish Armada.

From 1550 to the early nineteenth-century adventurers from all over the globe were drawn to the Caribbean and the Spanish Main in pursuit of plunder and the line between piracy and privateering was blurred more often than not. The Spanish had their own share of pirates which increased as other nations established settlements in the New World and sent ships to supply them, providing tempting quarry. By the late 1600s Greeks, Slavs, Corsicans and Italians joined the outlaw ranks. So did mulattoes, indentured servants, and transported felons from English colonies, particularly Jamaica, where the pirate loot which poured into Port Royal inflamed everyone's cupidity. Runaway slaves sometimes signed on pirate vessels. Slaves captured when a ship was seized were often invited to join the pirate ranks, although whole human cargoes of slaving ships were considered merchandise and disposed of accordingly.

Privateers, who operated under "no prey, no pay" were in effect legally sanctioned pirates. By law they were restricted to attacking enemy shipping and installations. Licensed privateers were required by the British Admiralty to put large sums, up to several thousand pounds sterling, in escrow before setting out to insure they would not commit acts of piracy. In reality privateers were often uncontrollable, their actions indistinguishable from outright piracy. Sometimes scale made the difference. Sir Walter Raleigh, old and obsessed, was released from imprisonment in the Tower by the Stuart king, James I, to lead an expedition to the Orinoco in search of the fabled gold mine at Manoa. The doomed adventurer was asked by Sir Francis Bacon what he would do if he failed to find the mine. Raleigh indicated he could then gain gold aplenty from Spain's treasure ships or in her ports. To Bacon's remark that James I forbade piracy, Raleigh scoffed "Did you ever know any that were pirates for millions? They only that work for small things are pirates."

Depending on the political climate men sailed as outright pirates or as privateers with genuine or forged letters of marque. Colonial officials were bribed to issue privateering commissions. But whatever they called themselves: privateer, pirate, buccaneer, corsair, freebooter, or flibustier the Spanish crown regarded all foreign seamen on the Spanish Main as *piratas*, loathsome interlopers. This book will examine what was the longest, most intense outbreak of piracy in history. It was global in nature and lasted from the early 1500s until the early 1800s. The pirates of the Spanish Main were united in their lust for booty and their hatred of Spain which controlled vast areas of the new world. Relying on stealth, trickery and terror they stalked their prey from Nova Scotia to Brazil and from the shores of the Americas to the malarial coast of Africa.

The pirates swarmed out of strongholds like Tortuga and Nassau in the Northern Hemisphere and Madagascar in the Indian Ocean scouring hundreds of thousands of square miles of ocean. The choice prey of the West Indies pirates was the Spanish galleon laden with gold and silver from Central and South America and precious gems, silks, drugs, spices, and porcelains from Asia and India which had been transported via Manila galleons across the Pacific to Acapulco and thence by mule train to Vera Cruz to be loaded onto the lumbering galleons en route to Seville.

The pirates raped and pillaged ashore as well, plundering outposts and ports—once even raiding a Spanish salvage camp on the coast of Florida where salvors had amassed a fortune in gold, silver and emeralds from the galleons of the 1715 treasure fleet which wrecked south of Cape Canaveral in a hurricane.

During the Golden Age of Piracy they preyed on the increasing volume of mercantile traffic between England and the American colonies. In 1717 James Logan, colonial secretary of Pennsylvania, estimated there were about fifteen hundred pirates lying in wait off the North America coast. The pirates weren't the only scoundrels. There was no shortage of dealers and clandestine markets where pirate prizes could be sold. The very officials charged with suppressing the pirates were often in on their deals for a "commission." The governor of North Carolina was in cahoots with Blackbeard and the governor of New York was in Captain Kidd's control for a while. The prosperity of the international pirate mart Port Royal, the "wickedest city in the world" depended on the collusion of Jamaican officials including the infamous Henry Morgan who served as lieutenant governor.

On occasion the sea wolves changed the course of history. A Dutch

anthem commemorates the privateer Piet Heyn, the only man to successfully capture an entire Spanish treasure fleet. He brought in enough gold
and silver to the government coffers that with loot from other Dutch
privateers, Holland was able to wrest its independence from Spain. Pirates
and privateers were responsible for the discovery of new lands and islands
around the globe. William Dampier, a British pirate who harried shipping
of all nations throughout the Indian and Pacific oceans, became one of
the most famous cartographers. He circled the globe twice and helped
map Australia and other parts of the Pacific.

The pirate has always exerted a fascination. He exudes a perverse
glamor. He is an outsider who refuses to play by society's rules. Often the
pirate's life, as portrayed in fiction and films arouses envy. Even today,
perhaps especially now in this age of pervasive technology and entangling
bureaucracy, people are enthralled by pirate stories. The pirate symbolizes
freedom from the constraints that harness most of us to routine lives. In
spite of his crudeness, the pirate appeals to something buried in our
psyches—the fantasy of sailing for distant horizons in quest of gold and
glory, heedless of the rules and ever hopeful.

Blackbeard, Captain Kidd, Henry Morgan, Montbars the Exterminator . . . they are names to conjure with and through the years so much
conjuring has been done that pirate mythology has obscured a far more
fascinating reality. Who were these larger than life sea raiders whose
images are etched in the popular mind? Where were they from and what
led them to the "sweet trade"? What was life like "on the account," and
what effect did pirates and privateers of the Spanish Main have on the
maritime nations whose fleets and colonial settlements they preyed on?

The romantic tradition which has shaped our vision of the Caribbean
pirate as a weather-beaten swaggerer with gold hoops in his ears, a pistol
tucked in his crimson sash and a gleaming cutlass in hand is not far from
the mark. In a memoir (a surprising number of sea rovers wrote of their
adventures) a seventeenth-century French buccaneer described his appearance as he disembarked to lead an attack on Caracas in Venezuela:
"I marched in front, as was right, with my pistols in my belt, my fine
deep boots and plumed hat, and a sword at my side."

His name was Louis Le Golif but he was better known as Borgne-Fesse,
or Half-Ass, since a cannon ball had deprived him of one buttock. Assumed names were preferred among the "Brethren of the Coast" as the
buccaneers called themselves. For three centuries the Caribbean was the
western frontier of Europe and like the wild west of the nineteenth century, the area attracted men of every ilk including those who wanted to
forge new identities. Seamen fleeing brutal and inequitable conditions in
the British navy, fugitive servants, escaped convicts, impoverished nobles,

unemployed veterans, and other restless souls gravitated to the uncertain life of the sea rover, risking "hempen fever" (the gallows) for the promise of booty and, just as important for many of them, the taste of individual liberty. For the most part they were French, Dutch and English. But there were among them Portuguese, Greeks, Germans, Africans and American Indians. Many men from the Thirteen Colonies went "on the account" in the years of the great "Pirate Round" sailing across the Atlantic, around the tip of Africa to the Eastern Seas and back.

With their bold and often bloody deeds the pirates and privateers of the Caribbean upset the equilibrium of Spanish and Portuguese rule, allowing other nations to gain a foothold in the Western Hemisphere. Piracy was a potent weapon, very much a part of imperialist policies. Spain's enemies pursued a three pronged attack in an attempt to dislodge her from her vast American empire. They sanctioned piracy in the form of privateering and tolerated outlaw pirates until they became too outrageous. Following Sir John Hawkins's slaving expeditions of 1562 and 1564 on which he profitably traded Africans for hides, gold and sugar, it was apparent there was a hole in the Spanish dike. English, French and especially Dutch privateers developed a lively contraband trade with the Spanish colonies, much to the fury of the Spanish government, and eventually established their own colonies in the islands and on the Main, the coast of Central and South America.

The treaty of Cateau-Cambresis signed by France and Spain in 1559 sanctioned an endemic state of nondeclared war which prevailed for centuries. "No peace beyond the line" was a treaty phrase which set the tone of tolerating hostilities west of the Azores. English privateers, Dutch zee-roovers, French corsairs and buccaneers, joined by seafaring adventurers of every nation subscribed to Queen Elizabeth's doctrine of Freedom of the Seas. "The use of the sea and air is common to all; neither can any title to the ocean belong to any people or private man." The daring exploits of the colorful pirates who roved the Caribbean furnished the stuff for countless novels, ballads and boyish dreams.

Generations of poets, playwrights and novelists have mined two particularly rich veins of Caribbean pirate lore. A. O. Exquemelin's *History of the Buccaneers of America* and Captain Johnson's *General History of the Robberies and Murders of the Most Notorious Pyrates* are beacons of pirate history. Both chronicle actual events and were written by men with first hand knowledge. Exquemelin's book deals with the buccaneer period in the seventeenth century whose most eminent figures were Pierre le Grand, Francois L'Ollonais, Henry Morgan, the Sieur de Grammont, Bartholomew Sharp and William Dampier. Captain Johnson's work chronicles the so-called "Golden Age" of Caribbean piracy which had two phases: the decade before 1700 when men like Thomas Tew, "Long Ben" Avery and Captain Kidd sailed the Pirate Round, a regular pirate route between the Indian Ocean and the North American seaboard, and the first quarter of the eighteenth century. This latter period furnished the most notorious and colorful of all pirate characters including Blackbeard, Bart Roberts, "Calico Jack" Rackham and the notorious female pirates, Mary Read and Anne Bonny.

Until recently the identity of Alexandre Olivier Exquemelin, (Esquemelin or Esquemeling as he is called in English), was a mystery. For years his writings were considered largely fictional but in fact, Esquemelin was a French Huguenot who went to the Caribbean in 1666 as an indentured servant with the French West India Company. He spent three years on the buccaneer stronghold of Tortuga Island and sailed with the pirates for five years as a barber-surgeon. Eventually he retired to Holland where, as a Protestant, he felt comfortable. His sparkling narrative combines eyewitness accounts of buccaneer derring-do with a dollop of exaggeration. In spite of historical inaccuracies *The Buccaneers of America* remains the most valuable record of seventeenth-century Caribbean piracy.

A number of sea rovers wrote fascinating, detailed accounts of their exotic landfalls and piratical adventures. Europe in the late seventeenth century was intrigued with scientific inquiry and lionized literary pirates like William Dampier and Lionel Wafer, darlings of the newly formed Royal Society in London. Their works along with those of Bartholomew Sharp and Basil Ringrose were among the first volumes in the British Museum Library and contributed to early knowledge of New World anthropology, geography, zoology and oceanography.

Esquemelin's book was first published in Amsterdam in 1678. It became an overnight bestseller and was issued in German, Spanish, French and English. The text of each edition was slanted to appeal to the chauvinistic prejudices of its readers. Morgan, for example, appears as the arch-demon in the Spanish edition and a protestant avenger in the English. Not surprisingly Morgan was unhappy with the way Exquemelin painted him as the most debauched and barbarous of a generally rough breed. He was so incensed at Exquemelin's eyewitness report of the sack of Portobelo that he sued the British publisher for "many False, Scandalous and Malicious Reflections." And he collected, because in English eyes he was a hero.

As the world developed and trade expanded piracy became a global affair with pirates operating in more than one area. In 1722 the last mass hanging of pirates took place signaling the end of piracy's Golden Age and the decline of large scale sea robbery. The British Admiralty tried 169 pirates at Cape Coast Castle on the Guinea Coast. Seventy-four were acquitted on grounds of having been forced into service, including musicians. Seventeen were sent to prison in London of whom all but four died on the long voyage. Twenty were sentenced to seven years' convict labor in the Royal Africa Company's Gold Coast mines, a slow death that claimed them all. Two men, sentenced to death, were reprieved but fifty-two others ranging in age from nineteen to forty-five were hanged in batches over a two-week period. As an example to others, the cadavers of eighteen of the most villainous were coated with tar, wrapped with metal bands and strung on chains. Their rotted, sun-dried bodies swinging from gibbets placed on hills overlooking the harbor presaged the demise of piracy's Golden Age with its stylish heroes who became legends in their own time.

In 1724 *A General History of the Robberies and Murders of the Most Notorious Pyrates* was published under the name of Captain Charles Johnson. The book recounted the misadventures and few stunning successes of the giants of piracy's Golden Age and was the literary event of the season, containing a rare wealth of information based on firsthand documents, gallows confessions and Admiralty trials. A second volume came out four years later. The authorship of these complex chronicles which are overlaid with the moralizing tone of the day was in dispute for a long time until it was proved that they were the work of Daniel Defoe, the prolific English author who wrote *Robinson Crusoe* and *Captain Singleton*. Defoe aimed at a public both fascinated and repelled by the outlaws who participated in the greatest rash of piracy ever known, plundering glittering prizes around the world, setting up pirate fiefdoms in the Bahamas and turning the Caribbean into a pirate sea. Defoe details the excesses of his "lewd and blasphemous" subjects. They were after all social anarchists who threatened bourgeois morality and order, but his subjects are treated in such a way that they become real and compelling.

Pirates were cutthroats and they were vengeful. They were outlaws who scorned civilized society and its laws. Yet they were passionate about their individual liberty and practiced a system of pirate democracy which offered a far better life than most had known before. Contrary to popular belief pirates were almost never the wayward sons of aristocrats in search of adventure.

They were ordinary seamen, most of whom had gone to sea as boys in an era when a man's fate was determined by the circumstances of his birth rather than by his abilities. Piracy offered an escape from the harsh discipline of naval ships and merchant vessels where a captain had the power of life and death over his men and brutal punishment was meted out on the whim of sadistic officers. The vast majority of those who joined the pirate ranks were naval deserters or mutineers or seamen who volunteered when their ship was captured, grateful to escape brutality. They were risk takers. As the Welsh pirate captain Bartholomew Roberts avowed: "Damnation to him who ever lived to wear a halter! . . . A merry life and a short one, shall be my motto!"

Life in the Royal Navy was hellish for ordinary seamen, many of whom had been press-ganged, that is snatched bodily and put aboard a ship where they were treated inhumanely. It was not unusual for the families of lowly seamen to starve because the men were paid a pittance, if at all and when a warship captured an enemy vessel the officers got the lion's share of whatever was aboard. Not surprisingly, desertion from the navy became such a problem that impressed seamen were sometimes shackled to prevent them from going ashore for a period of years. On some Royal Navy vessels crew members were maimed to keep them from jumping ship. On merchant and naval vessels ordinary seamen were forced to live like animals while the captain and officers lived in relative comfort.

Life at sea was never easy even on pirate ships. Once on board there was no escape from appalling living conditions. As many as two hundred and fifty men were sometimes jammed into the filthy fo'c'sle of pirate ships averaging 130 feet long and 30 to 40 feet abeam. They endured maggoty salt beef, weevily biscuits, storms, boredom, disease and inevitable battle wounds. Eye patches, wooden legs and hooks like Peter Pan's nemesis wore were common among veteran pirates. Pirate articles spelled out specific compensation for the loss of an eye or limb long before the Royal Navy.

Despite the hardships of life aboard a pirate vessel there was no shortage of recruits to the outlaw brotherhood from the disgruntled crews of the thousands of ships afloat in the expanding merchant and naval fleets of the civilized world. Conditions on those vessels were even worse than on a pirate ship and, in addition, there was brutal discipline and little prospect of financial gain. And a pirate enjoyed sexual freedom and could drink as much as he wanted when he wanted. Pirate grog was a great comforter and alcoholism was an occupational hazard.

The most obvious appeal of the outlaw life was the chance to make in one foray as much as an honest seaman would make in a lifetime. An equally compelling lure was personal liberty. As honest seamen most had been little better off than slaves. In fact, able-bodied African slaves were usually welcome to join a pirate crew. Signing the articles on a pirate ship meant joining a democratic brotherhood in which the officers and crew were equals and justice was meted out fairly. Pirates enjoyed individual liberty, an escape from the crippling strictures of a cruelly oppressive caste system in which the station of one's birth determined one's fate. Pirates were collective owners of their ships and independent operators. Except during attacks all decisions were made by one man, one vote. Even the captain and crew of a pirate ship were elected on the basis of merit and voted out of office if they displeased the majority of the crew.

Sifting fact from fancy means tossing out some cherished nuggets of pirate lore. Contrary to popular belief pirates almost never buried their treasure. They were wildly improvident and squandered their prizes on gaming, women and grog in between forays. Of those who escaped death in battle and the noose, most died in alcoholic poverty. A few, however, managed to put together a sizeable fortune and make prudent investments. Captain Kidd, for example, once owned several lots on Wall Street and adjoining lanes; now some of the highest priced real estate in the world. Unfortunately he failed to enjoy his investments. In 1701 Kidd was convicted of murder and piracy by the British government. He was hung twice—the rope broke the first time. In accordance with a thousand-year-old tradition his tarred corpse, preserved in an iron cage, was hung from a gibbet on the bank of the river Thames to warn would-be pirates.

There is no proof that pirates forced anyone to walk the plank. In fact, walking the plank seems mild compared to some of the atrocities pirates routinely committed. Pirates were vicious and vengeful, some pathologically so. Upon capturing a ship they routinely asked the crew whether their officers were fair with them and if the answer was negative, the captain and his officers were tortured or even disemboweled and decapitated.

Edward Low, an English pirate operating in the 1720s was barbarous to the point of psychosis. The particular object of his pathology were Portuguese captives. When the captain of a Portuguese vessel dropped a bag filled with gold escudos overboard to keep them from Low, the pirate had the man lashed to the mast of his ship and his lips cut off and broiled in a skillet in front of him. Few pirates were as mad as Low, but they all relied on a reputation for inspiring terror as a means of hastening the capitulation of a ship or a settlement. Sometimes the sight of the skull and crossbones on the black flag hoisted as a pirate ship closed in on a prize was enough to inspire surrender.

Mercurial, daring and prodigal, the pirates and privateers of the Caribbean were men who defied stereotyping. For centuries no one embarked on the Spanish Main without dreading attack but after the 1720s the risk was greatly reduced. The death knell for Caribbean piracy sounded in the 1820s. The U.S. Navy crushed several nasty operators in the Gulf of Mexico including the notorious Jean Lafitte and then Congress sent Commodore David Porter to the West Indies to mop up the vestiges of pirate activity. Privateering, although it continued for several decades, played a diminishing role in maritime defense as navies evolved into full scale professional force.

Piracy did not vanish from the Caribbean completely. As Dio Cassius observed, piracy will be with us until human nature changes and flare-ups of petty piracy occurred after 1825 whenever there was motive and opportunity as was the case during Prohibition in the 1920s. The most virulent outbreak in modern times began in the early 1970s when a new breed of pirate appeared in the Caribbean, attracted by proliferating shipments of drugs and arms. The area stretching along the Florida coast east and south through the Bahamas to the northern shores of South America became a veritable war zone. Thousands of craft disappeared and an untold number of people were murdered or thrown overboard by pirates who seized vessels for transporting marijuana, cocaine or arms, often abandoning them when they had completed their run. Pirates and drug traffickers operated with impunity despite U.S. government attempts to foil them with satellite detection, radar, electronic surveillance balloons and planes. In 1977 the U.S. Coast Guard, alarmed at what was happening, issued an official warning to recreational boaters contemplating a cruise in Bahamian or Caribbean waters. By the mid-1980s the danger abated because of increased governmental action and the changing nature of the smuggling itself, although drug smuggling still continues on a monumental scale.

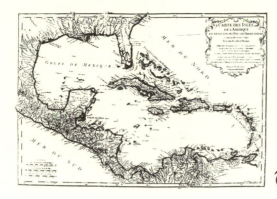

1

Europe

The Old World

The story of the pirates and privateers who infested the Caribbean for over three centuries is but one chapter in a fascinating three thousand-year saga of piracy. Outlaws of the oceans have preyed on mariners and plundered coastal settlements since antiquity. Inscriptions on Assyrian stone tablets complain of pirates plundering goods en route from Arabia to Africa in the Persian Gulf. In the fourth century B.C. sailors in the pay of Alexander the Great had to contend with Persian Gulf pirates. Homer's *Odyssey* describes a Mediterranean unsafe from pirates a thousand years before Christ. Sea outlaws were so pervasive that Cicero, the Roman orator called them *hostes humani generi*, "enemies of the human race." In 81 B.C. an arrogant young politician from Rome named Julius Caesar, was captured by pirates while en route to study rhetoric on the Greek island of Rhodes. He was held captive for six weeks during which he harangued his captors with speeches and poems. Released after a ransom of twelve thousand pieces of gold was paid he immediately raised a swift fleet and hunted down the pirate ship. Following a fierce battle Caesar had every surviving pirate crucified.

The word pirate comes from *peiran*, Greek for attack, although the first pirates were active long before the Greeks. No doubt the first mariners who put to sea with a valuable cargo found themselves set upon by brigands who were quick to see the relative ease with which they could appropriate a ship, its cargo and the crew to sell as slaves. Armed sea power, warships and navies were devised to combat piracy. However, until relatively modern times, a warship frequently turned pirate craft when it encountered a merchantman flying the flag of a rival state.

Piracy is inextricably entwined with trade. The conditions that nourished piracy in the modern world existed in antiquity as well. The first references to piracy are enmeshed in the history of early seaborne commerce. In the fifth century B.C. Thucydides, the Athenian historian, noted that sea trading has always been carried on in the shadow of fear. Piracy and maritime trade were born together. Piracy flourished as seaborne commerce increased and more of the world's cities participated in far flung trade. When control of the seas was contested by belligerent powers, pirates operated with impunity.

Ancient mariners were pioneers in a frightening, unfamiliar world. They used the watery medium as a road to take them to sources, first of food and then of coveted goods they could exchange for their local produce, but they weren't comfortable on it. Their vessels were crude and small. They had no navigational aids and sailed in sight of land, hugging the coast when possible. A course was reckoned by sighting familiar landmarks: headlands, hill profiles or other topographical features. At night they invariably anchored close to shore or pulled their light craft up on a beach to wait for dawn's light.

Historians conjecture that the first pirates were probably fishermen—inhabitants of an infertile area devoid of natural resources but lying on an established trade route. These men needed little cunning or equipment. Their boats were small, very light and built for speed. They lay in wait, hidden in a cove like those that serrate the Mediterranean coastline. Or their craft might have been disguised as a fishing boat to approach an unwary ship, although there were few boardings in the early days of navigation. It was much simpler to wait until a ship was pulled onto the beach at night and overwhelm its crew. The pirates typically left some of their number aboard a captured ship to make sure it was rowed to their lair where the prize was divided.

There was an evolution from single attacks on passing ships to larger-scale operations. Pirate organizations were formed which grew rich and powerful, thanks to profits from the sale of captives who were sold as slaves to insatiable markets in the developing world. Cunning pirate leaders sometimes became so powerful they headed quasi-states which extorted bribes from intimidated rulers and traders. Sometimes they became actual states like Samos, headed by the brilliant pirate chieftain Polycrates, which signed a treaty with Egypt in the sixteenth century B.C.

Piracy was accepted as a routine hazard of seafaring along with storms and treacherous reefs. As civilization developed, city-states like those of the Tigris-Euphrates Valley initiated far-flung international trade in metals, timber, cosmetics, perfumes and other luxuries. Mesopotamian merchants financed their voyages through loans from bankers. A syndicate borrowed the amount needed for a cargo, agreeing to repay the loan plus interest. If pirates captured the ship the partners paid the bill; the banker was guaranteed his money unless he had invested himself. Archaeological excavations in this century have furnished evidence of this trade. Decorative shells native to the coastal waters of India and Ceylon have been dug up in Mesopotamian cities of the third millennium B.C. along with fragments of statuary made of a hard rock called diorite which comes from Oman on the Persian Gulf.

Following the natural process of evolution which has characterized piracy throughout history, attacks by lone brigands on isolated ships increased in intensity as the tempo of commerce quickened. Pirate organizations operated out of strongholds where they enjoyed natural protection and political advantage. The first zone where organized piracy made voyaging hazardous was probably the Persian Gulf and the Arabian Sea along the 150 mile coastline from Qatar to Oman. By 5000 B.C. vessels had added sails to supplement oars and were trading between the west coast of India and the Indian Ocean. In the mid-third millennium merchants of Babylon dealt in goods from Arabia. By the end of the second millennium B.C. courageous traders from the Gulf of Oman were plying regular long-distance routes via Bahrain to China, the Indochina peninsula, Sumatra and Java.

Laden with copper, timber, gold, silver, jewels, silks, ivory, and exotic woods, trading ships headed for Mesopotamia. The fortunate ones sailed up the Euphrates where their cargoes were exchanged for the textiles, wool, leather and olive oil that Mesopotamia was famous for. Others fell victim to the pirates who haunted the treacherous Strait of Hormuz between the Oman peninsula and what is today the Iranian coast or were ambushed along the 150 mile stretch that follows, which since ancient times has been known as the Pirate Coast.

Toward the end of the second millennium this trade faded away. It revived under the Assyrian kings. Pirate fleets shadowed ships of the far-reaching Assyrian traders along the Pirate Coast and Sennacherib launched an offensive against them in the seventh century B.C. Pirate ships made incursions up the Tigris River until the Persians blocked its mouth. Alexander the Great's conquest of the Persian Empire in the fourth century B.C. made voyaging in the Arabian and Persian gulfs relatively safe for a time. Alexander asked a pirate taken in a battle between the Macedonian and pirate fleets: "What right do you have to infest the seas?" the pirate's alleged reply was: "The same right you have to infest the world!"

In the thirteenth century A.D. Marco Polo sailed around the Arabian Sea and Indian Ocean. He wrote of pirates from Malabar and Gujarat, on India's west coast, who sailed annually in a fleet with more than one hundred ships. Their wives and children accompanied them throughout the summer season as they preyed on merchant ships carrying spices, gold, silver, brass, cloth of gold and silks. One of their stratagems was to cruise in line, five miles apart so that twenty ships covered one hundred miles of sea. Once a merchantman was sighted, a signal was relayed by beacon so no ship could pass undetected. Polo reported the merchant crews defended themselves well and often escaped.

Polo called the corsairs of Gujarat the most notorious in the world. "Let me tell you one of their nasty tricks. You must know that when they capture merchants they make them drink tamarind and sea water so that they pass or vomit up all the contents of their stomachs. Then the corsairs collect all that they have cast up and rummage through it to see if it contains any pearls or precious stones. For the corsairs say that when the merchants are captured they swallow their pearls and other gems to prevent their discovery."

Pirates when caught were not treated gently. The Carthaginians and Etruscans stoned captured Greek pirates to death or tied the living to the dead and then threw them overboard. The Greeks responded by doing the same or by keel hauling captives. Two thousand years later seamen found guilty of murder in the English Navy were sometimes executed by keel hauling which involves dragging a man through the water under the hull of a boat so that his lungs fill with water and barnacles tear his flesh to ribbons. Several years ago workmen digging at Piraeus, the seaport of Athens, uncovered grisly evidence of another form of punishment. Buried in the sand were several enormous crosses, which must have been visible well out in the harbor. Fixed to them by bronze staples at the neck, wrists and ankles were the skeletons of ancient pirates. A fourth century A.D. Persian king named Shapur was dubbed Zulaklaf or Lord of the Shoulders because he destroyed pirate strongholds in the Gulf, stringing the captured pirates together through their shoulders.

Thanks to the precocious development of Egyptian civilization, the Red Sea was a focus of pirate activity in antiquity. Two thousand years before Christ, pirates were raiding ships traversing the Red Sea with cargoes of incense, resins and gold from southern Arabia and from Punt, probably where Somalia is today or perhaps East Africa. Pirates wearing high feathered headdresses and armed with large round shields are depicted in Egyptian friezes. About 1100 B.C., when the once mighty Nile kingdom was in decline, an envoy named Wen Amon was sent from Thebes to buy timber from the king of Byblos, one of the Phoenician city-states. A surviving papyrus tells how the unfortunate agent was robbed, shipwrecked and captured by pirates.

The Mediterranean was a focus of piracy from the dawn of sail with particularly intense periods of activity during the Greek, Phoenician, and Roman eras owing to the high volume of commercial traffic. In the violent world of early maritime commerce, naval operations and piracy in the Mediterranean were often indistinct from one another. The Phoenicians are found in almost every chapter of this early history. The Egyptians entrusted much of their shipping to these Semitic seafaring traders (and erstwhile pirates) who inhabited the coast of what is now Lebanon. Bronze Age pirates had their pick of booty. Phoenician ships delivered gold from Egypt's mines, papyrus, linen and other Egyptian produce to distant ports and brought back such diverse goods as timber, slaves, sumptuous textiles, copper and silver (highly valued because it was rare).

The Mediterranean was infested with pirates during the early Bronze Age, especially during the Minoan and Mycenaean periods. The pirate menace shaped the settlement patterns and architecture of coastal people. For safety the Minoan cities of Knossos and Phaestus were located miles from the barter posts on Crete's shore. Athens, Troy and Corinth were also established with an eye to protection from pirates. Ruined towers dot the Aegean, reminders of the perpetual pirate threat. The stone towers were lookout posts and also served as strongholds to which people could flee during a raid. When a pirate ship was sighted smoke signals or fire signals were given to warn the surrounding area.

The earliest effective suppression of piracy seems to have been organized on Crete, the mountainous Aegean island located at a natural crossroads of maritime traffic. From about 2400 to about 1400 B.C. Crete rose to prominence through highly organized piracy and was the center of the remarkable Minoan civilization which lay buried and forgotten until British archaeologist, Sir Arthur Evans excavated the palace complex at Knossos in 1900. The Minoan kings were undisputed masters of the sea during the centuries of their briskest trade. The Minoan navy, perhaps the world's first, was both a trading fleet and a war fleet, suppressing piracy on the one hand and engaging in it on the other. At their peak the Minoans controlled all the sea-lanes in the eastern Mediterranean and exacted trading concessions from other nations.

The palace complex at Knossos, like others on the island, was unfortified indicating it had nothing to fear from sea attackers. The Minoan rulers used their superior naval force to suppress rival pirates and keep competition at bay. The wealthy, pleasure-loving Minoans could afford cities filled with comfortable, highly decorated buildings because of their skill and daring as traders. Pursuing clues from pottery shards, archaeologists have traced the presence of Minoan goods in Asia Minor, Rhodes, Cyprus, Syria and Palestine to the east. They regularly went to Egypt and the North African Coast and got at least as far north of their island as Macedonia. They reached Sicily and may even have traded on the south coast of Spain for the copper needed in bronze manufacture.

A series of disasters—earthquakes and invasions around 1400 B.C.—
dimmed the brilliant Minoan civilization. Cretan culture had spread
throughout the Aegean to Greece and the coast of Asia Minor. Its chief
heir was the Mycenaean civilization (ca. 1500 B.C. to ca. 1100 B.C.) based
on the Greek mainland which was built on sea power and piracy. The
Mycenaeans were a warlike people whose history forms the background
of Homer's *Iliad*. Mycenaean towns, positioned on hilltops, were heavily
fortified and built at some distance from the sea for protection. The rulers
lived in stone citadels like the one discovered by Heinrich Schliemann
when he sought the bones of Agamemnon and found the famous shaft
graves filled with golden masks, jewelry and inlaid daggers. Their wealth
came from conquest and piracy in the early days and, later, from legitimate trade.

In the eighth century B.C., Homer wrote a lot about piracy. The Greeks
of the Homeric age considered trading beneath them. They preferred piracy which they practiced with particular relish on Phoenician merchant
vessels. Homer has nothing nice to say about the "Phoenician rogues"
whom the warrior Greeks regarded with contempt. In the *Odyssey* he
calls them "famous sailors, greedy merchantmen with countless gauds in
a black ship." In addition to metals and the luxuries of the east, the
Phoenicians supplied slaves. Phoenicians sometimes captured slaves by
dropping anchor in a bustling port, spreading their wares on deck and
inviting women and children to come aboard. As the unsuspecting brows-
ers fingered the beads, cloth and trinkets the Phoenicians offered, they
suddenly discovered they were bound for sea and slavery.

Thucydides, a historian not given to embellishment, wrote that "Even
kings (Greek) organize marauding expeditions, plunder towns and villages, and enslave the population. Indeed this (piracy) came to be the chief
source of livelihood among the early Hellenes, no disgrace yet being attached to such an occupation." The Laws of Solon, compiled by the Athenian lawyer, show that in the sixth century B.C. there were authorized
associations of pirates.

Piracy was viewed as a means of production, a source of slaves and
goods. Polycrates, the tyrant of Samos, was the most successful pirate of
that time. According to Herodotus, he was master of the Aegean and
commanded a hundred warships which were despatched to extinguish
lesser pirates. No ships sailed without paying him tribute. With the riches
he amassed, Polycrates who was an unusually cultivated pirate, built a
magnificent palace and attracted to his island the foremost artists, musicians, and thinkers of his time, but he never lost his desire for action.
Once he sallied forth and intercepted an Egyptian ship sailing on a diplomatic mission with gifts for the famous Lydian king, Croesus.

Piracy provided the stimulus for early alliances. In 477 B.C., the Delian confederacy of Greek city-states was organized under the leadership of Athens to combat Persia and to make the seas secure from pirates. Athens contributed ships rather than money and before long was able to control her allies through sea-power. The league of partners soon consolidated into the Athenian Empire. A highly disciplined fleet of some sixty ships patrolled the guarding against pirates from Phoenicia and the Peloponnesus. A naval base was set up on the Adriatic to protect shipping from sea robbers. During the Athenian Empire when commerce swelled to a new volume the Athenian Fleet swept the Aegaean relatively clean of pirates. The possibility of loss to pirates was taken into account in all contracts dealing with maritime commerce. For two generations mariners sailed with confidence until the pirate-cycle started anew.

The seas around Italy were always particularly dangerous with pirate nests all along the Adriatic. In 500 B.C., pirate adventurers from Cnidus in southeast Asia minor organized a communist pirate state in the Lipari Islands northeast of Sicily. They preyed on shipping in the Straits of Messina, not only sharing their prizes but dividing all land, goods and duties equally. Individualism eventually ended this communist experiment. Throughout history, however, pirates have tended toward communism, sharing responsibilities and rewards. As late as 1814 there was a pirate commune—the island lair of Jean Lafitte off the Louisiana coast.

Rome had its share of struggles with sea outlaws who at times prevented vital food supplies from reaching Italy. In the early days when Rome was developing from a collection of hill villages along the Tiber into a cohesive state with expansionist aspirations, the western Mediterranean was largely controlled by the Carthaginians who raided all shipping. Alexander's heirs controlled the Hellenistic east and there were pirates everywhere. Clearing the Adriatic of pirates in 230 B.C. was one of Rome's first steps toward maturity. The brigands of the Illyrian coast had raided the coasts of eastern Italy and northern Greece for ages. Their ragged native coast, with its many islands, was a pirate's paradise. The pirates were so powerful that they triumphed in a naval battle over the combined forces of the mercantile cities of Magna Graecia (Sicily and southern Italy) and occupied Corfu.

Rome sent two diplomats to Teuta, Queen of the Illyrians, to protest. She haughtily replied that piracy, according to their law, was a legitimate form of trade. One of the diplomats witheringly remarked that Rome would be happy to assist the queen in improving the law. When Teuta had the two envoys executed Rome responded by mounting a squadron of two hundred galleys which swept into the Adriatic purging the pirates and destroyed their breeding grounds. With this bold stroke Rome, a stripling nation of farmers, showed her naval prowess.

Piracy didn't disappear. In fact, the century before Augustus established the Empire, a pirate curse seemed to hang over the seas. Virulent bands of pirates operated independently but also hired out to Rome's enemies. By far the most ruthless and efficient of the pirates were those of Cilicia on the southern coast of Asia Minor, who captured Julius Caesar. In the early first century B.C. the Cilicians dominated the seas. Slaving was their stock-in-trade. For a time Cilician pirates supplied most of the human merchandise which went on the block in Italy. Rome, no longer a nation of free farmers, depended on slave labor for the vast Italian farms, the *latifundia* which were owned by a relative few. Roman planters weren't terribly interested in protecting trading routes but were vitally concerned with keeping the supply of human machines flowing since the brutal and wasteful system used slaves as disposable units. Consequently, they did little at first to urge the senate to take strong measures to control the Cilician pirates.

The Cilicians dealt with the Romans but had scant respect for them. When a captive announced he was a citizen of Rome, the pirates began a macabre charade by acting terribly contrite, falling on their knees to beg for mercy for their error. The Roman was assured he could now "make the trip home," with which he was pitched overboard and wished a safe journey. The Cilician pestilence eventually became intolerable. More than one thousand ships sailed under their flag, some with gilded masts, silvered oars and purple sails. They looted temples throughout Greece and controlled four hundred coastal towns. They were landing on the Italian coast and kidnapping patricians including the granddaughter of an admiral who had led an anti-pirate campaign. They even forced their way into Ostia, Rome's chief port, and destroyed the fleet of one of the consuls. Maritime commerce was at a standstill. Rome was in danger of starving since vital supplies of imported grain were cut off.

In desperation the Senate in 67 B.C. granted General Pompey, Caesar's rival, emergency powers to deal with the menace. Rome had such confidence in his skill that the day after his appointment the price of grain began to fall. The plan he conceived and carried out was brilliant. He divided the Mediterranean and Black seas into thirteen zones, appointing a fleet to each. In a beautifully orchestrated operation Pompey deployed one hundred and twenty thousand soldiers, four thousand cavalry and assembled five hundred ships drafted from Rome, Rhodes, Marseilles, the Phoenician city-states and other allies. Within three months he made good his promise to exterminate piracy, making the seas safer than they had been in centuries.

The Romans still had to cope with pirates from time to time. Barbarian pirates, originally from the southern Baltic area, destroyed Roman sea power and broke the back of the Western Empire. After the Fall, piracy declined. Without the Romans there were no insatiable markets for slaves and no rich towns to plunder. Sea trade and sea travel almost ceased. What little there was attracted the usual localized penny-ante pirates. In the centuries following the Fall of Rome, western civilization was plunged into barbarian gloom.

Almost four centuries later a fragmented Europe was subjected to an onslaught of piracy more explosive than any the world had ever seen. The Vikings with their sleek, swift, longboats stand out as history's consummate sea raiders. Between the eighth and tenth centuries they managed to sack (and settle) from England to Spain and from France to Russia. Swooping down like great predatory eagles from their icy stronghold at the top of the world, the Norse captains with names like Harald Bluetooth and Eric Bloodaxe led their warriors on a frenzied quest for the shining treasures of southern climes.

The Norsemen, or Vikings, as they have collectively been called, were pirates. The word *vikingr* is old Scandinavian for pirate. Scholars suggest that overpopulation of inhospitable lands spurred them to graduate from their early plundering for the love and gain of it to political expeditions, colonizing ventures and the establishment of commercial stations. They were superb naval architects and seamen. Viking mariners reached as far west as Minnesota and ventured south as far as Egypt in their flexible, undecked longships. Viking sea raiders; reckless, restless men who reveled in combat and lusted for women and gold, stripped the treasure houses of Europe, beginning with the Irish monastery of Lindisfarne in 793 A.D. The shining booty they took home precipitated 250 years of sea raids. Ireland, Scotland, Wales and Southern England were subjected to their rapine and slaughter. Norwegian pirates colonized the Orkneys, Faroes and Shetland islands.

Swedish pirates, known as Rus, spread east to found colonies like Kiev and Vovogorod. Before long they dominated the water routes from the Baltic to the Black Sea. They were traders dealing in slaves, furs and honey. Ibd Fadlan, a tenth century agent from the Caliph of Baghdad, was revolted by the Rus whom he described as filthy, wild-eyed drunks with a penchant for public sexual orgies. He observed a ceremony at which men prostrated themselves before totem poles praying "O Lord, I have come from distant parts with so many girls, so many sable furs. Please send me a rich merchant who will do business without too much haggling." The Vikings stormed Constantinople, the Byzantine capital and the world's most magnificent city, four times. Each time they were repulsed or bought off with payments of gold.

The Danes were less inclined to settle. Weaned on Baltic piracy they moved with lightning speed in their dragon-prowed ships set with blood red sails. Norse fleets of hundred-oared ships sailed up the Elbe to Hamburg and up the Seine, reaching Paris in 912. They settled what came to be known as Normandy on the French coast. The Italian goldworking centers of Rome and Milan were sacked and burned. Moslem Spain and Portugal were battered by Norse pirates the Moors called "Madjus"— heathen wizards. The Vikings tackled the North African coast at Morocco where they met stiff resistance from Saracen pirates who terrorized the Tyrrhenian Sea.

By the tenth century Norsemen ruled Sicily and England and were masters of Southern Italy and Normandy. Gradually the Vikings who settled were absorbed into the cultural mainstream. It was hard to recognize the Viking savages in their cosmopolitan descendants who embraced Christianity and the refinements of civilization.

Few pirates of note enliven the centuries of petty activity which followed the relative domestication of the Vikings. Long distance voyages all but ceased. The accumulated sea knowledge of the early mariners had been lost after the eclipse of Rome. Traders making coastal runs with unglamorous cargoes of fish, wine or wool encountered sea robbers who might well be traders themselves who were down on their luck. British and French outlaws predominated taking prizes in the narrow seas between Britain and the continent. A few operated far from home like Goderic, an Englishman who haunted the southern Mediterranean. The Cinque Ports of southeastern England, the towns of Hastings, Hythe, Dover, Sandwich, and Romney were pirate havens for centuries. In the early sixteenth century they were home to the King's Pirates, so-called because they routinely turned 20 percent of their take over to the crown, selling the remainder of their loot directly from the ships moored in port.

One of the very few who are remembered from the medieval era of petty piracy was the Black Monk, a former friar named Eustace who turned to piracy after being outlawed for murder during service in the private army of the Count of Boulogne. People believed the Black Monk could make his ship invisible with the aid of the Devil. He sailed for England's King John, seizing ships in the Channel and plundering up the Seine as far as Paris. In 1212 when King Philip of France made him a better deal he didn't hesitate to leave the palatial mansion in London King John had given him and turn his talents to English prizes. In 1217 he put together an armada to invade England. His ships faced a fleet from the Cinque Ports crewed by former colleagues. The English ships prevailed. The Black Monk was slain and his head carried from town to town in southern England and displayed to the accompaniment of admonitory sermons.

Gradually commercial activity increased. Cargoes of value attract predators. As seaborne trade expanded so did the pirate menace. During the Middle Ages pirate activity in the North Sea, the English Channel and the Baltic kept pace with the commercial growth of the northern European commercial centers and the development of the Hanseatic League. The Hanseatic League, the association of German free cities and expatriate merchant groups played the leading role in northern European trade from late thirteenth to fifteenth centuries. The cities joined forces for the express purpose of defending their monopolistic trading interests in the pirate infested Baltic and North seas. Ships with greater cargo capacity like the cog and the hulk were used to carry profitable shipments of fish and raw materials to the industrializing European area west of the Baltic. While nominally defending their trade, Hanseatic ships sometimes launched what can only be regarded as blatant pirate attacks on competitors.

In the late fourteenth century a band of Baltic pirates, known as the *Vitalienbruder* or Victualling Brothers for their aid to besieged Stockholm, took a number of Swedish towns and succeeded in capturing Bergen, Norway's chief city. Their depredations on merchant shipping pushed the price of herring to ten times its normal value in Frankfurt. Queen Margaret of Sweden's forces drove them from the Baltic but they regrouped under the banner of the *Likedeeler*, or Fair-Sharers, transferring their camps to the islands of East Frisia off the German coast from whence they plundered North Sea traffic.

Since the Crusades, pirates based on the North African coast had scoured the seas sweeping down on Christian shipping, seizing men and cargoes in the name of the avenging god of Islam. The Barbary corsairs took their name from the Barbary coast, the stretch of shore from Egypt west to the Strait of Gibraltar at the entrance to the Atlantic chiefly inhabited by the seminomadic Berbers. More than sixteen hundred years after Caesar's capture by Mediterranean pirates, Cervantes, author of the Spanish classic *Don Quixote* was captured by the dreaded Barbary corsairs in 1575 and remained a slave in Algiers for five years before he was ransomed by Trinitarian friars. Best known of the fraternity were the Turkish Barbarossa brothers, Aruj and Kheir-ed-Din, who was a cultivated patron of the arts whom the Ottoman Sultan appointed as Regent of Algiers.

The Barbary corsairs included renegade Christians and even some Jews. In the early seventeenth century Algiers, Tripoli and Tunis harbored English, Dutch and Flemish pirates including John Ward, Simon Danziker and Jan Jansz. The "Turkish Devils" harassed shipping far beyond the Mediterranean. Along with corsairs from Moroccan ports like Sallee and Mamurra they terrorized the Bristol and English channels, looting up the

Thames. They raided Portuguese, French and Flemish codfishing fleets off Newfoundland where they seized slaves and seamen with special skills. A number of times they made off with men, women and children from coastal settlements in Devon and Cornwall.

Driven as much by hatred of Christians, particularly Spaniards, as by greed, the Islamic corsairs were implacable—powerful enough to create their own pirate states and negotiate treaties with the seafaring nations of Europe, which often paid them tribute. Generally, capture, rather than destruction, was the goal. Dead captives were worthless; live ones could be sold and rich ones could be ransomed. In the first half of the seventeenth century the bagnios, or slave barracks, of Algiers held more than 20,000 captives. So many slaves were taken during a great sea battle off Algiers in 1541 when the corsair fleet challenged the combined forces of Christendom, that a "Christian was scarcely fair exchange for an onion," in the words of a contemporary. The English press made much of the sufferings of Christian captives. In 1622 English towns raised the huge sum of £70,000 to ransom native sons. The bulk of the funds, however, ended up in the Admiralty's coffers. It should be noted that the slave markets of Italy, Spain and Malta teemed with Islamic captives.

The scale of Barbary pirating was monumental. The great Italian admiral, Andrea Doria, led five hundred Christian ships against the corsairs in 1541 and lost 8,300 men to drowning or wounds in addition to the thousands taken as slaves. Three years earlier, sailing for the Spanish emperor, he led the combined Christian forces of Europe against Barbarossa's fleet. They met in the Bay of Preveza off the coast of Albania. Doria had eighty Venetian, thirty Spanish and thirty six papal galleys carrying a total of some 60,000 men and 2,500 guns. The pirates were outnumbered and outgunned in the ensuing battle, which pitted the world's greatest sea forces against them, but they fought with such skill and manic courage that the Christian fleet turned and fled.

Turncoat Christians were among the most dashing and successful of the Barbary pirates and were valued by the Moslems for their superior skill. It was a Christian, Simon Danziker, who early in the seventeenth century, introduced the corsairs to sailing ships, which with their mobility and speed were far superior to oar-powered galleys. John Ward was a Kentish fisherman turned English privateer, who joined the Barbary predators. He attracted other English pirates and gained control over a dozen armed ships. Their exploits were spectacularly successful. On one expedition Ward seized 400,000 crowns worth of booty—enough to almost collapse the mighty Venetian stock market. He boasted that if he met his own father at sea he wouldn't hesitate to rob and then sell him.

In the early seventeenth century a number of veteran British privateers who had sailed under Queen Elizabeth, joined the Barbary service. The Muslim pirates welcomed the advanced technology the English brought with them and the English unable to practice their craft under James I, who discouraged attacks on Spanish shipping, welcomed the chance to go "a roving." The Moors tolerated their guests for the most part although they were a scruffy lot. A French visitor in 1606 wrote that "They carry swords at their side, they run drunk through the town . . . They sleep with the wives of the Moors . . . in brief every kind of debauchery and unchecked license is permitted them."

Pirates and governments have often had a symbiotic relationship. Pirates, particularly if they were licensed privateers, received the sanction and protection of the flag they sailed under. Governments in return received licensing fees, a share of plunder and a free navy to direct against their foes, although they sometimes found their ungovernable mercenaries turned against them when there was a change in political weather. The Barbary corsair captains paid from 10 to 20 percent of their take to the local rulers where they were based. This gave them protection and a place to market their prizes. The governing beys or aghas encouraged piracy for the considerable revenues it produced. John Ward entertained bids from various potentates eager to attract his fleet, including the Grand Duke of Tuscany and the Duke of Savoy who offered Livorno or Villefranche as home ports.

Piracy flourished in times of war—both hot and cold. Pirates were generally an anarchic breed whose only lasting allegiance was to roving at sea. They were apt to turn and bite the hand that fed them and reveled in the inability of bickering allies to join forces to exterminate them. The Barbary pirates did so well for so long because the eras of active maritime commerce such as the Crusades, the Renaissance and the sixteenth and seventeenth centuries when gold and silver from the mines of Spanish America revitalized European commerce, were generally marked by dissension among the Christian powers which crippled efforts to exterminate them. Francis I went so far as to enlist the Muslim corsairs against the king of Spain, in an alliance even his own French subjects called unholy. The United States waged a series of little remembered but successful attacks against Tripolitania, a Muslim pirate state on the North African coast, in the 1820s and in 1830 a forty thousand man French force took Algiers, effectively ending six hundred years of Barbary menace, although Moroccan pirates from the Rif tribe continued to harass shipping in the western Mediterranean until the late 1860s.

The English furnished many of the most unforgettable characters in the annals of piracy. England was the first nation to develop laws dealing with piracy. Ironically, since the Middle Ages the English were generally lenient with their own pirates. "Now piracy is only a term for sea-robbery, piracy being a robbery committed within the jurisdiction of the Admiralty. If any man shall be assaulted within that jurisdiction and his ship or goods violently taken away without legal authority, this is robbery and piracy." What could be more straightforward than the definition delivered by Sir Charles Hedges, Judge of the Admiralty, at a pirate trial in 1696? Yet, time and time again from its inception in 1360 the High Court of the Admiralty found itself in a quandry when trying to determine whether or not a privateer had overreached his commission and committed an act of sea robbery.

The first English pirate was hanged in 1228. But few others went to the gallows until 1536 when Henry VIII who was appalled at the utter lawlessness which prevailed on the seas, enforced more stringent measures. More pirates were executed in the following two years than in the preceding three hundred. Until the end of the sixteenth century or later prosecution was uneven at best, intensifying or not according to questions of politics and economics.

From the thirteenth century on the south coast of England, the Welsh coast and the east coast of Ireland spawned innumerable pirates. Many operated from their native shores. Some were "wreckers." Whole villages often worked together setting up false beacons to lure passing ships to their destruction and pillaging the cargoes. A number of adventurous Britons plundered far from home—in the southern Mediterranean, the Red Sea or even the Persian Gulf.

Continual conflict with France led the English Crown to issue the first privateering commissions in 1243. Intense international rivalries during the Renaissance and Reformation coupled with the twin menace of Muslim pirates in the Mediterranean and continued raiding in northern waters gave a new impetus to privateering. Henceforth, governments relied heavily on privately owned ships which carried letters of marque, or reprisal, empowering their crews to plunder enemy shipping in the king's name. Contracts drawn before the start of an expedition stipulated what share the captain, crew, owner and Crown were to receive of the take. The theory was to recover compensation for enemy injuries. In practice, however, the distinction between reprisal, maritime trade and flagrant piracy remained somewhat hazy for the next 450 years.

French, Flemish, Frisian, and British corsairs clogged the sea-lanes during the late Middle Ages, preying on each other and the galleys of Italy's powerful maritime republics, particularly those of Venice. International trade was severely disrupted. In 1345, for instance, Edward III received a share of the booty taken when raiders from Bayonne captured the Hispano-Flemish wine fleet. Escort ships often raided their own convoys.

Rivalries among corsair ports such as Calais, Bayonne and St. Malo led to savage attacks on those fortified cities.

Privateers became indispensable to naval warfare. They cost the commissioning government nothing, in fact privateers provided revenues in license fees and plunder and they effectively weakened the enemy. The English Crown granted privileges to the Cinque Ports (Hastings, Romney, Hythe, Dover and Sandwich) in return for furnishing ships and mariners. This confederation to which Rye and Winchelsea were later added, enjoyed a monopoly on English seapower until after the fourteenth century. The men of these towns, fishermen and petty pirates by ancient custom, took to the privateering life with great relish, abusing their privileges. They even preyed on fellow Britons. All along the coast of the West Country coastal villagers joined the lucrative game and prospered long after the Cinque Ports had faded.

Governments withdrawing their blessings when peace had been made, found they had no control over their privateers who zealously continued to plunder not only their former enemies' shipping but sometimes that of long time allies as well. A privateer's allegiance, such as it was, was not to a flag but to the time honored "sweet trade." In those days when men were hanged for stealing a loaf of bread, life was harsh and short. So, not surprisingly, many men were willing to risk being "hanged like a dog and sun-dried," so they might have a chance for a better life.

Rulers found themselves in a quandry because in wartime they couldn't do without the privateers who, in effect, constituted the navy. Impoverished governments welcomed not only their share of swag but also the fees received. A study of English "roving," which falls outside the scope of this book, shows clearly how for four centuries pirates, calling themselves a variety of euphemistic names, flourished with the connivance and support of political figures and the establishment, whose prosperous members invested heavily in sea-robbery. If all those involved in piracy and the receiving and selling of pirate plunder in the Scilly Isles along the coasts of Ireland, Wales, Cornwall and England's southern shore in the sixteenth century had been convicted, the population would have been halved. Fisherman and country squire alike participated in what was the leading industry. Open markets of stolen goods were held on the decks of pirate ships all along the coast. Everyone attended, including the very officials who were employed by the Crown to police such activities.

The network of receivers and purveyors of pirate plunder seized from Spanish ships in the English Channel and even farther afield was extensive. So many fishermen went "roving" along England's south coast that their women had to take over at the nets. There was a glut of prizes and a shortage of warehousing until the large buildings of the religious houses dissolved under Henry VIII were turned into storage areas. The former Black Friars' Abbey was stuffed with dried figs and prunes; the Gray Friars' with stolen wine and the Austin Friars' with contraband dried fish. The British pirates attacked the French with whom they were at war and the Flemish, the Spanish and Portuguese as well, showing no prejudice.

With the death of Henry VIII in 1547 British piracy reached its peak. Thomas, Lord Seymour of Sudeley, brother-in-law of Henry's widow, Catherine Parr, was appointed Lord High Admiral. He flagrantly used his authority to be the greatest pirate of them all. He received half of what was looted and became so immensely wealthy that he was able to arrange with the Bristol Mint to coin 200,000 ducats for him. He sailed to the Scillies, a pirate redoubt, ostensibly to take the islands for the Crown but instead he seized them for himself. He wooed the young Queen Elizabeth with splendid stolen jewels. Under his misrule the Admiralty Courts, which under Henry VIII had begun to persecute pirates, became a farce. Henry's fledgling navy which had made some progress in protecting English shipping fell apart. Commerce was England's lifeblood and under Seymour it dried up. He was finally brought to trial, condemned and beheaded in 1549 but it was many years before the Admiralty recovered from his corruption.

Piracy in English waters was suppressed to some degree and it was to more lucrative though distant sea-lanes that adventurers looked. The development of trade in gold, ivory and slaves from the interior of West Africa lured European pirates to the South Atlantic to plunder Portuguese and Spanish vessels. And, of course, in the wake of Columbus, they flocked to the New World.

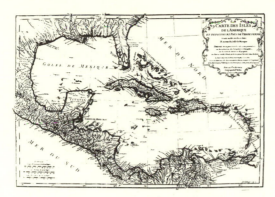

2

French Corsairs on the Spanish Lake

hen Christopher Columbus embarked on his first voyage of discovery he took with him a much-read manuscript of Marco Polo's Travels. He also carried a letter written by King Ferdinand and Queen Isabella to the Grand Khan of China. The Genoese mariner was sure if he sailed west he would encounter the fabled wealth of Cathay and Japan. It hadn't been easy for the Castilian monarchs to finance Columbus's expedition. The treasury was nearly empty but the possibility of cashing in on Portugal's trading monopoly with the East spurred Isabella to provide funds for the venture, although contrary to legend, she did not donate her personal jewels. Columbus had already been turned down by Portugal's king. His coffers overflowed with profits from the Guinea trade on Africa's Gold Coast where, as a young sailor, Columbus had visited the Portuguese enclave at Elmina. In 1488 a Portuguese voyage had reached the East African coast, opening the way to Portugal's lucrative spice and luxury trade with India and the East.

Columbus was seeking the gold-roofed palaces of Zipango (today's Japan) described by Marco Polo who had not seen them but reported what he heard from Chinese travelers. Columbus was disappointed at what he found in the Bahamas, his first landfall, where sunlight shining on palm fronds was the closest thing to gleaming golden roofs. His contract with the Spanish crown specifically mentioned gold. He was to retain a tenth of all revenues and precious metals derived from any islands and mainlands he discovered. "I was attentive and took trouble to ascer-

tain if there was any gold," he wrote in his journal. There were no golden
pavilions but he noted that the natives who went about naked, were
adorned with gold nose ornaments.

The first voyage, like those that followed, was a gold prospecting expedition and wherever there was promise of treasure there was the menace
of treasure hunters. Columbus sighted two French corsair vessels off the
Canaries as he sailed home in 1493, but because his ships were better
armed the corsairs gave him wide berth. A fleet of corsairs lurking off
southern Portugal's Cape St. Vincent almost took his flagship as he returned from his third voyage. Only a sudden storm which drove the corsairs off saved him. Interestingly enough Columbus had once been a free-
lance corsair himself, sailing for René d'Anjou who was based on the
Greek island of Chios. He apparently had no attachment to his birthplace
since he was part of a Portuguese corsair fleet which attacked Genoese
merchant ships off Portugal in 1476.

Columbus's discovery of the New World and the Portuguese discovery
of the sea route to India, marked a shift of world power and initiated a
new epoch in the history of piracy. On the eve of his first voyage, the
prevailing European mood was one of disillusionment. Most of the continent lay exhausted from years of costly wars. Christendom was in di-
sarray and the Papacy was in the corrupt clutches of a Borgia, Pope
Alexander VI. The forces of Islam haunted the sea-lanes and Christian
corsairs preyed on each other. Piracy made marine insurance rates so
astronomical that traders found it less expensive to ship goods from London to Venice via the overland route up the Rhine and across the Alps
than by sea.

The wealthy maritime republic of Venice, La Serenissima, suffered the
greatest depredations in the late fifteenth century. The corsairs of every
nation coveted the galleys of her annual Flanders fleet bound for the Low
countries, holds crammed with shimmering luxuries of the Orient: brocades, silks, damasks, cloth of gold, as well as jewels and a variety of gold
and silver currencies. Venetian ships everywhere were attacked, contrib-
uting to her decline and explaining, in part, why such an experienced
maritime state never participated in the expansion west of European horizons.

Piracy expanded westward in the wake of the conquistadores. The relatively modest amounts of gold—nuggets, fishhooks and ornaments—
Columbus brought back to the Spanish court from his first voyage
touched off the first gold rush in modern history. Rough and ready men,
many of them unemployed veterans of the Moorish campaigns in Italy,
flocked to Seville and to Sanlúcar de Barrameda, a port at the mouth of

the Guadalquivir River sixty miles downstream from Seville, to sign on ships bound for the Caribbean. The floodgates were opened. The inhabitants of the newly discovered islands and lands were helpless in the face of the conquistadores whose hunger for gold was insatiable. Native good will was rewarded with enslavement, exploitation and extermination.

In 1519 Hernán Cortés, a dapper plantation owner on Cuba, was sent to conquer Mexico. He landed on the Yucatán coast with six hundred men, sixteen horses and a few small cannons. Every school child knows the rest. The mighty Aztec civilization fell with lightning rapidity. Montezuma, the bewildered Aztec emperor, offered the "white gods" gold. But the massive amounts of finely wrought gold jewelry, plate and ornaments only inflamed their greed. The conquistadores were insensible to the beauty and refinement of Aztec goldwork. As tribute bearers brought it in it was thrown into furnaces, melting the genius of generations into small stamped bars.

By 1521 the Aztec Empire was no more and Spain had one of her richest prizes. Most of the Caribbean islands and coast had been explored and a few settled. Restless and reckless, the conquistadores plunged into the most forbidding jungles. They struggled across soaring mountain ranges and trackless deserts in the quest for treasure. Ranging farther south they found gold in Colombia, Panama and then Peru and in the Andes, the mother lode of the Inca civilization. Cuzco, a golden city which surpassed the treasure seekers' wildest dreams, fell to the illiterate conquistador, Francisco Pizarro and two hundred soldiers in 1531, who obliterated one of the world's most highly developed civilizations.

Pope Alexander VI confirmed Spain's claim of ownership in the Treaty of Tordesillas. For the next two and a half centuries the New World, chief source of Europe's gold, silver, emeralds and pearls, was a magnet attracting a multitude of daring pirates. French corsairs were the first to challenge "Adam's Will," as the Treaty of Tordesillas was called. They had hovered among the Azores and Canaries and about Cape St. Vincent at the southern tip of Portugal since before Columbus's voyages. In 1501 they were so numerous that the Spanish crown ordered the construction of warships to chase them away. In 1512 Ferdinand complained to the king of Portugal that they were so brazen as to wait right outside Portuguese ports for incoming Spanish ships and he dispatched two armed ships to the Canaries to escort returning Indies vessels.

The bold corsairs from St. Malo, Dieppe and other French corsair ports persisted. After 1520 when the prolonged warfare between the French and Spanish began, they redoubled their efforts with the royal blessing.

In 1521 they seized two of three caravels returning to Seville with valuable cargo. A Spanish squadron sailed in pursuit and managed to recapture one of the ships off Cape St. Vincent.

A squadron of warships known as the "Armada of the Ocean Sea" was organized in late 1522 to protect the Indies ships and a tax, the *averia* was instituted to finance it. The Armada met returning convoys at the Azores and escorted them to Spain. In the case of a threat to outward bound shipping, the Armada was to act as escort as far as the Canaries. The corsairs, far from being discouraged, simply extended their range farther into the Atlantic. In 1522 a fleet cruising off the Azores captured the richest prize yet to fall into French hands when they took two of three poorly armed caravels. The vessels were crammed with spectacular Aztec treasure Cortés was sending to the king. There were emeralds, one as big as a man's palm, multi-hued ceremonial robes fashioned of feathers, mosaic masks made of semi-precious stones as well as gold and souvenirs for the families of the conquistadores.

The third caravel escaped because it had anchored in a cove without being seen. Some months later the Armada arrived to escort the remaining caravel home. A corsair fleet organized by the Dieppoise ship owner Jean Ango and commanded by Jean Florin of La Rochelle (identified by some scholars with the Florentine adventurer Giovanni da Verrazano) lay in wait off the "cape of surprises," Cape St. Vincent, and nabbed not only the Aztec treasure, but another ship from the West Indies carrying 62,000 ducats in gold (the ducat was a monetary unit weighing an ounce and a half of silver), 600 marcs of pearls (a marc weighed half a pound) and 50,000 pounds of sugar. In 1527 Florin was captured after a fierce sea battle with Spanish ships off Cape St. Vincent and carried with 150 of his corsairs to Cadiz where they were all hanged at a public ceremony. The Spanish captain who captured him was knighted and the fleur de-lis, emblem of the French royal family, was added to his family's coat of arms.

Whenever corsair activity intensified another squadron would be organized to patrol the seas between southern Spain and the Azores. The *averia* tax, which supported the anti-piracy campaign, was levied on all ships, merchandise and bullion reaching Spain from the Indies or the Canary Islands and also on the coastal towns subject to corsair raids. The Crown, in an effort to thwart the corsairs, decreed that ships bound for the Indies must weigh a minimum of 80–100 tons, carry four heavy guns, arms, twenty-six soldiers and sixteen gunners.

During the first three decades of the sixteenth century virtually all the shipping between Spain and the New World was directed to Hispaniola, which today is divided into the countries of Dominican Republic and Haiti. The large, rugged island lying between Cuba and Puerto Rico in the West Indies was for sixteen years Spain's only colony. The number of ships sailing in both directions each year depended on their availability, the number of settlers and the volume of exports outward bound from Spain, and the volume of treasure and other New World produce going to Spain as well as on the degree of corsair threat between the Azores and the welcoming mouth of the Guadalquivir River on the coast of southern Spain. For instance in 1508, 66 ships sailed; in 1520 the number reached 108, but in 1529 when the corsair infestation was particularly severe, only 60 sailed, and of the 42 which attempted the return to Spain, 11 were taken.

When five corsair ships wrecked near Chipiona on the Spanish coast during the course of the winter of 1525 Spanish officials were amazed at the numbers of corsairs from prominent French families fished out of the waters. The lure of treasure was as powerful for second sons and impoverished nobles as for men who had never known the feel of silk or tasted fine wine. Increasingly, they moved "beyond the line" of demarcation set forth in the Treaty of Tordesillas and into the "Spanish Lake," as the Atlantic and Caribbean were known.

An occasional French corsair ship appeared in the Caribbean as early as 1506, nipping at Spanish settlements and attacking vulnerable vessels. In 1528, for instance, Huguenot pirates, *corsarios Luteranos*, as the Spaniards called the protestant French sea raiders, sacked and burned San Germain on Puerto Rico's west coast. But it was in the 1530s that large scale, organized corsair fleets moved on the scene. Spanish records reflect the mounting intensity of French raids on colonial island settlements and towns on the Spanish Main, the coastal region of the Americas stretching along the Caribbean. In letter after letter colonial officials pleaded for help from the motherland.

A letter written by Gonzalo de Guzman to the Empress in April of 1537, a year during which French corsairs threatened Havana and Nombre de Diós, sacked and burned La Yaguana and Port-au-Prince and blockaded Santo Domingo, describes the activities of a corsair vessel. In November 1536 it captured a Spanish ship carrying horses from Santo Domingo to the port of Chagres on the Isthmus of Panama. The pirates forced the horses overboard, landed the crew and made off with the ship, which was far more valuable to them. Next, they were spotted anchored in a bay uncomfortably close to Havana. The settlers there begged five Spanish ships then in port to go out and attack the corsairs. Assured the colonials would pay for their vessels in case of loss, three two hundred-ton ships approached the bay and launched a cannonade. They persisted for several days but the pirate craft was a *patache*, a small shallow draft boat, which easily ran inshore where the slower Spanish ships could not follow. Finally, the corsair vessel tried to make a run for the open sea. One of the Spanish ships cut its anchor lines and gave chase but foundered in heavy seas. The crew lowered small boats and made for shore, abandoning their vessel. The other two were also left adrift while their crews rowed for the beach. It was child's play for the corsairs to seize the empty ships. They burned two and sailed toward the Straits of Florida with the other.

For over three centuries the narrow, dangerous Florida Strait between the south tip of Florida and Cuba on the south and the Bahamas on the southeast was the route taken by Spanish shipping sailing for home. Hundreds of ships were lost there due to storms, faulty navigation and the predations of pirates. Fleets sailing from Havana generally turned north to head through the Straits. When they reached the latitude of Cape Canaveral, where the Kennedy Space Center is located today, the ships changed course to the northeast. They maintained this heading until reaching thirty-eight degrees of latitude, where they pointed in an easterly direction until the Bermuda Islands were sighted. Around Bermuda they picked up the prevailing westerly winds and made for the Azores. Fleets stopped at Terceira, one of the easternmost of the Azorean islands to pick up the Armada of the Ocean Sea escort. If the Armada wasn't there they either waited for it to arrive or proceeded alone, according to royal instructions awaiting them. From the Azores the usual route took the returning ships past Cape St. Vincent, on the southwest tip of the Iberian peninsula, where the Captain General of the fleet would dispatch a fast boat carrying mail and arrival notices to Sanlúcar de Barrameda.

The officer or midshipman entrusted with this duty landed at Sanlúcar, mounted a horse and traveled at breakneck speed, first to Seville where he delivered the mail for the House of Trade officials, and then on to the royal court at Valladolid (the court wasn't transferred to Madrid until the early seventeenth century) with news of the fleet's arrival. This was a journey of five to seven days, depending on the conditions of weather and roads. If he brought good news to the king, e.g., no ships wrecked, no losses to the ubiquitous pirates, and lots of treasure cramming the holds, the messenger was amply rewarded, perhaps even knighted depending upon how desperately the king needed to hear good news.

The Spanish monarch was almost always desperate. He needed every bit of treasure to carry on his wars with Protestant Europe and the Barbary pirates of North Africa; to maintain the Spanish occupation forces in Italy and the Low Countries; to support a colonial empire; defend the seas and to pay ever increasing amounts for imports of manufactured goods and even food. A poor country to begin with (when Ferdinand died in 1516 a chronicler noted that "it was difficult to procure money to furnish decent clothing for the servants at his funeral"), the rivers of shining wealth that poured back to Spain aboard the treasure galleons lulled Spain into misjudging its importance and effect. The New World treasure was to drain Spain of a large number of capable men, discourage industrial and agricultural development and spark an inflationary spiral which ultimately turned her into one of the continent's poorest nations. In fact, Spain and Portugal have only recently begun to emerge from four centuries in the shadow of industrialized Europe.

In the years following the early conquests the Crown was greatly enriched. It seemed inconceivable so much gold could do anything but ensure eternal wealth, power and prestige. However, after the colossally rich silver mines were opened at Potosí in 1545, little of the bullion that was transported to Seville remained in Spain. Most of it flowed right out again to the great merchant-banking houses of Germany, the Low Countries and Italy. Each monarch added to the mounting debt. The currency was repeatedly debased sending prices ever higher. Some years, fully two-thirds of the New World treasure production was mortgaged in advance to foreign creditors. Consequently, not only the Spanish government but every European power took great interest in the fortunes of the treasure fleets. The great banking and commercial houses of northern Europe received routine reports from agents and spies in Spain and the New World who monitored every aspect of the *flotas* and their cargoes.

In 1667 the return of a *flota* was delayed. The Venetian Ambassador to Spain wrote his sovereign:

> At the time of writing my last despatch to you, I informed you that there was great anxiety throughout Spain over the delay of the arrival of the treasure fleet from the Indies, and when the Genoese bankers informed the king that unless the *flota* reached port shortly they would be unable to negotiate any further loans for him, Philip fell into such a state that he had to be confined to bed by his physicians. The king then ordered about ten thousand ducats, which was about all the treasure left in the royal coffers, to be dispersed through his realm to various churches and monasteries for the saying of masses for the safe arrival of the treasure fleet. I am happy to inform you that news has just arrived from Seville that the *flota* has made port safely and that there is great rejoicing not only here at the Royal Court, but all over the land as well.[1]

Contrary to, widespread belief, only a small portion of the wealth from the New World came from gold—about 10 percent. The bulk of the gold was shipped to Spain in the Conquest period before 1550 when the golden legacy of the various indigenous civilizations was looted and god was panned by slaves on Hispaniola. The quest for gold spurred the exploration of the Caribbean islands and the Spanish Main but it proved disappointingly scarce or too expensive to mine save in a few places. One continuing source of gold was the silver mines of Mexico and Peru which were larded with rich gold veins. The real wealth of the Indies was in silver. So much was mined and put into circulation that its value, nearly equal to that of gold before the silver boom, dropped to a fifteenth of the value of the yellow metal.

Potosí, the vast silver filled mountain in Spain's colony of Peru (part of Bolivia today), was the chief source of Spanish silver. First worked in 1545, where an Inca Indian hunting a deer had found silver ore at a breathtaking 13,000 feet above sea level, Potosí became a mining and refining center. Three years later silver mines opened in Mexico and subsequently in other areas. Local Indians were enslaved to provide labor for mining and the mercury amalgamation process of refining low grade ores was introduced in 1556. When the Indian slave force was decimated by the harsh conditions imposed by colonial taskmasters, African slaves were imported in large numbers.

All gold and silver had to pass inspection by a royal assayer, who either sent it back for further refining or declared it pure, deducting from it the Crown's 20 percent, known as the "royal fifth," and a small fee for his services. A decade after the Potosí discovery, Mexico City and Lima each boasted a university and had populations of more than one hundred thousand—exceeding those of Seville or Toledo. By the end of the sixteenth century the Spanish had founded two hundred cities in the New World. A number of them had royal mints including Lima, Mexico City, Guatemala City, Bogotá, and Potosí.

Silver was minted into coins called reales in denominations of eight (the famed "pieces of eight"), four, two, and one—and gold into coins called escudos or doubloons of the same sizes and denominations. A portion of the Crown's share of bullion was minted to pay the salaries of royal officials and expenses for colonial garrisons, but the major portion was shipped to Seville in the form of bars, disks, wedges and coins. Except for nationalizing the mercury mine at Huancavélica, Peru, which supplied all South America's needs, the Crown left the American mining industry to private enterprise. The average mine owner was a businessman operating on a fairly large scale, although some Spaniards and Indians worked small claims by hand. Generally, considerable capital was required to mine, refine and then transport the metals to seaports either by llama, as in Peru, or by mule. The profits, however, more than compensated for the expenditures.

Fraudulent assaying and minting of the gold and silver was common although Royal officials were constantly on guard to make sure the Crown was not cheated of its share. Silver bars were sometimes found to have lead cores and "gold" coins were not infrequently made of an inferior alloy containing too much copper. Interestingly enough, silver coins were sometimes counterfeited in platinum, which was then considered an almost worthless metal.

During the sixteenth and seventeenth centuries the typical pay for a Spanish seaman was one piece of eight. A piece of eight was one ounce of silver. Monetary units of ducats and pesos were used for dealing with large sums. A peso was one and one-eighth ounce of silver and a ducat was one and one-half ounce of silver. The smuggling of gold and silver into Spain presented a constant problem. As early as 1510, years before the opening of the mines, an ordinance decreed that any unregistered treasure brought from the Western Hemisphere was subject to confiscation. Its owner was subject not only to a fine of four times the value, but any other punishment the Crown cared to mete out. It is interesting that gold jewelry worn at disembarkation was exempted which accounts for the heavy, elaborately wrought gold chains which have been found on Spanish shipwrecks, some of them exceeding six yards in length.

An elaborate procedure for registering cargo was developed to thwart smugglers. Every piece of bullion was stamped with its year of casting, a tally number, assayer's mark, total value in reales, weight and owner's mark. If the bullion was Crown property either the king's coat of arms or his name was stamped on it. All the information was recorded. Every chest of coins, precious gems or pearls was sealed by a royal official, and the value of its contents stamped on the outside and inscribed on the official record. Even ordinary cargoes such as barrels of sugar or bales of indigo were inspected, and their value stamped on the container and recorded. The records went into a registry on the ship carrying the cargo. Three copies were made of each register. One went aboard the *capitana*, the flagship of the fleet; another aboard the *almiranta*, a heavily armed galleon second in command; and the third remained in the port of embarkation until the following year, when it was sent to Seville to be checked against the original and the other two copies—a precaution against collusive tampering with the records during the long ocean voyage.

Anyone reporting a smuggling plot was awarded a third of the unregistered treasure involved. Yet, despite this inducement and the official safeguards on cargo shipments, a phenomenal amount of smuggling went on. Pirates seizing an eastward bound galleon almost always found more treasure aboard than was listed on the manifest. In 1551 a ship returning from Mexico wrecked off southern Spain. The king's divers recovered more than three times the amount of treasure that had been registered. The ship's unlucky officers were sent to the galleys for ten years.

No precautions, no punishments could deter smuggling. Everyone wanted as much as he could get of the fabulous treasures of the Indies. Fabulous they were: in 1508 the return of a ship carrying gold and pearls worth 50,000 pesos (pieces of eight) was cause for rejoicing in Spain. By 1523 a single ship carried as much as 400,000 pesos, and in 1535 four ships brought 2,500,000 pesos from Peru. Once the big mines began to produce, the amount of treasure funneled across the Atlantic soared astronomically, and in 1587 more than 16,000,000 pesos were shipped from Mexico alone.

Most of the time gold and silver contraband was scattered in the bales, boxes and chests of ordinary cargo since it was impossible for officials to search every inch on their *visita* or tour of inspection. Contraband was also concealed among the rounded ballast stones in the ship's bottom. Smugglers could be ingenious. Once an official scraped an iron anchor wondering why it had been painted and discovered an anchor of solid gold.

Spanish records show that between 1492 and 1830 a total of 4,035,156,000 pesos of gold and silver was produced in the New World. There is no way to determine the amount of unregistered gold and silver mined during this period, but it is estimated to have been between one and two billion pesos worth. The amounts of contraband found on Spanish galleons by modern shipwreck salvors attest to the volume of smuggled treasure. A lot of unregistered treasure went back to Spain but much was used locally in clandestine trade with European merchant ships which perpetually challenged the Spanish monopoly.

As early as 1503, commerce with the American colonies was tightly organized, with a virtual monopoly being granted to Seville, Spain's leading financial city and commercial port. Seville had the added natural advantage of being an inland port, safe from surprise attack by pirates or other hostile forces. The House of Trade was founded there to regulate navigation to and from the Indies, to see that all royal orders concerning conquest and colonization were carried out, to collect customs duties on outbound and incoming cargoes. Passage on ships sailing for the colonies was limited to Spanish citizens. An administrative body called the Council of the Indies organized expansion plans, appointed royal colonial officials and treasure fleet commanders, and acted as an intermediary between the House of Trade and the Crown. It also served as an advisory board to the king. In 1543 the large mercantile houses of Seville which monopolized the Indies trade received royal sanction to form a guild and became the clearinghouse for manufactured goods coming from the rest of Europe. The Merchant Guild had complete civil jurisdiction over its members. It supervised marine insurance which was compulsory, because of the mounting dangers of piracy and shipwrecks.

The French were the most pestiferous. In 1536 a corsair vessel succeeded in capturing Havana, leaving only when a large ransom had been paid and another expedition of 150 men in two swift vessels returned to Gascony in southwestern France with a great haul of gold and silver from the West Indies and French pirates attempted to attack the city of Santiago de Cuba on Cuba's southeast coast, but were driven off. That same year a French fleet under the command of Jean Ango plundered settlements on the coasts of Honduras, Hispaniola and Cuba, and captured nine treasure ships between Florida and the Bahamas.

In 1537, about ten years after merchant ships had been forbidden from crossing the Atlantic alone, the first of the fully organized and armed of the great treasure fleets sailed for the New World. The Emperor and Francis I had renewed their war and it was reported that a fleet of thirteen privateers was being outfitted in Brittany to attack shipping between Havana and Nombre de Diós on the Isthmus of Panama. The Spanish convoy consisting of six warships and twenty merchant ships sailed directly for Nombre de Diós to collect the treasures sent up from Peru, then proceeded to Cartagena on the Colombian coast to pick up gold and emeralds from the interior and pearls collected from the island of Margarita, located off the coast of Venezuela. Then it sailed for Havana where it met ships from Veracruz laden with treasure from Mexico. After taking on water and provisions at Havana, the fleet sailed for the Azores where it united with the Armada of the Ocean Sea which escorted it to Spain.

A certain number of single ships, called *sueltos* were permitted to sail on their own to the New World each year throughout the three centuries of the Indies navigation. Their number was restricted (seldom more than fifty per year) and depended on the current European political climate. The *sueltos* were easy prey for pirates but the Crown relied on them to afford a year-round communication system with out-of-the-way colonies not called on by the *naos*, larger merchant vessels of from two to four hundred tons. To protect the *sueltos* and the vulnerable fringe settlements, Spain maintained a Caribbean squadron of from four to eight galleons called the Windward Armada.

In the middle of the sixteenth century when galleons with their increased cargo capacity first came into use, superseding the *naos*, the convoy system was reorganized. Galleon size ranged from three hundred to a thousand tons. Two fleets were dispatched annually to the New World. Each had four heavily-armed galleons, two eighty-ton *pataches* and anywhere from ten to ninety merchant *naos*. The *pataches* were primarily used as official advice boats carrying messages from port to port or ship to ship but also to carry cargo to ports inaccessible to the larger ships. They might weigh up to one hundred tons and were of various types including pinks, tartans, sloops and pinnaces.

The two principal ships in each *flota* were the *capitana*, the flagship commanded by the captain general, and the *almiranta*, commanded by the admiral. When unusual pirate activity was anticipated extra warships accompanied each *flota*. All ships had to be armed. A merchant galleon of four hundred tons, however, might carry fewer than a dozen cannon, while a warship of the same size could carry as many as fifty large cannon, arranged in two or three tiers. Demiculverins, weighing two tons each and firing a ball of seven to twelve pounds were the largest guns the Spanish used. They had a range of a thousand paces at point blank range and more than twice that distance in trajectory. Brass cannon were preferred over iron since iron heated quickly and the guns tended to explode after repeated firing, inflicting more injuries on the cannoneers than on their enemies.

One *flota* generally left Spain in March and the other in September. The first landfall in the Indies was normally Guadeloupe or Martinique where the ships took on fresh water and fruits before going their separate ways. Those bound for Mexico sailed with the ships destined for Hispaniola, Puerto Rico, Cuba, Jamaica and Honduras. The four galleons and two *pataches* sailed with those heading for Venezuela, Colombia (then part of the vast Nuevo Reino de Granada), and the Isthmus of Panama. The galleons stopped at Nombre de Diós and Cartagena to collect treasure and then made their way to Havana to await the arrival of ships from all the other Spanish settlements before starting back for Spain.

After heavy losses to corsairs and privateers showed the vulnerability of the ships left to sail for Mexico without the protection of warships, the system was refined. For nearly a century after 1564 two *flotas*, the *Tierra Firme Flota* bound for Cartagena and the Isthmus of Panama, and the New Spain *Flota* bound for Mexico, sailed separately. The New Spain *Flota* which included ships for Honduras and the Greater Antilles was scheduled to leave Seville each April and proceed for the Mexican port of Veracruz. The ships seldom left on time. The crossing took from two to three months, depending on the condition of the vessels and the weather. They wintered in Veracruz avoiding the perilous "northers" which blew from October to February. In either February or March they made their way, already riding low in the water from the weight of precious cargoes, to Havana to join with the *Tierra Firme Flota* or sail alone for Spain.

The *Tierra Firme Flota* generally left Spain in August, taking under its protection all the vessels headed for ports along the Spanish Main. It loaded Peruvian treasure at Nombre de Diós, sailed to Cartagena and spent the winter there. In 1595 Sir Francis Drake, the English privateer sacked and burned Nombre de Diós and thereafter Portobelo became the main Caribbean terminus for the *flotas*. In the early Spring the *Tierra Firme Flota* sailed for Havana where it either rendezvoused with the New Spain Fleet or continued alone for home.

As time went on the frequency of pirate attacks, particularly by English buccaneers, forced yet another revision of the convoy system which was put into effect in 1591 and functioned until the mid-seventeenth century. The schedule was somewhat changed and a third *flota*, the *Armada de Tierra Firme*, also called the Silver Fleet, or simply The Galleons, was added. It consisted of eight to twelve galleons and two or more *pataches*. This fleet was forbidden from carrying anything but treasure. In contrast the other fleets transported both treasure and colonial products. The galleons weighed an average of six hundred tons, but the lead ships might weigh a thousand tons. Each carried a company of two hundred marines and a formidable arsenal.

The *Armada* of the South Seas, a squadron of from two to four armed ships, was instituted soon after the conquest of Peru in the early 1540s. Its function was to carry treasure from Peru to Panama City on the Pacific coast of the Isthmus of Panama, where it was unloaded, put on mules and transferred across nightmarish jungle terrain to Nombre de Diós or Portobelo on the Caribbean. The *Armada* was also charged with transporting European products and passengers from Panama to Peru. The fleet was based at Callao, a seaport only six miles from Lima.

The Crown was obsessed with treasure, the merchants and bankers of Seville with maximum profit and it was for their joint benefit that trade with the colonies was organized. The colonists' welfare was of minor concern. The islands along the outer fringe of the Caribbean were increasingly vulnerable to attack by corsairs and privateers. With the exception of pearls, once the early gold boomlet on Hispaniola and Cuba collapsed, their exports were such bulky, relatively low value goods as hides and sugar. The small population of planters on those islands were poor customers compared to those with fat purses on the mainland. Spanish merchants and ships much preferred to trade with the treasure ports of the Spanish Main where they could find silver, emeralds, gold, pearls and such valuable agricultural products as sugar, hides, and the dyestuffs cochineal and indigo. In those ports, too, there were more customers who could pay for imported European goods. In addition, they were well fortified and far safer than those of the neglected islands.

Inter-island shipping suffered accordingly from pirate attack as did those settlements left without adequate protection or transportation for the products of its plantations. In 1549, years before Havana was officially designated as the rendezvous for Seville bound ships, it was proposed but colonial officials representing the Audiencia of Santo Domingo, a regional administrative body with governing powers over Puerto Rico, Hispaniola, Cuba, Jamaica and Florida, voiced their fears that Spanish vessels gathering there would be easy prey to pirates and that Havana's port was an unprotected roadstead in the path of annual hurricanes. Eventually massive forts were constructed at the entrance to the port and a chain boom was strung across the mouth of the port to prevent undesirable vessels from entering.

A shadow of fear hung over colonial towns. They were poorly defended against pirate raids. Some had only the smallest, most rudimentary forts and no soldiers. Often the inhabitants had no guns or no ammunition. In one of innumerable reports which received scant attention from the Crown the Audiencia of Santo Domingo in 1541 noted the deplorable condition of Santo Domingo's chief fort which had been "built for defense against the Indians, not against corsairs, at a time when it did not seem possible for the latter to cross the seas" and went on to describe the plight of defenseless ports, robbed and burned in full daylight.

The settlement of Santa Maria de los Remedios, near Cape de la Vela on the coast of Venezuela, repulsed six French pirate ships in October of 1544. The colonists were better prepared than six months earlier when corsairs had swooped on the town sending them fleeing into the bush. Churches had been desecrated, houses stripped and even graves dug up by the Frenchmen who also maimed livestock and destroyed agricultural plots and chopped down fruit trees.

In 1543, Santa Marta, on the north coast of Colombia, was sacked for the first of several times. Four large ships and a *patache* appeared before the town at noon. In the face of the more than four hundred men, armed with pikes and arquebuses, who came ashore, there was nothing the inhabitants could do but flee inland leaving the pirates to pillage at will. The governor bravely went out to deal with the corsairs, trying to ransom the town and hoping as well to buy a few barrels of badly needed flour. He was rebuffed and for eight days the raiders burned houses and destroyed gardens, orchards and port facilities. When they sailed they took with them four bronze artillery pieces, Santa Marta's only defense which had proved woefully inadequate. In 1548 the local authorities warned the king that Santa Marta would be abandoned if a fort and artillery were not soon provided. A few years later, in 1551, Santa Marta was spared when corsairs accepted a ransom of two thousand pesos.

Most of the French corsairs were Protestant Huguenots, followers of Martin Luther, whose descendants centuries later left France because of Catholic persecution. These sea raiders continued to profit from the alliance between the Seville Monopoly and the Spanish Crown, which turned a deaf ear to the Audiencia of Santo Domingo's pleas for more soldiers, fortifications, supply vessels and the establishment of a naval squadron to protect the islands and police the waters between Hispaniola and Puerto Rico, the corsairs' chief rendezvous. In 1541 an audiencia report observed: "Although there is peace, they will not cease such robberies so long as rich prizes are available at such small risk." Perennial harassment from pirates eventually led the financially strapped Crown to adopt a policy of evacuating small settlements too costly to defend. Inhabitants moved inland or to other towns where coastal defenses were stronger.

However, even the chief ports of the Spanish colonial empire were not spared from attack by protestant French sea raiders known to the Spanish as the hated heretic *corsarios Luteranos*, who were attracted by the opportunities those towns offered. Cartagena, for example, first sacked by pirates in 1543, was plundered more often than any other important settlement in South America. In 1544 Cartagena was surprised on the dawn of St. James Day when three hundred corsairs, under the command of a Corsican who had lived there, stormed the town's weak defenses. A few Spaniards were killed and the governor was wounded. They sacked the place, making off with 35,000 pesos worth of gold and silver as well as other loot. Within two years of its founding in 1533, Cartagena superseded Santa Marta as the chief port on the Spanish Main, although the latter was closer to the mouth of the Magdalena, the river on which gold and emeralds were transported from Bogotá. Cartagena's harbor was more than ten miles long with room to anchor hundreds of large ships. It had only one small entrance, Boca Chica meaning Small Mouth. This would have made it one of the New World's most impregnable settlements if the Spaniards had constructed forts on both sides of the entrance and strung a chain across the opening.

The Spaniards, however, hadn't even completed the first fort by 1543 when the infant town was besieged and plundered by Robert Baal, a corsair. Needless to say, construction was speeded up thereafter and measures were taken to secure Cartagena since it was the first port of call for the majority of ships of the *Tierra Firme Flota*. Even more important, Cartagena was the rendezvous for all the ships of the *flota* once they had collected their treasure cargoes from the silver ports of the Spanish Main. When Francis Drake arrived in 1583 the chain across the harbor mouth still wasn't in place despite a royal order issued twenty years earlier. "El Draque," scourge of the Spanish Main, brazenly sailed in and took the town with relative ease.

As soon as a *flota* reached Cartagena a swift advice boat was dispatched to Nombre de Diós on the Isthmus of Panama with the news. From there a courier carried word across to Panama City. Colonial officials there immediately sent word by sea to Callao in Peru. Indians running in relays were also sent overland to the viceroy in Lima to make sure the amassed treasure would be loaded aboard the ships of the Armada of the South Seas for the first leg of its long journey to Spain.

Callao was a fine natural harbor protected by a large offshore island which boasted a fort and by a long promontory on the mainland, where another fort stood. All the silver from Potosí was shipped from Callao. It was transported by llamas from the rarified heights of the mines to Arica, the nearest seaport (part of modern Chile) and loaded on boats for the eight day trip to Callao. There were few piratical attacks on Callao since the only way to reach it by sea was to sail around the vast South American continent into the Pacific. Drake's successful raid in the year of 1579 was an exception, one that proved incredibly profitable to the English adventurer and his backers.

In the early days Panama City escaped pirate attack because of its location on the Pacific side of the Isthmus. The climate was torrid and unhealthy and the port was far from ideal but because it was strategically located to benefit from expanding trade with Peru, it grew into an important urban center with a huge cathedral, monasteries and handsome government buildings. Only small ships could use the port since it was extremely shallow, subject to great tidal variation and exposed to the sea. Large ships anchored in the harbor of Perico, six miles westward, where a group of small islands formed a protected anchorage. Cargoes had to be ferried by lighters to the port of Panama City.

Everything going to or coming from the Pacific coast of South America passed through Panama City and across the Isthmus to Nombre de Diós (or after 1596 to Portobelo several miles southeast). At first goods were transported on mule back across a forty eight mile trail hacked out of the jungle. To make things easier a staging point was established at the head of the Chagres River, fifteen miles from the city. Treasure from Panama City was taken by mule train (up to one hundred mules, laden with as much as three hundred pounds of silver each) to Veracruz, the staging point where it was put on small boats and carried down the river, a three to twelve day trip depending on conditions, to Nombre de Diós. Often, because of droughts or floods, the river was not navigable and the journey had to be made entirely overland across high passes where mules slipped to their death, and through thickly wooded areas where bands of runaway slaves known as *cimarrones* ambushed the mule trains.

Nombre de Diós had nothing to recommend it save its position at the narrow waist of the Isthmus. The port, slightly east of modern Colón, was located inside a shallow bay pocked with reefs so that ships had to anchor offshore. The gaping mouth of the harbor offered little protection from enemy attack or the elements. In 1565 during a violent norther an entire *flota* was wrecked at anchorage.

The climate was pestiferous, the terrain either swamp or jungle. It was said Nombre de Diós was so unhealthy that even Indian women and native trees bore no fruit there. Infamous as "the Spanish Graveyard" Nombre de Diós was unprotected by walls and never grew into an urban center. In fact, it was virtually a ghost town save when the Tierra Firme Fleet appeared.

At the first glimpse of sails the settlement was transformed into the bustling site of a fair at which the cargoes from Spain were exchanged for the precious metals and gems of Peru. Nearly every inhabitant of Panama descended on the squalid settlement, along with merchants from Peru, other South American colonies and even Mexico. During the tumultuous fair, which lasted from one to six weeks, the price of a meal or hammock in the primitive inns rose astronomically. Tropical fevers claimed the lives of many profit-hungry people.

The Spanish who were barred by the Portuguese from the southern route to Asia and its commercial marvels, launched the Manila galleons on a route that plied the Pacific between Acapulco and Manila in the Philippines. From 1565 until 1815 a few ships sailed almost every year from Acapulco. They were the largest of Spanish ships—averaging about 700 tons in the sixteenth century, 1,500 in the seventeenth and between 1,700 and 2,000 tons in the eighteenth. The voyage west took from eight to ten weeks and was not particularly arduous.

However, the return voyage which took from four to eight months was considered one of the most dangerous in the world because the great galleons had to beat their way as far north as Japan before catching the westerly winds which carried them across the Pacific until they made landfall on the California coast and worked their way south to Acapulco. On a typical eastbound crossing an average of from 100 to 150 of the 300 to 600 of the people aboard each galleon succumbed to epidemics, scurvy, starvation, thirst or exposure.

In spite of the great risks, which included the menace of Asian pirates close to the Philippines, the Manila galleons never lacked passengers or merchandise. The outward bound ships carried wine, olive oil, cloth and manufactured goods from Europe which the colonists craved and were forbidden from producing themselves. The galleons sailing to the Philippines also carried bullion and specie to pay for the exotic cargoes taken on in Manila. The faded inks of the manifests of the Manila galleons list a dazzling assortment of Oriental luxuries including silks, velvets, damasks, crepes, and taffeta from China and Japan, spices, pharmaceuticals, rugs, fans, gems, elaborate jewelry, Chinese porcelain ware, jewel-studded sword hilts, pearls, novelty items of ivory and sandalwood, and finely wrought religious articles in gold, silver, ivory and rare wood crafted by Asian artisans for European churches.

Over the centuries dozens of these galleons groaning under their precious loads were lost on the way to Mexico. The waters around Luzon Island were especially treacherous and quite a few wrecked shortly after leaving Manila. Those that made it across the Pacific anchored at one of the world's finest natural harbors, a deep, semicircular bay which is nearly landlocked. On a narrow strip of land between the bay and the encircling mountains, Acapulco was founded. Little more than a tropical village with a scattering of shacks, one church and a small fort during most of the year, Acapluco came to life whenever the Manila galleons arrived and a fair was held where the wares of China, Japan, Java, the Moluccas, India and even Persia were unloaded and displayed along with goods destined for the East which had come overland from Veracruz.

Veracruz, named by Cortés when he landed there in 1519, became Mexico's leading seaport. Again, it was location rather than natural features which were responsible for its development. The harbor was open and unprotected, leaving anchored ships exposed to the brunt of hurricanes in the summer and northers in the fall and winter. Only small ships could cross the shallow bar at the harbor entrance; larger vessels anchored at San Juan de Ulúa, a small fortified island fifteen miles south.

Veracruz was the first port of call for the majority of the ships of the New Spain *Flota* and served as the clearinghouse for the treasure of Mexico and the portion of the Manila galleon goods destined for Spain. In addition, the town was the center of trade in cochineal, a costly scarlet dye made from the desiccated bodies of female insects. Save for the bustle of the trade fair, Veracruz was a sweltering, sleepy town where few Spaniards chose to live.

Havana was altogether different from the majority of New World seaports. It became a truly splendid city, boasting magnificent public buildings and a sophisticated populace, although its beginnings were hardly auspicious. In 1536 the settlement at Havana was considered of so little account that a French pirate who captured the town accepted a mere one hundred pieces of eight for its ransom.

Once trade with the Indies was in full swing Havana blossomed, attracting settlers who appreciated the breeze-tempered climate. Its deep water harbor, the finest in the West Indies, could accommodate a thousand ships with ease, and the entrance to it, a narrow channel, could easily be defended.

All ships sailing for Spain passed within sight of Havana. Most of them put in for provisions, water, and perhaps a fresh crew to replace those who had died or deserted. Havana also supplied timber becoming the most important shipbuilding center in the Western Hemisphere. Havana was the only port consistently visited by both the *Tierra Firme Flota* and the New Spain *Flota*. It took the *Tierra Firme Flota* ten days to two weeks to reach there from Cartagena. The other *flota* battled contrary winds and currents, heading north from Veracruz as far as modern Pensacola, before being able to come about. The fleet then sailed south, hugging the coast of Florida as far as the Keys, before sailing directly for Havana.

The pirates and privateers who shadowed the treasure galleons craved Havana's riches. In the early days before the fortifications were completed the city was sacked and burned many times. However, by 1586 it was so strongly defended that even Drake, the most daring of all sea raiders, was dissuaded from attacking.

Permanent lookouts were stationed at Cape San Antonio, on Cuba's western tip, and elsewhere around the island. As soon as a pirate fleet was sighted, news was relayed to Havana by smoke signal. When a *flota* passed Cape San Antonio, the captain general sent a small boat ashore to receive word from the island's governor on whether the coast was clear. If it was not, the captain general had to make the decision to sail directly for Spain, to head for another safe port, or to prepare to fight his way into Havana harbor. Once inside the *flotas* were safe enough, protected by the best forts in the New World. During the long period of Spanish dominion in the New World, Havana was the least attacked seaport.

Prior to 1552 when war broke out again between Spain and France, most corsair raids had been carried out by one or two armed ships, accompanied by a smaller pinnace with both sails and oars which could maneuver close inshore. Although such forays continued, large corsair squadrons which sometimes had royal warships among them, cruised the Caribbean raiding shipping and pillaging Spanish ports. In general, these corsairs were sailing as privateers rather than pirates since they had been issued letters of marque by the Henri II the French king. These were documents which authorized them to capture enemy (i.e., Spanish) ships and cargo. In 1553 Vincent Bocquet of Dieppe with two ships captured eight of fourteen ships in a *flota* bound for Spain. King Henri granted letters of marque in the same year to François le Clerc, a Huguenot from Normandy better known as Jambe de Bois or Pie de Palo (Wooden Leg). With his lieutenants Jacques Sores and Robert Blondel, Pie de Palo had a fleet made up of three royal vessels, several privateers and a number of smaller, faster boats. They sacked La Yaguana, San Germán, the islands of Mona and Saona and a number of other settlements. In the following year Pie de Palo, who had a deep seated hatred of the Roman Catholic Church, led a band of three hundred corsairs on Santiago de Cuba. They held it for a month, terrorizing the populace and treating the Catholic clergy with extreme cruelty. When they left they took eighty thousand pesos worth of plunder and left the town a wasteland which never recovered.

In 1555 corsairs captured Havana, after sacking Santa Marta, La Margarita and Rio de la Hacha, and left it "no better off than the Greeks left Troy." Pie de Palo landed two hundred men a little distance from Havana in the predawn darkness of a July day and marched on Havana with flags flying and drums beating, taking the fort as well as the town. The Spanish governor disregarded the agreed upon truce and vainly tried to surprise the privateers during the night with a small motley force of Spaniards and slaves. Several of the *corsarios Luteranos* were killed, including a relative of Pie de Palo's.

In revenge he had all Spanish prisoners massacred. Refusing to ransom the town, he burned it to the ground and desecrated the cathedral. He distributed the priests' richly embroidered vestments as cloaks for his men. The Protestant corsairs then paraded through the ruined town in a mock religious procession mutilating sacred statues. They ravaged the surrounding countryside and burned all the boats in the port. A number of captive slaves were hung simply because they were Spanish property. Then the French left, taking with them a rich haul of booty. As if poor Havana hadn't suffered enough, another expedition of 120 corsairs led by Jacques Sores landed in early October, destroying buildings under construction, and capturing a caravel loaded with leather. Then, they fanned out into the countryside destroying whatever plantations the previous raiders had overlooked and sailed off with everything they found of value.

These attacks were followed by many others and inspired a French royal plan that was never carried out to shatter Spain's naval capability and economy by seizing Panama and the Southern Sea *Flota* and the New Spain *Flota* as well. Basque pirates from Bayonne and St. Jean de Luz sacked Puerto de Caballos on the coast of Honduras in 1558. Inter-Caribbean trade was paralyzed. Corsair activity escalated to the point that ships cowered in port, or made desperate runs, shadowed by the ubiquitous and arrogant corsairs. Spanish defenses remained weak, as Jacques Sores's Havana foray had shown, and Spanish silver very tempting. The Treaty of Cateau-Cambresis of 1559 which established peace between France and Spain had little effect on the Caribbean which lay "beyond the line" of amity. It was tacitly understood that French and Spanish ships might take each other as if war were still underway. Almost ten years later a Spanish colonial official reported that: "For every two ships that come thither from Spain, twenty corsairs appear. For this reason, not a town on this coast is safe, for whenever they please to do so they take and plunder these settlements. They go so far as to boast that they are lords of the sea and the land, and as a matter of fact daily we see them seize ships, both those of the Indies' trade and also some that come here from Spain itself."[2]

Most of the corsairs were Protestants whose hatred of Catholics added to their ferocity. They relied on Catholics, however, to pilot their ships through the shoal and reef-strewn waters of the Caribbean. Renegade pilots, including the Italian Abagni family from Lucca in Tuscany, settled in ports like La Rochelle. Francisco Dias Mimoso, a one-eyed Portuguese, was the most notorious. He was highly successful at seizing homeward bound Spanish vessels in the tricky waters of the east Florida Channel between Havana and the Florida coast. The Spanish sovereign was obsessed with getting rid of Dias Mimoso. Twice he prevailed upon the French king to try him. Both times he was condemned to death and reprieved. He was finally hanged in France in 1569.

The sixteenth-century corsairs were drawn to the islands and coast of eastern Venezuela because of the pearl fisheries where slave divers working from lateen-rigged frigates brought up beautiful lustrous pearls called *margaritas* in Spanish. The frigates and the seaside *rancherias* or camps where the slaves were kept were easy prey for pirates who stole harvested pearls, held the frigates for ransom and made off with the slaves.

La Barburata, one of the pearling settlements on the Venezuelan coast was evacuated in 1553 on account of the corsairs. It was an excellent port, large and secure. Juan Lopez de Velasco, sixteenth-century Spanish author of *Geography and Description of the Indies* wrote that " . . . it is of very great importance to keep it because it is the seaport for the New Kingdom of Granada (which encompassed modern Colombia) and all the provinces of Peru and if the French take possession of it, it will be difficult to recover."

Later, the Spanish did retake Barburata, but for years it served the French as both a corsair base and a center for *rescate*, an ambiguous form of contraband trade they engaged in with the Spanish settlers. The word covered a host of activities including ransom, smuggling, barter and exchange. A French ship laden with slaves and other goods might trade straightforwardly one moment and use armed threats the next to exact its own terms. The colonials winked at French claims of having been "blown across the Atlantic by tempests" into the forbidden Spanish Lake. They were willing to break the law and risk being victimized by a French trader/pirate rather than dangle at the mercy of official trading policies which delivered too little, too late and at too high a cost. They much preferred trading with the French and the Portuguese and later the English and Dutch to avoid the onerous Spanish regulations and taxes. In addition, the colonials' products fetched higher prices from the interlopers than from the monopolist Spanish traders.

The French set up raiding and trading bases not only on the Venezuelan coast but in other mainland harbor areas as well as on a number of islands including La Margarita, Trinidad and Curacao, which very nearly became a permanent station in the 1560s. To the north the French, like the Catholic Portuguese whose smuggling was a little better tolerated by the Spanish than that of the largely Protestant French, generally made landfall at Puerto Rico. They picked up fresh water and provisions in one of the island ports where they learned what Spanish warships were prowling in the area and then made for Hispaniola to trade on the northern and western coasts attacking any Spanish or Portuguese ships they encountered. The small islands of Mona and Saona lying east and southeast off Hispaniola served as dual purpose bases for the Protestant trader/corsairs. They lay in wait to intercept boats carrying sugar and hides, sometimes paying for what they took but more often not.

Spanish colonists didn't always welcome the illicit traders. In 1568 for example a Protestant ship from LeHavre called at La Margarita, off Venezuela. Captain Burgoyne requested permission to come ashore to trade and was invited to disembark. His crew traded for about ten days with the Spaniards who then turned on them, killing sixteen or seventeen, capturing and hanging the rest and distributing their merchandise and whatever else they found aboard the ship.

A little after mid-century the French government awakened to the possibilities of making an official try for some portion of the New World and its riches. In 1562 Admiral Coligny, the Huguenot leader, sponsored a French settlement at Port Royal on the coast of what is now South Carolina. The colony failed, but in 1564 a second attempt to establish a Protestant colony under the command of René de Laudonniere was made at the mouth of the St. Johns River on the northeast coast of Florida. The little Protestant colony struggled to survive. Many of the men abandoned the settlement for a life of piratical raiding on Spanish settlements.

The Spanish Crown greatly feared the effects of a French colony in such a strategic location so close to the Florida Straits. Previous efforts under Ponce de León, Panfilo de Narváez and Hernando de Soto to gain control of the area had failed and the king gave Pedro Menéndez de Avilés, an Asturian *flota* commander and naval genius, a commission to conquer and colonize the Land of the Flowers as Ponce de León had named the peninsula. Menéndez was an experienced conquistador who used his own funds to outfit the expedition which was empowered to claim Florida for Spain and dislodge the French. He had an ulterior motive. His son had been on a ship which was lost at sea between South America and the Bahamas some years earlier and he hoped that perhaps he would find his son who might have been shipwrecked on the Florida coast and captured by natives as other Spaniards had been.

The Spanish admiral found the little Huguenot colony freshly reinforced by the arrival of Jean Ribault, the founder of Port Royal, who had arrived with an infusion of ships, men and supplies; however, they succeeded in destroying the settlement slaughtering every single Frenchman they came across. Inflamed by the memory of the atrocities the Protestant corsair Sores had inflicted on Havana a decade earlier, they justified the massacre with labels on some of the corpses stating they had been killed "not as Frenchmen but as Lutheran heretics."

Menéndez secured the Florida Straits, establishing a settlement at St. Augustine in 1565. As *adelantado*, or governor, of Florida, Menéndez was responsible for providing the colonists with supplies and food. He was entitled to a fifteenth of whatever wealth Florida might produce, but it soon became apparent that it had neither gold nor shining prospects of any kind.

Menéndez was Spain's most powerful naval representative in the Caribbean until his death in 1574. He was dedicated to protecting the *flota* system, Spain's lifeline, and the treasure ports. At the same time he used his office to chase down corsairs for the prize money. He wrote Philip II of his intention to rid the Caribbean of the predators: "so that Your Majesty may have the Indies and Florida secure, and that no corsair shall come to these parts without being lost, nor any ship trading without license."

The next Fall, October of 1566, Menéndez began a pirate hunt with six warships, a frigate and a *patache* around Puerto Rico, Santo Domingo and Cuba. In Santo Domingo he received word of the imminent arrival of a great French armada of three squadrons. He was ordered to direct the fortification of Puerto Rico, Havana and other ports and then return with all speed to Florida. Menéndez was disappointed at this development since "it had been his wish to scour the seas and fall upon one of the corsair squadrons, which should afford very rich booty."

Menéndez faced a thankless task. Four of the towns he went to prepare for defense were unwilling to assist him since they profited from contraband trade with the French. Fifty of the soldiers he had left in Puerto de Plata on Hispaniola's north coast had to fight off an attack led by the corsair Jean Bontemps when the citizens refused to defend themselves. Thus encouraged, Bontemps led his corsair band on Monte Cristi, La Yaguana and Puerto Real. He seized twelve ships carrying gold and silver in the three harbors and burned Puerto Real. Menéndez finally gained a measure of revenge taking five richly laden corsair ships off the coast of Cuba which helped defray the expenses of the expedition.

Menéndez's passion for sweeping the sea clean of pirates led him to develop a modified galleon design. Spanish ships were generally no match for swifter French or English vessels. Built to carry as much cargo as possible, they were big, heavy, unwieldy craft which fared poorly in rough seas. Menéndez designed a smaller, lighter ship, with a lower deck for oarsmen so that it could navigate in shallow coastal waters and penetrate the winding creeks and mangrove-choked areas the pirates favored as hiding places. However, these *galeoncetes* as they were called, were discontinued after an initial trial because they were expensive to build, maintain and crew and rode too low for the rowers to maneuver. Once again, the Spanish had to rely on an inadequate number of oared galleys stationed at Cartagena and Santo Domingo for coastal defense.

In the latter half of the sixteenth century the pirate menace in the Caribbean and on the Spanish Main continued unabated. Spanish territorial expansion was arrested and when corsairs destroyed established colonies they were often abandoned rather than rebuilt. Trujillo and Puerto de Caballos in Honduras were abandoned and no further settlements were made on that coast leaving the route to the riches of Guatemala and the Golfo Dulce open to enemy ships. Thousands of head of Spanish livestock on Curacao, the largest of the islands off Venezuela's coast, were slaughtered by French corsairs who took their hides. The pearl beds of Cubagua were no longer worked as before because of the pirate threat.

A contemporary chronicler, Antonio Barbudo, wrote that "Throughout the 150 leagues of the province of Venezuela there is not a single settlement by the sea, nor any man who would settle there, because of the robberies and burnings of the corsairs." Barbudo noted "the continuance of the attentions of the English pirates and French Lutheran corsairs to that coast and nearby waters for twelve years." describing how the pearl fishery on La Margarita was robbed and burned so many times that the settlers abandoned the coast, leaving their houses and farms, and retreated two leagues inland. Even there, he wrote "the enemy have not left them alone, but have gone to seek them out setting fire to their church and to some of their houses."

The Caribbean islands fared little better than the Spanish Main. Apart from the town of Puerto Rico and the city of Santo Domingo all the settlements had either been abandoned or had been moved inland because they were sacked and burned so many times by the French. The Spanish king, self-appointed guardian of Catholic Europe, had committed his very limited resources to warring on the Turkish infidels, leaving the New World possessions to fend for themselves. Undermanned and poorly supplied with war galleys, they couldn't hope to combat the French corsairs, although they made valiant attempts. One Spanish captain wanted to station divers on war galleys and in ports where corsair ships anchored. He suggested they could dive at night to strip the caulking from the hulls of corsair ships or drill holes in them.

The corsairs continued to attack Spanish shipping and settlements and threatened to seize the Isthmus itself, Spain's essential link to the wealth of Peru and the Pacific. In the late 1560s and 1570s English sea raiders, the Elizabethan sea dogs, swarmed through the hole in the Spanish dike the French Protestants had made to plunder the West Indies and the Spanish Main on a grand scale.

NOTES

1. Venetian Ambassador to Spain in 1667 letter, Duro, Fernández Cesareo de, *La Armada Española*, Vol. V, pp. 219–20.
2. Spanish official in 1569, Linage, Joseph de Vieta, *Norte de la Contratacion de las Indias Occidentales*, Vol. II, ch. XXXIX, p. 29.

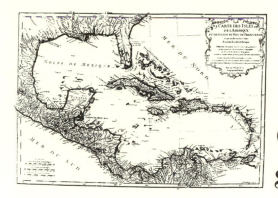

3

Elizabeth's Sea Dogs

hile French corsairs plundered the Spanish Main in the first half of the sixteenth century, England's mariners were lured by other opportunities. Sea rovers from the West Country reaped fat profits from traditional piracy in the Narrow Seas between Great Britain and the continent. The fishermen of Bristol had worked the great schools of cod and ling in Icelandic waters in the fifteenth century until the Hanseatic fleet all but chased them away and had to search for new fishing grounds.

Master mariners like John Cabot and his son Sebastian, sought the fabled northerly passage to Asia. During the reign of the Tudors, and even later, the English were convinced the passage existed. They believed discovery of this route would furnish England with her rightful share of the seemingly inexhaustible supplies of gold, silver, precious stones, silks, spices and Eastern luxuries which Spain and Portugal plucked from their colonies with apparent ease.

A few English adventurers made random voyages to the New World but neither the Crown nor England's powerful merchant class seized the initiative. It was motivation not ability that was lacking since the English were consummate mariners. England sat out the first round of discovery and colonization, preferring to invest in the relatively secure commerce with northern Europe. Henry VII rewarded John Cabot's planting of an English flag on the shore of Nova Scotia with a meager ten pounds.

Henry VIII was even less interested in oceanic voyages and aggressive expansion, although he stimulated European maritime enterprise. Henry's fine navy, boasted men-of-war and armed merchant ships constructed at his great, new dockyards. The navy was created to keep the English Channel free of pirates so English woolens and other merchandise could be freely shipped to the Netherlands and other markets including Spain.

Until Elizabeth came to the throne in 1558, trade with the distant Caribbean was considered far too risky. During Henry VIII's reign (1509–47) England was engaged in an intermittent war with France and so found herself uneasily allied with Spain. She was, consequently, unwilling to openly poach on Spain's New World preserve. Queen Mary, a Catholic, who ruled from 1553 until 1558 was married to Philip II of Spain. Elizabeth, a Protestant, maneuvered skillfully to preserve nominal peace with Spain although it was increasingly difficult for the champion of Protestantism and the bulwark of Roman Catholicism to remain friendly. In 1585 open warfare erupted between England and Spain. Merchants, even in Elizabeth's reign, who might have provided backing for oceanic voyages or transatlantic pirating expeditions participated indirectly in trade with the New World and felt little motivation to change the status quo. English goods found their way to the Caribbean via English traders who lived in southern Spain, some of whom had representatives in Mexico (circumventing Spanish prohibitions) and managed to visit the area.

After Henry VIII declared war on France in 1543 privateering reached a new peak in European waters. English privateers, limited by their letters of marque to taking certain amounts of goods from French ships, grew so bold they seized entire cargoes of any vessel carrying French merchandise. The English markets were glutted with goods from dried fish to fine lace. There was scarcely room to store it all before selling it for bargain basement prices. William Hawkins, who had made three pioneering voyages to Brazil in the 1530s, took a Spanish ship off the English coast and sold the cargo before the British Admiralty Court gave him permission. Spain was England's nominal ally at the time and Hawkins was jailed briefly at the insistence of the Spanish Ambassador but there was no stopping the English pirates, although hundreds were hanged. In 1563 more than four hundred known English pirates were operating around the British Isles and many more to the south.

The increased traffic between Spain and the New World stimulated a period of intense piracy in European waters which was initiated in 1545 by Robert Reneger of Southampton when he took the *San Salvador*, a Spanish treasure ship on its way to Seville from Hispaniola. This act of piracy was in retaliation for the loss of a French vessel Reneger had captured and taken into a Spanish port, expecting to receive a large share of the cargo as a reward. The Spanish prize court seized the vessel. An infuriated Reneger set out to capture a Spanish ship. His ship lay off Cape St. Vincent, the southernmost point of Portugal, with four other English vessels waiting for a homebound Spanish treasure ship. When the *San Salvador* appeared they boarded her and found gold, hides and sugar worth 7,243,075 maravedis. The captain pleaded with Reneger not to mention the gold which was contraband and not listed on the manifest. The gold was stored in the Tower of London for eight years when about a third of it was finally returned to Spain.

The Spanish ambassador was enraged at the hero's welcome Reneger received when he returned to England. The final straw as far as the Spanish envoy was concerned was that Henry VIII, who had officially professed to have been "greatly annoyed" at Reneger's insolent stroke of piracy on a allied ship, named him to a command in his fleet. Henry's promise to the Spanish ambassador to halt attacks on allied shipping meant little. Reneger's exploit, so amply rewarded, motivated legions of Anglo-English freebooters to have a go at Spanish shipping not only off the English coast but even near ports in Spain and Portugal.

With such rich pickings close to home, few English mariners cared to roam in distant seas. There were exceptions. The first mention of an English ship in the New World was made by Alonso de Ojeda who encountered one off Venezuela in 1499 while exploring the northern coast of South America. In 1516 Sebastian Cabot and Sir Thomas Pert voyaged to the Brazilian coast, and a few hazy references indicate there may have been another venturesome English explorer or two in those early years.

The first detailed account of an English ship in the Caribbean concerns John Rut's expedition of 1527. Spanish documents report that a well-armed ship of about 250 tons appeared in the Mona Passage between Hispaniola and Puerto Rico on November 19, 1527. A caravel loading cassava watched as a pinnace was launched with about twenty-five armed and armored men in it. The Spaniards dispatched a small boat at the same time, thinking the other ship was also Spanish. The two boats met and Rut, the English captain identified himself, explaining that he had been en route with a second ship to discover the land of the Great Khan (China) when a storm separated the ships. Ice filled seas prevented Rut's ship from proceeding westward so he turned south, touched at Bacallaos (Newfoundland), where his pilot was slain by Indians, and then sailed down into the Caribbean.

The English spent two days on Puerto Rico and then sailed for Hispaniola. At Santo Domingo Rut went ashore with a few of his men, requesting permission to bring his ship into port to trade. The local authorities told him to enter the following morning and sent pilots to help bring the ship in. However, during the night they reconsidered, fearing that if one English ship were cordially received, an English invasion might follow. So next day when Rut approached, the Spanish commander gave an order to fire on the ship. The English returned to Puerto Rico where they traded cloth and pewter for fresh supplies and then sailed for Europe but were apparently lost at sea. The Spanish commander was subsequently imprisoned for driving the ship away rather than allowing it to enter the port where it could have been captured.

Rut's was the last English sail sighted in the Caribbean for some years. William Hawkins, father of the renowned Sir John Hawkins, launched the next wave of oceanic voyages by the English sea dogs, as the English called seasoned sailors. William served as Henry VIII's chief naval advisor and established Plymouth as England's maritime center. Queen Elizabeth based her navy at Plymouth and it was home port to the greatest of the sea dogs—John Hawkins, Francis Drake (his cousin) and the ill-starred Walter Raleigh.

The elder Hawkins had pioneered the trade in ivory and gold dust with Upper Guinea (Liberia). Between 1530 and 1532 he made three voyages to trespass in Brazil which the Pope had assigned to Portugal. He followed a triangular route, sailing to Upper Guinea on the first leg. In 1530 he traded for ivory and pepper and then crossed to Brazil, landing near Bahia. He traded for brazilwood, a red dye wood prized by English cloth manufacturers. Profits were so good that he repeated the triangular voyage the following year, returning with a native chief from Brazil to show to the king and leaving one of his men there as hostage.

Hawkins hoped to persuade Henry VIII to support his transoceanic voyages. The king and his court were fascinated by the exotic chieftain, who had a jewel set in his lower lip and bones piercing his cheeks. Henry, however chose not to back Hawkins. When he sailed on his third voyage, it was still with his own ship and funding. The poor chieftain didn't survive the trip home but his people didn't hold the English responsible and allowed Martin Cockerham, the English hostage who had spent the year preparing a shipment of brazilwood, to leave.

Hawkins himself made no more voyages but sporadic trade between Plymouth, Upper Guinea and Brazil continued until 1540. Robert Reneger was one of the men involved. French pirates were a menace to ships off the Brazilian coast and in 1542 English interests were substantial enough to warrant private construction of a fort near Bahia. The Caribbean was still forbidden territory to the English although in 1540 a captain named John Philips sailed from London with the *Barbara* directly to Hispaniola. Piracy rather than trade seems to have been his object for near Santo Domingo he seized a Spanish ship laden with sugar and hides. The *Barbara* had struck a reef and begun leaking so the crew put the Spanish prisoners ashore, sunk their damaged ship and sailed off in the prize, rechristened the *Barbara*. They sailed in such haste that their French pilot, who had been taken on because of his familiarity with Caribbean waters, was left behind. Back in England, Philips was arrested on charges of piracy at the insistence of the Spanish ambassador who, three years later, was pointedly ignored when he pressed for action against Reneger for a similar act of piracy.

The rulers of England and Spain were able to feign a tolerance for one another's affairs that their subjects did not share. Jealousy of Spain's new "golden world" wasn't the only cause of the average Englishman's hostility. The flames of hatred were fanned by reports of Spanish oppression, cruelty and treachery in the New World. The greatest factor, however, was the growth of bitter religious differences born of the Reformation and compounded by the Counter Reformation. Sea dogs, like Drake, were to make their attacks on ships and settlements in the Caribbean a holy mission aimed at the Evil Forces of the Apocalypse. After Reneger's provocative piracy was rewarded by Henry VIII, Spain imposed suffocating new restrictions and fines on English traders. English merchants were no longer welcome as residents. They were harassed and many were brought before the Inquisition. Some were convicted of heresy and thrown into dungeons where they encountered captured English privateers who were luckier than many of their fellow sailors who were burned at the stake or condemned to short lives as galley slaves. It wasn't surprising that staunch Protestant sea dogs believed they had God's blessing for their zealous Caribbean marauding. Nor was it surprising that Queen Elizabeth, while publicly condemning the spectacular piracies of Hawkins and Drake, secretly rejoiced at the sapping of Catholic Spain's strength and was a share holder in some of their ventures.

From the vantage point of 1690 Dalby Thomas wrote *An Historical Account of the Rise and Growth of the West India Colonies.* In it he expressed the general English feeling toward Spain and sharp annoyance with England's lack of initiative in the first flush of transoceanic enterprise:

> We will make a short reflection on the unaccountable negligence, or rather stupidity, of this nation, during the reigns of Henry VII, Henry VIII, Edward VI and Queen Mary, who could contentedly sit still and see the Spanish rifle, plunder and bring home undisturbed, all the wealth of that golden world; and to suffer them with forts and castles to shut up the doors and entrances unto all the rich provinces of America, having not the least title or pretence of right beyond any other nation; except that of being by accident the first discoverer of some parts of it; where the unprecedented cruelties, exorbitancies and barbarities, their own histories witness, they practiced on a poor, naked and innocent people, which inhabited the islands, as well as upon those truly civilized and mighty empires of Peru and Mexico, called to all mankind for succor and relief against their outrageous

avarice and horrid massacres . . . (England) slept on until the ambitious Spaniard, by that inexhaustible spring of treasure, had corrupted most of the courts and senates of Europe, and had set on fire, by civil broils and discords, all our neighbor nations, or had subdued them to his yoke; contriving too to make us wear his chains and bear a share in the triumph of universal monarchy, not only projected but near accomplished, when Queen Elizabeth came to the crown.[1]

Thomas lauded Elizabeth for letting loose "those daring adventurers, Drake, Hawkins, Raleigh, the Lord Clifford and many other braves that age produced, who, by their privateering and bold undertaking (like those the buccaneers practice), now opened the way to our discoveries, and succeeding settlements in America." Under Elizabeth, England took the lead in challenging Spanish pretensions to sole ownership of the lands and wealth that furnished the means to maintain the fleets and armies of the Catholic Cause. After England helped the Netherlands escape Spanish rule, Dutch freebooters (from *vrijbuiter*, the Dutch word for both pirate and buccaneer) joined the English and French in making the far-off Caribbean the scene of international piracy aimed at the treasure ports and treasure fleets.

Philip II had inherited the Netherlands under feudal law. When the inhabitants resisted his imposition of Catholicism, he sent his son Don Fadrique and the Duke of Alva with twenty thousand soldiers to bring the country to heel. During the five years after 1567 more than sixty thousand people in the Low Countries were condemned by the Council of Blood and beheaded, hanged, or burned at the stake. Many thousands of others fled to the Rhineland and England. Many of the Dutch freebooters had waged guerrilla action against Spanish shipping during this period. They were part of a patriotic underground organization of men calling themselves sea beggars or woods beggars faithful to William, Prince of Orange who had taken refuge in German principalities to the north.

During the latter sixteenth-century economic depression in north western Europe, religious strife and political instability created ideal conditions for the pursuit of piracy as a national policy. In England countless unemployed men, many of them naval veterans, signed on as privateers. They had little to lose and much to gain in the tropic waters far from harsh European naval discipline. The sixteenth-century sea dogs made little pretense of engaging in trade or colonization although they professed strong nationalistic ties. They were bold, opportunistic predators backed by shipowners and investors attracted by the profits from plunder. In addition to the famous sea dogs who are remembered for the style and scope of their activities, there were hundreds of others whose small scale, independent raids had a cumulative effect, opening the Caribbean to new-comers and halting the advance of the Counter Reformation.

On September 26, 1583, the Fugger newsletter, an economic report produced periodically by spies for the great German merchant banking concern, noted the arrival at Seville of the Spanish treasure fleet bearing fifteen million pesos, having left a million in Havana because the ships were in danger of sinking under the weight of their precious cargo. "This is a pretty penny which will give new life to commerce." It was shipments like this that aroused England's envy and led Elizabeth to encourage her sea dogs. Drake's circumnavigation of the world which she helped fi-nance, yielded an enormous 4,700 percent return on her investment. Her "chested treasure," as she called it, permitted the queen to tax her subjects lightly, to come to the aid of the Dutch, to crush the Irish rebellion and to fund routine administrative and military expenditures. John Maynard Keynes, the British economist, felt that Elizabeth's share of the treasure Drake brought back from his circumnavigation furnished the "origins of British foreign investment," the seed from which the Levant Company and then the East India Company grew.

The first English interloper in the Caribbean was John Hawkins, who had sailed as a young boy to Brazil with his father. He was also the first Englishman to engage in the transatlantic slave trade. Backed by a London syndicate whose members included Sir William Wynter, the Surveyor of the Queen's Ships, and Benjamin Gonson, his father-in-law and Treasurer of the Queen's Navy, Hawkins proposed establishment of triangular trade with West Africa and the West Indies. The syndicate members were either prominent London merchants or naval men. The merchants had the capi-tal and an interest in the profits to be made from gold and slaves which they shared with the naval backers who owned private ships which were suited to long ocean voyaging and sea battles.

In 1562 Hawkins embarked on his first voyage with three ships. He sailed for Sierra Leone where "partly by the sword and partly by other means" he managed to load about three hundred Africans and other mer-chandise. He also seized a Portuguese slave ship and took it with him. From informants in the Canary Islands where he stopped to trade and take on provisions, Hawkins learned the neglected settlers on Hispaniola were desperately eager to buy contraband slaves, although the settlers at Santo Domingo, anxious not to anger the Crown, made a show of sending troops against the English.

Hawkins explained to the Spanish commander, who pretended to be-lieve him, that his ships had been blown across the Atlantic by foul weather. He needed supplies and had only African merchandise to barter for them. The Spanish commander agreed to let Hawkins sell two-thirds of his human cargo and leave the remaining Africans on deposit with the town council. Hawkins loaded four ships with hides and a small amount of gold, silver, ginger, sugar and pearls and sent two of them to England where their cargo brought a good profit for the investors. The other two he sent to Seville on consignment to an English merchant living there with a Spaniard as a front man.

These two ships, the Portuguese slaver with its original crew, and a caravel Hawkins had hired in Hispaniola, were seized by the Portuguese and Spanish governments. Thomas Hampton, the English captain of the caravel barely escaped the Inquisition, and the English merchant and his Spanish associate were imprisoned for illegal trade. Hawkins protested the seizure, although he knew he had been breaking Spanish law by infringing on the New World monopoly. Perhaps he hoped to show Philip II that England, Spain's traditional ally, could be of service in providing essential supplies, particularly slaves, to Spain's agricultural colonies which the Seville traders neglected in favor of the wealthier ones. A Spanish report in 1568 stated, "the colonists' needs are very great and neither penalties nor punishments suffice to prevent them from buying secretly what they want." Despite diplomatic pressure on Spain and offers of assistance in ridding the Caribbean of French corsairs if he were allowed limited trading privileges, Hawkins received neither his impounded cargo nor permission to trade.

Profits on the portion of hides and sugar taken to England were high enough, however, that in 1564 he sailed again with four ships for West Africa and then the Caribbean. This time his backers included a number of courtiers including Lord Dudley, the Queen's favorite. Elizabeth herself participated, supplying the *Jesus of Lubeck*, one of her largest warships and allowing Hawkins to sail under her personal flag. She commanded him to serve "in the interests of the King of Spain" while in the West Indies. The Queen hoped Philip would change his mind about reaching a mutually beneficial agreement. The two nations, after all, were still allies. They needed each other's support in the fight against the French and were deeply involved in Anglo-Spanish European trade vital to both their economies. Philip II, a fanatical Catholic, was held back by an unwillingness to allow "heretic" sea traders into his overseas domain. Then, too, the plundering of Spanish ships by English privateers in European waters made him very wary of letting an English foot in the New World door even though he needed help to oust the French interlopers.

Philip, far from being moved by Elizabeth's offers of assistance, had his ambassador protest strongly against Hawkins's voyage. The English expedition traded and raided on the West African coast until they had amassed six hundred slaves, some gold and ivory, and seventeen Portuguese ships. Hawkins crossed with seven ships to the Spanish Main where he was greeted as a corsair despite his petition to trade peaceably. At Barburata, where his formal petition for a license was rejected, Hawkins threatened to attack the town. The governor then offered to let him trade if he paid exorbitant customs duties. Hawkins refused and "the sixteenth of April hee prepared one hundred men well-armed with bowes, arrowes, harquebuzes and pikes, with which hee marched to the townewards." After some negotiation, the governor lowered the duties and Hawkins proceeded to trade, receiving gold and silver in exchange for his slaves. He repeated this performance at Rio de la Hacha. He then set a course for Hispaniola but missed both it and Havana, his next objective, and ended up on the coast of Florida at the remnants of the French colony at Fort Caroline. He gave the pathetic colonists a ship to sail to France, food, shoes and other supplies, an act which he can't have imagined would please Philip.

In fact, the Spanish ambassador kept Hawkins under surveillance after his return to England. When it appeared he was preparing a third voyage, he prevailed upon the queen to forbid him to go. So he stayed home while his ships, under the command of John Lovell, stole out of Plymouth harbor in 1566. Aboard one of them was his twenty-one-year old cousin Francis Drake. The expedition's sailed for West Africa, seizing several Portuguese ships off the Cape Verde islands which were laden with slaves, sugar, wax and ivory.

One ship took the pirated wax and ivory to sell in Plymouth. The other ships crossed to the Caribbean. Lovell wasn't as forceful as Hawkins and didn't do much trading. However, he met the French corsair, Jean Bontemps, who had recently led a pirate raid on Santa Marta, and together the two sailed to Barburata where they sold a small number of slaves. This was the first of many Anglo-French pirate alliances in the 1560s and 1570s. However the expedition was a financial disaster for which Hawkins never forgave Lovell. Drake, who made a fortune on subsequent voyages didn't make a shilling on his first Caribbean excursion.

Hawkins begged Elizabeth to let him sail again with slaves to the West Indies "in truck of gold, pearls and emeralds." In 1567 she permitted Hawkins to embark for the Caribbean. She even lent two of her warships but warned him not to give the Spanish any cause for complaint which was somewhat ridiculous since she knew that his very presence in the area was a red flag to the Spanish Crown.

Francis Drake was given command of the *Judith*. The squadron sailed to the African coast where they joined with some French corsair vessels. They obtained some slaves by seizing Portuguese caravels carrying Africans and involved themselves in a tribal war on behalf of the King of

Sierra Leone to get others. The king promised them prisoners if they would help him attack a rival chieftain's town. There was fierce fighting and Hawkins watched horrified as the Sierra Leone warriors massacred their prisoners, leaving him 260, a number he felt hardly merited the effort and the loss of nine of his men.

With the French ships, Hawkins sailed west to the Caribbean arriving in April of 1568, seven months after leaving England. He managed to trade with several settlements on the Main, despite official reluctance. At Rio de la Hacha, however, where the timid Lovell had been forced to leave one hundred slaves without receiving payment, Hawkins was refused point blank. When Miguel de Castellanos, the settlement's treasurer wouldn't even permit the English to refill their water casks, Hawkins fired two shots at his house. The next day he landed two hundred men a couple of miles from town, giving the Spanish one last chance to change their minds. When they didn't, his men marched on the town, easily capturing it and the port. The inhabitants fled to the woods with whatever valuables they could carry. Hawkins sent an intermediary to warn those in hiding that he would burn the town if not granted permission to trade. Castellanos replied he'd rather "see all the Indies afire" than submit. However, when the English began to set fire to some buildings the treasurer agreed, at the urging of his people, to allow the English to trade. They stayed a month and Castellanos himself acquired twenty slaves for whom he paid 1,000 gold pesos and another sixty for whom he paid Hawkins 4,000 pesos from the King's treasure.

At Santa Marta, Hawkins's next port of call, he negotiated with the governor for a sham capture of the town followed by "forced" trade so that the authorities in Spain couldn't find fault with the colonials. This ploy soon became common. His hopes of trading at Cartagena were dashed by Spanish gunfire so he decided to head for home before the onset of the hurricane season.

Soon after, the disastrous battle at San Juan de Ulúa, marked the end of English attempts at peaceable trade in the Caribbean. For the next three decades the Elizabethan sea dogs had revenge on their minds as they surpassed the French and Dutch in plundering the Spanish Main, swarming over the Caribbean like "so many roaches," as one Spaniard commented.

The incident which inflamed the sea dogs' vengeance began innocently enough. As Hawkins's squadron rounded Cuba's western end on its way into the Florida Channel, a storm forced the ships to run for shelter on the west coast of Florida. The *William and John*, separated from the rest, managed to limp back to England alone, arriving in February of 1569 which was a month after Hawkins himself got home. The storm drove the other ships southward into the Gulf of Mexico. The queen's battered old ship *Jesus* was in dire need of repair so Hawkins headed for the nearest port which was San Juan de Ulúa, the port of Veracruz, Mexico. This was where all the Mexican treasure was collected for shipment to Spain and where mule trains carried the oriental treasures brought to Acapulco on the Manila galleons.

The Spaniards there thought his ships were the flota whose arrival was imminent and allowed him to enter the port. Hawkins's fame had spread throughout America and when they realized whose ships were anchored at the off shore island which formed the harbor they were aghast, although Hawkins assured them his intentions were peaceful.

The very next morning thirteen sails of the plate fleet's ships appeared on the horizon. Hawkins was in a difficult position. Unsure of the flota commander's reaction to the presence of English ships, he could secure his safety by denying them entrance. If, however, he forced them to anchor outside their own port, exposed to strong winds, he risked igniting a political powder keg. He dared not refuse them entry. The Spanish ships anchored and hostages were exchanged along with mutual promises of peace. Hawkins was to leave as soon as he could and not disturb the treasure-laden merchant ships lying at anchor waiting for transfer of their cargo to the flota galleons.

It so happened that the newly appointed Viceroy of New Spain, Don Martín Enriquez, was aboard the *almiranta* of the fleet. Philip II had specifically ordered him to curb English freebooters in the colonies so he immediately planned to break the truce and seize the English corsairs. The hostages he had put in English hands were not the men of quality they were dressed up to be but ordinary seamen in borrowed velvets.

During the night Hawkins noticed Spanish ships maneuvering in violation of the truce agreement. When Robert Barrett, his second-in-command who spoke Spanish, was sent to the Spanish flagship to complain he was clapped in irons and at dawn the Spaniards launched a dual attack, firing from their ships and from shore batteries. The harbor battle went on for most of the day with guns firing at point-blank range. The English fought bravely, aided by the crews of the two French privateering vessels accompanying them. They sank two Spanish ships, including the flagship and set the vice-admiral's ship afire. In hand-to-hand combat they kept Spanish boarding parties at bay but were no match for the overwhelming superiority of their adversary's manpower and artillery.

As cannon balls crashed all about him, Hawkins kept his men's spirits up. His page brought him beer in a silver mug. The moment he set the empty charger down it was hit by a shot. "Fear nothing," he shouted "for God who hath preserved me from this shot will also deliver us from these traitorous villains." Unfortunately, the Spaniards captured one of the

French privateers, dismasted the other, immobilized the *Jesus* which had to be abandoned, and wreaked such havoc that by evening only the *Minion* and the *Judith* remained. Under cover of darkness they moved out of firing range.

At dawn Hawkins, aboard the *Minion* saw that Drake's *Judith* had disappeared. Evidently his cousin thought it his obligation to get his men and ship away from a hopeless situation and headed away from Ulúa. Hawkins later forgave Drake's abandonment, attributing it to youthful misjudgment of the situation. Neither of the great sea dogs relented in their consuming hatred of the treacherous papists whose surprise attack cost the expedition all but two of its ships, some hundred thousand pounds worth of treasure and the lives of three quarters of the four hundred men who had set out from Plymouth.

All but fourteen men aboard the *Minion* died on the passage to England. Food and water were so scarce aboard the ship that Hawkins acceded to the pleas of one hundred men who begged to be left on the Mexican shore. Many of them died from malnutrition; others were captured and brought before the Inquisition. Robert Barrett and another English Protestant who refused to renounce his faith were burned alive in Seville's market plaza and the rest were condemned to two hundred lashes each and, then, if they survived, eight years in the galleys. One man, David Ingram, evaded the Spaniards and succeeded in trekking across the vast continent from Tampico, Mexico to what is now St. John, New Brunswick, Canada—an amazing journey. He was rescued by a French trader and eventually returned to England.

The Ulúa debacle marked the end of sixteenth-century English trading voyages in the Caribbean and the beginning of a relentless campaign of plundering waged by the sea dogs. The Elizabethan pirates outstripped the French corsairs in their predations. Before 1585 Spain and England were nominally at peace but there was no peace "beyond the line." During those years Hawkins's cronies, ever mindful of Spanish treachery and cruelty, launched private missions to avenge their lost comrades. They had the Queen's secret encouragement and after 1585, when open hostility broke out with Spain over the Netherlands, they had her full public support sailing with official letters of marque as privateers.

Documentary evidence from the Spanish archives in Seville indicates that there were some fourteen notable piratical expeditions and an unknown number of smaller ones to the Caribbean in the aftermath of the battle at San Juan de Ulúa. Ten of them took place between 1570 and 1574 as the epidemic of piracy, which had been ravaging European shipping lanes from the North Sea south to the Canaries and Azores, spread across the Atlantic. After the rupture of Anglo-Spanish relations, the number of ships questing after a share of the gold and silver of Mexico and Peru multiplied. During the eighteen years prior to Elizabeth's death in the Spring of 1603, there were at least seventy-six West Indian raiding expeditions which involved 235 large ships plus a larger number of smaller boats such as pinnaces, barges and launches. Details of additional English expeditions are bound to turn up as historians comb archives and private libraries.

The members of these marauding voyages were recruited from every level of society from the dregs to the upper crust. The life of the sea rover offered adventure and the possibility of golden dreams fulfilled. It offered escape to the desperate, the fugitive, the unemployed and redemption and glory to debt-ridden nobles like Sir Walter Raleigh and the Earls of Essex and Cumberland who hoped to distinguish themselves as patriots and gain gold into the bargain, although they were generally regarded as rank amateurs by veteran sea dogs. English ports were crowded with cowherders and runaway apprentices eager to go "on the account." Gambling on the chance of making in a day's plundering what they would have to toil years for ashore, they were willing to endure overcrowded, filthy conditions, risking death from dysentery, scurvy, tropical fevers, gangrene or wounds. Capture and subsequent hanging or burning were hazards, like shipwrecks, which they faced without flinching.

Not every crew member was aboard by choice. The demand for seasoned shipwrights outstripped the supply so they were sometimes shanghaied or lured aboard by a false itinerary listing European ports of call. It wasn't unusual for an English ship to have a Dutchman, Frenchman, Turk or even African on a voyage. These men were generally either pilots, interpreters or seamen with essential knowledge of foreign shipping practices, routes and ports.

Every privateer received a share of the crews' third of the value of each prize taken under the terms of a privateering contract. Traditionally the crew also had the right to pillage all valuables and goods not part of a ship's actual cargo, including the personal belongings of the crew and passengers and whatever was found above deck. These items were brought to the mainmast and distributed according to rank with the officers receiving the largest share. Sometimes it was impossible for the captain to restrain his rough and ready crew from breaking into the actual cargo and looting it as well. Captains of privateering vessels were sometimes in collusion with their crews to "break bulk"—that is to rifle a cargo before it was officially inventoried. Some captains were forced to put up a bond to insure this didn't happen. The Admiralty and the financiers who backed privateering expeditions were frequently cheated when cargoes seized by their privateers were smuggled ashore in the British Isles or marketed elsewhere.

The life was hard and the men were rough. Discipline was always a problem, despite such gruesome punishments as flogging or marooning for falling asleep on watch, gaming (gambling), or blasphemous talk at mess. Drake who never permitted "filthy talk at mess" was one of the few Elizabethan sea dog captains capable of controlling his men. Most privateering captains had to resort to brutal punishment. A man who pulled a knife on an officer was liable to have his hand "strook off." If he assaulted a fellow crew member he was ducked three times from the yardarm, and if he stole, his head was shaved and rubbed with a mess of boiling oil and feathers. Discipline in the Queen's Navy, however, was even harsher and there was not even the hope of gain.

With time privateering voyages assumed a democratic character. Illiterate plunderers and their gentlemen shipmates were equals with a common goal. In the 1590s the crew had a voice in selecting the course and objectives of an expedition. Sir Richard Hawkins, only son of Sir John, complained the crew was like "a stiff-necked horse which, taking the bridle between his teeth, forceth his rider to do what him list."

Returning from the Caribbean with their prizes, these sea rovers flocked to harbor taverns where they mingled with pirates fresh from Brazil, West Africa, the North Sea and the Mediterranean. Smugglers and middlemen frequented these smoky haunts where, amidst raucous drinking and gaming, they swapped tales of high adventure and bargained for Peruvian silver, Guinea gold from Africa, French satins, Brazilian parrots and other exotic goods. Tavern keepers and legions of willing wenches soon parted a sea rover from his booty.

Pirates celebrating their lucrative exploits during this era enhanced their reputations for flamboyance by dressing far above their station. Some decked themselves out as lawyers in fur trimmed gowns and spectacles. Others wore the silks and satins of men they had murdered or bought magnificent outfits with plumed hats and jeweled scabbards. They sported sumptuous cloaks and gem-studded jewelry to impress the world and prospective backers. Pirates provided a source of entertainment for the masses. A favorite pastime in London was to attend a pirate hanging at Execution Dock, Wapping, where one might see a character like Thomas Walton who, as he was about to hang for piracy in 1583, stood beneath the gallows and "rent his Venetian breeches of crimson taffeta and distributed the same to such of his old acquaintances as stood about him."

Ostentation was a hallmark of the Elizabethan age and the pirates who dressed in outlandish costumes were only imitating their betters. The height of extravagance was reached by Thomas Cavendish, a sea dog born of a gentle Suffolk family. In competition with other upper-class sea dogs for the Queen's favor, he repeated Drake's circumnavigation of the world. It cost him a fortune to outfit the voyage during which he captured the *Santa Ana*, a Manila galleon, off the coast of California. She carried 22,000 gold pesos and six hundred tons of costly cargo, which was more than ten times what Cavendish's two ships could hold so he set fire to the great ship with five hundred tons of valuables still aboard. In a letter to Lord Hunsdon, his patron, Cavendish wrote "Along the coasts of Chile, Peru and New Spain I made great spoils. I burnt and sunk nineteen ships, both great and small. All the villages and towns that I landed at, I burnt and spoiled."

Cavendish made a triumphal return, entering Plymouth harbor in September of 1588. The *Desire*, his flagship, had gilded bows, damask sails and the topmasts were wrapped in cloth-of-gold. All hands paraded the deck dressed in gorgeous silk brocades. Two years later Cavendish sold off much of his estate to finance a second voyage. His appetite for Spanish booty had not been satisfied with the great dividends he'd earned. The bulk went to pay numerous creditors and the rest evaporated, squandered in much the same manner as the prizes of illiterate pirates vanishing in whoring and gaming. Fortune no longer smiled on Cavendish and broken in mind and body, he died at sea during his second voyage which was marked by tempests and starvation.

The one sea dog on whom fortune and royal favor shone most warmly was Sir Francis Drake, knighted for his voyage of circumnavigation. He was the embodiment of Elizabethan maritime enterprise. The Virgin Queen who fondly called Drake "my pirate," relished the Spanish loot he poured into her treasury and the lavish presents he gave her such as a diamond cross valued at five thousand crowns. The wealthy men who participated in his ventures rejoiced at his successes and all England hailed him as the national savior. His name was on the lips of every Englishman and he was notorious as "the terrible dragon" to every Spaniard.

Drake, the quintessential sea dog was a self-made man who became England's greatest seaman, a millionaire and a noble at a time when knighthood was not lightly conferred. He was born about 1543 of humble Devon stock. His father, a religious zealot, imbued Drake and his eleven brothers with Protestant dogma. Drake's family fled his West Country birthplace because of religious persecution and lived in the hulk of an abandoned ship near Chatham in Kent, so love of the sea and loathing of the papists were second nature to him. From the age of thirteen Francis was apprenticed to the coasting trade and learned so well that when his old master died he bequeathed him his small trading ship which plied the English Channel.

Drake, like all young mariners who heard of John Hawkins's transatlantic voyage, dreamed of venturing to the Indies where he heard the rivers were spangled with gold and the earth yielded emeralds. He sold his coaster and gravitated to Plymouth finding employment in the Hawkins's family business. He sailed with Lovell's pirating-cum-trading expedition and then signed on with Hawkins for a voyage to the Caribbean. As a youth he already displayed the characteristics that were to ensure a brilliant career. He was able, resilient, adventurous and blessed with an intuition for making lucky decisions. His men loved him. Although he was a stern disciplinarian and had a violent temper, Drake rewarded a job well done and was gentle with inferiors including the blacks and Indians he met in the New World. Even Spanish captives remarked on his courtesy and charm. If he had a weakness it was the common Elizabethan love of flattery, fame and nouveau riche ostentation.

Francis Drake was passionately devoted to his God and his queen, and after Ulúa he was equally devoted to revenge. He had grown up amid the persecutions and Protestant burnings of Mary's reign when England was a bitterly divided country living in the shadow of Spain, whose ruler was Mary's husband. He never forgot a friend and he never forgave an enemy. At the age of forty he had the deep satisfaction of returning to the West Country area from which his poverty stricken family had fled and buying Buckland Abbey, which had once been a powerful center of English Catholicism.

As a man he waged a personal war against Philip II, his ships, treasure and empire. Drake was not rash. He prepared his campaigns with infinite care. In 1570 and again the following year he made reconnaissance voyages to the Caribbean. As carefully as any general, he studied Spanish America, looking for the Achilles' heel. He found it in the narrow Isthmus of Panama, which was vulnerable to a well-orchestrated strangling maneuver.

In the spring of 1570 he slipped quietly out of Devon with two small ships "to gain such intelligence as might amend him for his loss . . . not only of goods of some value but also of his kinsmen and friends . . . " No record exists of this voyage but the following year he sailed on the twenty-five-ton *Swan* to the Isthmus to further study the possibilities of an attack on Nombre de Diós, terminus of all the Peruvian treasure. On the steamy coast of Darien he discovered a small, hidden natural harbor. It boasted a narrow, defensible entrance screened by thick vegetation which concealed ships anchored within. There was abundant fruit and fish and so many pheasants in the surrounding forest that Drake named his hideaway Port Pheasant.

From this secret base right in his enemy's vitals Drake sallied forth with a crew of about thirty bold men striking at Spanish ships. A Spanish document entitled "A summary relation of the harms and robberies done by Fr. Drake an Englishman, with the assistance and help of other Englishmen" recounts how they robbed numerous vessels in the Chagres River that were transporting merchandise worth "forty thousand ducats of velvets and taffetas, besides other merchandise, besides gold and silver in other barks, and with the same came to Plymouth where it was divided among his partners . . . " Drake and his men were pirates in anyone's judgment and knew the scaffold or stake awaited them if they slipped one time.

While he was at Port Pheasant Drake befriended local Indians and escaped Negro slaves called Cimaroons or Maroons who had intermarried with Indians and lived in concealed jungle communities. The Cimaroons shared Drake's loathing of the Spaniards and furnished him with a great deal of detailed information. He learned a lot about the treasure routes and administrative details from captured Spaniards, whom he mercifully released before leaving even though he knew they compromised his future plans. He was so daring that he once disguised himself as a Spanish merchant and visited Nombre de Diós to familiarize himself with the port, street plan, shore batteries and treasure warehouses. The *Swan* sailed for Plymouth late in 1571 after Drake had buried surplus stores at Port Pheasant in anticipation of his next move.

In May of 1572 Drake sailed on the third of his private expeditions. This time he had two small well-equipped ships, the *Swan* and the seventy-ton *Pasha* which had three prefabricated pinnaces stowed aboard in sections. Seventy-three men sailed with Drake, only one of them was over thirty. Their mission, amazing in its daring, was to capture Nombre de Diós the principal city of the Spanish Empire and reap the "golden harvest" stored there awaiting transhipment to Seville.

When the pirate band reached Port Pheasant six weeks later they found a message "on a plate of leade, fastened to a very great tree." It was signed by his "verie loving friend, John Garret," who had been with him the year before and had remained in the Caribbean with a small trading vessel. The message read "Captain Drake, if you fortune to come into this port make haste away; for the Spaniards which you had with you here last year have betrayed this place, and taken away all that is left here . . . "

Rather than "make haste away" Drake set his men to work erecting a log stockade. Port Pheasant had become a rendezvous for French and

English pirates and almost immediately an English privateer appeared. She was under the command of James Ranse, a former officer with Hawkins who had worked the English Channel with Huguenot privateers and then sought more golden pastures in the Caribbean. He and his thirty men teamed up with Drake for the attack on Nombre de Diós.

The stockade was completed and the pinnaces assembled. Then the three large ships sailed up the coast to the Isle of Pines where they planned to leave the ships and swoop down on Nombre de Diós in the swifter pinnaces which could be better maneuvered than the others because they had oars. With his usual luck, Drake found some African slaves on the islands who had been sent to cut wood. From them the English pirates learned that because the town had recently been attacked by Cimaroons, Spanish reinforcements were on their way from Panama City.

Drake decided to act at once before the troops arrived. He kept the two boats the slaves had used to come to the islands, setting the men ashore to join the Cimaroons. Ranse stayed behind while Drake took seventy men, including his brother John and John Oxenham, his chief lieutenant, one of the two prize boats Ranse had brought with him to Port Pheasant, and the pinnaces on a surprise predawn raid on Nombre de Diós. The trumpeter, a boy, was killed and Drake himself was wounded in the knee. The Spaniards were in a state of panic, unable to tell in the darkness whether this was a Cimaroon or pirate attack. Drake had his men loose volleys of flaming arrows and magnified the English presence by beating drums and blaring trumpets. Arrows, as Caribbean corsairs had found, were far more reliable in the humid tropics than the arquebus, which had to be ignited by a slow match.

The English pressed on to the governor's residence where Drake knew the bulk of the treasure lay. The residents had fled leaving behind a heap of large silver bars piled twelve feet high and stretching seventy feet or so along the wall to a depth of about ten feet. They hurried along to the King's locked Treasure House as Drake told his force "I have brought you to the mouth of the Treasury of the World and if you do not gain you have none to blame but yourselves."

As the pirates tried to break into the Treasure House a violent tropical thunderstorm broke, paralyzing the attackers and the attacked. As soon as the enveloping torrent abated, Oxenham and John Drake battered at the doors. Drake moved into the open to offer covering fire and suddenly crumpled to the ground. The great loss of blood from the leg wound, which he had hidden from his men, "soon filled the very prints which our footprints made, to the great dismay of our company, who thought it not credible that one should be able to lose so much blood and live," wrote one of the men who helped carry him to the pinnaces.

Drake urged his men to carry on looting but they hadn't the heart to continue without him, so although some made off with "goodly booty," they abandoned some 360 tons of silver and untold quantities of gold, gems, jewelry, porcelain and other treasure. Disappointment at leaving such riches behind diminished somewhat when they captured a Spanish ship laden with fine Canary wines.

The English retired to a little islet provocatively close to the town. A Spaniard carrying a flag of truce was sent to survey the pirate band under the pretense of inquiring if the English arrows were poisoned and, if so, how were such wounds cured. He asked Drake if he were the same Drake who had been on the coast before. The emissary found Drake full of confidence, anything but ready to admit defeat. Drake answered his queries stating that "he was the same Drake they meant; that it was never his custom to poison arrows; that their wounds might be cured with ordinary remedies; and that he only wanted some of that excellent commodity, gold and silver (which that country yielded), for himself and his company; and," he added insolently, "that he was resolved, by the help of God, to reap some of the golden harvest which they had got out of the earth, and then sent into Spain to trouble the Earth."

Now that the Spanish knew the extent of the English force, Ranse decided it would be prudent to plunder elsewhere and left. Drake, hearing from an escaped slave that it would be some months before the arrival of the Peruvian treasure, took his squadron south to molest the Colombian coast. Displaying characteristic arrogance, he entered Cartagena's outer harbor and captured four ships. The largest was a richly laden merchantman about to sail for Spain. In full view of the city Drake and a small party of his men approached the two hundred-ton ship in three pinnaces, which were basically open rowboats and took her without a struggle while the unwary crew was having a siesta.

Drake towed the big ship just out of port, locked the crew below and transfered her valuable cargo to the hold of the *Pasha*. By this time the alarm had been given in the city and soldiers rushed to the shore, firing over the water too late to be of any help. Drake added two smaller prizes to his catch and then sailed back to the Isle of Pines near Nombre di Diós to get on with his main objective.

Drake secretly had a shipwright scuttle the *Swan* because he hadn't sufficient men to crew the ships and the pinnaces. He only needed one large ship to serve as a command post and supply vessel. The pinnaces, light, fleet and able to row or sail into the shallowest reef water, were to be his most effective weapon.

The charred remains of the *Swan* were left on the beach at the Isle of Pines to mislead any Spanish vessels that sailed by into believing the English had given up and sailed for home. It wasn't long, however, before all Spanish America knew "El Draque" was still around. In the months while he waited for the rainy season to end and the treasure convoy from Panama City to arrive at Nombre de Diós, Drake used his pinnaces to terrorize the Main. From a new mainland base, patterned on a Cimaroon village where his men played bowls on their off-hours, Drake made lightening swift raids on settlements and ships. The sea dog's name sent shivers up and down the coast. A ballad describes "The Dragon that on our seas did raise his crest, and brought back heaps of gold unto his nest, unto his foes more terrible was than thunder . . . "

He paid dearly for his successes, however, watching his brother Joseph and many other of his brave young men die in an epidemic. Another brother John, was killed in an attack on a ship. It was Drake's practice to seize a ship, help himself to her cargo and then release it with its crew unharmed. He buried caches of plunder up and down the coast at strategic locations so that he could stock up whenever he ran low on food (which often happened), powder, naval stores or other supplies.

"El Draque" plundered hither and yon in an attempt to divert the Spanish from his designs on Nombre de Diós and the treasure. Following the advice of a fugitive slave he forged an alliance with a band of Cimaroons who were delighted to join forces with the renowned pirate. In February of 1573, the Cimaroon jungle-telegraph brought news that the mule train carrying treasure was about to leave Panama City. Drake plunged into the tropical forest moving toward Panama with eighteen English pirates and twenty-five Cimaroon guides. One day the guides halted before a mighty tree on a jungle ridge and urged him to climb it. From his lofty perch he saw the Pacific Ocean for the first time. It was a dramatic moment. Behind him lay the shimmering softness of the Caribbean, ahead the deep oceanic blue of The Great South Sea. Drake prayed aloud "to Almightie God of his goodness to give him life and leave to sayle once in an English ship in that sea." Oxenham who was with him and echoed the prayer actually sailed into the Pacific before Drake but was captured by the Spanish and executed.

The party pushed on, descending from the mountains to the dangerously open grasslands. As they approached Panama City the men caught glimpses of its gilded spires and the harbor stippled with ships. A Cimaroon scout ventured into the town and returned with exciting news. Two mules trains, one laden with silver, were leaving that night. With them were the Treasurer of Lima, his daughter and his private mule train carrying gold and gems.

Drake prepared an ambush, deploying half his men on one side of the track and the others in the long grasses opposite. The men wore their long shirts outside their trousers so they could distinguish friend from foe at a glance. They lay hidden for hours and as night fell they finally heard the cling-clang of the mule bells announcing the convoy's approach. Drake was sure that within minutes he would have sweet revenge and a king's ransom in precious metal and jewels. Once again, success slipped through his fingers. A drunken Englishman, named Robert Pike, betrayed the pirates' presence when he jumped up for a second at the sound of a horse going in the direction of Panama. The Spanish rider glimpsed him and warned the mule train he had seen a disturbance in the grass behind him.

The English pirates and their Cimaroon companions retreated to the small town of Venta Cruz, halfway between Panama and Nombre de Diós, where treasure was transferred from mules to barges for the trip down the Chagres River. Tired and frustrated they looted the town but at Drake's command didn't harm women and unarmed men.

Once again Drake returned to his base, redoubling the hit-or-miss pirate raids designed to keep the enemy off balance. He wanted them to think his failure to take the treasure train had made him abandon that goal. Oxenham captured a supply ship. Drake added a Spanish frigate to his fleet which had some gold among its cargo.

A Huguenot corsair named Guillaume Le Testu and his seventy men joined forces with the English pirates. Testu who was a brilliant hydrographer as well as a corsair was cruising the Caribbean with letters issued by Catherine de Medici's relative, the Florentine, Filippo Strozzi. Drake's hatred of Catholics was rekindled by news Testu brought of the Saint Bartholomew's Day massacre when an estimated fifty thousand French Huguenots had been killed by French Catholics with the Pope's blessing.

Drake came up with a new plan to rob the treasure caravan. The pirate force went ashore near Nombre de Diós, trekked inland and ambushed the treasure trains when they were so near the town that the Spaniards never expected an attack. The guards were not vigilant and the mixed pirate force overwhelmed the train which was made up of two hundred mules, most of them carrying three hundred pounds of silver apiece. There was gold too. It was far more than they could carry so the bulk of the treasure was buried at various spots in the jungle.

As the last of the treasure was being hidden the pirates heard the sound of approaching soldiers. Grabbing as much gold as they could stagger under, the men headed toward the Río Francisco where they were to meet the pinnaces. Drake planned to load the open boats and then go back and retrieve the cached silver and gold. They also had to rescue Le Testu, who had been severely wounded and remained in the jungle with two French corsairs who refused to leave him alone.

What greeted their eyes as they reached the Francisco River was the sight of seven Spanish vessels in the distant bay. Their frigate and pinnaces were nowhere in sight. His men were desperate, sure their craft had been captured. Drake, however, correctly surmised that strong westerly winds had delayed the English. Soothed by his strength and confidence, Drake's men constructed a log raft from flotsam pulled out of the storm swollen river and raised a makeshift sail from a piece of sacking. The idea was to search for the pinnaces at the mouth of the bay. Three men sailed with Drake down the turbulent river and into the bay. The frail craft battled huge sea swells for six hours before they spotted two pinnaces coming toward them and beached the raft to wait, parched and exhausted, for the pinnaces.

The pinnace crews feared the worst when they saw four sun-blistered, tattered figures. What had happened to all the others? Drake had a sense of humor which seldom deserted him and when his rescuers asked what had happened, he shook his head as if to confirm their apprehensions. Then, reaching under his shirt, and breaking into a wide smile, he pulled out a large gold ring, declaring "Our voyage is made."

The success of the expedition was marred by two things. Captain Le Testu and his two faithful comrades were never found and most of the treasure buried in the jungle was gone; dug up, most likely, by Spaniards who must have captured the Frenchmen and tortured them to reveal the treasure's location. Drake gave half the plunder to his French allies who sailed off to fresh horizons. The pinnaces were broken up and the fittings and nails given to the Cimaroons, to whom utilitarian metals were far more valuable than soft gold. The *Pasha*, too old and worm eaten to make the Atlantic crossing, was also broken up. One more sizeable ship was needed as a storeship for the voyage home so Drake, with the bravado which made him a living legend, cruised up the coast looking for a suitable prize. The harbor of Cartagena was crowded with Spanish ships including treasure fleet galleons. Drake thumbed his nose at the Spanish by sailing close by Cartagena "in the sight of all the Fleete, with a flag of St. George in the maine top of our fregat, with silk streamers and ancients downe to the water, sayling forward with a large wind." He captured a frigate off the Magdalena river which turned out to be filled with "hens, hogs, honey" and abundant other foodstuffs.

Bellies full of fresh food, their ships' holds overflowing with gold and silver, Drake's young men, the thirty-three who survived the fifteen-month adventure sailed round the western end of Cuba, into the Florida Channel and home. The English pirates had seized more than a hundred ships, plundered dozens of settlements and dealt a serious blow to the Spanish Empire. Back in England, where his name had become a household word, Drake got a full measure of adulation from the public but not from his sovereign.

Unfortunately for him, the political climate had changed during his absence. Philip and Elizabeth agreed that the embargo on trade must be lifted to the mutual benefit of both their economies and negotiations were underway to resume normal relations. The fact that the pirate Drake had robbed the king of Spain of some 150,000 pesos of gold and silver, a monumental sum, and spent the past year stinging the Spanish Main made him an acute embarrassment to the queen. He faced possible arrest and the confiscation of his treasure, which was enough to make him the Elizabethan equivalent of a millionaire in his early thirties. He quite literally disappeared for the next two years before turning up with the Earl of Essex's forces in Ireland.

It was a dozen years before Drake again raised his dragon's crest in the Caribbean. In 1577 he embarked on his greatest feat—the circumnavigation of the globe in the *Golden Hind*. John Oxenham, who had first glimpsed the Pacific with Drake from the Panamanian jungle, preceded him in the Great South Sea by a year and a half. His objective was plunder; his destination Panama. Oxenham stunned the Spanish by landing on the Isthmus near Nombre de Diós and crashing through the jungle with fifty men and Cimaroon guides to reach the Pacific near Panama City. The Spaniards knew of his plan from pirate prisoners taken at La Margarita. They mistakenly believed it was part of a concerted English offensive, rather than an isolated piratical foray. The president of the audiencia of Panama informed the King that "it was learned that they and another captain with four ships, and another with more, sixteen sail in all, are all out with the intention to sack these cities of the Main and to cross to the Pacific; and that there are among them captains and men who, allied with the Cimaroons, in the year '73 made those famous assaults on the highway from this city to that of Nombre de Diós."

The Spanish report exaggerated Oxenham's force partly in ignorance but also to shock the Crown into reinforcing the Isthmus. He had only one ship of a hundred tons, a small frigate he had captured and two launches. His force consisted of 50 not 250 men. There were other English pirates around and they did join forces from time to time but there was never the great pirate navy the audiencia imagined. Captain Philip Roche "traded the seas for piracy" in the islands and along the coast. Andrew Barker of Bristol, financed by the Earl of Leicester was off Panama with the *Ragged Staff* and the *Bear* about the same time as Oxenham but they didn't meet. Barker seized ships along the Main and off Margarita until mutiny weakened his vigilance. A Spanish patrol surprised the squabbling pirates at a little island off the Honduran coast. Barker and many of his men were killed. Some escaped but perished later. Only a few got home safely.

Oxenham built a pinnace on the Pacific shore and sailed with his men to the Pearl Islands in the Gulf of Panama. From there they lay in wait for treasure galleons coming up from Peru and pillaged Spanish settlements at will. Their crude behavior was in contrast to that of Drake's men. Witnesses who observed the sack of a settlement told how they made sport of a Franciscan friar, forcing him to march about with an overturned chamber pot on his head, how they turned the church into their cook house and then set it on fire, and how gleefully they destroyed religious articles in private houses.

Oxenham netted 60,000 gold pesos and more silver than his men could carry, enough to make them unquestionably rich. Their fatal mistake was lusting for more. They robbed the Pearl Island natives of a great many pearls which they buried in the jungle along with other loot until they could transport it across the Isthmus to their big ship. In retaliation the islanders told the Governor of Panama about the English pirates. The governor dispatched two search parties. One found Oxenham's ship and base on the Caribbean coast. The other patrol tracked down Oxenham, his men and their two hundred Cimaroon companions as they were struggling back across the Isthmus with their booty. A number of the English sea dogs were killed in the ensuing fight. Oxenham led the remnant toward Nombre de Diós. When they discovered their ship was in Spanish hands, the pirates took to the mountains to hide. They were betrayed by some Cimaroons and captured. Some were hanged in Panama and Oxenham with his officers was taken to Lima for questioning by the Inquisition about English designs on the Pacific.

One of Drake's goals, when he sailed into the Pacific more than a year later, was to rescue his old friend Oxenham from Lima which was only a few miles inland from the treasure port of Callao. His declared objective was to explore the southern coast of South America with an eye to eventual English settlement although he, no doubt, had plunder and revenge uppermost on his mind. The politically powerful members of the syndicate that backed the voyage, wanted Drake to lay English claim to Terra Australis Incognita, the unknown land mass believed to lie south of the Straits of Magellan, which were named for the only navigator to precede him around the world.

Elizabeth, who may have had a secret share in the expedition, received Drake before he sailed. She pleased him greatly when she declared: "I would gladly be revenged on the King of Spain for divers injuries that I have received." Drake took her remarks at face value and attacked ships and settlements on the west coast of South America with great zeal. He sailed from Plymouth in mid-December of 1577 with four ships and 164 men and boys including musicians, a chaplain, and a number of younger sons of land owning families. Two years, nine months and thirteen days later he returned to England aboard the *Golden Hind*, the only vessel of the expedition to complete the voyage around the world. Fifty-nine survivors of the crew of ninety were aboard.

Before reaching the Pacific "El Draque" took two Spanish caravels off the African coast near the Tropic of Cancer and seized a Brazil bound Portuguese ship laden with wine and cloth. He rechristened her the *Mary* and took Nuño da Silva, her pilot, aboard his ship, pressing him into service for fifteen months to aid in navigating the South Atlantic and South American coast.

Dissension broke out provoked by Thomas Doughty, a courtier who dabbled in the occult and claimed that he, not Drake, was responsible for persuading the Queen and backers to let Drake sail. The undercurrent of sedition increased to the point that Drake brought his former friend to trial before a jury of forty men on charges of mutiny. The trial was held on the bleak Patagonian shore at St. Julian where, ironically, Magellan had executed mutinous crewmen in 1520. Doughty was found guilty and given the choice of being executed immediately, marooned ashore or taken home in chains to face the Privy Council. He elected execution as befitted a gentleman. He was beheaded after sharing Holy Communion with Drake and talking to him privately in the latter's cabin and his severed head was held aloft by Drake who warned his men "Lo, this is the end of traitors."

Doughty's beheading seemed cruel but Drake knew how crucial naval discipline was on such a perilous voyage. In spite of his severity, the men were devoted to their brilliant leader. He dismissed all his officers' expressing the pirate's hallmark spirit of democracy: "I must have the gentlemen to haul and draw with the mariner, and the mariner with the gentlemen, I would know him that would refuse to set his hand to a rope." Dangers and prizes were to be shared without class distinction.

Valpariso on the coast of Chile was unprepared for the appearance of the English who sailed into the harbor on the fifth of December, almost a year after leaving England. The sea dogs made off with 25,000 gold pesos from one anchored ship alone. The *Golden Hind* proceeded up the coast as the pirates raided coastal towns and shipping, collecting silver and other booty.

Some prizes were more easily taken than others. In northern Chile some of the crew went ashore at the Pisagua river to replenish their water supply. They found a snoring Spaniard asleep on the river bank and without disturbing his siesta managed to relieve him of his pack which contained thirteen silver bars worth nearly 4,000 ducats.

Another time a watering party came across a train of eight strange looking beasts such as they had never seen, guarded by a lone Spaniard. They were llamas, each laden with a hundred pounds of silver bars. "We could not endure to see a gentleman Spaniard turned carrier," wrote one of the pirates, so they offered to drive the beasts for him, "only his directions were not so perfect that we could keep the way he intended." The poor Spaniard was left to rant and rave as the English adventurers herded the llamas to the coast and loaded the silver into their pinnaces.

In early February Drake reached Callao, taking his ship under cover of darkness right into the harbor where he anchored among some thirty unsuspecting ships. At dawn's light, the Spanish vessels seeing that Devil Drake was in their midst, frantically cut their moorings and raced for the open sea. Drake approached the largest ship in his pinnace, boarded her and discovered a black leather chest crammed with treasure. He took a brigantine carrying "25,000 pesos of fine gold to the value of above 37,000 ducats, a richly decorated gold crucifix and some emeralds and pearls" but all this paled in comparison with what was about to fall into his hands for he learned that a galleon laden with some of the annual Peruvian treasure had just sailed for Panama.

The *Golden Hind* gave chase. The quarry was the *Nuestra Señora de la Concepción* more commonly known by the somewhat obscene nickname *Cacafuego*. The captain offered a gold chain to the first man who spotted her. Drake's nephew John won the prize. As soon as John shouted she was on the horizon, Drake slowed down to make the Spanish think his ship was a lumbering tub. He left the sails up but reduced her speed by dragging mattresses, water filled casks and iron cauldrons affixed to cables tied on the stern.

San Juan de Anton, Captain of the galleon hadn't the faintest suspicion of the ship he saw behind him. In fact, thinking it was a Spaniard, he came about hoping to enjoy the latest news from Callao. When he was almost alongside the *Golden Hind*, de Anton heard Drake identify his ship as Chilean. Drake shouted: "Strike sail, unless you wish to go to the bottom." The courageous Spaniard replied "What, English? Who bids me strike sail? Never! Come aboard and strike sail yourself." The battle that followed was brief. The galleon was poorly armed, her guns unmanned, and the first English volley shattered the mizzen mast. The captain surrendered and was brought aboard the *Golden Hind* where Drake was already shedding his coat of mail and helmet. Speaking as one valiant mariner to another, Drake put his hand on the Spaniard's shoulder saying: "Accept with patience what is the usage of war."

The officers, crew and passengers aboard the Spanish ship were placed under guard. Then Drake and the crew turned to the cargo, examining with wonderment the fabulous array of treasure they had won. It surpassed their wildest dreams and included "fruits, conserves, sugars and a great quantity of jewels and precious stones, thirteen chests of royals of plate, eighty pounds of bar gold and twenty-six tons of uncoined silver," worth an estimated thirty-five million dollars in present day value. The treasure was inventoried as the two ships sailed side by side for several days and then transferred to the hold of the *Golden Hind*. There was so much silver that it had to be stowed in the bilges as ballast. Drake gave de Anton his ship back with a message for the Viceroy warning that if John Oxenham were hanged "I swear it will cost the heads of three thousand men of Peru, all of which heads I will cast into the port of Callao." This threat gave Oxenham a reprieve but a year later, after Drake sailed out of American waters, he was hanged.

The news spread like wildfire. The haul which made Drake one of the richest men in England in a matter of a few hours, stirred the whole of Spanish America against him. Attacking the Isthmus was out of the question but his thirst for plundering the Main was not yet slaked so he preyed on towns and ships in out of the way places. Off Nicaragua the sea dogs seized a Panama bound ship which yielded a priceless collection of charts, including some of the route to Asia. Off Guatemala they took the *Espirito Santo* whose captain Don Francisco de Zarate was a cousin of the Duke of Medina Sidonia who later commanded the Spanish Armada. The vessel carried Chinese silks, taffetas and porcelains. Zarate who was treated with great courtesy and released by Drake presented the Englishman with an emerald-beaked gold falcon as a parting souvenir.

Zarate wrote a lengthy intelligence report to Drake's arch enemy Don Martín Enriquez about Drake and his ship. The first question Drake had asked on boarding was whether there were any relatives of Enriquez aboard, for he hadn't forgotten the treachery at Ulúa. "This Drake," Zarate reported, "seems to be about thirty-five and has a reddish beard. Of middle height and thickset, he is one of the greatest sailors in the world, both in his skill and his command of men—He treats all his men with affection, and they treat him with respect. On every occasion, however unimportant, he calls them together and listens to what they have to say before giving his orders—although, in fact, he pays no real attention to anyone." He mentioned that Drake had no favorites but invited all men equally to dine with him at an elegant table where he ate delicacies to the accompaniment of violins and he marveled that a pirate could be such a gentleman.

Before heading across the Pacific to the Spice Islands, Drake made a last stab at Philip's dominions, sacking the Guatemalan port of Guatalco. The English burst into the town hall during the trial of three African slaves who were charged with plotting to burn the settlement. They freed the men, allowing two to join the crew for awhile. Drake spoke with a Spanish merchant who afterward remembered he had said, "you will be saying now that this man is a devil who robs by day and prays by night . . . (yet) I am not going to stop until I have collected the two million crowns that my cousin John Hawkins lost for certain at San Juan de Ulúa."

Once again the triumphant welcome home Drake expected was muted by current political conditions. The Spanish Crown suspected that the Privy Councillors and the Queen herself were involved in Drake's pirating expedition which had cost them so dear. They had no proof and Elizabeth was careful not to give them any. The treasure was put into safekeeping at Plymouth Castle and Drake sent word of his arrival to the Queen and his backers. He prepared to go under cover as before, having heard rumors the Queen and the London merchants whose trade with Spain had been jeopardized by his exploits, were not at all pleased with him.

Much to his surprise he received a summons from Elizabeth who was eager to see his "curiosities." The Queen and her pirate spent six hours at Richmond Palace pouring over samples of gold and jewelry. She openly showed her delight at what he had brought her from Philip's Treasure House. Drake was permitted to keep a large amount of treasure and to divide an equal amount among his crew. The remainder was clapped into the Tower of London until Elizabeth could figure out how to avoid giving it back to Spain, whose ambassador was raging against "the plunders committed by this vile corsair."

The Queen badly needed to replenish her treasury and she was very leery of Philip who had become the most powerful ruler in all Christendom. He was abetting the Irish rebels and had ordered construction of a mighty fleet of warships, claiming they were to be used against the Barbary pirates plaguing Spanish shipping in the Mediterranean. Elizabeth feared, however, that they were destined for use against Protestant rebels in the Netherlands, and perhaps ultimately against England. Far better she have the treasure, worth as much as twenty-five million dollars than Philip. So she kept it, using much of it to pay for the warfare which marked the last years of her reign. The syndicate members received the previously mentioned 4,700 percent return on their investments. Drake was knighted before a great throng as the Queen dubbed him "The Master Pirate of the Unknown World."

Spain's ambassador protested bitterly. "Her majestie could finde no reason why Spaine should hinder her subjects and those of other princes, from sayling to the Indies; that she could not bee perswaded that they were his owne." Elizabeth's action inspired a spate of English privateering expeditions to the Indies. Spanish documents of the period are filled with incidents such as one in 1580 when a band of English pirates landed at the mouth of Colombia's Madalena River. After the colonists fled, the settlement was looted and burned. One prize was a chest containing 125 pounds of gold nuggets which had been hidden in a well.

The English were openly aiding the people of the Netherlands in their rebellion against Spanish rule, as well as assailing Spain in the Caribbean. War was inevitable, and was formally declared in 1585, the year Sir Francis Drake sailed again to "impeach the King of Spain in his Indies." In May, Philip had ordered the arrest of all English ships in Spanish ports in retaliation for English piracies "beyond the line." Elizabeth sent Drake off in September with a commission to make limited reprisals in Iberian ports and freeing English ships and men held by the Spaniards. She knew, however, that he would unofficially head for the Indies to plunder and, if possible, intercept a treasure fleet. The Queen provided ten thousand pounds and two navy ships which she valued at an exaggerated ten thousand pounds, so as to claim a larger share of the plunder. The usual conglomerate of navy officers, courtiers and tycoons subscribed to the joint-stock enterprise.

Drake sailed with twenty-nine ships, a force of soldiers and a distinguished company of officers including Martin Frobisher, the renowned Channel pirate and explorer, Richard Hawkins's son John, and Drake's brother Thomas. They hit several places on the Spanish coast, taking booty after finding the arrest had been lifted and no Englishmen wanted to be rescued. At the Cape Verde Islands the expedition looted and burned several small towns. On the passage to the Indies nearly three hundred men died of a virulent fever and many more were stricken but survived. The pirate fleet reached Santo Domingo on New Year's Day 1586. At night a force was secretly put ashore out of sight of the city. Next morning while Spanish attention was occupied by a fierce bombardment from the English ships, the landed soldiers seized the elegant city and its castle. Drake sent a black boy, his personal servant, with a truce flag to the enemy commander with an offer to negotiate. A Spanish officer, insulted that a black should be a messenger, killed the boy. Thereupon, Drake in a rage, hanged two friars and threatened to keep on hanging men until the officer responsible for the murder was executed. The Spaniards hanged the officer and ransom talks began.

The Spaniards refused the amount Drake demanded so the town was looted and ships anchored in the port were seized. The pirates' determination to burn the city, quarter by quarter, until the Spaniards paid up was thwarted by the solid stone construction of the buildings. "And albeit for divers dayes together we ordeined each morning by daybreake, until the heat began at nine of the clocke, that two hundred Mariners did nought else but labour to fire and burne the said houses . . . yet did wee not . . . And so in the end, what wearied with firing, and what hastened by some other respects, wee were contented to accept five and twentie thousand ducats." The English stayed a month, liberating one hundred Moorish galley slaves before departing.

Drake bypassed many ports on the Spanish Main because of his reduced force, and proceeded to Cartagena. He had wanted to attack Spanish America's second most important city ever since he had brazenly sailed by a decade earlier. His men took the gold and emerald capitol easily but were disappointed at the amount of plunder they found. The inhabitants with a month's warning that El Draque was once again on the prowl had hidden their valuables well inland. After six weeks only a quarter of the ransom he demanded had been produced, so Drake sailed off with one hundred and ten thousand ducats and the city's guns.

The plan to leave a permanent garrison in Cartagena was abandoned because a new epidemic, most likely malaria, had erupted among Drake's men. So many died or were "decayed in their wits" that he had a mere seven hundred left, making it impossible to pursue his old dream of seizing Panama by marching overland with the Cimaroons. Instead the fleet headed for home, destroying the Spanish Florida settlement at St. Augustine and picking up the survivors of Virginia's failed first colony.

Financially the expedition which cost the lives of almost half its participants was not a success. The plunder, including two hundred bronze cannon Drake brought home, didn't begin to cover the cost of outfitting the fleet. Politically, however, it was a triumph. Drake had once again sent shock waves through the Spanish Empire. Colonial defenses were weakened, commerce shattered, and crucial Spanish credit with European financiers terribly damaged. The Bank of Seville collapsed, the Fugger Bank at Augsberg withheld credit and the Bank of Venice, whose principal debtor was the King of Spain, was on the verge of bankruptcy.

The stunning blow to Spain's prestige couldn't go unpunished. Philip sent his instrument of revenge, the Invincible Armada, to invade England in 1588. Drake, abetted by foul weather, led England to victory over the Armada but it wasn't the end of the Spanish threat. Elizabeth heard that Philip was preparing another invasion fleet and redoubled her efforts to staunch the flow of vital bullion from the Spanish mines which nourished her enemy. She sent her privateers against the treasure fleets. In 1589 Clifford, Earl of Cumberland, was waiting off the Azores and managed to snatch a straggler, the returning New Spain Flota. She carried nearly one hundred thousand pounds sterling in treasure, which would have delighted the Queen whose Armada victory had depleted the treasury. However, as they neared England a squall hit Cumberland's squadron and the galleon and her precious cargo sank.

Cumberland was a courtier, a gambler and a dandy who had run through his inheritance in a hurry. In his hat he wore a discarded glove of the queen's, in which he had diamonds set, as a good luck token. His privateering exploits in the Caribbean and in European seas were undertaken as much for glory as for gain. Elizabeth was a major shareholder in his ventures and was fond of her "Right trusty and well-beloved cousin." The chief accomplishment of Cumberland and his fellow sea dogs was to disrupt the sailing of the treasure fleets. In 1589 the Crown ordered the homeward bound flota to lay over at Havana until spring, causing great hardship for Spain.

In 1592 Christopher Newport, known as "One Hand" having had the other "strooken off" during a daring attempt to capture a treasure galleon off Cuba, pillaged the Caribbean and the Main with four ships. He seized Ocoa and Yaguana in Hispaniola, Trujillo in Central America and captured two large ships and seventeen smaller ones. Newport had taken a daughter of the Glanville family as his third wife. The Glanvilles were leading London goldsmiths and in a position to back privateering expeditions and make the most of the gold, silver, gems and pearls they yielded. Newport made a fortune in the course of some ten privateering voyages to the West Indies. He became an admiral of the colonizing Virginia Company and later sailed to India.

In the 1590s sea dogs like Myddleton, Hippon, Preston and Sir Anthony Shirley, operated from bases including Guadeloupe, an island unclaimed by Spain which lay at the entrance to the tropical sea. Its lofty volcanic peaks made it easy to sight. There was abundant water and the sandy beaches were perfect for careening ships after the trans-Atlantic run, a process which involved dragging the ships up on the beach and turning them on their sides so they could be cleaned, caulked and repaired. In 1592 Captain William King sailed to the Caribbean with two ships. He took a number of prizes including a slave ship with 270 Africans aboard. He reported meeting other English privateers off Cuba's north coast.

Pirates who fell into enemy hands could expect the kind of treatment described in a 1604 report from the Venetian Ambassador in London. "News arrived yesterday," he reported, "that the Spanish in the West Indies have captured two English vessels. The Dons (Spaniards) cut off the hands, feet, noses and ears of the crews and smeared them with honey and then tied them to trees to be tortured by flies and other beasts."

It was a brutal world but Elizabeth's sea dogs were not deterred. In 1593 the Venetian Ambassador at the Spanish Court wrote that "The

West India fleet has never at any time of its history been so harried by the English and exposed to such danger of capture as at this present moment." Between 1589 and 1603 there were at least 160 privateering voyages to the Caribbean, with the late 1590s witnessing the most intensive activity.

In most cases two or more large ships joined forces. Agreements to sail together and share prizes were often broken provoking lawsuits whose records make fascinating reading. "One Hand" Newport sued his former partner Captain Michael Geare because when they were raiding in 1596, Geare's pinnace failed to rendezvous with Newport's *Neptune* which was "the overthrow of the voyage and cause that the ship came home without purchase, for that the said pinnace was the hope of the voyage," since it could enter shallower waters than the *Neptune*. Geare chose to operate on his own and made seven known Caribbean cruises with his versatile little ship.

The Elizabethan privateers were individualists and opportunists who vied for prizes and royal favor. They acted in concert only as long as it was to their advantage. Sometimes they fought among themselves over booty. A privateer fleet under John Watts joined the *Lion's Whelp*, an admiralty ship in ransoming the pearling station of Rio de la Hacha. The *Lion's Whelp* started to speed off with more than their share of the ransom and were chased down by Watts's men.

John Watts was the most ambitious and successful of the group of wealthy London shipowners and merchants who promoted privateering ventures to the Caribbean. These were sophisticated operators with long experience in Mediterranean trade. At the beginning of the war they received official sanction to take Spanish ships and cargoes in reprisal for losses of their property in Spain. With ships, capital and marketing connections they were ideally prepared to cash in on West Indian plundering. Watts's fleets cruised the Caribbean in 1588, 1590, 1591, 1592, 1594 and 1597. He sent out many smaller raiding expeditions as well. Four of the ships in Drake's 1595 fleet belonged to Watts as did six in Cumberland's Puerto Rico venture of 1598.

Many wealthy aristocrats also promoted privateering ventures. Lord Charles Howard of Effingham, the lord admiral, organized one expedition himself and bought stock in several others. The joint stock companies underwriting privateering voyages generally issued "bills of adventure" stating an investor's share of the profits, which depended on how much money, ships or supplies he had put up. Courtier-promoters who hadn't the experience or connections of London merchants occasionally sought loans from friends or even bore all expenses themselves. Those few who gambled their own fortunes in the hope of even greater gains and glory were derided as amateurs and often lost all. When an expedition was well organized, however, and commanded by an able captain, members of a joint stock company could expect some dividends. In the year 1591 John Watts admitted to netting thirty-two thousand pounds sterling in plunder, after the crew had exercised their traditional right to "pillage," although it was thought the actual profit was far greater.

With such likelihood of gain it was no wonder the Caribbean swarmed with English privateers whom the Spaniards lumped with their French and Flemish counterparts, calling all of them *corsarios* or corsairs. In the 1590s there were so many English sails buzzing around the Cuban coast waiting for the arrival of the treasure flotas that Juan de Tejeda, the governor, lamented, "These English are losing all respect for me, for every hour they sail under my nose . . . In the future I would like to be prepared, that the enemy may not so insult me without my being able to get at him. I am asking his majesty to exchange these two galleys, which have proven so fruitless, for four of the frigates I am building here." In 1590 English privateers blockaded Havana Harbor, capturing two rich vessels of the New Spain flota and a number of smaller ships. The next year a fleet of thirteen large privateers paralyzed Havana, plucking seven rich ships from Santo Domingo as they came into port and two galleons of the New Spain flota, one laden with treasure.

In 1595 Sir Robert Dudley sailed to Trinidad and then proceeded to pillage up the Spanish Main and through the Caribbean before heading home. The same year Sir Walter Raleigh, who was to lose his head because he failed to find Eldorado and feed the royal appetite for gold which Drake had so increased, seized the town of San Josef on Trinidad. Amyas Preston and George Somers, two other privateering captains who sailed about the same time as Raleigh with plans to join him for the Eldorado search, elected instead to raid along the Main. They had great success along the coast and even captured the inland town of St. Iago de León in Venezuela.

The sea dogs failed, however, with the exception of Cumberland, to capture any of the treasure galleons, but not for want of trying. Elizabeth commissioned a succession of privateering attempts on the flotas. For years her advisers had counselled attacking and capturing the Indies flotas as the best way to bring Spain to its knees. She had ignored advice such as Raleigh's: "Whosoever commands the trade of the world commands the riches of the world, and consequently the world itself. Only by England having a powerful navy and stopping Spain from benefitting of the riches of the Indies, can Spain be humbled."

The Armada defeat had redoubled Philip's determination to invade England and Elizabeth had been forced to spend a fortune in building and maintaining warships to guard her shores. She sent fleets to cruise off the

Azores in wait for the returning flotas. After Cumberland's capture of the treasure ship which sank, Elizabeth sent two squadrons, under old John Hawkins and Martin Frobisher, to cruise in the Mediterranean between Cape St. Vincent and Cádiz. Philip learned of their presence at once and sent word to the Indies commanding the flotas and all other ships not to sail. So the two squadrons spent seven months cruising at their respective stations without sighting a single West Indies vessel.

In 1591 the Queen was determined to recoup the losses incurred by her squadrons. In March, aware that Philip would have to risk bringing the New Spain ships and the Tierra Firme flota home to ease his painful financial situation, Elizabeth sent out a powerful fleet of twenty-four warships under Lord Thomas Howard with Sir Richard Grenville as vice-admiral. They were to intercept the two flotas as they passed the Azores. It was common knowledge that Spain's coffers were empty and that this double shipment of treasure was critical. What the English didn't know was that Philip had ordered that the treasure shouldn't come on the galleons but on swift vessels called zabras, especially designed for its transport.

Some treasure had already arrived in Spain before Howard reached the Azores. Philip didn't want to lose his flota ships, even if they had no silver and gold aboard. Normally the Armada of the Ocean Sea would have chaperoned the flotas on the last leg of their voyage, but since the defeat of the Invincible Armada in 1588, this armada had ceased to exist because all available warships had been pressed into forming a second great armada for an English invasion. News of Howard's hovering in the Azores forced the King to abandon his grandiose plans for the second Invincible Armada in favor of restoring the Armada of the Ocean Sea.

After almost five months at sea off the Azores, Howard's ships and men were in dire straits. Sickness, hunger and thirst plagued the crews aboard the foul, cramped ships. Just as he was about to give up and return to face Elizabeth's wrath, six English supply ships brought relief. Spirits rose and dreams of gleaming treasure were renewed. The men were confident the convoys would sail into view before long. They had no idea that a fighting fleet of fifty-five ships, under the command of Alonso de Bazán, was on its way to destroy them and then escort the approaching flotas to Spain.

Bazán tricked the English into thinking his fleet was the combined flotas by sailing at them from the west. The late afternoon of August 31, the whole English fleet was anchored off the island of Flores taking on water and changing the ballast stones which served as a ship's septic tank.

A lookout saw distant sails and gave warning. Howard at first believed the flotas were approaching and ordered preparations for battle and capture. Within a few hours it was clear from their alarming size that the vessels were warships and he gave orders for flight.

All the ships weighed anchor save Grenville's *Revenge* which tarried to pick up a large number of the crew who were ashore. The *Revenge* had no choice but to run the gauntlet of Spanish ships. The account of Grenville's incredibly brave fight and the *Revenge*'s ultimate capture, as written by Raleigh who interviewed the survivors, is one of the most stirring episodes in English naval history. Even the Spanish, who lost two ships in the battle, greatly admired Grenville's heroism. Grenville died of wounds a few days after the honorable surrender of his splintered ship. Queen Elizabeth, once again deprived of a golden harvest, alone belittled Grenville's action.

Elizabeth persisted, sending privateering fleets financed by private capital to go after the treasure flotas in 1592, 1593 and 1594, although she refused to lend her own ships or money. It must have seemed to both the Spanish and the English that the riches of the colonies were under Divine protection. These private expeditions had no better luck than Howard's fleet. Each year the Spanish ships were forewarned of English ships lying in ambush and took alternate routes home.

In 1595 the queen mounted an official expedition that appeared to have every chance of success. She assembled a fleet of six of her best ships and others financed privately. She named John Hawkins and Francis Drake, her two most experienced sea dogs as joint commanders. It was the first time since Ulúa that the two had been raiding together. It was to be the last voyage for each of them. Drake came out of relative seclusion as a country gentleman to join Hawkins, now aged and cranky, to plunder the Main and specifically to capture the almiranta of that year's treasure fleet which had lost masts and rudder in a storm in the Florida Straits and was stranded in San Juan, Puerto Rico with more than three million pesos aboard. In addition, El Draque still harbored the dream of taking the Isthmus. He wanted to prevent a Peruvian treasure shipment from reaching Spain by seizing Nombre de Diós and Panama which could then be held for ransom payable in money, or perhaps with a permit allowing free English trade.

The race was on between the English fleet of twenty-seven ships carrying 2,500 men and Spain's five swift zabras sent to collect the treasure in San Juan. The English might have won, had it not been for the inability of the joint commanders to agree. Each of the two great sea dogs considered himself supreme. The friction almost led to disaster the day the fleet left Plymouth. Drake and Hawkins each tried to be the first ship out of the harbor, traditionally the privilege of the flagship of any fleet, and almost collided. Ill omens continued. Against the advice of Hawkins,

Drake insisted on raiding Grand Canary island, which wasted time and yielded little. One of the fleet's smaller ships was captured by the zabras between Guadeloupe and Dominica as they sailed into the Caribbean. A surprise attack on San Juan was now out of the question.

By the time Drake and Hawkins arrived at San Juan the Spanish had prepared a warm reception, opening fire from the fort, from shore batteries and even with the guns of the stranded almiranta. They had also sunk a couple of ships at the harbor mouth to block the entrance. There was little the English could do but withdraw, sailing to an uninhabited part of the island to repair their ships and bury John Hawkins, who had died of a wasting illness at San Juan, and about fifty others who died of battle wounds. With his last breath Sir John had asked his friend, Captain Troughton, to convey to the Queen his regret at the failure of the voyage, which he felt was inevitable owing to Drake's misjudgments. In a codicil to his will Hawkins left Elizabeth two thousand pounds as partial atonement for the loss of her investment.

Drake proceeded southward, returning to his old haunts. He sacked the oft-raped settlements of Ranchería, Santa Marta and Rio de la Hacha but came away with little to show. It may have been frustration at the lack of plunder that led Drake to order the burning of the settlements and the destruction of the surrounding countryside. He hadn't lost his renowned compassion, however, and forbade the molestation of women and the destruction of the church at Ranchería. Next Drake made for Nombre de Diós. He found the town almost deserted, the inhabitants having had adequate warning to take themselves and their valuables across the Isthmus to Panama. How things had changed. Settlements which had once been fertile ground for plundering were now barren. Drake's former allies the Cimaroons had been crushed. Colonial shipping had been reorganized so that Drake on his final voyage saw few Spanish ships, none carrying prize cargoes. English pirates had forced the Spanish to improve coastal defenses and to develop new types of ships. Thanks to Drake and his ilk, Philip had even reorganized the flota system and strengthened his navy.

Drake made Nombre de Diós headquarters for his planned attack on Panama. He sent 750 men under Baskerville overland to Panama. Another party was sent up the Chagres River to Venta Cruz to await the arrival of Baskerville's men with whatever treasure they might have. Nothing was as before. The trail had reverted to jungle because the Spanish had established a new base at Portobelo, twenty miles west on the coast where a new pack-trail began.

The English fought their way, foot by foot, through the torrid jungle combating fever, torrential rains, snakes, insects and sniper-fire, only to find a new Spanish fort barred their way at the place where Drake had once climbed a tree and seen the Pacific. A vain attack on the fort resulted in many casualties. Their food and ammunition had been ruined by the constant rain so the remaining English force hobbled back to Nombre de Diós.

Drake had no option but to give up his grand plan for Panama. To the last his spirit was indomitable. He showed his men a map of the Central American coast, promising them the riches that would be found in the towns along it. His men, ever faithful, were willing to follow but before they sailed far bad weather forced the fleet to anchor by a small island near Portobelo.

To keep his men from losing heart he had them set to work careening the ships. The tropical climate which had proved so unhealthful to the Spaniards took its toll on the English as well. One of the many who died of dysentery was Francis Drake who struggled from his pallet to put on his armor, insisting he "die like a soldier." On August 28, 1595 the greatest sea dog of them all was cast into the sea in a lead coffin. His long vendetta against Philip II was over, Ulúa more than revenged. No single man did more than Drake, the Queen's own "pirate" to halt the Counter Reformation and the Spanish king who was its leader.

This last raiding expedition of Drake and Hawkins brought the epoch of the adventurous Elizabethan sea dogs almost to a close, although individual, private voyages continued to plunder the Spanish Main for quite some time. The most ambitious of these was the Earl of Cumberland's 1598 attack on Puerto Rico which crowned a dozen years of Caribbean plundering. In 1598 he mounted an expensive operation involving twenty ships with which he attacked San Juan. He succeeded in taking the city but sailed off to ambush treasure ships near the Azores. The contingent he left in San Juan was decimated by fever and before long the island was abandoned. Sir Robert Dudley, the Queen's pet, cruised through the Indies at the end of the century with a Captain Popham. In 1595 Dudley had claimed Trinidad for Elizabeth, where he found what appeared to be a gold deposit, although he cautiously noted that "all is not gold that glistereth." The two privateers seized a Spanish ship near the island of Grenada which they brazenly tried to sell to the Spanish at San Juan. They cruised north near Bermuda and eventually encountered a six-hundred ton Spanish ship. After a two-day battle the Spanish ship sank in deep water so that Dudley complained "in this voyage I and my fleete, tooke, sunke and burnt nine Spanish ships which was losse to them, though I got nothing."

Captain Amyas Preston and George Somers were also in the Caribbean in 1595, having sacked Porto Santo in the Madeiras on the way over. They took and plundered the towns of Cumaná, Caracas, Coro and Coche, a little island near Margarita. To get to Caracas their small force had to struggle over a high mountain chain and through stoutly defended territory. The ransom Caracas was able to produce was so disappointing that the English privateers burned the city to the ground. They did the same thing in Coro. A number of ships were taken off the Main before they turned northeast toward Hispaniola and Jamaica, where they landed for several days to hunt wild cattle.

Another Caribbean privateer at the end of the Elizabethan age was Sir Anthony Shirley. In May of 1596 his fleet of six ships set out for a raid on Sao Thomé in the Gulf of Guinea. He changed course because of sickness and bad weather and sailed instead for the Caribbean. Arriving at Dominica, between Guadeloupe and Martinique, in mid-October Shirley and his sickly men rested a month, receiving aid from the friendly Caribs. At Margarita they were disappointed not to find any pearling boats. They did take some small Spanish vessels and captured Santa Marta. A Flemish ship carrying valuable cargo was spared, although they were tempted to seize her, because the captain showed a pass signed by England's Lord Admiral. Shirley was a privateer but not a pirate and had no quarrel with the Flemish.

Proceeding to Jamaica, Shirley's fleet took the small Spanish settlement at Villa de la Vega, now Spanish Town, without difficulty. They stayed there a month resting and gathering foodstuffs. Jamaica pleased them with its abundant fruits and flowers. "We have not found in the Indies a more pleasant and holsome place," wrote Shirley. They were joined by Captain William Parker of Plymouth, a highly successful privateer who made at least six extremely profitable West Indies raids. Parker, like Michael Geare, Christopher Newport and others in the years of Anglo-Spanish hostilities enriched himself and made his backers very happy. Geare was rewarded with a knighthood and Parker became a founder of the Virginia Company.

Together, Shirley and Parker sailed to the Central American coast. Their fleet attacked Trujillo in the Bay of Honduras but retreated in the face of a strong defense. They did take Puerto de Caballos, now Puerto Cortés in Honduras, and sent a small ship up the Dulce River from there in a fruitless search for a passage to the Pacific. Shirley sailed back to England but Parker continued on to Campeche in the Gulf of Mexico. His small force took the town by surprise but was so outnumbered they eventually had to flee to their ships. Parker then resorted to a new stratagem. "For having divers of the townsmen prisoners," he wrote, "we tied them arme in arme together, and placed them in stead of a barricado to defend us from the fury of the enemies shot." In 1668 Sir Henry Morgan was to use the same ploy at Portobelo in Panama. Parker returned home with a prize ship laden with silver, dyewood and other costly cargo but fourteen of his men who had been captured in the Gulf of Mexico were hanged by the Spaniards. In 1601 Parker was back in the Caribbean and executed a daring raid on Portobelo. He seized the town, made off with a rich haul and then plundered coastal trading ships south to Cartagena. This was the zone best protected by the Spanish who had improved coastal defenses as a direct result of years of corsair depredations. In 1592 one of John Myddleton's privateers was captured by a patrol galley and in 1601 Captain Simon Boreman's ship was seized along with a pinnace and a Spanish ship he had recently captured. Yet the governor of Cartagena didn't send a galley to chase Parker because by the close of the war Spain's resources were so overtaxed he no longer had adequate patrol boats.

Cumberland's 1598 raid on Puerto Rico signaled the close of large English privateering ventures in the Caribbean. The turn of the century saw continued small-scale raiding by English ships, often in conjunction with French or even Flemish vessels. Settlements along the Main continued to suffer. Poor Rio de la Hacha, which had been burned by Drake in 1595 was hit again and again. In 1597 the ranchería, or pearling station there was robbed of five pearling canoes and more than a hundred slaves. Three months later Watts's fleet swept through the ranchería, stealing food and equipment and burning three large canoes. Pearl fishing was all but abandoned for the next three years because of the numbers of French and English raids which persisted until the end of the war in 1604.

Continued predation along the Spanish Main led to abandonment of some settlements and the isolation of others. None could flourish as long as they were so vulnerable to the privateer menace. In an official Spanish report to the Crown, Francisco Mexia de Godoy, governor of Caracas, wrote that La Guaira, the new port for Caracas, was "a nest of enemy robbers, to which they regularly repair so regularly that they obstruct the trade by sea and land." He complained that Caracas and other settlements needed essential supplies because pirates had seized over sixty ships and sacked the port's warehouses.

Colonies like this which were off the beaten track found it didn't pay to produce goods for export. They were isolated, poor and ignored. The governor of Cumaná on the Venezuelan coast noted in 1600 that trading ships dared not come into port. Honduras, Guatemala and many of the island settlements were also cut off. Puerto de Caballos in Honduras, where goods bound for Spain were brought for trans-shipment, was sacked three times in 1594 alone and cargo was seized from vessels being loaded to join the New Spain Flota. In 1603 Captain Newport and a corsair from Bordeaux joined forces and occupied Caballos for eighteen days. They left with one of the New Spain galleons filled with hides, indigo and other valuable merchandise.

The Spanish Crown was, for the most part, unable to protect or supply her colonies. The sea dogs and corsairs thus laid the foundations for the development in the seventeenth century of English, French and Dutch trade with the Caribbean. Elizabeth's sea dogs set England on her course as a maritime nation with far flung interests. They stimulated changes in ship construction and made contributions to navigation and astronomy.

The close of the sixteenth century brought an end to the glorious Elizabethan age. Philip II died in 1598, his "papal inheritance" of the New World threatened but still intact. Five years later Queen Elizabeth died. Thanks in large part to her pirates, she left no national debt to James VI of Scotland, who succeeded her as James I of England.

James's accession brought a peace treaty with Spain in 1604. In 1598 the French had signed the Treaty of Vervins agreeing to an end of the war but with a secret clause permitting hostilities as usual "beyond the line." England's treaty was ambiguous in regard to the Caribbean but James made it clear he would not sanction the kind of plundering raids his predecessor had taken such an interest in. Trading and colonizing efforts, rather than privateering, received his royal favor. During the seventeenth century England developed maritime power as a means to a distant end. American and West Indian colonies were established and in the following century Canada and India and then bases in Africa and the Far East came under British hegemony as the British flag followed trade.

King James's desire for peace gave birth to a new phase in the history of sea robbery. In June 1603 he outlawed all privateering ventures. He curtailed the Royal Navy, mothballed much of the fleet and dismissed thousands of seamen. Ironically, during the next twenty years of tenuous peace, English merchants lost more ships than during the years of war with Spain. The king's ban on privateering and the loss of naval employment had the effect of stimulating a rise in piracy. Operating from bases along the North African coast and Ireland, pirates ravaged shipping in the English Channel, in the eastern Atlantic and the Mediterranean. They continued marauding in the favorite pirate playground, the Caribbean, as well.

Mariners were forced to compete with unemployed soldiers for a pitifully inadequate number of jobs. Sailors, who knew no other life, offered to serve aboard merchant ships without pay just to have food and a hammock to sleep in. But there weren't enough berths available so many turned to piracy, preying not only on foreign ships but on English merchantmen too. During this period the Barbary pirates began to plunder Channel shipping as well, so that England's vital trade was crippled. Not even King James's relatives were safe at sea. In 1614 pirates attacked his brother-in-law, the King of Denmark, who was sailing to Yarmouth. Some of the king's courtiers circumvented his ban by financing privateering ventures under letters of marque bought from foreign authorities. In 1616, for example, an East Indies privateering expedition with a commission from the Duke of Savoy was outfitted by Sir Robert Rich, heir to the earldom of Warwick and later Lord Admiral. His partner was a rich Genoese living in London.

Captain John Smith explained why so many men turned to piracy: "King James who from his infancie had reigned in peace with all Nations had no imployment for those men of warre so that those that were rich rested with what they had; those that were poore and had nothing but from hand to mouth, turned Pirats; some, because they become sleighted of those for whom they had got much wealth; some, for that they could not get their due; some, that had lived bravely, would not abase themselves to poverty; some vainly, only to get a name; others for revenge, covetousnesse, or as ill."[2]

NOTES

1. From Dalby Thomas, *An Historical Account of the Rise and Growth of the West India Colonies, and the Great Advantage They are to England in respect to Trade*, London, 1690.

2. From Captain John Smith, Arber, E., editor, *The True Travels and Adventures of Captaine John Smith*, Birmingham, England, 1884, p. 15.

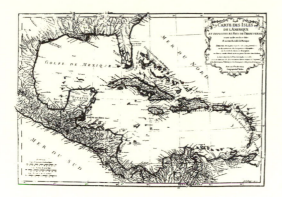

4

The Sea Beggars

he seventeenth century brought an onslaught of vengeful Dutch pirates to the Caribbean. The Spanish called them *pechelinguas*, a name allegedly derived from Vlissing or Flushing, their chief port. The rest of Europe, envious of their success, knew them as the "sea beggars." They were heirs of the audacious *vrijbuiters* who bedeviled Spanish America in the previous century. Many of them were former "sea beggars," veterans of the guerrilla campaign against Spanish occupation of the Low Countries. Sailing from Brill and Zierickzee under the flag of William, Prince of Orange, the "sea beggars" had pioneered privateering as a tactic of war in the fight to end Spanish occupation of the Low Countries. By any name the seamen of the Netherlands were unsurpassed as privateers and traders. In the course of the seventeenth century, which marked the Netherlands' Golden Age, the sea beggars transformed the Caribbean from a Spanish lake into a Dutch canal filled with contraband-laden ships flying the new flag of the tiny Netherlands. Dutch privateers inflicted more damage on the war-weary Spanish Empire than either France or England. At the turn of the century the Dutch, already the principal sea carriers along the coasts of Europe, were raiding and smuggling with increasing frequency in the New World. They soon outstripped the French and English whose corsairs had been the first to raid the King of Spain's "golden orchard." By mid-century the ships of the Dutch West India Company and independent Hollander vessels accounted for a volume of illicit trade almost six times that of legitimate trade with the West Indies.

The French and English complained bitterly that they had plucked Spain's golden fruits only to find them put in a Dutch sack. Dutch ships were everywhere, providing slaves, supplies, credit and encouragement to fledgling colonies in exchange for tropical produce. Their commercial rivals noted that, like the bee, the free trading Dutch sucked honey from all parts. The earliest mention of the Dutch in the Caribbean appears in a Spanish document of 1569 which notes a squadron of sea beggars cruising among the Bastimentos, a group of islands off Nombre de Diós, Panama. In the mid-1580s Dutch smugglers were operating on the Brazilian coast, buying sugar and selling cloth and slaves. About 1595 Dutch ships began contraband trade with ports in Cuba and Hispaniola. Early in the seventeenth century Dutch ships were raiding throughout the Caribbean and up and down the Atlantic and Pacific coasts of Central and South America. Sea beggars took Santiago de Cuba in 1602 and successfully attacked a Spanish fleet off Mexico in league with disaffected Spanish colonials in 1605.

Deeply committed to maritime commerce, the Dutch were traders first and foremost. They combined traditional maritime prowess with brilliant business acumen and a virulent hatred of their former overlords to catapult them into prominence in the Spanish Indies. The sea-oriented men of the tiny United Provinces succeeded where the great kingdoms of France and England had failed, breaking down the Spanish colonial system and irrevocably upsetting the equilibrium of the Empire. In the process they opened the way for French, English and Danish settlement, introduced the cultivation of sugar cane to the Antilles and gained a virtual monopoly of trade in the Caribbean.

By 1623 some eight hundred Dutch vessels plied the trans-Atlantic run on a regular basis. A twelve-year truce between Spain and the Netherlands expired in 1621 and the sea beggars eagerly resumed hostilities, combining trade with piracy and attacks on Spanish coastal towns. In 1624 they seized the Portuguese colonial town of Bahia and briefly held Pernambuco while consolidating a hold on Brazil's sugar rich northeast which lasted almost three decades. A brisk trade in slaves for sugar also flourished in the Greater Antilles where the first Dutch smugglers had appeared at Spanish ports in the 1590s.

From the 1620s to the 1640s permanent colonies were established on the small islands of the Lesser Antilles as England, France, Denmark, Sweden, Brandenburg-Prussia and Courland, a duchy in Western Latvia all scrambled for tropical island possessions. The single most important factor allowed interlopers to claim bits of Spain's formerly ironclad domain was the Dutch West India Company. Chartered in 1621 it was dedicated to waging maritime war against Spain, "our hereditary enemy" and to making profits by plunder as well as by trade. The Company's fleets ravaged Spanish settlements in the Caribbean and Portuguese shipping and towns in Brazil. The damage they inflicted on Iberian interests served their own commercially oriented ends and also allowed other nations to claim a place in the sun.

The first islands settled were in the Lesser Antilles, members of the Windward and Leeward Island chains which the Spanish had ignored for over a century and which they were no longer in a position to defend, even if they had wanted to. These small islands, most inhabited by Carib Indians, were peripheral to Spain's economic interests but lay at the heart of her watery overseas kingdom and were well suited as the corsair and smuggling bases their claimants initially intended them for.

St. Kitts, Nevis, Santa Cruz and the Virgin Islands—members of the Leeward Islands, had become corsair haunts in the second decade of the century. They were outside the perimeter of Spanish patrols and were strategically located as staging areas for attacks on the prosperous Greater Antillean islands of Hispaniola and Cuba. The English and French had partitioned St. Kitts. Beaten away from Dominica and St. Lucia by Caribs, English settlers occupied St. Croix with the Dutch and claimed Barbados, Nevis, Antigua and Montserrat. The French took Martinique and Guadeloupe, exterminating the Carib inhabitants. The Dutch laid claim to islands which fitted in with their pursuit of commercial monopoly. They shared St. Croix in the Virgin Islands with the English and claimed Saba, St. Eustatius and St. Maarten in the Antilles to serve as trading stations and naval bases. They also positioned themselves in the southern Caribbean on Curacao, Bonaire and Aruba. The Dutch are tenacious. They still have a relationship with all those islands except St. Croix.

Since 1648 St. Maarten has seen sixteen changes of flag. Today the island, largest of the six Dutch Antilles, is amicably divided with France. Perpendicular Saba, spiraling out of the sea to a height of three thousand feet, was the most impregnable of Holland's island possessions. Despite an unusually effective defense system which involved rolling stones on invaders as they climbed the steep ravines leading from the island's landings to the few mountainside villages, Saba changed hands a dozen times. St. Eustatius, so incredibly crammed with valuable trade goods in the sixteenth and seventeenth centuries that it was world renowned as "The Golden Rock," was a thorn in the side of every colonial power competing with the Dutch. A haunt of privateers and pirates, and the Caribbean's second largest slave mart, Statia, as it was known, changed hands a record twenty-two times, ten of them between 1665 and 1696.

Dutch commercial interests dictated the need for a base in the southern Caribbean, one closer to the Spanish Main. A mainland settlement would have been too vulnerable so in 1634 a Dutch fleet took the barren island of Curacao off the coast of Venezuela. It had the added attraction of lying among islands whose natural salt deposits would be available when the traditional source in southern Portugal was off limits because of war. Curacao has been the center of Dutch activity in the Caribbean ever since.

"Jesus Christ is good but Trade is better" was a proverb much quoted by those who profited from Holland's raiding and trading in the Caribbean. Not colonizers, planters or proselytizers themselves, the Dutch encouraged and nourished the fledgling plantations of others. They bought the first tobacco crops and when the world market crashed they introduced sugar cane cultivation to the English and French islands, supplying plants and technology from Portuguese plantations in Brazil and making capital, credit, laborers, and imported manufactures available to settlers on far more generous terms than their own government regulated traders did.

The Dutch traded with Spanish colonials as well; crossing the fine line between privateering and piracy when they encountered reluctance. In the process they became the Caribbean's foremost commercial magnates and raiders, incurring the envy of the governments whose colonists they aided. Until the eighteenth century most of the chocolate used in Spain came from cacao beans bought illegally, or pirated, from Spanish sources in the West Indies and sold to Spain via Holland at prices six and seven times what they should have cost. The Dutch made a profit at whatever they turned a hand to. In 1662 about 120 of the 150 ships trading with the French West Indian islands were Dutch; only three or four were French. No wonder the smug merchants of Flushing called the French, English and even Spanish colonials "our planters." An English political scientist, James Harrington, said that the Dutch sweated more gold (from the New World) than the Spaniards were able to dig.

Profits from the West Indies, the spice-rich East Indies and the historically lucrative Baltic trade ushered in Holland's Golden Age, a miraculous blossoming which lasted about a century before succumbing to bourgeois contentment and inertia. During that time the watery little nation was the financial, cultural and intellectual capital of the world and Amsterdam, in the words of poet Consantin Huygens, was "a golden swamp with heaven's plenitude replete, storehouse of east and west, all water and all street."

The well-spring of the Dutch miracle was the sea. The Netherlands had thrown off Spanish rule in 1579, after years of revolt sparked by the semi-piratical Calvinists who came to be known as the Sea beggars, the name perpetuated by later generations of Dutch sea rovers. In 1572 these sons of sons of sailors, whose ancestors had organized North Sea fishing fleets in the fourteenth century and whaling expeditions to the Arctic in the fifteenth, seized Den Briel and a number of other towns in the north provinces. This was the beginning of armed resistance to Spain which culminated in freedom for the seven breakaway provinces which formed the Netherlands.

The Netherlands was a little nation of disparate people united primarily by a talent for seaborne commerce and a hatred of Spain. Fortunately, there were some astute men with money to invest in relatively long-term ventures and many others with consummate sea skills. The Calvinist oligarchy was committed to a seaborne empire and was able to pay for superb merchant fleets and navies out of taxes. Dutch naval architecture was so good and Dutch shipwrights so skilled that even Denmark, Sweden and France had their navies built at Amsterdam, even though the timber had to be imported from the Baltic and Norway. The introduction in the 1590s of a cheaper, more efficient cargo ship called the *fluit*, or flyboat, had the contradictory effect of stepping up the pace of Dutch maritime trade but also throwing large numbers of mariners out of work, some of whom joined the Barbary pirates.

The ultimate goal of the men who sailed for the Dutch West India Company was the capture of a treasure fleet, Drake's unfulfilled ambition shared with virtually every privateer. In 1623 in the Pacific a Company admiral, Hugo Schapenham, narrowly missed taking a flota carrying two years' accumulated treasure off Callao, the port for Lima, Peru. Others tried but none came close until 1628 when the ablest admiral of them all, Piet Heyn, commanding a fleet of thirty-one ships, took the annual home-bound convoy off Matanzas on the Cuban coast. Heyn's spectacular stroke put every ship in the Spanish fleet: merchantmen, treasure galleons and escorts into his hands with hardly a shot fired.

The cargoes which were taken to Havana consisted of 177,357 pounds of silver, 135 pounds of gold, 2,270 chests of indigo, 735 chests of cochineal, 37,375 hides, logwood, 235 chests of sugar, together with spices, pearls and the personal treasures and effects of the Spaniards aboard the flota's ships. It was a triumph not to be repeated for thirty years. The haul of treasure and other goods from the New Spain flota recharged the coffers of the Company, providing funds for further plunder, conquest and commerce in succeeding years and producing a dividend of 50 percent for jubilant stockholders.

It was a tragedy for Spain, the first time the treasure had not been carried up the Guadalquivir to be unloaded before Seville's Tower of Gold. Her credit, never strong, received a ruinous blow. The psychological effect of the capture, so close to Havana, was stunning. Shippers were ever more reluctant to send out their vessels. Dutch privateers had already swept local Spanish shipping from the Caribbean and plundered port towns, leaving them in flames. Now, the Crown was under redoubled pressure to find armed escorts for trans-Atlantic sailings. Freight and insurance charges were astronomical. After Heyn's brilliant exploit the Spanish watched with impotent rage as more and more foreign vessels made the Caribbean an international sea.

Heyn's capture of the treasure fleet spawned another series of Dutch raids. Doggedly, the Spanish hung on, in spite of paralyzing wounds, to Caribbean defense and communications. Attempts were made to create a navy to patrol the Indies. Warships, equal in number to the merchantmen they escorted, were dispatched across the Atlantic. Sailings were increasingly irregular, less frequent and more costly. Defense requirements of the mainland treasure zones further drained strength from the Spanish islands. Yet Spain relinquished no significant claims in the period following Heyn's exploit and somehow managed to continue siphoning the shining treasures of the Americas across the Atlantic although she was powerless to turn back the tide and keep the Caribbean for herself alone.

It wasn't until 1648 that Spain officially recognized the independence of the Netherlands, the existence of Dutch West Indian colonies and the right of Dutch ships to trade in the Caribbean. Until then all Dutch activities in the area were technically illicit acts of privateering or, in time of truce, of piracy. Dutch raiders who had been active since the beginning of the century, treated the Caribbean to a relative period of calm during the Dutch-Spanish truce, although Dutch pirates, sometimes in league with those of other nations, made raids and persistently engaged in forced trade with settlements along the Main and on the coasts of Cuba and Hispaniola. After 1618, during the Thirty Years War, corsair activity in the eastern Caribbean accelerated. Dutch marauding reached an intense level once the Spanish-Dutch truce ended in 1621, although it was technically no longer piracy but privateering, a distinction lost on its hapless victims.

The Dutch West India Company was responsible for altering the balance of power in the Caribbean in the years following the capture of the treasure fleet. The modern world had never seen such an effective union of governmental geopolitical objectives and private commercial interests. The Dutch maritime offensive proved that plunder and conquest could be organized to furnish the foundation for long-range commercial gain and the domination of lucrative colonial trade.

Dutch involvement in the Western Hemisphere began on a very modest scale. Zeelander traders who had initiated early trade with Portuguese colonists in the Amazon Delta expanded their operations westward toward the mouth of the Orinoco in 1580. They traded with Indians along the Guiana coast exchanging European manufactures for tobacco and captives. By 1600 Dutch agents were stationed on several rivers to negotiate exchanges. The Spanish made little effort to oust the Dutch since Guiana was a buffer zone between Portuguese Brazil and Spanish Venezuela.

Spanish authorities viewed with great alarm, however, the appearance of Dutch ships at the vast salt pans in the lagoon of Punta de Araya on the coast of Venezuela near Cumaná. Dutch prosperity had been built on herring fishing, an industry requiring colossal amounts of salt. For generations Dutch seafarers had sailed to Setubal on the southern coast of Portugal for salt to supply their own fisheries and for the rest of northern Europe. War forced them to look elsewhere, first to the Cape Verde Islands and then to desolate Araya, which Dutch traders dealing in cloth and slaves had noted earlier.

The salt cost nothing. Dutch ships anchored at the eight-mile long lagoon and used their own crews to hack out blocks of solar salt left by the evaporation of seawater. Araya became the rendezvous for Dutch corsairs and a lively contraband center attracting an ever larger number of traders. The Spanish Indies had never seen such intense illicit trade. The Dutch were supplying cloth and slaves to sugar planters to the south, loading tobacco in Guiana and exchanging cloth, slaves and other goods for Spanish pieces of eight, gold, emeralds and pearls at ports like Rio de la Hacha, Maracaibo and La Guaira. Dutch ships ranged north, too; twenty ships loading hides and sugar alone each year on Hispaniola and Cuba. They raided where they didn't trade and greatly contributed to the decline of the Cumaná pearl fishery.

The situation became intolerable. In 1600 the governor of Cumaná wrote to the King proposing the salt deposit be poisoned to destroy the "pirates." Antonelli, the military engineer who designed the massive fortifications on Puerto Rico and other anti-corsair defenses in the Spanish Indies, suggested flooding the lagoon. Neither plan was executed and in 1603 more than sixty ships were anchored in the lagoon at one time, many of them large hulks or *urcas* of two hundred to four hundred tons. Between 1600 and 1606 the governor calculated that upwards of one hundred interlopers visited his province annually, most of them Dutch. Their total tonnage was about equal to that of the annual combined flotas sailing to Veracruz and Portobelo. Many of the Dutch ships carried letters of marque. They were lightly armed, however, better equipped for swooping down on a lone ship than mounting a shore attack, and so they made few forays ashore.

In the face of continued corsair raids and illicit trading, the Spanish dispatched an armada in 1605 to oust the interlopers from Araya. Luis Fajardo, one of Spain's most capable generals, led a force of twenty five hundred men in fourteen galleons and four other vessels in a surprise attack on nine Dutch ships and a French ship which they found at the lagoon. The ships were burned and most of the crewmen murdered, many of them horribly tortured. Those who survived were carried to Lisbon and ended as galley slaves. The Spanish gained heart from Fajardo's success. The king issued a *cedula*, or royal decree, ordering the extermination of all pirates and corsairs. Fajardo's armada sailed north to the Antilles where, on February 6, 1606, seven of his ships engaged a combined corsair fleet of twenty-four Dutch, six French and one English ships off Cuba's south coast. The encounter ended inconclusively with three Spanish ships lost and one corsair vessel burned and sunk.

Even after the truce in 1609 when Portugal's salt pans were once again open to the Dutch, they continued to put in at Araya on occasion. In 1621 with the expiration of the truce, the Dutch erected a small wooden fort which housed a permanent garrison of thirty soldiers. On a moonless night in November 1622, two hundred Spanish soldiers overwhelmed the fort, beheading all the Dutch, save one man who hid and was later picked up by a salt hulk.

News of this atrocity caused a great outcry in Holland. The public shouted for retaliation. In May 1623 a fleet of 104 Dutch ships reached Araya and while the majority began loading salt, twenty sailed for the pearling island of Margarita. The Dutch force descended on the island with cold fury, razing every building. All but a hundred of Margarita's twelve hundred inhabitants were slaughtered. The rest, women and children, were taken back to Europe and sold to the Barbary pirates.

Subsequently, the Dutch looked elsewhere for salt, finding ample supplies around Curacao, Bonaire and Tortuga off Venezuela and on lagoon-laced St. Maarten in the Leewards to the north. Wherever they went they carried on their dual raiding and trading. The Spanish rallied to prevent their seizing mainland territory but couldn't stem the tide that carried more and more "*pechelinguas*" into the Caribbean where they terrorized coastal settlements along the Main and in the Greater Antilles. In their wake came the ships of other European corsairs who established lairs in the outer islands and paved the way for the colonizing efforts of the 1620s and 1630s in the Lesser Antilles.

In 1598, the year King Philip II died, the Dutch mounted a number of exploratory expeditions seeking commercial opportunities in distant regions which had previously been off limits including the Portuguese-dominated East Indian Spice Islands, the West African coast and South America. Two fleets attempted to reach the Spice Islands by sailing west around the dreaded Straits of Magellan. The first squadron, comprised five ships with 547 men, purported to be heading for the East Indies, but the Spanish suspected it was planning to circumnavigate the globe since it took on a pilot who had sailed with Cavendish.

Once across the Atlantic, one of the ships penetrated up the Rio de la Plata as far as Buenos Aires where it requested permission to buy provisions and sell cloth and other merchandise. The governor of the isolated settlement denied the Dutch although he had abundant food to trade and his people were in dire need, reduced to wearing animal skins because their cloth garments had rotted away. The governor seized the Dutch captain and officers and, according to documents, the ship sailed away without them. The fleet was plagued by bad luck. Only two ships made it across the Pacific. One of them was captured by Portuguese in the Moluccas and the other strayed to Japan where the fourteen mariners who had survived the voyage abandoned ship.

The other squadron led by Olivier van Noort completed the first Dutch circumnavigation of the globe but not without many harrowing incidents. Van Noort also carried a pilot who had been with Cavendish, a man named Melis, whom they picked up in Plymouth. Off the coast of Chile they seized a Spanish coastal vessel, putting the captain and all the crew save the pilot and four slaves ashore.

One of the slaves blurted out the fact that his ship had been carrying fifty-two cases of gold weighing a total of 5,200 pounds and 500 bars of gold weighing a total of over 15,000 pounds. The Spanish captain had thrown it overboard when Dutch sails were sighted. The captive pilot was tortured and allegedly confessed. If this was so it would have been the richest prize ever taken, but there is doubt about the veracity of the slave and the worth of a confession obtained by torture. In any case, a fine-toothed combing of the ship turned up no more than a small gold nugget wedged between the keel and ballast.

In 1615 a squadron commanded by Joris Spilbergen, a German in the Dutch service, sailed into the Pacific. Like the Dutch expeditions before him, he plundered Spanish shipping off Chile and Peru and raided little settlements but failed to intercept a Manila galleon or take a treasure ship from Callao even though he defeated a small armada dispatched against him by the viceroy of Peru. Dutch sources claimed their five ships were attacked by seven large galleons and after a fierce, protracted battle four galleons were sunk and a thousand Spaniards lost, including the Admiral and the General. Very few Dutch were killed they said, although Spanish sources claimed at least 180 deaths versus 500 for their side. In his multi-volume work *Armada Española* Fernando Duro, the nineteenth-century Spanish historian, attributed the low Dutch claim to their penchant for distorting history, "trying to make their men better fighters than they really were," a charge which might be equally valid in regard to the Spanish.

The projectiles in Spilbergen's first cannonades against the Spanish armada weren't normal cannon balls but Spanish coins called *patacones* or *pesos duros* which he had taken from a merchant vessel captured at the port of Canete the day before. This odd cannonade, illuminated by lights hung from the masts and yards of the Dutch ships, took place at nine p.m., five hours after the two fleets had sighted each other, and was accompanied by the playing of music as a morale booster. The battle continued throughout the night and all the next day. In a freak incident a Spanish cannon ball zoomed into the bore of a Dutch cannon, blowing it up and killing seven men.

When the Dutch sank the Spanish flagship at nightfall on the second day, all hands aboard were drowned save four who were picked up by the Dutch and later put ashore. Among the survivors was the celebrated Military Nun, the Monja Alferez, Doña Catalina de Erauso who passed as a male soldier for years in the New World and who published an autobiography in 1646 describing her exploits.

In 1623 the most ambitious Dutch effort to date was mounted to capture a treasure flota. The expedition was under the auspices of the Dutch West India Company which had as its chief objectives the seizure of the flotas which would cut the sinews of war by ending the flow of American gold and silver the Spanish King used to finance anti-Protestant actions all over Europe. Attacks on the flotas and the New World colonies would serve a double advantage: Spanish naval forces would be too preoccupied with protecting their own flotas to harass Dutch merchant fleets and the attacks on Spanish settlements would deflect the Crown's energy from the shores of the Netherlands, enabling the Dutch to employ all available forces in a rigorous offensive.

In 1621, the year the truce expired, the Dutch West India Company was chartered and immediately sent a hastily organized squadron to intercept the returning flotas off the Azores. From the crew of a captured fishing boat the Dutch Admiral Villebrins learned the flotas had sailed past the area four days earlier. Hoping to catch up with them, the Dutch headed toward Spain, all canvas flying, but the flota ships slipped into Cádiz a mere eight hours before Villebrins sighted the port. The following year fate once again smiled on Spain. Villebrins commanded a fleet of warships which cruised off the Azores in wait for the homebound treasure galleons. For seven tedious months the Dutch waited before they learned that the flotas, devastated by a hurricane which sunk nine ships soon after they left Havana in September, had limped back to the Cuban port to wait for spring.

After these fruitless attempts, the Company formulated a new plan of attack on the flotas. In 1623 Spanish spies in the United Provinces reported that a war fleet was being prepared. The embarkation of a great quantity of provisions, unassembled launches and galliots (light galleys), campaign artillery and soldiers, led the Spanish to believe the Dutch were about to launch an offensive against the Portuguese East Indies, where they had already taken over the Moluccas and other spice islands. Consequently, the Crown took no action to warn American officials.

The Dutch squadron sailed from the port of Texel on April 29, 1623 with the intention of sailing to the Pacific and intercepting the Armada of the South Seas which was bearing gold and silver from Callao to Panama. Jacques l'Hermite, an extremely capable Dutch West India Company admiral, was entrusted with the enterprise. He had lived in Madrid for seven years, spoke fluent Spanish and understood the Spanish mentality. The action began before the Dutch even crossed the ocean. Off Portugal l'Hermite took four caravels returning from Brazil with sugar and sent them to Holland. Near the Barbary Coast l'Hermite took a Flemish merchantman, easily persuading most of the crew to join his squadron by hanging four men who steadfastly swore their allegiance to the King of Spain.

The Dutch fleet spent a month at the Cape Verde Islands making hardtack from goat meat, stowing the heavy cannon in the hold, and taking on fresh water, fruit and vegetables. The Portuguese crewmen of the captured caravels were left behind when he sailed except for three who were pilots. L'Hermite headed south along the Guinea coast and put in at the port of Farallones, where the Portuguese settlers surrendered to the Dutch and were turned over to the local African chieftain who promptly slew them all.

While they were at Farallones the Dutch fleet's chief surgeon was tried on charges of killing some two hundred seamen and soldiers with his medications. Found guilty, he was promptly hanged much to everyone's delight.

The squadron then headed across the southern Atlantic and into the grueling passage through the Straits of Magellan. After battling the pitiless elements for three months they finally succeeded in rounding Cape Horn on February 2, 1624, although two ships sank with all hands. An additional nineteen men were killed by Patagonian natives when they landed to gather firewood. They stopped at Juan Fernández Island, off the Chilean coast, to get fresh water and provisions, repair damages and to mount their cannon in anticipation of attack.

L'Hermite profited from the experience of his English predecessors in the Pacific. Instead of sailing up the Chilean coast, thus giving notice of his presence, news which would have travelled swiftly to Peru, he took a longer route planning to make landfall at Callao and take the Spaniards by surprise. This circuitous route, however, took him a month longer than anticipated. Near Callao he captured a Spanish coastal trader and tortured its crew until he was told the Armada of the South Seas, laden with not one but two years' accumulated silver, gold and emeralds, had sailed thirteen days earlier from Callao. In fact, however, the extraordinarily treasure-laden Armada made up of four large galleons and several smaller ships had sailed on the third of May, not thirteen days but three days before the Dutch fleet's arrival. L'Hermite discovered the truth too late. Had he known at once he could easily have pressed on and overtaken the armada.

When the news reached Lima on May 6 that a Dutch squadron had been sighted and was preparing landing launches, the Viceroy of Peru was at a bullfight with the country's most prominent nobles. The announcement precipitated great confusion. The Viceroy urged the populace to mobilize but everyone was concerned only with escaping to the interior with as many possessions as possible. Callao was so off guard that the forts had no powder to fire their artillery. L'Hermite resolved to land troops and take both Callao and Lima. Unfortunately, instead of launching an offensive at once to press home the Dutch advantage, he waited four days allowing the Spaniards valuable time to prepare their defenses. Consequently the colonials were able to repel a month-long series of assaults, each of which cost the Dutch heavily.

L'Hermite died on June 2 of an illness contracted on the voyage. He was succeed by Vice Admiral Hugo Schapenham, who immediately lifted the siege of the port. The Dutch had lost more than two-thirds of their original force and relinquished any hope of success. They set fire to the seventeen Spanish merchant vessels in port as they sailed away but they had gained nothing. Schapenham sailed up the coast to Guayaquil, Ecuador, where he sacked the town and destroyed a five hundred-ton galleon under construction. The booty was pathetic, the inhabitants having fled into the countryside with their good, slaves and animals. As a farewell gesture the frustrated Dutch privateers hanged thirteen prisoners they had captured from coastal fishing vessels.

The trip home wasn't easy. The squadron, which had set out with such high hopes, reached Holland after two years at sea. Schapenham was aware that an exact account of the costly, disappointing campaign would hardly be welcome news, especially to the Company shareholders. So, to salve national pride even though it would fill no pockets, Schapenham invented a great naval battle which resulted in a resounding Dutch victory. Later, when the truth was learned, the commander was demoted to the rank of seaman and banished to the East Indies for the remainder of his life.

The year of the Pacific fiasco wasn't a total loss for the West India Company which launched the first of a series of naval attacks on Portugal's possessions in Brazil and West Africa. From 1581 until 1640 Spain ruled Portugal whose overseas territories were considered the most vulnerable part of the Empire. Control of Brazil's northeast coast where African slaves on Portuguese owned plantations cultivated most of the sugar consumed in Europe was crucial to long-range Company plans as was control of the Portuguese slave stations on the Guinea coast of Africa. In 1624 a mighty expedition of thirty-six ships and sixty-five hundred men seized Sao Salvador (Bahia), Portugal's chief settlement in Brazil. There was plenty of booty—half a million pesos in treasure, as much again in merchandise and two hundred tons of sugar, all of which was shipped back to Company warehouses in Holland.

When word of Sao Salvador's capitulation reached the King, nineteen-year old Philip IV, he burst into tears and refused to see or speak with anyone for a week, including his closest advisor. News of jubilant celebrations in Holland and the hasty departure from the court of a group of Italian and Austrian bankers with whom the King had been negotiating desperately needed loans, deepened his depression. Count-Duke Olivares, Philip's Rasputin, hastily organized the Armada of the Ocean Sea, fifty-two Spanish and Portuguese ships under Don Fadrique de Toledo and ordered it to Brazil to oust the Dutch.

In the Spring of 1625 the combined Iberian fleet took Sao Salvador from the Dutch netting over half a million pesos in treasure and goods, six hundred slaves, 260 pieces of artillery and other war materials. Soon after a Dutch fleet of thirty-four ships entered the bay of Sao Salvador unaware it was again in the hands of the enemy. Toledo sent six warships out of the bay to get behind the Dutch fleet, trapping it in a cross fire. Once the Dutch ships caught on they started frantically out of the bay, escaping with the aid of a favorable wind.

The Dutch commander, Boudewijn Hendricksz, then split his fleet, sending nineteen ships back across the Atlantic to storm Elmina, the chief Portuguese slave depot on the Guinea Gold Coast. The Dutch prepared to land a force of two thousand soldiers, confident of victory over Elmina's fort which was garrisoned with a mere fifty-seven Portuguese troops. A large quantity of gold dust stored there for shipment turned the tables, however. The Portuguese distributed the gold to local chieftains to buy the aid of nine thousand African warriors. The Dutch were repelled with heavy losses.

Five years later, the Dutch who by then controlled much of northeastern

Brazil after capturing Pernambuco (Recife), successfully assaulted and held Elmina. They became the New World's chief slavers, supplying Africans to the Iberian colonies and to the developing French and English settlements in the West Indies and the North American seaboard.

The remainder of Hendricksz's squadron, seventeen ships under his command, had sailed toward Cuba, planning to lie in wait for the treasure flotas as they sailed into Havana. Near the Virgin Islands he captured a Spanish coastal trader whose captain deceived him into believing the flotas had already left Havana and were well on their way to Spain. In fact, none of the galleons had even reached Havana and if Hendricksz had been less gullible and proceeded with his plan, the treasure flotas would almost certainly have been captured.

Instead he made an ill-advised attack on San Juan, Puerto Rico, which the mendacious Spanish captain told him was poorly defended. San Juan was indeed a bedraggled settlement, weakened by hurricanes, epidemics and struggles with the Caribs. Only two hundred men and boys were capable of bearing arms but the town boasted a fine fort, Morro Castle, designed by the renowned military architect, Antonelli, at the orders of Philip II after Drake sacked the town in 1596. Hendricksz landed without opposition and sent an emissary demanding immediate surrender. If not forthcoming, he threatened "We will not spare one person on your island; old nor young, women nor children . . . "

The Governor replied: "I have read the paper you sent to me and am shocked you would waste time asking me such a stupid question. Here I stay with all the advantages on my side and with thirteen years of hard fighting experience behind me from the wars in Flanders. Actually the tables are turned. You will give over all your ships to me but one, on which all of your men will return, after first leaving your weapons behind, otherwise you will suffer severely."[1]

The Dutch were not deterred by this ultimatum and opened fire from a six-cannon battery they constructed on a hill, high above Morro Castle. That night a Spanish patrol silently crept up the hill and massacred twenty-five sleeping Dutchmen without incurring any losses. The following night Spaniards stole aboard two of the smaller Dutch ships and slit the throats of the men on watch. They overpowered the rest of the crew, threw them all overboard and moved the two prizes further into the harbor. A Dutch attack on the town next day was driven off but on October 21 Hendricksz landed all his men and marched into San Juan, whose residents had fled to the adjacent hills. The Dutch, who at this juncture were sorely in need of food and supplies, burned the town to the ground in revenge for finding neither food nor booty.

The Spaniards strengthened by indignation counterattacked and drove the more numerous Dutch back to their ships. Hendricksz decided to retreat but as the first Dutch ship started through the passage to the open sea it was struck by fire from a Spanish battery. The vessel went out of control and ran aground on a shoal blocking the exit of the rest of the fleet. Efforts to dislodge the stranded ship were fruitless. Finally smaller ships in the fleet were used to tow the larger warships around the derelict and out to sea as Spanish settlers on the shore called out derisive remarks.

Hendricksz's fleet returned to Texel with its tail between its legs. Far from the easy capture of a treasure fleet he had planned on or the seizure of San Juan which he had been willing to settle for, the Dutch commander had to report the loss of three ships, six cannon that had been placed ashore at San Juan and four hundred men. Since no significant plunder had been taken, the loss was even greater for Company shareholders. The fleet had taken a number of Spanish ships but their cargoes of manioc flour, hides and dried fish were hardly the shining bullion they hoped for.

The most gratifying prize Dutch privateers took in the Caribbean was a richly laden galleon from Honduras which fell, almost by accident, into the hands of a three ship reconnaissance expedition in 1624 led by Pieter Schouten as it cruised off Cuba's Cape San Antonio, the point all the flotas and Honduran galleons passed on the way to Havana. Once Pernambuco was occupied by the Dutch, privateers sailing singly or in small groups began to step up the pace of plundering in the Caribbean and along the Main. In 1626 and 1627 sea beggars sailing up from Brazil did quite well for themselves. The Spaniards especially feared a privateering captain named Hendrick Jacobszoon, known as Captain Lucifer, whom they called "the worst shark in the sea."

In 1626 three Dutch privateering fleets cruised the Gulf of Mexico and hung off the Florida coast waiting to pounce on the silver flotas, but the galleons eluded them and the great Dutch dream of capturing the treasure flotas seemed more of a mirage than ever. The commander of one of the Dutch squadrons was Piet Heyn, a former corsair, who had been named the captain-general, or supreme commander of the Dutch West India Company's navy for his brilliant service in the capture of Sao Salvador.

Pieter Pietersz Heyn, was the greatest threat to the Spanish who both feared and grudgingly admired him for his consummate sea skill. He was the outstanding contributor to the overall success of the Dutch West India Company and the only man ever to have captured an entire treasure fleet. Even today his exploits are remembered in a popular national Dutch song. Heyn was born to a seafaring father in 1577 in Delfthaven. He followed his father to sea at an early age. In 1592 the entire crew of his father's ship was captured by the Spanish. Fifteen year old Heyn and his father spent the ensuing four years chained to a bench on a Spanish galley, working the long sweeps amid filth and stink. Father and son were eventually freed in a prisoner exchange but in 1598 they were captured again and served another four years as galley slaves. Piet Heyn somehow managed to sustain his physical and mental health despite the spirit-breaking toil he was subjected to. He even earned a bit of extra rations by knitting stockings, a skill he had learned as a child.

Released once more, Heyn tasted freedom for a year and then had the misfortune of being taken captive yet again, this time while on a voyage to the Caribbean. His third stint in the galleys was served in the West Indies where he acquired invaluable information about Spanish shipping practices and the flota system. Ironically, the captain on whose galley he was enslaved was a certain Don Juan de Benevides y Bazán, from whom he was to exact a full measure of revenge in 1628 when he encountered him serving as general of the silver flota. The years spent in chains and the cruelties he had suffered and witnessed were branded on the young Dutchman's mind forever, inspiring a consuming hatred of the Spanish.

In 1607 when he was thirty, Heyn sailed as first mate on a Dutch East India Company ship. During the next five years he captured countless Portuguese ships and led incursions throughout the Far East and in the Indian Ocean, making a name for himself as a brilliant strategist and tough adversary. His fame grew when he returned to Holland and embarked on a period of raiding Spanish ships in European waters. Once again he sailed to the East Indies to bait the Portuguese. In 1622 he went home and was elected a city-father of Rotterdam. Soon after Heyn was named vice-admiral of the West India Company's 1624 expedition to Sao Salvador, during which he greatly distinguished himself.

In 1626 Heyn was dispatched to the Caribbean with command of a fleet of nine warships and five fast sloops. He had orders to rendezvous with a fleet of twenty-three warships under Admiral Witsen which had been cruising off Cape San Antonio at the west end of Cuba waiting for a treasure flota on its way to Havana. Heyn left Holland, unaware that Admiral Witsen had died on July 11 and that his second-in-command had opted to head for home, a decision that lost the Dutch another golden opportunity to capture the flotas. When Witsen's fleet was sighted near Havana in mid-June, the governor of Cuba had sent fast boats to warn the galleons then loading in the ports of Cartagena, Portobelo and Veracruz. The flota ships were ordered to remain in safe ports until notified of the Dutch departure. Witsen's expedition had little luck. Not only had they been seen but their efforts to secure provisions either through illicit trade or raiding were thwarted. Each time they tried to land Spanish soldiers repelled them with considerable force and then Witsen died.

Heyn found no sign of the other Dutch fleet in the Caribbean and correctly assumed it must have headed for home despite orders to remain until a flota was captured or contrary instructions were received from Holland. Heyn knew he had neither the men nor the ships to attack an entire flota but he decided to lie off Cape San Antonio in hopes of picking off a rich straggler or two when the flota passed. After a month he moved near the Dry Tortugas off the southern tip of Florida, an island group which the New Spain flota habitually sailed close to on the way to Havana.

Captured crewmen from a Spanish merchantman told Heyn the Tierra Firme Flota was already in Havana Harbor and the other flota was expected at any moment. On August 9, two days after reaching the Tortugas, the Dutch saw the New Spain Flota on the horizon. Sailing in tight formation some of the forty large treasure ships passed so close to Heyn's that lilting Spanish voices floated across the water. Heyn was heartsick at having to forego this rare opportunity but his small squadron was dwarfed by the mighty flota. With tears of frustration on his cheeks, Heyn retired to his cabin where he remained in melancholy solitude for two days.

His instructions from the Company, taking into account the possibility of Witsen's premature return to Holland, ordered him to cruise off the coast of Brazil and harass Portuguese shipping until further notice. The prevailing easterly winds in the West Indies forced Heyn's squadron to cross the Atlantic twice before reaching Brazil. The majority of his men were suffering from dysentery and scurvy so he put in at Sierra Leone on the West Coast of Africa to let them recuperate. At the beginning of March, almost seven months after he had wept as the silver fleet sailed past, Heyn appeared at the Bay of All Saints (Bahia).

Unable to surprise the Portuguese, Heyn's fleet boldly swept into the port even though the potential prizes of twenty-six large merchant ships lay at anchor very close to several of the almost forty forts encircling the great bay. No one but dauntless Piet Heyn, or perhaps Errol Flynn, would have dared such a move. With total disregard for the barrage of cannon fire from Portuguese ships and the forts, Heyn took his ship into the midst of the enemy, dropping anchor between the Portuguese capitana and almiranta—the two largest and best armed of the Portuguese vessels. While half his men answered fire, Heyn and the other Hollanders scrambled into small boats and boarded the two ships. In less than ten minutes both massive galleons struck their colors and surrendered. Heyn spurred his men on to take another twenty-two ships right under the noses of the Portuguese ashore. His flagship the *Hollandia* was left within range of the main fort to draw fire while the Dutch ships and captured prize vessels were moved farther from shore. The *Hollandia*'s guns slammed cannon balls into the fort without a break but took such return fire that by sunset the flagship was battered almost beyond recognition, riddled with more than five hundred holes. At midnight Heyn set the remains of his ship ablaze and escaped in a sloop with the surviving members of his crew. Thirty-seven of his men had died and seventy-seven had been wounded. The other Dutch ships lost a total of some one hundred men. A large number of French, English and German mercenaries from the captured prizes, many of them Baltic traders and not Portuguese ships at all, enabled Heyn to crew his expanded fleet.

For ten days Heyn hovered near the mouth of the Bay of All Saints, making repairs and transferring plunder for shipment to Holland. There was lots of it. This was the most rewarding Dutch privateering enterprise to date. The booty amounted to more than two million guilders in gold and silver specie and bullion, worked silver, hides, tobacco, valuable dye-woods, cotton and twenty-five hundred tons of sugar. A Company administrator rejoiced that: "The Company begins to breathe again . . . thanks to that courageous sea beggar Piet Heyn."

Success whetted Heyn's appetite for revenge against Spain. Rather than sail home in triumph, he elected to cruise along the South American coast plundering Spanish and Portuguese ships. Off Rio de Janeiro he took seven ships but was disappointed in their cargoes. So he returned to the Bay of All Saints, once again dashing in under the fortress's cannons. He captured two ships—the only large ships in port. He interrogated men on the vessels and learned that at news of his approach all ships then in port had been towed by galleys into several concealing river mouths around the bay.

Heyn was determined to go after the ships, fully aware the Portuguese had deployed more than two thousand musketeers on both sides of the main river emptying into the bay and set up shore batteries. With characteristic bravado he led the attack, captured the shore batteries and fought on despite two musket balls lodged in his chest. In a savage, bloody battle that raged for more than eight hours, the Dutch took one ship after another, until all thirteen were theirs. The captured vessels yielded half a million guilders worth of additional booty to Heyn's already impressive take. The Dutch fleet reached Holland at the end of October 1627, a year and a half after setting out. Heyn was given a hero's welcome, presented with a massive ceremonial gold chain and given a standing ovation—normally reserved for monarchs—by the delegates of the States-General.

Piet Heyn couldn't rest on his laurels. He was more determined than ever to capture a silver fleet. As eager as he had been to get home after Brazil, Heyn hadn't been able to resist the temptation to lie in wait for any laggards in the 1627 treasure flotas. After two weeks he learned from the crew of a captured fishing vessel that the flotas had passed by the Azores a week before his arrival. Luck had been with Spain yet another time. The flotas had eluded the grasp of navies, privateers and pirates so many times. Could such luck last?

The safe delivery of the American treasure in 1627 was scant cause for celebration in Spain. The Crown tottered on the brink of bankruptcy once more, so Philip IV appropriated all the treasure, including that belonging to private citizens of various nations, to partially repay some of Spain's staggering debts. The cost of maintaining the Spanish Empire, which had almost one hundred and fifty thousand troops stationed in several countries, far exceeded the total value of New World treasure which reached Seville. During 1627 the Spanish and Portuguese lost over two hundred and fifty ships to storms and the ravages of the sea beggars—more than twice the number of ships both countries had built in the previous decade. Unfounded rumors of a hundred ship Dutch fleet on its way to attack Portobelo and news of England's organizing a great fleet to attack the returning treasure flotas caused general panic in Spain.

Philip IV entrusted command of the New Spain Flota to the brother of his mistress, Don Juan de Benevides y Bazán, none other than Piet Heyn's former galley master. Benevides, a member of one of Spain's wealthiest families, had little to recommend him other than his connections. He was a man of fifty-seven, with long record of undistinguished naval service and a reputation for having amassed a large fortune by carrying contraband goods to the West Indies and smuggling unregistered treasure back to Spain. Accusations of flight before the enemy had been quashed thanks to his sister's influence. In a formal ceremony Benevides took the oath administered to all captain generals before receiving command of a flota. It ended with the phrase: "The captain general swears to always bring honor and glory to Spain and the King's name upon pain of death." At the time this vow seemed a mere formality to Benevides. He couldn't foresee it would cost him his head.

Most of the flota preparation was left to Admiral Leoz, while Benevides concerned himself with the purchase of contraband cargo to sell in Mexico. Leoz had to deal with an alarming scarcity of ships, men, arms and funds. Ships were commandeered from protesting private owners and a thousand convicts let out of the dungeons of Andalusia to crew them. Both the capitana and the almiranta had to sail with less than half of the requisite number of cannon and some of the merchantmen had none at all.

The merchants of Seville at first refused to send any cargoes to the Indies, sure the flota would be captured before reaching Veracruz. Only a royal edict threatening imprisonment and seizure of all their possessions persuaded the merchants to prepare cargoes. There were other delays, one caused by seamen on several ships who mutinied when they discovered greedy ships' pursers had watered their wine rations. The mutiny was not quelled until Benevides hung three pursers and replaced the questionable wine. The final delay occurred when the newly appointed archbishop of Mexico, who was late in arriving at Sanlúcar, refused to embark on Benevides flagship, the six-hundred-ton *Santiago*, unless Benevides relinquished his own spacious quarters. Benevides refused to accommodate the prelate who then refused to board. A compromise was finally reached which left Benevides his quarters and pushed Admiral Leoz out of his cabin on the six-hundred-ton *Santa Gertrudis* in favor of the archbishop.

The flota of thirty-one ships sailed on July 20, 1627, four months behind schedule. Because of the critical shortage of money and bullion, the King ordered the flota not to winter in Veracruz, as was the usual practice, but to sail home immediately with the treasure. The combination of a late departure and the approaching storm season in the Gulf of Mexico kept Benevides from following his instructions. In fact, in pursuit of his business deals, he was to disregard most of the orders issued by the King and the House of Trade officials. Against orders, he stopped at the Canaries for six days to trade illegally with Dutch, French and English merchant vessels. The Atlantic crossing was marred by hunger because all the provisions turned putrid and had to be thrown overboard, leaving little but hardtack and fish, when they could be caught. Benevides ignored orders not to put in at Guadeloupe for fresh water and fruit. Many men from the three previous flotas had been killed there in Indian attacks and Benevides too lost twenty-six of his crew.

The flota reached Veracruz on September 16. Normal procedure called for immediate unloading of Mexico City-bound mercury, which was essential in separating gold and silver from their ores. Instead, Benevides who placed his private interests above all else, had his contraband goods unloaded first. To get a jump on the Spanish merchants and their agents who had sailed with goods, the captain-general commandeered all of the mules which were waiting to transport the 250 pounds of Hungarian mercury, to carry his trade goods to Mexico City. Consequently, the mercury arrived in Mexico City three months late. Adding insult to injury Benevides bribed Veracruz authorities to impede the departure of all the Spanish merchants and their goods until he had completed his profitable dealings in Mexico City.

Admiral Leoz oversaw the unloading of the ships and made preparations against the northerly storms which were expected to batter the coast throughout the winter. Then he set off for Mexico City, abandoning the seamen to their fate since there were neither provisions nor money to buy any. No wonder more than half the men had deserted by the time the flota sailed the following summer. The skeleton crews on some of the ships could barely work the sails, let alone defend the ships from pirates or privateers.

In mid-December 1627, Benevides received an order to sail at once for Havana with whatever treasure was available. Comfortably ensconced in a palace in Mexico City, he chose to ignore it. The King wrote to him personally, a letter that reached Benevides in mid-June and forced him to return to Veracruz and the shambles of his flota. A high mass for the safety of the flota's voyage to Spain was held in the Veracruz Cathedral. At the conclusion of the service an enormous bell toppled from the belfry crushing two Spaniards to death. This portent of disaster caused some passengers to remove their baggage and wait for the next eastbound flota. As the flota's thirty ships filed out of port a squall struck. Benevides's capitana ran aground on a shoal and was lost. It took eighteen days to transfer treasure and cargo from the ruined ship to the *Santa Ana Maria*, the newly designated capitana.

It was during this time that a Dutch fleet of thirty-five sail with more than four thousand men under the command of Piet Heyn was first spotted off Cuba. The island's governor sent nine small boats to search for the flota and warn Benevides but all nine fell into the hands of the Dutch, so the treasure fleet had no suspicion of what was about to strike.

Heyn had left Holland vowing he would return with the shining plunder from a Spanish treasure fleet or not at all. His admiring employers gave him the means to make his life's ambition a reality. He had the best ships and armament and the country's best seamen and officers. Men flocked to sail with Heyn, who had achieved great feats with relatively light losses. His stern but just treatment of his crews and the fairness with which the booty had been distributed made men so eager to serve under Heyn that some even offered to sail without pay. He left nothing to chance. Discipline was strict and a Calvinist minister sailed on each of the large ships to attend to spiritual needs. Weapons, including the cannon, were cleaned daily and arms drills were held for an hour each day in good weather.

When he sailed on May 20, 1628 all but a few trusted officers believed the fleet was bound for the East Indies or to recapture Sao Salvador. Off the south coast of England Heyn encountered a squadron of English ships. They exchanged salutes and then Heyn pulled alongside the English flagship for a chat with the commander, during the course of which he confided that his destination was the East Indies. Just as he expected, this misleading information soon reached the Court at Madrid and so lulled the Spaniards into false security that no word was sent to warn the flotas and no armada was organized to protect them. He made sure his fleet was sighted off the Canaries as if making for the East Indies and then changed course to cross the Atlantic.

The Dutch fleet reached St. Vincent, west of Barbados, on July 12 and remained there a week to refresh the crews and take on water and fruit. The next stop was Isla Blanca, off Venezuela, where Heyn replaced putrid salt beef and pork with fresh goat meat from the large population descended from a flock put ashore by sea beggars at the turn of the century. The ships then sailed across the Caribbean expecting to encounter the Tierra Firme Flota carrying the treasure from South America.

The situation in Spain was desperate. A smallpox epidemic killed more than one hundred thousand people between April and July. Lawless bands terrorized the countryside, robbing and killing. As news of Spain's moribund condition spread throughout Europe her enemies gathered to strike. The Barbary pirates who had plagued Spanish shipping in the past, stepped up attacks on seaports carrying off booty and men, women and children to sell in the slave markets of North Africa. An alarming rumor reached Madrid in June that the English planned an attack on Seville, the heart of the nation's commerce and banking.

One disaster built on another. When Philip issued an edict that anyone caught trading with the Dutch would be put to death, more than half the Seville merchants left the country, pointing up the fact that without the Dutch there would be no profitable trade. The final blow occurred in early August when bankers in Genoa, Vienna and Antwerp announced there would be no further loans to the Crown until they had been repaid the colossal sums already owed them. Dutch attacks on the East and West Indies were expected. The money markets were closed and the wages of his soldiers were more than two years in arrears. Philip was in desperate trouble and ordered the Spanish governor of Flanders to initiate peace negotiations with the Dutch, who refused to entertain any such proposal.

Turning to God, Philip IV ordered the last coins in his coffers distributed to churches throughout the land for special masses to be said for the speedy and safe return of the treasure flotas. Ironically, this happened on the very day that Heyn seized the New Spain Flota. The anticipated meeting with the Tierra Firme Flota had not materialized. Escorted by the *Armada de Tierra Firme*, or the Galleons as they were better known, under Captain General Tomás de Larraspuru, the treasure ships had been warned of Dutch presence in the Caribbean. Larraspuru ordered all the ships under his command to remain in port at Cartagena until they had news from Havana that all enemy ships had departed.

When he saw no sign of the Tierra Firme galleons, Heyn headed for Cape San Antonio, past which all the flotas and Honduran galleons sailed on the way to Havana. He arrived on August 7, unaware his fleet had been sighted by a lookout on the Cape and word sent to Havana. When the Dutch intercepted the nine boats dispatched by the Cuban governor to warn the treasure fleet, Heyn learned that the commander was none other than Benevides whose brutalized galley slave he had once been. Heyn thanked God for the imminent opportunity for revenge. He issued fighting orders to his captains, reserving for himself the first shot against the flota and the right to initiate the attack on Benevides's capitana.

Heyn gave detailed orders. The Dutch ships were to deceptively fly Spanish colors until the battle began and only then to raise the flag of Holland. Cannon fire was to be judicious so that the galleons riding low in the water under the weight of gold, silver, emeralds and pearls would not sink. Barrels of water were placed on deck to extinguish any fires. Patches of lead were prepared to cover any cannon shots below the water line and scaffolding was constructed over the open decks to protect the cannoneers. The most skilled marksmen were stationed in the mast tops with hand grenades and blunderbusses. The rest of the crew was issued muskets, pikes and boarding axes. Each officer received two pistols in addition to his sword. Heyn told his men that anyone displaying cowardice would be shot by an officer on the spot as would anyone killing a Spaniard after he surrendered. There would be prayers and a stout ration of confidence-bolstering rum as soon as the enemy was sighted. Heyn also offered a reward of one hundred guilders and a half pound of precious tobacco to the first man who spied the flota's sails.

The fact that Benevides was in command of the New Spain Flota drove away all thoughts of intercepting the galleons and the Tierra Firme Flota which would be coming up from Cartagena. It seemed that Divine Providence decreed his golden opportunity for revenge. He divided his fleet into two squadrons, one under his command and one under Admiral Loncq and hovered in the vicinity of Dry Tortuga Island, west of present-day Key West, Florida. The still air that presages a hurricane and the strong easterly current conspired to move the Dutch fleet farther and farther from the island. On August 22 they passed within sight of Havana, still at the mercy of the current which threatened to ruin plans to intercept the flota. Heyn sent his smaller ships, which could be rowed when becalmed, to the west looking for the flota. By August 25 the main body of the Dutch fleet was off Matanzas Bay, forty-five miles east of Havana which the flota would be approaching from the west.

The Dutch were still becalmed on the twenty-ninth. Heyn was sure a hurricane was in the offing and called a meeting aboard his flagship. Many of the captains urged a return to Holland, fearing it was too dangerous to linger. Heyn listened thoughtfully and then told them nothing was going to stop him. Later that day a small Spanish boat was captured by a Dutch launch. Its crew said the New Spain Flota was expected momentarily, probably slowed because of the same calm which gripped the Dutch.

For the next eight days the Dutch ships maneuvered to the west, trying to keep within sight of Matanzas Bay during alternate periods of calm and gusty winds. At sunset on September seventh a light breeze lifted spirits and sails and the ships eagerly began tacking toward the west. Around midnight men aboard the *White Lion* one of the swifter ships, suddenly heard voices. Thinking it was a Dutch ship, the captain called out a warning lest the two vessels collide. "*Que quieres?*" responded someone in Spanish, "What do you want?" The Dutch seamen, hearing the musical foreign words, were overjoyed. The long awaited moment had arrived. They quickly jumped into small boats and captured the ship without firing a single shot.

Meanwhile another Dutch ship flying the Spanish flag sailed into the main body of the flota and remained there undetected through the night. At dawn it escaped, firing several broadsides into Benevides's capitana, rousing the captain-general from dreams of contraband profits. Benevides came on deck to discover that during the night his flota had drifted right by the entrance to Havana and was close to Matanzas. As he fumed and raged at the flota's chief pilot, lookouts shouted down that a fleet of thirty-two warships was bearing down on them from the northwest and that there were several other Dutch ships between them and the shore.

The captain-general's actions hardly inspired his men. Abandoning all composure, he rushed babbling to his cabin, locked himself in and began to swill brandy, refusing to talk with anyone but a judge, his personal guest who knew nothing of naval warfare. It wasn't until sometime in the afternoon of that bright, cloudless day that Benevides ordered his ships to prepare for battle. His capitana was groaning under such a load of treasure and cargo, much of it unregistered, that only ten cannon could be readied; the rest were buried under tons of treasure in the hold.

The weeks of little wind had scattered the Spanish fleet. Twelve of the smaller ships were ten miles from the main body of the flota. When it appeared that a fresh east wind might enable them to make Havana, Heyn sent Loncq's squadron to give chase. By noon, nine had been taken. They were all merchantmen with cargoes of hides, cochineal, indigo and the like that fell short of Dutch hopes. Loncq placed Dutch crews on the prizes and then hurried back to join Heyn who was closing in on the flota's treasure-crammed galleons.

In mid-afternoon the wind picked up and the torrential rains, typical of a summer squall, began to fall. Heyn's squadron, only three miles from the flota, lost sight of it in the downpour. Not since Drake had a Protestant *pirata* struck such terror in the hearts of Spaniards. Piet Heyn's ships were invisible but so very close. Benevides's intake of brandy may have given him courage, for during the storm he called a meeting to decide what to do. Opinion was divided. Some captains favored engaging in battle and then trying to make it into Havana, others including Benevides, wanted to make for the closest port and get the treasure ashore. The chief pilot suggested entering the Bay of Matanzas at nightfall when the sea breeze subsided and the land breeze commenced. Then, the Dutch could not follow them into port and would be blown farther out to sea until the following day, giving them time to unload and hide the treasure.

The flota headed for Matanzas with the Dutch in hot pursuit. The pilot's stratagem almost succeeded. As the last rays of the sunset shot the western sky with violet and emerald, the Spanish ships began entering the bay. Suddenly the capitana ran aground and then the almiranta which was just behind stuck fast with a sickening lurch. The next two large galleons were unable to veer off in time and also stuck fast in the shallow water. The remaining thirteen ships squeezed past them and landed their crews and panicky passengers who disembarked carrying whatever they could.

The gold and silver were all stored aboard the four galleons grounded near the mouth of the bay, their bows pointed inshore so that only the cannon on the stem could be used for defense. Heyn's ships reached the bay as the sea breeze died out, just after the galleons had entered. They fired on the four stranded ships until Heyn realized they were helpless. Aided by a full moon, launches carrying eager boarding parties approached the stricken treasure ships. A volley of Dutch musket fire over their heads reminded them their commander was to be first to board the capitana and confront Benevides.

Pandemonium reigned aboard the stranded ships. Benevides attempted to restore order by announcing that anyone attempting to abandon ship would be summarily executed. Once he saw, however, that the Dutch were preparing boarding launches he forgot the oath of office he had taken in Seville and ordered a general retreat to shore, leaving an officer on each galleon to set it afire. Benevides was one of the first to reach the beach. When the crews of the boats bringing the first party of Spaniards ashore refused to return for the rest, Benevides was unable to compel them to follow his weak commands. However, with sword in hand, he forced several soldiers into one of the boats and ordered them to take him up a nearby river. By nine that night, just as the Dutch were boarding his galleons, Benevides was more than five miles from the beach, well on his way to refuge in Havana.

The first ship Heyn boarded wasn't Benevides's capitana as he first thought but the almiranta. Admiral Leoz was still aboard, but like his craven commander, he preferred life to honor and disguised himself in the clothes of an ordinary seaman. The entire crew surrendered and Heyn left men to guard the treasure while he rushed for the capitana. It was taken after a few salvos of musketry with no bloodshed on either side. His fury at Benevides's escape almost overshadowed his joy at seizing the New Spain treasure. On board he found Benevides's mistress, a beautiful eighteen-year old mulatta from Veracruz, whom he had callously abandoned. Her terror subsided when Heyn didn't lop off her head as she anticipated but sent her ashore with the other Spanish prisoners. Heyn took a moment to enjoy his victory. The crusty old sea beggar drank wine from his enemy's private stock out of Benevides's gold goblet, which bore the crest of Philip IV and the Benevides family. Had he known that a mine was set to explode in the stern castle, he might not have relished his drink quite so much. Fortunately, some of his men discovered the charge, which was directly below him, only minutes before it went off.

Heyn directed his launches in capturing the remaining thirteen ships and by midnight it was all over. "Thanking the Almighty God for the good victory he had given," Heyn retired to his ship after posting guards on the treasure galleons to prevent looting, although some of his men managed to siphon off and hide large amounts of treasure. When the fleet was forced by privateers to stop in England on the way home, a number of Scottish sailors who had served with him deserted. They had so much stolen booty they didn't even bother to go to Holland to claim their legal share. One Scot arrested by English customs' officers had fourteen pounds of gold and a large sack of pearls in his possession.

That was but a drop in the bucket. When Heyn's fleet reached Holland, after a difficult crossing and a series of battles with Dunkirk privateers in the English Channel, the Dutch nation rejoiced. Church bells all over the country rang out and mobs of ecstatic people descended on the small port of Hellevatolnis to welcome the nation's hero and gape at what had never been seen before. It took five days to unload the colossal amount of gold, silver and other plunder. More than a thousand mule carts from throughout the province gathered to carry the booty to Amsterdam. It took five hundred to transport the hundred tons of silver bullion and chests of coins. The masses of sugar, indigo, cochineal, chocolate, nearly two million hides, amber, musk and spices, all valuable but less dazzling, were later transported to Amsterdam by sea.

The march to Amsterdam was like a great Roman triumph. Heyn led the procession in a magnificent coach which the directors of the Dutch West India Company had sent for him to ride in. The next three carts bore "such great treasures as few men outside of Spain have ever lain eyes on." They were piled high with chalices, candle sticks, church plate and jewelry, all of gold; hundreds of pieces of wrought silver, including a six-foot high crucifix, a silver chain over two hundred feet long; chests overflowing with magnificent Chinese silks and embroideries, porcelain and other art works and caskets filled with emeralds, pearls and other brilliant stones.

Benevides's personal possessions, including the gold goblet and a gold crucifix which had hung over his ship-board bed, lay at Heyn's feet in the triumphal coach. Ten Jesuits who had been captured at Matanzas brought up the rear, tethered by their necks to the last cart of the mile long procession as it wound its way across the country. Tormented by vengeful Protestants along the way, they were close to death by the time they reached Amsterdam a week later.

Heyn was feted and presented with golden ceremonial chains and gold medals. He was appointed Lieutenant-Admiral of Holland, the nation's highest office after the Admiral-General, who was the Prince of Orange. Meanwhile the booty was locked away in the vaults of the Dutch India House. An accounting indicated the value exceeded fifteen million guilders. This was more than enough for the Company to repay all outstanding debts, recover the cost of the expedition, present the Prince of Orange with 700,000 guilders for his one-tenth share of the booty and furnish the shareholders with a 75 percent dividend. The Company directors awarded themselves 1 percent each, or 7,000 guilders.

This same amount was given to Piet Heyn. His officers and seamen were awarded seventeen months' extra wages. Considering the extraordinary value of the plunder they had worked so long and risked so much to take, Heyn and his men felt cheated at their paltry shares. A band of angry seamen tried to break into India House in a vain attempt to get a share of loot. The honors heaped on Piet Heyn didn't take the edge off his disgust at receiving such a small share of the spoils. A captain in the service of the Dutch East India Company had received 31,000 guilders in prize for taking a Portuguese ship valued at a mere 500,000 guilders in 1606 and had he been an English privateer Heyn's share would have been at least 200,000 guilders. However, his patriotism prevailed. He buried his resentment and responded to the States-General's request that he leave the West India Company to become the supreme commander of all Dutch naval forces. His brilliant career was cut tragically short when he was killed in action against three Ostend privateers on June 18, 1629. He lives on in the hearts of his countrymen who still sing in praise of his spectacular exploit in capturing the Spanish treasure fleet.

It was Christmas Eve 1628 before Philip IV learned of the loss of the flota. He was attending a ball when Count-Duke Olivares gave him the appalling tidings. The king fell to the floor, foaming at the mouth and muttering incoherently. He was carried to his apartments and put under sedation. The Venetian ambassador who was present wrote to the doge that the Dutch capture "has agonized the whole country, made the businessmen tremble, endangered the fortune of them all, and caused the greatest anguish to the rest, not so much because the treasure meant such a great loss, but because of the affront which permitted the enemy to deal the final stroke of destruction to Spain."

Five days later the king emerged from his apartments. His first order was to send the fastest vessel available to Havana with instructions to have Benevides "immediately beheaded and his head sent back to Seville where it shall be placed on display for all to see what befalls cowards who do not defend my honor and treasures." Benevides was already on his way to Spain where, thanks to the intercession of his sister, he managed to keep his head for six years. As soon as she died, however, he was executed.

The Tierra Firme treasure which Larraspuru had set out to escort home eight months before eventually reached Spain safely but not before Philip sold most of the queen's jewels and obtained a loan from Genoese bankers at a usurious 40 percent interest rate to outfit an armada of eighteen ships for the purpose of finding the Tierra Firme Flota and the galleons and bringing them to Seville. Larraspuru arrived with Benevides and Leoz, who were immediately imprisoned as public demonstrations were held calling for their execution. When the Seville merchants learned that the king had ordered that all treasure coming back from the Indies for the next three years was to be handed over to him, many left Seville to set up business in other countries.

Spanish prestige and power had been shattered by little Holland. Heyn's colossal capture had not been the only capture of rich galleons in 1628, a most profitable year for the Dutch West India Company. A squadron of twelve ships spent eight months off Brazil and came home with the cargoes from thirty-eight Portuguese merchantmen valued at over a million guilders. Another squadron of twelve warships under the command of Admiral Pieter Adrianzoon Ita had been secretly ordered to capture the two Honduran galleons which sailed every year in May or June from Trujillo, Honduras to Havana where they waited to rendezvous with the returning New Spain Flota.

On the way to the Caribbean, Ita's fleet captured four Spanish ships laden with Dutch goods off the Canaries. The cargoes were sent to Holland, no doubt for resale to Spain which depended greatly on Dutch manufactures. After an aborted attack on the port of Santiago, Cuba which was Spain's chief copper shipping center, Ita's squadron took up station out of sight of land between Yucatán and Cuba. Somehow the

Honduran galleons slipped past Ita's ships one dark night, and the following morning one of the Dutch ships which had been sent to cruise near Cuba, appeared with the news that the Spanish ships were approaching Havana.

Ita gave chase and caught up with the great galleons when they were less than two miles from port. The Spaniards were at home in the treacherous reef strewn waters and moved close to shore hoping the Dutch would not risk losing their ships. But the wind shifted suddenly enabling several of Ita's ships to get between the galleons and the harbor entrance. A bloody battle ensued ending in a Dutch victory. The cargo of silver, indigo, cochineal and hides aboard one of the galleons which had run aground was transferred to Dutch ships and Ita headed for home and congratulations.

Spain was completely demoralized by the Dutch. In 1629 the Spanish Empire was at lowest ebb. For the first time since the flota system had been introduced, no treasure fleets sailed. There were no funds and too little cargo. In fact, that year only four small advice ships went to the New World and three of them were captured by the Dutch. In June the Crown declared bankruptcy. Gold and silver coins were debased by the addition of copper and all but disappeared from circulation to be replaced by worthless copper coins called *billon* which no other country would accept. At home it took nearly four hundred pounds of these coins to purchase a hundred pounds of cheese.

The blows the sea beggars dealt Spain in the Caribbean area transformed the New World from a private Spanish estate where trespassers were not tolerated, to a land of opportunity where other European nations staked their claims. Dutch hatred of Spain generated by years of oppression and religious incompatibility coupled with Dutch naval and commercial skill made the Dutch unbeatable. The triumphs of Piet Heyn and Ita renewed the sea beggars energies and in the following years they unleashed one privateering fleet after another on the Empire's shipping and settlements in the Caribbean. The Netherlands had proved that keeping blood (the riches of their overseas domain) from the wasting continental body was the best way to battle the Catholic empire.

The Dutch solidified their control in Brazil, took Curaçao and then colonized Bonaire, Aruba, St. Maarten, St. Eustatius and Saba as bases for raiding and trading. Between 1623 and 1636 Dutch privateers deprived the Spanish Crown of an estimated 120 million guilders by tne systematic plundering of ships, the looting and burning of towns, ransoms and by contraband trading and smuggling. By 1634 the Dutch were in such firm control of the Caribbean that Spain was unable to send over a single ship during the entire year. It wasn't until 1655, however, when the English captured Jamaica that Spain actually lost an occupied possession.

In 1648 after almost eighty years of intermittent warfare the two enemies signed the Treaty of Munster by which the Spanish king recognized the independence of the United Provinces, giving the Dutch officially what they had in reality enjoyed for years. The treaty also gave Dutch vessels the right to navigate and trade in the Caribbean and recognized the existence of Dutch colonies. Dutch interlopers and privateers had brought Spanish prestige to an all time low in the Caribbean and gained for their new nation maritime and commercial supremacy of the zone which was to turn friendship with France and England, whose fledgling settlements they did so much to foster, into fierce rivalry. The Munster Treaty ended sanctioned Dutch privateering in the Caribbean but the threat of corsairs beyond the line didn't fade. As one chapter came to a close another, that of the buccaneers, an even more dangerous breed of predator, had already begun.

NOTES

1. Governor of Puerto Rico's reply to Hendricksz, de Laet, Joannes, *Le Linschoten-Vereeniging*, 1624–36, Amsterdam, 1638, Vol. IV, p. 234.

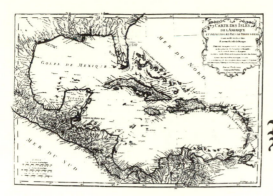

5

Buccaneers, the Brethren of the Coast

Poor Spain. What had seemed like Midas's Golden Touch bestowed by Pope Alexander following Columbus's fateful voyage, proved more a curse than a blessing with each passing year. The lure of treasure drained the motherland of able men. The administration of the new golden lands proved wasteful and fatally costly in political, economic and human terms. Pirates and privateers had thumbed their noses at Spain since the early sixteenth century. Their relentless plundering of shipping and settlements in the Caribbean was an important factor in Spanish colonial history. Chronically inadequate defenses at sea and on land forced the Crown to concentrate on maintaining those bases vital to the treasure flow at the expense of their other settlements. Even in the best of times the peripheral settlements suffered from benign neglect, their planters and hunters left largely to their own devices.

While places like Havana and Cartagena flourished, colonies along the Main and in the Antilles withered. Some were even evacuated; their inhabitants forcibly removed to diminish opportunities for pirates and smugglers. Colonial participation in illicit trade was so widespread that the Crown prohibited the lucrative cultivation of tobacco at the beginning of the seventeenth century, leaving Venezuela, Nueva Andalucia and the Islas de Barlovento in commercial isolation.

The north coast of Hispaniola, the Banda del Norte, had long been a haunt of maurauders and smugglers. In 1603 the Council of the Indies issued an edict ordering removal of the population from several towns to two locations near Santo Domingo. Island authorities procrastinated, fearing that renegades and freebooters would fill the vacuum, carry on the *rescates* (ransoming), the illicit trade, and eventually take possession. In 1605 the governor, Antonio Osorio, aided by 150 troops sent over from Puerto Rico, finally implemented the two-year old edict.

"I resolved to enter the settlements in person and make them take away their women and belongings, compelling them to move to the new settlements and setting fire to their houses . . . I went myself to their ranches and rounded up their cattle . . . At every stage throughout they tried all sorts of tricks and schemes to distract me from my purpose . . . " Osorio's report to the king is chilling. No wonder there were those who fled aboard French, English or Dutch ships to Cuba or hid from the governor's hunting parties in the area's densely forested hills. As predicted, the evacuated areas of the north and west did become a haven for foreign interlopers. They were the buccaneers who brought seventeenth century plundering in the Caribbean outrageous new levels.

Buccaneering was a peculiar form of sea robbery which dominated the Caribbean in the second half of the century once maritime supremacy passed from the Dutch to the English and French. A blend of piracy and privateering in which the two elements were often indistinguishable, buccaneering was encouraged by Spain's enemies who used it as a weapon as they established their own territorial claims in once exclusively Spanish domains. The French governors of Tortuga and the English governors of Jamaica fostered the activities of the colorful buccaneers, pleased at the weakening blows they dealt Spain and thankful for their share of the prizes which flowed into Tortuga and Port Royal, Jamaica: gold doubloons, silver coins, gold and silver church plate and jewelry from the churches of the Main, pearls from the coasts of Venezuela and Panama, emeralds from the mines of New Granada as well as commercially valuable hides, dyewoods, ginger and other agricultural products.

The Brethren of the Coast, as the buccaneers styled themselves, were a powerful force in the Caribbean. They formed a roving sea republic which did as much as any nation to further erode the Spanish monopoly of the New World. A shifting confederation of English, Irish, French and Dutch buccaneers with a sprinkling of Portuguese, Scots, Indians, mulattoes, blacks and a Turk or two who had a mutual loathing of the Spanish dons attacked without respite. Crews were international because able-bodied seamen and slaves on a prize were strongly encouraged to sign articles joining the buccaneer crew. The alternative was to labor as a captive without enjoying a share of plunder. Passengers of means were allowed to pay ransom, whereas pirates regarded sick or feeble men found aboard captive ships as liabilities and seldom hesitated to kill or abandon them.

Piet Heyn and his fellows had forced a drastic curtailment of Spanish shipping. Sailings were primarily restricted to the heavily protected treasure flotas. As long as the buccaneers limited their prey to Spanish ships pickings were slim at sea and they turned increasingly to land raids in the fashion of Drake. The raids were so frequent and so brutal that Spanish colonists took to the hills in reflex action at the mere sight of an unexpected sail on the horizon. In the six years following English occupation of Jamaica in 1655, Port Royal buccaneers ravaged eighteen cities, four towns and some three dozen smaller settlements. Some villages were assaulted again and again including a number far inland where sea robbers would hardly seem likely to venture.

The buccaneers had a modest beginning in what is Haiti today in the northwest sector of Hispaniola, where vast numbers of feral pigs and cattle roamed the rolling savannahs. The animals were descended from abandoned Spanish stock which had been introduced at the turn of the century by the settlers who had eventually been forced to evacuate the island by the Crown. They attracted French hunters, scarcely less wild than the animals they hunted who camped in the wilds, sleeping on the ground. They covered their faces with rendered fat to repel insects and were called *boucaniers* (hence buccaneer in English). The word *boucan* is derived from an Indian word for a wooden grill made of sticks upon which wild hogs were broiled and which the *boucaniers* adapted to smoke strips of beef and pork in making jerky. These rough men sometimes remained in the bush for a year or more, preparing a store of smoked meat and hides to be bartered with the crews of passing ships which put in at Tortuga or the Banda del Norte. Men who had been at sea craving variety from the staple fare of hardtack and dried fish bartered gunpowder, shot, brandy, tobacco and other provisions for the jerky.

The *boucaniers* or buccaneers were savages in dress and habits, wearing rough linen homespun garments steeped in the blood of slaughtered animals. They lived in shacks covered with palm leaves and slept in sleeping bags to keep insects off. A Frenchman who observed them returning from the hunt said they looked like "the butcher's vilest servants, who have been eight days in the slaughter house without washing themselves." No amount of bathing could eradicate the stink of guts and grease which clung to them. Their round hats, their boots and belts were made of untanned hogskin or cattle hide. Each man generally carried a firelock rifle and had an axe and a cutlass or two stuck in his belt. Marrow which they ate straight from the bones of freshly slain beasts was their favorite food and drinking and gambling their favorite pastimes. The early buccaneers typically lived in groups of six to eight, sharing almost all they had and abiding by mutual agreements. Some of them lived in a kind of homosexual union known as *matelotage* (from the French for sailor and a possible origin of the word mate meaning companion). The two *matelots* held their meager possessions in common with the survivor inheriting. After the buccaneers established themselves on Tortuga and women joined them, *matelotage* continued with a partner sharing his wife with his *matelot*.

The *boucaniers* shifted like nomads across the wilds of northwestern Hispaniola, an area remote from the Spanish occupied southern part of the island and Santo Domingo, the only large town. Initially, they caused no trouble but the Spanish authorities found their presence intolerable, considering them poachers in their God-given preserve. The Audiencia of Santo Domingo ordered five hundred lancers to hunt down the *boucaniers* but they were defeated by the vastness of the territory and its rugged terrain. Next, the Audiencia hired Spanish and mestizo hunters to exterminate the feral cattle and hogs. This campaign was successful in its expressed intent but precipitated unforeseen consequences. By depriving the hunters of their cattle and hogs, the Spanish forced them after new quarry—the ships and settlements of the mortally ill Spanish colossus.

The mass slaughter of cattle and hogs initiated a new phase in the history of the *boucaniers*. In the past, in the rainy season when hunting was at a standstill, the boucaniers had sometimes practiced piracy. They set out in their rude open boats to attack a passing ship, relying on surprise to offset their primitive piratical capability. In 1630 they settled across the channel on Tortuga, a small island off the northwest coast of Hispaniola which was named for its resemblance to a sea turtle. It offered fresh water and fertile ground. Best of all it offered good anchorages, defensible harbors and an ideal position on the Windward Passage between Hispaniola and Cuba through which the Spanish treasure flotas sailed.

On Tortuga random buccaneering activity matured into organized large-scale operations as outlaws, marooned men and deserters of various nationalities joined the roving French hunters on Tortuga. Many of them were English buccaneers. At their urging the Royal Providence Island Company which had a colony off the Mosquito Coast of Honduras and Nicaragua (on the island of Providencia today owned by Colombia) obtained a revised charter from Charles I which gave them nominal claim to Tortuga. In the two decades following 1636 the island's ownership was hotly contested among the Spanish, French and English. The populace frequently sought refuge from the commotion by fleeing to the hills of Hispaniola. The French authorities on St. Christopher controlled the island for awhile and in 1659 Spain relinquished her claim in favor of France.

Initially the buccaneers plundered passing ships from small open boats, equipped with oars and sail. Eventually they were able to mobilize hundreds of buccaneers under the command of leaders such as Henry Morgan. Early Jamaica, taken by the English in 1655, depended on the buccaneers of Port Royal for its very existence. They brought in such a volume of gold and silver that the English government proposed establishing a mint at Port Royal as early as 1662. Jamaica was known as "a citadel over all the Spanish West Indies." Rivalry between the two leading buccaneering bases stimulated even greater marauding activity. Letters of marque were handed out freely by island authorities who wanted the Spanish kept at bay.

The intermittent wars which convulsed most of Europe from mid-century on gave added impetus to buccaneering exploits "beyond the line." The prey was not always Spanish. Between 1672 and 1678 Tortuga buccaneers played a prominent role in attacks on Dutch settlements and shipping which led to the bankruptcy of the Dutch West Indies Company. Ever opportunists, the French governors of Tortuga didn't let peace stand in their way either but sent to Portugal for commissions when Spain was at peace with France but not with Portugal. When English authorities on Jamaica were forced to curtail their handing out of licenses the French on Tortuga and at Petit-Goâve on Hispaniola were only to happy to oblige. Once Henry Morgan had been knighted and traded piracy for politics he served as lieutenant-governor of Jamaica. Charles II prohibited Morgan from issuing letters of marque so he sent men applying for privateering commissions to Governor d'Ogeron in Petit Guavos, who paid him a fee for each recruit. D'Ogeron, of course, sold his questionable commissions at a tidy profit. It was reported that the French governor of Tortuga "never refuses commissions, whether before or after capture of a prize, provided he receives some present, as, for instance, a tenth share." So many English buccaneers carried commissions from the French that King Charles angrily declared that he was determined Jamaica be a plantation and not "a Christian Algiers."

The officials who attempted to use the buccaneers to their own ends discovered that they were not easily persuaded to change their ways when national interests dictated a change in tactics. A partial list of buccaneer prizes indicates why their activities were encouraged for so long. In 1666 buccaneers brought back 260,000 silver eight reales from the pillaging of Maracaibo plus a huge amount of other booty. Devout ruffians, they also plundered the bells and treasures of the city's cathedral to furnish a church they were building on Tortuga. In 1668 Henry Morgan, the most famous of them all, led an outnumbered band to attack Portobelo urging the men on as his countryman Drake had done a century before: "If our number is small, our hearts are great; and the fewer persons we are, the more union, and the better shares we shall have in the spoil!" They came away with half a million pieces of eight.

Five years later the sack of Trinidad furnished a buccaneer band with more than 100,000 pieces of eight to divide and the 1683 sack of Veracruz, one of the wealthiest cities in the New World, yielded the equivalent of more than six million dollars to a mixed expedition of French, Dutch and English buccaneers. Traditional enemies thought nothing of uniting under their chosen chief to attack His Catholic Majesty, their common foe. As Brethren of the Coast they trusted and obeyed their democratically elected leader during a campaign, risking all for a share of Spanish treasure.

The last great buccaneering raid was a joint French naval-buccaneer expedition which held Cartagena for a huge ransom. The incredible treasure included over a thousand pounds of fine emeralds, a large silver-robed Madonna studded with gems, church plate and seven million and a half francs in gold and silver bullion. Undertaken in 1697 when most of Europe was allied against France, the raid was at first abetted by Jean-Baptiste du Casse, the ex-buccaneer governor of Santo Domingo who brought the French freebooters to heel when they became too unruly. After Cartagena, the buccaneer force was ordered to disband. Those who persisted in their calling were branded as outlaw pirates.

Baron de Pointis, the naval commander, had shown contempt for his buccaneer allies from the beginning of the expedition, scorning them as "the refuse of all the kingdom, without honor, without virtue." The buccaneers cared little for his high-flown patriotism but he was not immune to the same treasure fever that seized them and flimflammed them over the division of the spoils and sailed off. The cheated buccaneers swooped back on poor Cartagena and extracted a further million crowns' worth of treasure in a four-day orgy of rapine. Du Casse pleaded for his buccaneer contingent's fair share in France and won at least a moral victory, if indeed plundering could be so judged. He was knighted and promoted to admiral. Ironically, in 1702 he returned to Cartagena as an ally of Spain commanding a French squadron bringing a thousand fresh troops to Cartagena and Portobelo. Ten years afterward Philip V of Spain, the new Bourbon king, bestowed one of Spain's highest orders, usually reserved for the nobility, on the former buccaneer in recognition of his safely escorting a treasure flota home.

Three decades before the French cracked down on their buccaneers, the English government had recognized the harmful effects of their activity on the development of Jamaica as well as on diplomatic relations with Spain. Despite the prize money they brought in, the buccaneer presence discouraged the establishment of a viable society with a sound economic base. Quality settlers were scarcely attracted to the Babylon of the New World. Port Royal's brothels, gaming houses and taverns were as notorious as the prodigious appetites of their customers. Efforts to turn the reckless denizens of Port Royal into sober planters aroused little enthusiasm in the sea-seasoned men who knew full well that a lifetime of mucking in the tropical soil would never yield what they might gain in a single successful raid. Planters complained that "all servants that can, run away and turn pirate."

After Morgan led fourteen hundred men on a harrowing march across the Isthmus to sack and burn Panama in 1671, buccaneering was officially discouraged by Jamaica, although it wasn't until 1685 that the first English naval squadron was sent to Jamaica to suppress the buccaneers. No more commissions were passed out, but Port Royal remained a buccaneer roost until the mid-1680s. Morgan's exploit, occurring after the 1670 signing of the Treaty of Madrid, which recognized English territorial claims in the West Indies in return for English suppression of the buccaneers, proved a great embarrassment to England.

Morgan pretended ignorance of the document. Buccaneers typically refused to recognize European treaties which might curtail their plundering. French freebooters claimed the 1688 peace Treaty of Aix-la-Chapelle between France and Spain didn't apply to them since they had neither negotiated it nor signed it. The rough-and-ready breed of Caribbean buccaneers cared little for newly forged alliances and even less for the commercial opportunities they made possible which were to prove far more valuable to the national interest than piracy. Suppressing the buccaneers was no easy task. Several governors of Jamaica succumbed to the temptation to allow outlawed activity and corrupt officials in the Bermudas, the Bahamas, St. Thomas and elsewhere didn't scruple to issue commissions. Sea rovers often carried no commissions, or used letters of marque which were woefully out-of-date or forged such as one a Jamaican naval captain recognized as fraudulent because in it Governor Lynch, the only one of the first four governors to wholeheartedly attempt turning Jamaica from a pirate den into a plantation colony, was called Gentleman of the King's Bedchamber, rather than Privy Chamber.

Throughout the 1670s and 1680s buccaneering verged increasingly on piracy, with proliferating attacks on non-Spanish prey. Setting a thief to catch a thief, Charles II appointed Henry Morgan lieutenant-governor of Jamaica, barely two years after he had been brought to England as a prisoner to appease Spanish anger at his buccaneering exploits. For several years the ambitious ex-buccaneer, now Sir Henry Morgan, publicly espoused the official antibuccaneering line and sat as judge of Jamaica's

Vice-Admiralty Court which tried pirates. "Nothing can be more fatal to this colony," he noted in 1680 while acting governor, "than the temptingly alluring boldness of the privateers which draws off white servants and all men of unfortunate or desperate condition." It is believed, however, that even as he sat on the bench he continued to covertly broker commissions between buccaneers and his old ally Governor d'Ogeron, in French Hispaniola.

Morgan, of course, was correct about the drain on Jamaica. The colony depended on its men for defense and in the years between 1668 and 1671 some 2,600 Jamaicans were lost in the buccaneering raids against Tobago, Curacao, Portobelo, Nueva Granada and Panama. Seventeen centuries after the Roman general Pompey's experiment to turn pirate swords into plowshares, a similar program on Jamaica offering each man who had "followed the Course" a free pardon and thirty-five acres of land failed to lure many buccaneers into the agricultural life. A few accepted Sir Thomas Lynch's offer but a considerable number of buccaneers turned to outright piracy or accepted commissions from corrupt officials in Bermuda and the Bahamas or sought refuge on Tortuga or other French islands until the Treaty of Ryswyck in 1697 by which Spain formally ceded Santo Domingo to France, ended the buccaneering phase of Caribbean piracy.

Bermuda and the Bahamas were centers of piracy and privateering almost from their beginnings. Robert Rich, Earl of Warwick and owner of England's biggest pirate fleet was a principal in the establishment of Bermuda, the Virginia Colony and the settlement on Providence Island. His ships used Bermuda as a base. The island's governors were usually acquiescent, accepting letters of marque of dubious authenticity and sometimes taking bribes offered in lieu of a letter. Governor Butler when asked permitted a pirate into port in return for fourteen African slaves.

The Council for Trade and Plantations which sat in London was slow to comprehend the abuses of privateering commissions in the Caribbean. Once they did, however, they applied sufficient pressure to drive some adventurers out of the business. More intrepid adventurers moved into the Pacific. Toward the end of the century, the North American seaboard became a mecca for outlawed buccaneers foreshadowing the eighteenth century's Golden Age of piracy.

The Buccaneer Hall of Fame, or Infamy, boasts as colorful a group of characters as ever went to sea. Whatever their class, background or personality, they shared quick wits, astonishing courage and an insatiable hunger for gold. Men like Pierre le Grand who retired after a singularly successful exploit were rare; generally the appetite for plunder increased with each feeding. Le Grand, a native of the corsair port of Dieppe, and his handful of men sailing in a little pirogue had captured the straggling Vice-Admiral of a flota near Cape Tiburón off the western coast of Hispaniola in the dead of night. The buccaneers sailed straight for Dieppe with their rich prize and Le Grand never sallied forth again. The buccaneer and his twenty-eight men had been in desperate condition when they first sighted the galleon. After a long cruise they were near starvation, weakened by thirst and exposure. To enhance the do-or-die nature of their assault, the men voted to have the expedition's surgeon bore holes in their little craft. Thus motivated, they stealthily approached the ship and boarded. They found the captain playing cards with several of his officers. "Jesus bless us!" the surprised Spaniards shouted, "Are these devils or what are they?"

Le Grand's exploit, one of the first successes for the Tortuga-based buccaneers, benefitted from a relatively low level of Spanish vigilance. News of this "happy event" precipitated a rush to the sea among the hunters and planters of Tortuga. Esquemelin wrote that men were so eager to emulate those pirates that they left whatever work they had and sought boats "wherein to exercise piracy." Such vessels were in short supply and some bold buccaneers set out in their canoes to capture Spanish trading ships off Cuba's Cape d'Alvares. They sold the cargoes of tobacco, hides and other goods to ships, most of them Dutch, calling at Tortuga. With the proceeds they outfitted their prizes and set off "cruizing." In the first couple of years they took a lot of Spanish ships, some of them with exceptional cargoes like two silver-laden galleons sailing from Campeche to Caracas. Their successes attracted more of their ilk until the Spaniards moved against Tortuga and assigned two men-o-war to patrol the zone.

Not every buccaneer was lucky. Twenty-six men cruising with Pierre Francois in an open boat encountered no Spanish ships near home so they headed south to the pearl fisheries which the pirates of the previous century had so often plundered. Off Rio de la Hacha they came upon the pearling fleet comprising a dozen large canoes protected by two men-o-war. To deceive the Spaniards into thinking they were a local craft from Maracaibo, they took down their sails and manned the oars, rowing directly alongside the smaller escort ship which, with sixty armed men and eight cannon, was still a formidable opponent. The buccaneers demanded surrender and a fight followed. Amazingly, the buccaneers prevailed and had they been content with the fortune in pearls they found aboard, valued at 100,000 pieces of eight by the Spaniards, all would have gone well. They tempted fate by assaulting the larger man-o-war and were themselves captured. Sometime later a Scot nicknamed "Red-Legs" Greaves who escaped from forced labor on Barbados made a lightning raid on the pearling canoes off Margarita, darting off with enough booty to buy a fine plantation on Nevis.

One of the most blood thirsty buccaneers was a Gascon of good family called "Montbars the Exterminator." Louis le Golif, the French buccaneeer-memoirist known as Borgne-Fesse because of his mutilated buttocks, noted that Montbars's eyebrows were wider than his moustache, "which gave him such a terrible air that his aspect alone assured him of victory before a fight was joined." Montbars went to the Caribbean as a midshipman on a Royal French Navy frigate commanded by his uncle. He had witnessed the frigate, with his uncle on board, explode when the French set fire to their own powder magazine rather than surrender to encircling Spanish ships. Montbars swore an oath to revenge his uncle and never spared a Spaniard.

He became a full-fledged member of the buccaneer confraternity and joined with an English captain and the Chevalier de Grammont, one of several buccaneers of noble birth to lead an attack on Maracaibo, Venezuela. Most of the population fled to the wooded hills with many of their valuables. Montbars tortured a number of prisoners to discover where gold and silver were hidden. Maracaibo lay on a lake with a narrow fortified entrance where three Spanish frigates blocked Montbars's escape. Bold buccaneers never surrendered in the face of certain defeat and the Exterminator ordered his ships to attack. The Spanish flagship was set on fire. Another vessel was boarded by the pirates as the third hastily cut its anchor cables and escaped, whereupon the buccaneers rendezvoused at Vache Island, off Hispaniola, to divide the booty.

Further exploits of Montbars have been lost in the mists of history but de Grammont's name appears again and again as one of the principal figures in buccaneering. Following a scandalous duel in Paris he joined the Royal Marines and sailed to the West Indies as a naval officer. De Grammont distinguished himself at sea as commander of a privateer, capturing a rich Dutch merchantman near Martinique. He got the equivalent of 400,000 livres for his prize at Hispaniola where, according to the Jesuit historian Charlevoix, he proceeded to disgrace himself gambling, wenching and drinking until he had not a penny left and dared not return to France.

He joined the Brethren of the Coast where in the words of an anonymous admirer, his "grace, generosity, eloquence, a sense of justice . . . and courage soon caused him to be regarded as the chief of the *filibustiers.*" A surprisingly religious and superstitious lot, they flocked to sign on with de Grammont, although shocked by his professed atheism.

In 1678 de Grammont and 700 men established a base on Lake Maracaibo where they spent six months. From there they sallied forth to ravage coastal settlements and seize Spanish vessels. The spoils were disappointing. In the old days even a modest haul could make a group of 20 or 30 marauders happy. It took far more to content a volatile pirate army of 700. The same year another noble, the Marquis de Maintenon, sailed with almost 800 Tortuga buccaneers and French privateers to plunder the Venezuela coast. They, too, found the spoils far from what they had hoped for as did other expeditions which descended like locusts on Campeche on the Yucatán Peninsula, Cuba's Puerto Principe, Trujillo in Honduras and the town of Santo Tomás on the Orinoco River in Venezuela. The Chevalier de Franquesnay led a buccaneer multitude on St. Jago de Cuba but was repulsed by the Spanish.

In 1680 de Grammont was badly wounded in a daring attack on La Guaira, the seaport of Caracas, when he and fewer than 50 of his audacious "brothers" landed at night and overwhelmed the town. They took the two forts and the batteries mounted on the city walls, seized the governor and other officials as hostages but had to retreat swiftly to their ships when the inhabitants rallied, strengthened by news of 200 troops on their way from Caracas. De Grammont and his buccaneers fought brilliantly, keeping the Spaniards at bay for two hours while they all embarked. Again, however, the spoils were bitterly disappointing.

In 1683 de Grammont joined an international buccaneering expedition against Veracruz which made up for past disappointments. With de Grammont were an English captain and five Dutch captains including the leaders Laurens de Graaf and Vanhorn, a pirate who posing as a merchant captain had captured prizes around the Canaries and seized blacks on the Guinea Coast of Africa whom he brought to sell in the Caribbean. De Graaf's reputation as a successful leader had been boosted by his seizure of a ship laden with 120,000 pieces of eight en route from Havana to pay off the garrison at Puerto Rico. Each of his crew had received 700 pieces of eight and the French Governor of Petit-Goâve, who had supplied a license was in for a share as well.

De Graaf was an interesting man, veteran of many raids. He pioneered the French claim to Louisiana and was such a bogey-man to the Spanish that coastal colonists prayed at public masses for God to spare them from his savagery. He had been a Dutch gunner in the Spanish Navy, working his way up to commander. On his first tour of duty in the Caribbean he was captured by buccaneers and became one of them. His second wife, Marie-Anne Dieu-le-Veult, was the widow of one of Tortuga's first settlers. De Graaf was smitten by her when she confronted him with a loaded pistol, demanding an apology for an offensive comment he had made about her. He admired her spirit, she couldn't resist his handsome mien, and they ended in each other's arms or so the story goes.

The eight captains of the international expedition rendezvoused off Cabo Catoche, Yucatán in mid-May. With them were a thousand men. Aware that the city was awaiting the arrival of two ships from Caracas the buccaneers crammed about 800 men on two of their ships, hoisted the Spanish flag and calmly sailed into the harbor where the misled populace lit bonfires to guide them in. What followed was the familiar litany of rapine and pillage which went on for four days. The governor fled but was found by an English buccaneer hiding in a hayloft and ransomed for 70,000 pieces of eight. The expedition yielded 1,300 slaves, enough booty for each of the thousand participants to receive a share of 800 pieces of eight. Vanhorn, whose two ships had been used for transporting the buccaneers to shore, demanded thirty shares. He and de Graaf got in a fight over the division and Vanhorn was wounded on the wrist. What seemed like a mere scratch turned septic and two weeks later he died of gangrene.

The Governor of Veracruz was beheaded for allowing the *piratas* to take the city with such ease. The Spanish Crown requested the King of England to order Governor Lynch of Jamaica to assist a Spanish Commission of Inquiry in studying the raid which had forced cancellation of the annual Veracruz Fair with the result that the Cadiz-bound Mexican flota was less than half normal size. In spite of Spanish objections both Governor Lynch and the French governor on Hispaniola courted de Graaf to make his headquarters with them.

By this time the French King had ordered a halt to buccaneering on his islands and at least one governor tried valiantly to comply. De Franquesnay, while temporary Governor of Hispaniola really cracked down on the buccaneers who threatened to rise up in arms. It was during this period that Governor Lynch, empowered by the Privy Council, which was disturbed by increased French attacks on English fishing sloops and traders, tried to entice de Graaf to Jamaica. Before de Graaf made a move de Cussy, the new Governor of Hispaniola, arrived.

He assessed the situation and realistically determined that no matter what the King commanded, he could not afford to alienate the buccaneers if he wanted to protect Hispaniola. So he invited de Graaf back with ceremonies befitting a hero and urged the return of all those who had been chased away by his predecessor. De Cussy dispensed commissions freely until forced by the King to repress the buccaneers although de Cussy argued they were the best defense against Spanish attack.

At this juncture many of the buccaneers began to operate off the Pacific coast of the Main where neither French nor English governments would harass them. Others set up on Petite-Goâve ignoring French authority. De Grammont teamed up with de Graaf again in 1685 for an attack on Campeche which no amount of pleading by de Cussy could dissuade them from. More than a thousand rough and ready men sailed with them to Yucatán. They marched inland to Mérida where they were repulsed by the Spanish.

At Campeche, they had better luck, holding the town for six weeks during which they blew up the fort, leveled the city, and generally acted like the diabolic butchers the Spanish called them. Before leaving they lit monumental bonfires to celebrate the feast of their patron Saint Louis. They fueled the fires with 200,000 crowns worth of logwood which they couldn't carry away. This raid caused a terrible uproar in diplomatic circles. De Grammont was offered an attractive government post as King's Lieutenant for the coast of Santo Domingo by de Cussy who preferred to have him where he could keep an eye on his activities. De Grammont was flattered but couldn't resist one more raid so he mounted an expedition of some 180 adventurers and sailed off never to be heard of again.

Jean-David Nau, called L'Olonois or L'Olonnais after his birthplace at les Sables d'Olonne in Brittany, makes a striking contrast to the buccaneers of gentle birth. He was a sadist, a psychopath; the most notorious of the old guard, the original *boucaniers* of Tortuga. Born at the bottom of the social ladder, he was transported to the West Indies as an engagé or indentured servant. At the expiration of his term of indenture he drifted to Hispaniola and started hunting with the boucaniers. Eventually he joined the Brethren of the Coast on Tortuga, carrying out a number of successful assaults against Spanish ships which brought him to the attention of the Governor of Tortuga, de la Place. The Governor provided L'Olonnais with a ship and he began his career in earnest, plundering shipping, torturing and committing such atrocities that Spaniards preferred to die fighting or drown rather than fall into his hands.

L'Olonnais behavior was that of a psychopath. "It was the custom of L'Olonnais that, having tormented any persons and they not confessing, he would instantly cut them in pieces with his hanger, and pull out their tongues," wrote Esquemelin who also described other of his fiendish tortures including "burning with matches and suchlike torments, to cut a man to pieces, first some flesh, then a hand, an arm, a leg, sometimes tying a cord about his head and with a stick twisting it till his eyes shoot out, which is called woolding."

L'Olonnais wearied of plundering ships and turned his barbarous attention to the towns of the Spanish Main. In partnership with Michel le Basque he equipped a fleet, crewing it with seven hundred Tortuga ruffians. On the way to Maracaibo, their first objective, the buccaneers captured a Spanish vessel carrying 40,000 pieces of eight and a shipment of gems in addition to a large cargo of cacao. L'Ollonnais sent the prize to Tortuga where the Governor later bought its entire cargo, reputedly for less than one- twentieth of its worth. The Buccaneers next unleashed their savagery on Maracaibo which they sacked for two weeks, torturing prisoners over and over to discover every bit of hidden treasure. They then moved on to the town of Gibraltar and repeated the orgy of pillaging and carnage.

L'Olonnais's force stayed a month at Gibraltar extracting great riches and many slaves and then returned to poor Maracaibo, refusing to quit the city until a further ransom of 20,000 pieces of eight and five hundred cows was paid. Much to the consternation of the dazed inhabitants, three days after the buccaneers had lifted anchor their sails appeared again at the port entrance. A launch came ashore with a message from L'Olonnais requesting a pilot to guide his largest ship over the treacherous bank at Lake Maracaibo's entrance. Needless to say, one was dispatched at once. The people of Maracaibo began to rebuild their city and restore their fortunes, resigned to the endless cycle of rapine, ruin and rebuilding which the Spanish settlements were subjected to for three centuries by the pirates and privateers of the Caribbean.

L'Olonnais's reputation for daring and the dazzle of booty his men spread around Tortuga's taverns and brothels had men clamoring to sign on with him. He raised a buccaneer army of over a thousand men which descended on the coast of Nicaragua. On the way they detoured to Matamaná, a turtling port on the south coast of Cuba, where they stole a number of canoes, useful for shallow waters. On the Main, L'Olonnais and his savages destroyed the villages of Spaniards and Indians alike. They cruised the Yucatán coast and the Gulf of Honduras committing everywhere their "horrid insolencies."

In one place, L'Olonnais was so enraged at the lack of information elicited from a Spanish prisoner that he ripped open the man's chest with his cutlass and began to gnaw ravenously on the still beating heart, shouting to the other prisoners "I will serve you alike if you do not show me another way." L'Olonnais met a fitting end. He and a remnant of the buccaneer force, which survived an engagement with a Spanish flotilla which killed most of the buccaneers, were captured by Indians. They were cannibals and made a meal of the bestial psychopath and all but five of the survivors.

One of the most revolting of the buccaneers was a squat, powerfully built Hollander called Roche Braziliano by virtue of having lived in Brazil during the period the Dutch held part of the coastal area. He moved to Jamaica where Esquemelin says he at first comported himself so well that he was elected to lead a buccaneer band. One of his first prizes was a Spanish galleon coming from Mexico with a cargo of treasure. Admiration for his feat was tempered with apprehension at his behavior when drunk. He "would oftimes shew himself either brutish or foolish . . . he would run up and down the street, beating or wounding whom he met, no person daring to oppose him or make any resistance." He behaved even more brutally with Spanish prisoners once ordering some to be roasted alive upon wooden spits when they refused to tell him where his men could steal hogs.

After a raid Braziliano and his accomplices "wasted in a few days in taverns all they had gained, by giving themselves to all manner of debauchery," according to Esquemelin and then they set off again. Once they were shipwrecked on the coast of Campeche but managed to survive one peril after another until they chanced upon several vessels loading logwood which they were able to take, stocking them with slaughtered Spanish horsemeat which they salted. Thanks to their new little squadron they managed to seize a vessel on its way to Maracaibo from Mexico which carried a gratifying amount of silver coinage. Once Braziliano was captured near Campeche and carried before the Governor who threw him and his men into the dungeon to await execution. Braziliano couldn't have been too foolish for while in prison he succeeded in forging a letter addressed to the governor which purported to come from a powerful pirate force hovering off the coast. It warned the governor not to treat his prisoners harshly or the pirates would wreak vengeance on Campeche. The governor rescinded the execution order and sent Braziliano and his men to Spain aboard the galleons to serve as galley slaves. Before long Braziliano escaped and returned to Jamaica and his cronies. They put to sea again "committing greater robberies and cruelties than ever they had done before." Later, captured and tortured by the Inquisition in Campeche, Braziliano admitted to having buried treasure on the Isle of Pines. Spanish soldiers sent to dig it up found over a hundred thousand pesos which was most unusual for, contrary to belief, pirates seldom buried their treasure, although they might hide it for a short period of time.

Another infamous character was Bartholomew el Portugués, a Portuguese buccaneer plagued with bad luck. He once captured a large ship against all odds, pitting thirty buccaneers and four small guns against seventy Spaniards with twenty cannon. He lost this rich prize with its cargo of 70,000 pieces of eight and a huge amount of valuable cacao pods when three galleons on their way into Havana from Mexico happened upon the scene and gave chase. He also lost his freedom and was taken as a prisoner to Campeche. The governor was delighted to detain the Portuguese pirate who had committed "innumerable excessive insolencies upon those coasts, not only infinite murders and robberies, but also lamentable incendiums, which the people of Campeche still preserved very fresh in their memory."

His luck wasn't all bad, though, for on the eve of his execution, as a gibbet was being erected in the public square, el Portugés escaped from the ship where he was being held. His method was novel. Like many of his mates the bold buccaneer was unable to swim. He was a terror on the sea but helpless in it. Undaunted, he plugged the mouths of two large earthen storage jars. In the middle of the night he stabbed a guard with a concealed knife and jumped overboard with the jars which he used as flotation devices. He made his way to shore and into the jungle where he eluded search parties the following day. Eventually el Portugués reached the Cape of Golfo Triste, 140 miles from Campeche, where he boarded a buccaneering ship which took him home to Port Royal.

The history of the buccaneers is well known thanks not only to Esquemelin but also to the journalistic bent of a few of the protagonists and several close observers. There are also official papers, such as the Spanish documents yellowing in the archives at Seville, that chronicle the suffering of the colonists and the Crown's rage and frustration. The English Calendar of State Papers and other publications in archives in Paris and the Hague add another dimension to the history.

Three Jesuit missionaries, Labat, Dutertre, and Charlevoix, who were in the Caribbean in the late 1690s also chronicled the close of the buccaneer era. Père Labat's lively memoirs include a description of his passage from Martinique to Guadeloupe aboard a pirate craft commanded by one Captain Daniel, a genial host and devout Catholic. Landing at a small island to take on provisions, the pirate and his crew of ninety captured a number of inhabitants, including the local priest whom they took aboard while searching the village for wine, brandy, chickens and other supplies. The pirate captain asked the priest to conduct mass. An altar was set up on the poop deck and all the pirates ordered to participate. The mass was punctuated with cannon salvos fired at significant moments. "Only one incident," Labat writes, "slightly marred this ceremony." One of the pirates made mocking gestures during the elevation of the host and cursed the captain when he rebuked him, so Daniel drew his pistol and shot the pirate through the head, swearing by God he would do the same to anyone else who showed disrespect for the "*Sainte Sacrifice*." "Quite an effective method, as one perceives," commented the missionary, "to prevent the poor fellow repeating his offense."

Labat's voyage to Guadeloupe aboard the buccaneer ship took a surprising fifty-two days to cover ninety miles, because the captain detoured to take several prizes. The buccaneers also rescued two English ladies of quality from little Avis Island between Martinique and Dominica, where the ship they were taking to Antigua foundered. The ladies accompanied by eight slaves and fourteen English sailors had been stranded for eleven days waiting for a small boat that had been with them to return with a new ship. The buccaneers coerced the shipwrecked soldiers to help them in a futile attempt to refloat the foundered ship, now a pirate prize and Daniel prepared to seize the rescue vessel as soon as it appeared. For a price Labat managed to negotiate safe passage to an English island for the ladies and their retinue.

Labat gives a charming account of how he showed the women to cure turtle meat while they were on the deserted island and how they reciprocated by teaching him the English way of cooking a beef brisket with potatoes and—"I don't know how many ragouts. In fact I could write a volume on the subject telling how to serve one hundred twenty-five covers at no cost on a desert island in magnificent style."

The buccaneers seized the rescue ship when it appeared. The following day they took a small English cacique which sailed near the island by flying English colors from Daniel's ship to lull its crew into thinking it was a friendly vessel. Daniel let the two captured English captains load the cacique with as much cargo as it would hold for which they agree to pay ransom. The buccaneers kept the most valuable cargo which included some silver, brocades, gold trimmings, ribbons, and Indian silks as well as wine, and food. Slaves told the buccaneers that items of great value had been buried ashore. Daniel tallied his take with the bills of lading of the wrecked ship and persuaded the English cargo officer to reveal the cache. Labat brings the buccaneers to life in his writings, describing how "the men dressed themselves up in all kinds of fine clothes and were a comical sight as they strutted about the island in feathered hats, wigs, silk stockings, ribbons and other garments."

Captain Daniel headed next to the Danish controlled island of Saint Thomas which welcomed buccaneer business. Labat accompanied the English gentlewomen to the governor's and the Danish Company's offices. Labat wrote "The ladies said the kindest things you can imagine about our captain, nor did they omit the small services I had done for them." The women ransomed their slaves but one refused to leave the buccaneer ship explaining she was a French slave, married with children on Guadeloupe who had been seized by the English in 1703. Labat offered to buy the woman but her mistress freed her giving her some money and dresses and arranging her passage to Martinique. Labat described the moving scene as the two women parted, embracing and weeping. The former slave stayed with her mistress until the ship sailed, which it did once every last pirate penny had been squandered on drink and women "according to custom" which forbade the taking to sea of any money. Labat adds that Daniel, who was impatient to get on with the voyage, got his men aboard by circulating a rumor that a well-laden merchantman was in the area.

Labat relates that soon buccaneer luck did bring a two-hundred ton merchant ship their way. Flying English flags they took an English ship laden with rum, syrup, sugar, a little cotton, some hides and two cases of chocolate. She was bound for Virginia where she planned to exchange her cargo for saltfish, dried beans and lumber to take to the English settlers on Antigua. The captain agreed to a ransom of 25,000 francs payable, as so many were during this last fling of buccaneering enterprise, on St. Thomas. Daniel got part of the sum in cash and the rest drawn on letters of change payable in Martinique. After the transaction, the two captains dined amicably together aboard the buccaneer ship and the English captain was handed back his vessel intact save for four casks of rum, a case of chocolate and a few "souvenirs."

Before reaching Guadeloupe, a destination that seemed to recede with each piratical exploit, Daniel anchored at St. Maarten, the French-Dutch island. Labat was pressed into service to perform weddings, christenings and sundry masses for the islanders who had no priest among them. He was impatient at the delays but pleased to be of service to needy Christians. He attended a very ecumenical Sunday dinner given by the Dutch governor to which Captain Daniel and the captain of an English buccaneering ship anchored in port had also been invited.

Daniel's penultimate deed before bringing the weary priest to Guadeloupe was to storm the tiny island of Barbuda where General Codrington, governor of Antigua, had an estate. The buccaneers burned houses, looted and took fifteen slaves. They also liberated a number of indentured servants, who were little better off than slaves in the early West Indies. These "unfortunate Irishmen" joined the buccaneer crew. A large English ship with thirty-two cannons appeared on the horizon and Daniel attacked although Labat felt "she appeared too tough a morsel for our digestion." The buccaneers prevailed in a raging battle that left the prize's sails and riggings in a shambles. The buccaneers counted one man dead and five wounded. The English had eight dead and fourteen wounded. The captain, who had sustained an arm wound, and his wife were brought aboard Daniel's ship. Their personal belongings were transferred too since Daniel "never allowed any prisoners to be robbed, but was as kind to them as he could be."

The obvious sympathy and affection Labat has for the buccaneers contrasts sharply with the harsh but compellingly realistic description of them given by Esquemelin, the buccaneer barber-surgeon whose book, first published in French in 1684, has been published in many English editions.

The classic English edition of *The Buccaneers of America* is subtitled *A true account of the most remarkable assaults committed of late years upon the coasts of the West Indies by the Buccaneers of Jamaica and Tortuga* (both English and French) and credited to John Esquemelin, "One of the Buccaneers who was present at those tragedies." It is generally published with the account of Basil Ringrose, who was part of the famed buccaneer expedition led by Sharp and Coxon across Central America which was chronicled in no less than five published journals.

Esquemelin's history of a quarter century of buccaneering crackles with deeds of derring-do and details the nefarious careers of some of history's blackest villains but it isn't limited to blood and booty. The author fills page after page with discerning observations of the geography, flora and fauna of Hispaniola and environs. There is not dull passage in the whole work. Esquemelin's lively curiosity led him to examine native American customs as well as those of his fellow buccaneers. Certain Indians allied themselves with the buccaneers joining them "on the account." The natives of Cape Gracias a Dios on the East Coast of Nicaragua sometimes spent years with pirate crews, learning French and English and teaching pirates their language. Esquemelin mentions two buccaneers who were fluent in the native tongue. The Moskito Indians were highly regarded for their skill with a spear fitted with alligator teeth. One man could provide enough turtles and fish for a crew of one hundred men.

These Indians were "very unskillful in dressing of victuals" and Esquemelin, in what must be the first description of an American cocktail party, explains they seldom invited friends to their house for a banquet but asked them instead to come over "and drink of their liquors." Before the guests arrived the women combed their lustrous black hair and painted their faces red while their husbands daubed themselves with black makeup. The host welcomed his friends by falling to the ground on his face in front of his cottage. They picked him up and reciprocated by falling down themselves, after which everyone went inside and proceeded to imbibe one drink after another. "Hereunto follow many songs and dances and a thousand caresses to the women that are present," wrote Esquemelin.

Spanish documents relate the plight of Spanish shipwreck victims who ran afoul of buccaneers in 1641. A fleet of thirty-one ships sailing from Havana to Spain was caught in a hurricane. Some ships were blown clear of danger, some sank and others were dashed to pieces like eggshells on coastal reefs. The almiranta, torn apart at the seams, managed to make it to the Abrojos (Spanish for "open your eyes"), north of Hispaniola, where it wrecked and sank. Over 300 of the 514 people aboard drowned. The survivors lowered rafts and abandoned ship. The admiral, Juan Villavicencio, forced his way onto the only launch. English buccaneers coming across survivors adrift on rafts stripped their prey naked to get what was in their pockets and then cast them up on the nearest coast. Less fortunate souls, clinging to overcrowded rafts, were picked off by sharks.

The Spanish Crown was alarmed at more than the mounting tempo of piratical attacks in the Caribbean and along the Main. A major concern was the growing numbers of interlopers, especially English and French, who were settling in the islands as planters. In 1629 the outbound treasure flotas were instructed to call at the infant English settlements on St. Kitts and Nevis and drive out the "trespassers." Admiral Fadrique de Toledo took Nevis easily when the island's indentured servants, many of them Irish Catholics, refused to fight alongside their planter-masters. John Hilton, a storekeeper said that "our servants proved treacherous, running away from us and swimed aboard and told them where we hid our provissions and in what case our islands stood." St. Kitts, which had both French and English settlers, surrendered, too. Most of the French had escaped but the English were taken prisoner. Their homes and crops were destroyed although de Toledo treated them humanely, sending the majority back to England and taking only a few to Spain as hostages. Some of the former settlers of Nevis and St. Kitts despaired of restoring their plantations and drifted to Tortuga where the majority took up the buccaneering life.

The most distinguished of these was Anthony Hilton, the former Governor of Nevis who became Governor of Tortuga in 1631, but most were fugitive indentured servants and transported convicts whose lives had been brutish. For half a century, until the Africa-American slave route was well established, it was thousands of European indentured servants who furnished the colonies with labor. They came from the lowest classes and belonged to four categories. There were "free willers" who sold themselves for a period of five to seven years in payment for transportation to the Indies. They were free men at the end of their terms. There were "redemptioners." A redemptioner signed indenture papers with a ship's captain with the understanding that once he or she reached the West Indies he would have a given number of days to find a "redeemer," that is, a planter who would buy his papers from the captain. What happened all too often, however, was that the captain detained the servant aboard ship until the days expired and then sold him at auction to the labor-starved planters. This meant, of course, a profit for the captain and a longer period of servitude for the wretched redemptioner. The most piteous indentured servants were children and youths snatched or lured from backstreets and alleys. Experience proved that children under the age of eight or nine often perished on the crossing, so the "spiriters" learned to concentrate on older ones. One Englishman claimed to have kidnapped five hundred children a year over a twelve-year period. Most of these were orphans or children of abject parents who had no recourse. Society cared little for these wretched creatures. When a sixteen-year-old Londoner named Alice Deakins escaped, she was bold enough to press charges against her abductor. He was tried and found guilty of kidnapping and the sale of a human being. His mockery of a sentence: to pay a twelve-pence fine. A third category, the "transportees," comprised convicted felons, vagrants, prostitutes and political undesirables who were sold by the government. At the expiration of their bondage they were forbidden from returning to their native countries.

Servants whose terms had expired and were free but had no land or hopes of any added to the English buccaneer population on Tortuga. So did political and religious dissenters and adventurous, vigorous young men seeking a life free from the restrictions of organized society. The women who became camp followers were escaped slaves, Indians, transported prostitutes or workhouse maids who had been brought to the Indies as indentured servants. Many of the French buccaneers were escaped *engagé* laborers whose treatment was no better than that of their indentured English counterparts.

Esquemelin, who had been ill-treated as an indentured servant himself, wrote wrenchingly of the plight of bound servants. "Their masters used them harder," he wrote, "than they did their slaves," since the slave was a lifetime possession and the indentured servant would be free after a certain number of years. They succumbed to malnutrition, overwork and the rigors of the tropical climate or were literally flogged to death. Men with no prospects at home signed on voluntarily for the Caribbean but others had been shanghaied by gangs roaming seaports for strong, young men or boys to transport to the islands. In 1640, two-hundred French youths were kidnapped by their own countrymen and carried to Barbados where each was sold for a term of at least five years. The going price was nine-hundred pounds of cotton per youth. Once in the islands indentured servants were sometimes sold again or their contracts were illegally extended. This happened to Esquemelin when it appeared he would die of a tropical fever. Indentured servants with no recourse to injustice and no means were ideal buccaneer recruits.

With the arrival of the British on Tortuga the buccaneers became a more disciplined group capable of planning bigger raids. In 1631 when Tortuga was taken under the wing of the Providence Company Hilton was named Governor. The Providence Company, chartered in 1630, was established by English Puritans who settled on Providence Island and Henrietta Island (Providencia and San Andrés off Colombia) in 1629. The two beautiful

islands lay more than a thousand miles from the nearest English settlements on St. Kitts and Nevis yet, at the time, their colonies were considered more likely to succeed than the fledgling Massachusetts settlements which were being financed by many of the same English investors.
The islands never fulfilled their expectations. There was dissension in the
Providence colony from the beginning between the fanatical Puritans and
settlers from Bermuda.

Providence had been suggested as a location for English expansion by
Daniel Elfrith, a privateer captain who sailed out of Bermuda for Robert
Rich, Earl of Warwick, the privateer magnate. Rich, one of the original
members of the Somers Islands Company which settled Bermuda in 1612,
had received a commission in 1616 from the Duke of Savoy and used it
to plunder Spanish ships throughout the Caribbean.

He wasn't overly fussy about abiding by its terms. In 1620 for instance,
when Spain and England were nominally at peace, Elfrith brought a captured Spanish prize with a cargo of slaves into Bermuda. The governor, a
friend of Rich's managed to hush up the affair. Bermuda throughout its
history was sympathetic to privateers and pirates.

Elfrith had explored Providence on one of his privateering junkets finding fertile ground and sufficient fresh water on the six-mile long island.
A company was formed to settle it in hopes that the cultivation of tobacco,
which had proved disappointing on Bermuda, would flourish. The island's
chief attraction, however, was its ideal location on the direct route of the
treasure galleons which sailed from Portobelo up the Isthmus to Havana,
through the Yucatán Strait. The shortage of laborers and the island's isolation from other English colonies doomed the tobacco project but by
1634 Providence was a pirate haven where Puritan injunctions against
cards, dice, "stinkinge tobacco" and strong drink were scoffed at. Slaves
taken from small Spanish merchantmen were sold cheaply to the planters
and Dutch privateers brought in captured cargoes which they sold openly
to the great displeasure of the Puritan faction.

When the first English settled on the island they found a Dutch freebooter named Blauvelt, or Bluefields, already headquartered there and in
1637 the Dutch, who wanted an exclusive privateering base, offered the
Providence Company 70,000 pounds sterling for it. The Company wanted
to accept but King Charles I, preferring an English privateering base to a
Dutch one, refused to sell. After an Anglo-Dutch privateering expedition
exacted a ransom of 16,000 pieces of eight from Trujillo on the coast of
Honduras, the Spanish decided the buccaneers must be dislodged. In 1641
a Spanish force captured the island which Spain held until Jamaica buccaneers under Edward Mansfield, or Mansveldt, a seasoned freebooter,
recaptured it in 1666.

Mansfield was the first of the notable buccaneer captains to command big expeditions from Port Royal. He was a Hollander who led the sack of Santo Spirito town on Cuba. In a letter of March 1, 1666 to the Duke of Albermarle, Sir Thomas Modyford writes "that every action gives new encouragement to attempt the Spaniard, finding them in all places very weak and very wealthy. Two or three hundred privateers lately on the coast of Cuba, being denied provisions for money, marched forty-two miles into the country, took and fired the town of Santo Spirito, routed a body of two hundred horse, carried their prisoners to their ships, and for their ransom got three hundred fat beehives sent down." He added that the privateers, under Mansfield's leadership, were then bound for Curacao. Modyford who was not permitted to issue privateering commissions despite repeated appeals from the Council of Jamaica to the Crown mentions that the privateers were sailing with Portuguese-issued letters of marque.

Mansfield also ravaged Granada in Nicaragua and with Henry Morgan as his lieutenant plundered Providence Island which was then in Spanish possession. He left a garrison on the island and Modyford sent a Governor down but within a year the Spaniards had retaken it. Mansfield dreamed of establishing a pirate colony on Providence soon after leading the buccaneer seizure of Curacao he was captured and executed by the Spanish.

Tortuga remained in English hands until fifteen months later when a Spanish force took it back. In 1670 Morgan and his Port Royal contingent who wanted the island as the base for an attack against Panama, found the small Spanish garrison so demoralized that they easily forced a surrender. After a very brief spell they left and the island lay abandoned for almost seventy years save for the rare visit by a pirate ship taking on fresh water.

While they administered Tortuga, which they rechristened Association, the Providence Company had transported slaves they bought from privateers on Providence to Tortuga to cut logwood. This enterprise proved unprofitable. Nor did Governor Hilton have much success interesting free men in planting. Plundering was much more to their taste. The majority of the islanders were French so Hilton was hardly a popular man. In 1634 the Spanish launched an offensive to root out the "pirate nest." In a surprise attack the six hundred Europeans and an unrecorded number of slaves were overwhelmed by a force from Santo Domingo. A renegade Irishman named John Murphy, whom they called Don Juan Morf, helped them. Murphy, a Catholic, was one of the indentured servants the Providence Company had sent to cut logs on Tortuga. He escaped to Santo Domingo and furnished the Spanish with valuable information about the English settlement. Spanish soldiers who took part in the attack testified that Murphy stabbed the English governor during the fighting. Most of the buccaneers were slaughtered. Slaves who hid in the forest were little better off as they were recaptured by the English who took the island back because the Spanish left no garrison. It didn't take long for buccaneers to gravitate back to Tortuga but few were English. In 1638 the Spanish raided the island again, killing many of the inhabitants and then departing. Like weeds, the buccaneers sprang back, this time both English and French drifting to Tortuga in greater numbers than ever before. The English now outnumbered the French but the minute the balance was reversed the French buccaneers requested de Poincy, the French governor of St. Kitts, to send them a French governor.

De Poincy killed two birds with one stone by sending them Monsieur Levasseur, a Huguenot gentleman grown wealthy in the colonial trade, who was regarded with suspicion on St. Kitts because of his Protestantism. During the twelve years of his administration, Levasseur repelled Spanish attacks and managed to keep a rein on the undisciplined buccaneer population while allowing them to operate until his murder 1652 at the hands of two Frenchmen. His first move was to construct an impregnable fortress atop a rocky promontory near the harbor. Within its walls he built a battery, a powder magazine and his residence, which he called his "dovecote."

It soon became clear why the Protestant Levasseur had been so heartily disliked on St. Kitts. As Governor of Tortuga he had the sanction to indulge his venality and his fanatical brand of Protestantism. Catholics were forbidden to attend mass. He burned their chapel and deported the priest. With one hand he collected a share of every transaction that was carried out on the island. With the other he cruelly repressed growing numbers of enemies, locking them in what he referred to with black humor as his "purgatory," a dungeon in his lofty fortress or in "hell" an iron cage too small for a man to sit or lie in. The Huguenot governor's tyranny aroused the buccaneers ire and alarmed de Poincy who had appointed him but no longer had any control over him.

His arrogance rankled the Governor of St. Kitts too, who wrote asking him for a Spanish statue of the Virgin worked in silver, which he heard a buccaneer had given him. De Poincy wanted it for his chapel and mentioned that certainly Lavasseur, a Protestant, would have no use for such a Catholic devotional object. On the contrary, Lavasseur replied, writing that Protestants adored silver Madonnas and that he was sending de Poincy a Virgin of painted wood since he knew that Catholics were too spiritual to care about material things.

Before de Poincy could muster an expedition to oust him, the insufferable Levasseur was shot and stabbed to death in a quarrel over a mistress by two buccaneers named Thibault and Martin whom he had appointed his heirs. The murderers hoped to rule but settled for a pardon when a French force from St. Kitts arrived to restore order. De Fontenay was made Governor, Catholicism was restored and the buccaneering business went on as usual. Before long, however, five Spanish ships with four hundred infantrymen were sent against the island in November of 1653, driving the French out once again. Official Spanish reports complain that there would have been a terrific amount of rich booty if Dutch ships then in the harbor hadn't sacked the island and made off with it all. De Fontenay made a futile effort to recapture Tortuga from the garrison of 150 Spaniards left to hold the island. Only 130 of De Fontenay's men would join him, the rest took off to join the buccaneers who had taken refuge on western Hispaniola where they settled at Port Margot and Port de Paix.

The Royal Council of the Indies had ordered that all vessels plying the Caribbean were to carry a minimum of two large bronze guns, six iron guns and a certain quantity of small arms. Spanish shipowners often failed to meet these requirements, which certainly made it easier for the buccaneers in their small boats to take a hefty prize.

Although they sometimes used larger ships of thirty or forty guns, the buccaneers of the old guard favored smaller, easily-maneuvered boats holding as many as fifty men and eleven to fourteen guns. These had both oar and sail and could operate in shallow or shoal water. Bermuda-built boats were thought the best. French buccaneers preferred small arms and knives. The English liked cannons. The buccaneers, particularly the veteran *boucaniers* hunters, were superb marksmen. In their swift cedar sloops they would sail right up to a crowded merchant vessel. The crew lay prone to avoid enemy grapeshot. By aiming their sights at the helmsman and any mariners in the rigging, the buccaneers established an immediate advantage over the larger vessel. They followed it up by lowering the mast and triangular sail, just as pirates had done in the Mediterranean thousands of years earlier, and zoomed in on the stern to incapacitate the rudder before swarming aboard with pistols ready and knives clenched between their teeth. After fierce hand-to-hand combat, victory was often theirs.

Homebound vessels were preferred as prey because their crews and passengers were fewer and their cargoes more valuable—gems, metals and dyewood as opposed to wheat, wine and cloth. The periods before dawn or after dusk were favored for their attacks because it was during those hours that ships tended to sail past Tortuga taking advantage of the winds which blew them toward the Atlantic by night but reversed by day. Also, they could paddle silently up to an unsuspecting ship in the darkness. They seldom left any Spaniards alive.

It was about 1640 that the Tortuga buccaneers began to call themselves the Brethren of the Coast. To become a member of this democratic confraternity a man vowed to subscribe to a strict code called the Custom of the Coast. Among the fiercely independent buccaneers this took precedence over any national code of law. By crossing the Tropic of Cancer they had, according to superstition, drowned their former lives. Last names were taboo, generally known only if a man was married. Before setting out on an expedition the buccaneers agreed to the *chasse-partie* or articles describing the conditions under which they were to sail. In the days of the early *boucaniers*, before the huge expeditions organized by leaders like Mansfield or Morgan, the men generally selected their leader from among themselves. This system didn't die out altogether and in the 1740s Admiral Vernon, the controversial naval officer who inflicted great injury on the Spanish Empire during the so-called War of Jenkins's Ear (which broke out in 1739 precipitated by an English captain who claimed Spanish pirates had boarded his ship and cut off his ear), expressed an opinion that it must be insufferable to be the captain of a privateer vessel, "lorded over by the company's quartermaster, supported by the crew, who have chosen him for their champion . . . " and who could at any time demote him.

Setting out on an expedition, the participants assembled on a given day, each with his quota of powder and bullets. In a council held aboard ship the men decided where to head for provisions, "especially of flesh, seeing they scarce eat anything else," wrote Esquemelin who gives us fascinating details of buccaneer preparations. Their chief meat was pork which they generally obtained by raiding Spanish hog ranches. Turtle meat ranked second and was eaten fresh or salted. When they could they ate manatees, the gentle sea cows which are an endangered species today. Sometimes they made the six hundred-mile trip to the Cayman Islands northwest of Jamaica where turtles abounded. They also turtled on the south coast of Cuba, harpooning the creatures by the light of candlewood torches. They also kidnapped turtle fishermen from that area and made them work for them "so long as the Pirates are pleased."

The buccaneer council next decided where to go to "seek their desperate fortunes" and precisely what share of the booty each man was to receive. The Brethren of the Coast pioneered workmen's compensation, drawing up a schedule of awards to wounded members, according to the severity of their loss. Esquemelin's account of these negotiations states that like all pirates the buccaneers adhered to the law of "no prey, no pay." "In the first place, therefore," he observed, "they mention how much the Captain ought to have for his ship. Next the salary of the carpenter, or shipwright, who careened, mended and rigged the vessel. This commonly amounts to 100 or 150 pieces of eight, being according to the agreement, more or less. Afterwards for provisions and victualling they draw out of the same common stock about 200 pieces of eight. Also a competent salary for the surgeon and his chest of medicaments, which is usually rated at 200 or 250 pieces of eight. Lastly, they stipulate in writing what recompense or reward each one ought to have, that is either wounded or maimed in his body, suffering the loss of any limb, by that voyage. Thus they order for the loss of a right arm 600 pieces of eight, or six slaves; for the loss of a left arm 500 pieces of eight, or five slaves; for a right leg 500 pieces of eight, or five slaves; for the left leg 400 pieces of eight, or four slaves; for an eye 100 pieces of eight or one slave; for a finger of the hand the same reward as for the eye."

Whatever remained in the pot after paying out the above was divided into shares. The buccaneer leader got five or six times what the ordinary crewmen received. The officers received an amount proportionate to their position and the lowest ranked boys were awarded a half share "by reason that, when they happen to take a better vessel than their own, it is the duty of the boys to set fire to the ship or boat wherein they are, and then retire to the prize which they have taken." The first to sight a prize won an extra share. The buccaneers swore not to steal from one another nor conceal any plunder. No locks or keys were allowed on board. Any man found stealing from a brother had his nose and ears sliced off. Following a second offense, a man was marooned on a deserted shore with nothing more than a jug of water, a musket and shot.

Throughout history pirates have been renowned for their debauched tastes and prodigality. The buccaneers were no exception. "My own master," observed Esquemelin, "would buy, on like occasions, a whole pipe of wine (126 gallons) and placing it in the street would force every one that passed by to drink with him; threatening to pistol them in case they would not do it. At other times he would do the same with barrels of ale or beer. And, very often, with both in his hands, he would throw these liquors about the streets, and wet the clothes of such as walked by, without regarding whether he spoiled their apparel or not, were they men or women." Women and wine soon parted the swaggering buccaneer from his last piece of eight but tavern keepers and brothel owners extended long lines of credit to their dissolute customers in anticipation of their next visit. Esquemelin's master, so generous with his liquor, fell hopelessly into debt and, like other heedless pirates, became an indentured servant at Port Royal.

The Spanish were chronically short-handed in their defense of the Caribbean. When in 1655 the Tortuga garrison was recalled to deal with the threat of an English attack on Santo Domingo, the buccaneers filtered back to their old haunt, English as well as French. The same year, after the capture of Jamaica, the English commanding officer there gave a prominent buccaneer named Elias Watt or Ward a commission as Governor of Tortuga. About the same time, a commission from Louis XIV appointed a French noble, Jeremie Deschamps, Sieur de Mousac et du Rausset, to the same post. For a while, they presided together over a community of some 150 buccaneers of both nationalities.

Du Rausset proved a more able politician than Watt. His adroit manipulations led to an order from the Commonwealth Government of England to General Edward D'Oyley, who governed Jamaica in 1659, which named him Governor of Tortuga, provided he maintain English interests. Watts, who had been outmaneuvered sailed with his family and some English followers for New England. Du Rausset promptly showed his contempt for English interests by raising a French flag over the fortress and making it clear English buccaneers were unwelcome. The English made several attempts to get Tortuga back but it remained firmly in French hands vying with Port Royal as the buccaneer capital of the Caribbean.

During this period a buccaneer force of four hundred men sailed for Puerta de Plata on the coast of Hispaniola in a commandeered French ship which had anchored at Tortuga and several smaller vessels. Their objective was the town of St. Iago which lay some twenty leagues inland. They marched through the forest for three days. They arrived in the night, surprising the governor asleep at home. For a ransom of 60,000 pieces of eight the marauders spared his life and then devoted themselves to an orgy of pillaging. Loaded with valuables from private homes and all kinds of ecclesiastical treasures, including the church bells, they set out for the coast taking the governor and other notables as hostages. A Spanish force managed to outflank them and ambush them but withdrew when the pirates threatened to slay their prisoners.

The English buccaneers driven from Tortuga found an ideal base at Port Royal—"a citadel over all the Spanish West Indies." The early governors welcomed Dutch, Portuguese and French freebooters too, freely issuing letters of marque to anyone who would aid the vulnerable new colony by harassing the Spaniards so they could not descend upon the island. Jamaica fell into English hands in a round about way when Lord Protector Oliver Cromwell's grandiose Western Design misfired. Despite the poet Milton's Latin eulogizing of the Caribbean project, Cromwell's plan to have an English armada take Hispaniola was nothing more than a piratical expedition, launched with no declaration of war while English and Spanish diplomats were discussing a possible alliance.

Cromwell had grossly underestimated Spanish force and overestimated his own. The attack on Hispaniola was a debacle. The fleet, under command of Admiral William Penn, was too hastily organized. The army was hopeless; composed of undisciplined former Parliamentary forces, forcibly drafted vagrants with no training and recruits picked up at Barbados, St. Kitts, Nevis and Montserrat. The Caribbean recruits, some of them buccaneers, were, if not better trained, at least more eager to avenge themselves against the Spaniards, many of them having suffered at their hands. A number of the recruits had fled Providence Island in 1641 when the Spanish attacked.

The level of recruit was not high. Henry Whistler, who had come with Penn expressed his contempt for the population of Barbados in general, writing that "This island is the Dunghill wherine England doth cast forth its rubidg: Rodgs and hors and such like people are those who are generally Broght heare. A rodge in England will hardly make a cheater heare; a Baud brought over puts on a demuor comportment, a whore if hansume makes a wife for sume rich planter."

They were a mutinous rabble, hardly an army. The officers didn't inspire confidence either. A Captain Butler, sent on a recruiting mission to St. Kitts was so soused with drink that he toppled from his horse and vomited at the feet of a couple of appalled French officers. During the battle on Hispaniola General Venables, the British Army commander, hid behind a tree "soe much possessed with terror that he could hardlie spake." The English troops dropped like flies from battle wounds, dysentery and exhaustion. After two and a half humiliating weeks the survivors sailed away in defeat.

An anonymous chronicler wrote "God was not pleased to deliver it up unto us though with 9,500 men and 80 saile of great ships and small vessels, soe that never were men more disapoynted than some of us, nor did the hearts of English men faile them more than in this attempt."

Returning to Cromwell without some kind of territorial acquisition was unthinkable so the motley expedition set its sights on Jamaica which lay at the very core of the Spanish Caribbean. They somehow succeeded in wresting the island from the Spaniards despite one of the most inept military campaigns in British history. Jamaica was sparsely settled. The hereditary proprietors of the island were the Dukes De la Vega, descendants of Columbus. They were harsh administrators demanding high rents from the planters, many of whom were Portuguese. Spanish colonists preferred to live on Hispaniola or on the Main where they were closer to the sources of mineral wealth.

The English had, of course, been there before. Sir Anthoney Shirley on his pirating expedition of 1596 and then Colonel Jackson who sacked and ransomed St. Iago (modern Spanish town) in 1642. On the same voyage Jackson, who held a commission from the Providence Company which had suffered the loss of Providence the year before, sacked Puerto Caballo, Maracaibo, and other settlements on the Central American coast terrorizing the Spanish for three years with the help of almost a thousand men recruited from the pool of perennial adventurers on St. Kitts and Barbados. A large number of these ruffians found Jamaica so beautiful that they deserted and stayed on. In 1655 when Venables accepted the Spanish surrender of the island, he insisted on being handed these men.

Nearly the first thing the unruly troops did upon entering St. Iago was to start digging for buried treasure. They found almost none and took out their anger by destroying churches and other buildings. They spread out over the countryside wantonly killing cattle and hogs. In a couple of weeks they slaughtered some 20,000 cattle. The stench of rotting carcasses filled the air. Soon there was not enough meat so they dug up immature crops.

Men died of disease and starvation or ate lizards and unripe fruits. The English managed to hold on to their acquisition, but just barely. From the beginning most colonists preferred plundering to planting, despite the beautiful island's fertile soil. "Dig or plant they neither will nor can, but are determined rather to starve than work," wrote Major-General Robert Sedgewicke, left in charge after Venables returned to England and a brief sojourn in the Tower. Before long Sedgewicke died in an epidemic of dysentery which felled the weakened English like flies.

Time and more able administration consolidated English control. In an effort to establish a plantation colony, prisoners captured in Royalist uprisings, felons and other undesirables were transported from England to work as servants. The Council of State ordered the importation of a thousand Irish girls and a thousand boys under the age of fifteen and a few months later issued another order for twelve hundred men from Ireland and Scotland. These immigrants did little to help. Many died, others fled to the buccaneering life rather than face the rigors of tropical farming. Only when experienced planters from Nevis, Barbados, Bermuda and other islands moved to Jamaica did the new colony gain vigor.

It was piracy, however, which protected Jamaica and made it prosper for the first thirty years or so. Port Royal was the key to island prosperity. The buccaneer port lay on a small cay at the tip of a long sandspit which curves away from the southern coast of Jamaica in the shadow of the lush Blue Mountains. The sandspit, called the Palisadoes, forms Kingston Harbor. It is one of the finest natural seaports in the Western Hemisphere, judged capable in the view of one seventeenth century visitor of "holding all the ships of Christendom." In 1692 Port Royal was twice as large as New York was at that time.

It would be hard to imagine a less favorable location for the settlement which toward the close of the century ranked as one of the richest cities in the world. The cay, separated from the Palisadoes by a mangrove marsh, had no fresh water. No crops could grow on its barren sand. The only things the site had in abundance were pestilential insects. It enjoyed, however, an unrivaled geographical advantage as a port at the very center of Caribbean maritime traffic. During its heyday, more than five hundred ships, some of them thousand tonners, called at Port Royal, focal point of the Caribbean's contraband trade. Many of the vessels were the smaller, faster vessels of the buccaneers, privateers and pirates who made Port Royal "the most wicked city in the world" and one of the most flourishing.

In 1683 resident Francis Hanson, a lawyer, wrote:

> The town of Port Royal, being as it were the Store House or Treasury of the West Indies, is always like a continual Mart or Fair where all sorts of choice merchandises are daily imported, not only to furnish the island, but vast quantities are thence again transported to supply the Spaniards, Indians and other Nations, who in exchange return us bars and cakes of gold, wedges and pigs of silver, Pistoles, Pieces of Eight and several other coins of both metals, with store of wrought Plate, Jewels, rich pearl necklaces, and of Pearl unsorted or undrilled several bushels . . . almost every House hath a rich cupboard of Plate, which they carelessly expose, scarce shutting their doors in the night . . . in Port Royal there is more plenty of running Cash (proportionally to the number of its inhabitants) than is in London.[1]

In the seventeenth century the Caribbean was the world's Wild West and Port Royal its boom town with an international reputation for godlessness, profligacy and wantonness. A clergyman cut short his intended ministry in Port Royal, returning to England aboard the same ship he had sailed on because: "This town is the Sodom of the New World and since the majority of its population consists of pirates, cutthroats, whores and some of the vilest persons in the whole of the world, I felt my permanence there was of no use." Not many in the Caribbean Babylon quibbled about the pursuit of worldly gain and worldly pleasures, however. In 1661 the Council granted forty new licenses for grog shops, taverns and punch houses in the month of July alone. The taverns were filled nightly with roistering mariners; free-spending buccaneers flush from recent raids with gold hoops glinting at their ears and a strumpet on either arm. The prodigal pirates spent as much as two or three thousand pieces of eight in a night's carousing.

The buccaneers favorite drink was a punch called "kill-devil" which must have been potent indeed. Governor Modyford wrote that "the Spaniards wondered much at the sickness of our people, until they knew the strength of their drinks, but then wondered more that they were not all dead."[2] King Charles took advantage of the unquenchable thirst of Port Royal's denizens by establishing a royal monopoly on the sale of spirits. The revenues financed the town's impressive fortifications. As late as 1690 when buccaneer patronage had waned somewhat, an observer noted that still one out of every four or five buildings in the teeming city consisted of "brothels, gaming houses, taverns and grog shops."

Port Royal's brawling, bawdy history came to a cataclysmic end. On a sultry day in June 1692 the air was absolutely still and at noon the sky turned red. The earth shook and within two minutes nine-tenths of Port Royal was swallowed by the sea. Houses sank thirty or forty fathoms deep and the ground opened and swallowed buildings and people in one street and threw them up in another. Ships and sloops in the harbor were overset and sank. A contemporary chronicle described how "All this was attended with hollow rumbling noise, like thunder . . . The earth heaved and swelled like the rolling billows . . . in many places the earth crack'd, open'd and shut, with a motion quick and fast and of these openings two or three hundred might be seen at a time; in some of these people were swallowed up, in others they were caught in the middle and pressed to death, and in others the heads only appeared, in which condition the dogs came and ate them . . . Scarce a planter's house or sugar-work was left standing in all Jamaica." Two thousand people died in the earthquake, three thousand more perished in the epidemic which followed. Many survivors were reported murdered by drunken mobs of men and women who looted what remained of the pirate lair. The earthquake and tidal wave which destroyed Port Royal were thought by many to be a punishment for wickedness meted out by an avenging God.

There were few pirates left at that time. Although the colony could not have survived without the buccaneers in its infancy, they had come to be an embarrassment. A 1670 treaty of peace between Spain and England prompted the English government, after years of vacillation, to enforce a vigorous antibuccaneering policy. Gone were the days when Jamaican authorities made every effort to attract and placate the buccaneers. The very rovers they had welcomed with open arms they took to hanging. In 1687 the infamous Buccaneer Captain Banister and three of his brethren were brought back to Port Royal dangling from the yardarm, "a spectacle of great satisfaction to all good people and of terror to the favourers of pirates," reads Governor Molesworth's report in the Calendar of State Papers.

Domination of the Spanish-American trade routes was a primary English objective in the Caribbean. Cromwell authorized attacks on Spanish territory and shipping right after the taking of Jamaica. A few months later Vice-Admiral Goodson led a force which sacked and destroyed Santa Marta on the Main, an action which acting-Governor Robert Sedgewicke disapproved of. "This kind of marooning cruising West Indian trade of plundering and burning towns, though it hath been long practiced in these parts," he wrote, "yet it is not honourable for a princely navy . . . "

There wasn't much of a "princely navy" however, so buccaneers were set on the Spaniards. Governor D'Oyley, appointed after Sedgewicke's death, strongly supported the buccaneers who began to flock to Port Royal from throughout the Caribbean and Europe as well. No buccaneer captain of ability ever had difficulty crewing his ship. In the latter part of the seventeenth century there was no shortage of vigorous unemployed men in the West Indies. In 1650 St. Kitts and Barbados were the most densely populated areas in the world. Shut out of a reasonably prosperous settled existence by slave labor and the plantation system which concentrated land and wealth in a few hands, unskilled whites drifted from one Caribbean port to another. With nothing to lose they were quick to sign on to "go a roving" on the Main.

D'Oyley sent Captain Christopher Myngs to terrorize the southern Caribbean. His buccaneer force of three hundred devastated Cumaná, Puerto Caballo and Coro where they made a spectacular haul by trailing some of the escaping inhabitants into the forest. They found twenty-two chests of royal treasure each filled with four hundred pounds of silver coins as well as plate, gems and cocoa. It was Port Royal's first great booty—worth as much as half a million pounds. Myngs was hailed as a returning hero until it was discovered he had skimmed 12,000 pieces of eight for himself and he was sent to England in disgrace. Apparently, he didn't give an accounting to officials before dividing up the booty among his officers and crew. In addition, there was a question about pillaging six Dutch ships he had seized for illicit trading at Barbados on his way from England to Jamaica. In any case, he, like so many of his ilk, had a cat's nine lives and despite banishment to England was soon back at Port Royal.

In 1660 Charles II was proclaimed King of England. With his coronation, hostilities against Spain which Cromwell had illegally provoked ceased—at least officially. It appeared briefly that the King might even hand Jamaica back to Spain but Charles soon made it clear that the buccaneers who had sailed with commissions from the Commonwealth could carry on. Buccaneer ranks grew with former Republicans taking to "roving" after the Restoration. To appease Spanish complaints a show of curbing their predations was made from time to time.

Governor Modyford, appointed in 1664, received a royal command to forbid buccaneering, punish offenders and make restitution to victims. Modyford obediently posted the proclamation, the first of many, which went unheeded. In 1660 the last English naval frigate had been recalled, leaving the island virtually defenseless, save for its buccaneers. Modyford couldn't afford to alienate them, nor could any other governor for the next quarter century. Modyford granted letters of marque for a fee, generally twenty pounds, and once accepted a leopard pelt filled with gold coins from a buccaneer. Spanish settlers lived in constant dread of buccaneer invasion. Captain Barnard sacked San Tomé on the Orinoco in 1663. In the same year Lewis Scot, a Welshman, destroyed Campeche. In 1664 John Davis, a buccaneer of reckless courage, led eighty men up Nicaragua's San Juan River in canoes to loot the city of Granada and torture and kill its population. They made off with 50,000 pieces of eight in cash and a great deal of other plunder. Davis's next foray was the sack of the Spanish city of St. Augustine in Florida.

King Charles recognized the necessity of tolerating the buccaneers despite the diplomatic quandary their actions put him in vis-a-vis Spain. A 1664 report from Modyford states there were "no less than 1,500 lusty fellows abroad" at Port Royal. When war broke out against Holland and France they were enlisted to aid the English in taking the Dutch islands of Tobago, St. Eustatius and Saba in 1666. A buccaneer force sailing from St. Kitts plundered the Dutch half of St. Maarten and a band from Barbados attacked Dutch settlements in Guiana at Pomeroon and Esequibo so that by the close of 1665 the Dutch were left with only Curacao. However, English governors in the Caribbean were still prohibited from licensing privateers.

Minutes of the February 22, 1666 Council meeting enumerate the reasons why letters of marque were needed. Jamaica needed the buccaneer force to defend it and also depended on the abundant supply of reasonably priced goods which they brought into Port Royal, including currency, bullion, cocoa, logwood, hides, tallow, and cochineal. These items attracted ships from as far away as New England and provided a living for many merchants. Poorer planters needed the privateers to sell provisions to and planters needed the slaves they brought in.

The Council mentions the need for intelligence about the Spanish which the buccaneers could provide as they did during Governor D'Oyley's administration. They mentioned that privateers and buccaneers kept the French pirates of Tortuga, Hispaniola and the little cays off Cuba at bay. The Council went on to say that furthermore, "They are of a great reputation to this island and of terror to the Spaniard, and keep up a high and military spirit in all the inhabitants." The profits they bring in, including those for "His Majesty and Royal Highness" were invoked and in concluding the Council stated that "it seems to be the only means to force the Spaniards in time to a free trade, all ways of kindness having produced nothing of good neighborhood, for though all old commissions have been called in, and no new ones granted, and many of their ships restored, yet they continue all acts of hostility, taking our ships and murdering our people, making them work at their fortifications and then sending them into Spain . . . "[3]

The most celebrated of all the buccaneers was the ruthless and clever Henry Morgan who garnered 105 million dollars in booty from the sack of the Spanish Empire's principal cities. Little is known of Morgan's boyhood, except that he was born in 1635 in Glamorganshire Wales. Esquemelin wrote that he was son of a yeoman farmer. This prompted Morgan, after he had made the transformation from pirate to Lieutenant-Governor of Jamaica, to sue two London publishers of Esquemelin's book, as much for what he considered a slur against his father, who he said was a gentleman with a modest estate, as for describing him as a debauched and barbarous pirate. Morgan was probably transported to Barbados as an indentured servant and may have gone with the Cromwellian forces to Jamaica and subsequently with Myngs on the raids against Santiago de Cuba and Campeche in 1662–63. It is certain that he was the nephew of Colonel Edward Morgan who led the buccaneers who looted and captured St. Eustatius and Saba.

Morgan's fame rested on his skill as a tactician, his courage, the scale of his expeditions and their phenomenal success. In 1668 he led seven hundred buccaneers in a dozen ships to Puerto del Principe, Cuba (now Camaguey) where torture of captive citizens produced an abundance of valuables. Later that year he launched his first great venture, an attack on Portobelo. Mansfield and Morgan had aimed at the treasure port in 1666 but finding it too well fortified had seized Providence Island as a consolation prize. Next to Havana and Cartagena, Portobelo was the strongest city in the Indies.

It was so heavily fortified that the only hope of taking it lay in complete surprise. Morgan, accordingly, landed 460 men a hundred miles up the coast from the city. The buccaneers transferred to large canoes and sailed south, approaching the city at dawn. Morgan's men captured a sentry before he could give the alarm and forced him to call upon the defenders of the fort to surrender or die. The answering fire of Spanish muskets sent the intrepid buccaneers over the walls to overwhelm the sleep-slowed enemy. True to his word, Morgan had the Spanish soldiers locked in a single building which he blew up with gunpowder. The second of the three forts was taken with ease, but the third, where the governor commanded, proved another story. Vowing to die rather than give in to the *piratas ingleses*, the governor organized a staunch defense which all but forced Morgan to retreat.

The battle raged from dawn until the midday sun burned overhead. The population took advantage of the fighting at the fort to bolt for the woods with their valuables. This sight inspired Morgan to redouble his efforts. He employed a novel, and terrible, stratagem. He had his men construct siege ladders. Then he corralled all the priests, friars and nuns who could be found. Relying on the Spaniards' reputation for reverence, he forced the servants of God to carry the ladders to the ramparts and set them up against the walls. To Morgan's consternation the governor, torn between duty and piety, ordered his troops to keep up their barrage of fire. Despite the governor's decision, the fort soon surrendered.

Once the city surrendered the butchery began. Buccaneers in a perpetual state of drunkenness indulged in an orgy of rape and murder. Esquemelin, who was among the buccaneers on this expedition, writes that Morgan had citizens tortured on the rack to reveal where their valuables were hidden. From gardens, cisterns and caves a stream of gold, silver, plate and jewels poured into the buccaneer headquarters. Valuable merchandise was systematically collected from the warehouses along the waterfront and the buccaneers returned to a rousing welcome at Port Royal with half a million pieces of eight, a mountain of merchandise and three hundred slaves. For a month the great event was celebrated in the taverns and brothels of Port Royal.

The following year Morgan mounted an attack on Cartagena. It got off to an inauspicious start. At the conclusion of the preparations, Morgan held a wild bon voyage party aboard his flagship the *Oxford* at Cow Island off the south coast of Hispaniola, where his force of English and French buccaneers rendezvoused. To add to the festivities drunken gunners shot off muskets and a spark ignited a powder barrel, blowing up the *Oxford* and killing 350 men, including those across the table from Morgan. The sea turned red with blood from dismembered corpses. Buccaneers from the other ships rowed among the bodies in small boats stripping them of valuables, even hacking off fingers to salvage the gold rings buccaneers liked so much.

Eventually Morgan got underway with a fleet of fifteen ships and about 600 men. He turned away from Cartagena when he realized its fortifications were invincible and moved against Maracaibo, which had barely recovered from previous attacks. Maracaibo was protected by an impressive fort. But Morgan was able to sail into port at the end of a long day's fighting because, as had happened many times before, the garrison had abandoned the fort and slipped off in the night.

It was the same old story. Most of the terrified populace had fled with whatever they could carry at the first sight of buccaneer sails. Thirty men, women and children were captured and tortured for three weeks. Morgan's brutes also terrorized the town of Gibraltar farther up the lake and altogether extorted about a quarter million pieces-of-eight from the inhabitants of both towns.

This exploit, which involved a brilliant escape from the lake, the exit from which was blocked by three enormous Spanish warships, added to Morgan's already considerable fame. In late 1670, when he organized the greatest expedition of his career, he had no trouble in raising a fleet of about forty ships and two thousand bold buccaneers to take Panama, the golden warehouse of the Indies. It would have to be reached overland and taken by surprise from the rear, a challenge even for the toughest adventurers. Morgan landed at Fort San Lorenzo on the Caribbean side of Panama. The Spanish commander of the fort agreed to surrender to Morgan if the buccaneers would stage a sham assault. He promised to use no shot in Spanish guns returning fire. This way he would retain his honor and avoid punishment by the Spanish Crown. After the mock attack, however, the Spaniards resisted and the garrison of 350 soldiers managed to kill 100 buccaneers and severely wound 70 more, before surrendering.

Morgan left a contingent to hold the fort and men to guard the anchored fleet and embarked 1,400 of his best men in thirty-six canoes they had constructed to sail up the Chagres River. They took no provisions because they expected to procure them from Spanish and Indian villages along the route. However, they found little or no food at the few settlements they passed on the tedious seven day voyage up the river to Venta Cruz. Weakened by hunger and dysentery and dropping from fever, the buccaneers were in poor condition for the next stage of Morgan's plan—the grueling march through the jungle. But march they did, their progress impeded by Spanish ambushes. Again they found no food and crazed by hunger some men resorted to eating their shoes and leather bags. They prepared these morsels by first cutting them into bite size pieces, then beating and boiling them. After more than a week of pushing through the hostile jungle, the famished treasure hunters sighted Panama City from a hilltop. In the distant bay they spied the billowing sails of a great galleon headed toward the open sea. Later, to their great sorrow, they learned it was on its way to safety with nearly five million pieces of eight. Another ship also carried away gold, plate and jewels.

On the outskirts of the city the buccaneers found herds of cattle. They halted their march to slaughter and roast some of them and then lay down to sleep. In the morning as they prepared to march on the city, 2,100 Spanish infantrymen and 600 cavalry troops appeared in battle formation on the plain in front of the city. Outnumbered but undaunted, Morgan didn't hesitate. He ordered an advance judging that the rising sun shining in enemy eyes would offset their great advantage.

The entire Spanish cavalry charged the buccaneers who held their ground and repelled the charge with deadly accurate volleys of musket fire. The Spanish infantry massed for another advance. At the same time they had Indians stampede two thousand head of cattle at Morgan's rear guard. The maneuver might have worked but again buccaneer fire effectively dispersed the charge. The Spanish infantrymen, now within range of the buccaneers' fire, lost their impetus. Most of them fired once, then flung their heavy, cumbersome muskets to the ground and ran for the city, where fresh troops waited to defend the barricaded streets.

The President of Panama could have staged an effective defense but chose instead to destroy his city, rather than have it fall into the hands of the buccaneers. The principal buildings were set on fire. The fort was blown up in such haste that forty soldiers inside went with it. The populace escaped to the woods according to standard procedure so that Morgan and his men met little resistance as they came through the city gates. By the time they extinguished the holocaust, three quarters of the city had been leveled, including the majority of the more than two hundred richly stocked warehouses and the homes of the wealthiest citizens. When Morgan learned that the galleon they had seen departing had made off with the bulk of the city's treasure he sent boats in pursuit but they failed to catch up with it.

Throughout their ordeal the buccaneers had been sustained by visions of the riches that were going to fall into their hands when they took the town. When they failed to find the coffers overflowing with gold, pearls and gems, the bullion and coin they had dreamed of, they were bitterly disappointed. They spent a month entrenched in the ruins, sending out parties to hunt down Spaniards whom they tortured to find out where valuables had been cached. Ironically, the buccaneers overlooked the greatest treasure of all which was right in their midst. They had been outfoxed by a resourceful friar who, as soon as he heard of the buccaneer's approach, hastily slapped a coat of whitewash on the great golden altar of Panama's Cathedral.

The booty, although less than hoped for, was substantial. Most of it came from ransom of prisoners. It included 750,000 pieces of eight, some gold doubloons, silver bars, gold ingots, pearls, jewelry, silks and spices. Morgan had it loaded on 175 mules and carried across the Isthmus, where it was divided up. Dissension had broken out in the buccaneer ranks during the expedition. There was constant friction between the predominantly Catholic French group and the Protestant English. It was aggravated when Morgan insisted that the French, like the English, although it was not their custom, be searched to ensure there was no holding back of booty. While in Panama, a separatist faction had secretly provisioned a ship to be used on an independent plundering cruise in the South Seas. When Morgan got wind of the plot he scuttled the ship.

When the treasure haul was divided up at Chagres River, rebellion flared into mutiny. Morgan, the mutineers claimed, had kept the lion's share of the spoil and the best jewels for himself. The two hundred pieces of eight each man received seemed far too little reward for the privation and suffering they had endured. Morgan refused to listen to complaints. He ordered the destruction of the Chagres fort when the Portobelo authorities refused to pay ransom. While the general burning and destruction of the fort and surrounding buildings was being carried out, Morgan lifted anchor and sailed off, leaving his buccaneer force without a word of good-by. Legend has it that he buried a king's ransom in treasure somewhere on the way back to Port Royal. Today there is scarcely an island in the Caribbean which doesn't claim to be the very one on which the terrible Captain Morgan hid his treasure. Esquemelin was one of those left on the shore in Panama. Faced with a lack of provisions the remaining buccaneers split up and went their various ways. Esquemelin's ship cruised for plunder along the coasts of Costa Rica and Cuba before returning to Jamaica.

By the Treaty of Madrid, signed in 1670, Spain recognized England's holdings in the Caribbean and the two countries were at peace. Considering the Treaty was already in effect, Morgan's welcome home ought to have been restrained. Jubilation reigned nonetheless and the Colonial Council of Jamaica even issued the buccaneer a vote of thanks. When word reached Spain the king was livid. He threatened to declare war on England if the pirates who destroyed Panama were not punished. Charles II was anxious to preserve the peace and sent former Governor Sir Thomas Lynch to Jamaica to replace Governor Modyford who had countenanced Morgan's venture, and ordered both men to be transported to England in chains.

Morgan had a talent for turning disaster into triumph. He avoided both a trial and prison. Upon his arrival he was lionized by the English public and cosseted by the King. The less fortunate Modyford was held in the Tower until 1674, when tensions with Spain had eased. Morgan was knighted and returned to Jamaica as Lieutenant-Governor under newly appointed Governor Vaughn. Vaughn replaced Lynch, whose stern measures against the buccaneers had made him extremely unpopular.

As governor, Sir Thomas Lynch was committed to building the base of Jamaica's prosperity on agriculture rather than plunder. The trial of Peter Johnson is an example of the lengths he sometimes went to in his aggressive prosecution of buccaneers. Johnson had sailed from Port Royal when Spain and England were already at peace and both nations agreed

to revoke all commissions and cease countenancing pillaging. He set out
with ten men and a seized Spanish ship, whose crew of twelve he killed.
Before long he led a band of a hundred men. They captured a Spanish
galleon from the Canaries near Cuba and murdered the crew.

When Johnson, who had amassed some 30,000 pounds worth of plunder, learned the governor had sent naval frigates after him he returned to
Port Royal sure he could strike a bargain with the authorities. Lynch had
him brought to trial for piracy before a commission presided over by
Colonel Modyford, the son of the former governor. Lynch instructed the
commission not to acquit Johnson. Despite the confessions of Johnson
and two of his cohorts which were "enough to hang one hundred honester
persons," he was found not guilty and within an hour was celebrating in
a grog shop with the commssion members. Lynch was infuriated. He had
Johnson arrested again and sat as judge in a trial convened in the governor's council room, coercing the jury into a verdict of guilty of piracy.
While there is no doubt Johnson was a pirate his execution was lamented
by many at Port Royal "as if he had been as pious and innocent as one of
the primitive martyrs."

In spite of harsh measures, an estimated four thousand buccaneers were
still operating out of Port Royal at the time of Sir Henry Morgan's appointment. England had begun to awaken to the fact that Adam's will
was no longer valid and that France posed more of a threat to her New
World ambitions than Spain. Buccaneering could no longer be tolerated
and Charles expected Morgan to persuade his former comrades to change
their ways. Existing commissions were called in and no further commissions were issued. Recently rewarded activities became outlaw piracy pun-
ishable by death. Morgan was empowered to hunt down and hang the
very men whom he had led.

The campaign signaled the end of large scale buccaneering but Port
Royal continued to prosper, profiting from the volume of contraband
trade with the Spanish colonies and the sale of slaves. Morgan did persuade some buccaneers to take up the agricultural life. A larger number
of men joined the rugged logwood cutters in the forests of Honduras and
Yucatán where they had to fight off frequent raids by Spanish pirates who
continued to be active along the Main.

Some of the pirates who preyed on the English were English themselves.
A mysterious and much dreaded character of uncertain nationality called
Captain Yellowes or Yallahs, was supported by the Spanish. An Englishman named Captain Bear, who had once held a commission from the
Governor of the Leeward Islands continued his piratical career, moving
to Havana with his mistress, whom he introduced as the daughter of a
great English nobleman. The people of Havana were delighted to welcome

this pair and the leaders of colonial society attended the wedding of the pirate and his "noble" lady. There were others too who formerly held English commissions and turned pirate, preying on English ships. Philip Fitzgerald, an Irish Catholic, was one who operated out of Havana with a Spanish warship. Armed with twelve cannon and a commission from the Spanish Governor of Campeche, Fitzgerald set on English vessels plying between Jamaica and the Windward Islands, Virginia or London. Once, Fitzgerald came into Havana Harbor with five captive Englishmen tied to the yardarms, and as he approached the fort he ordered his victims swung off with nooses around their necks as he and his scurvy crew shot at the twitching bodies. His sadistic treatment and slaughter of English mariners prompted protests to the Spanish authorities who made little effort to bridle the pirate and others like him.

The Spanish authorities refused to halt such outrages because they still attributed every attack on their ships and settlements to the English, even though the buccaneers had been publicly disavowed. Pirates continued to plague the seas from scattered bases throughout the Caribbean and some of them were, in fact, former English denizens of Port Royal.

One of the first episodes of the new brand of piracy had its beginning in 1682 in Jamaica when a merchant ship flying the colors of Louis XIV dropped anchor at Port Royal. Pierre Le Pain, the captain of *La Trompeuse* told Sir Henry Morgan that he came from Cayenne in Guiana and was a Protestant seeking asylum. He was granted permission to settle and his cargo was allowed in duty free. He chartered the ship to two Jamaican traders who dispatched it to collect logwood in Honduras and then sail for Hamburg where it was to be turned over to a French agent.

The Jamaica Council discovered to its chagrin that their refugee had stolen the ship and cargo in Cayenne. The King of England, responding to pressure from the French ambassador ordered Le Pain (or Paine) arrested and shipped to France. Getting *La Trompeuse* back to its rightful owners wasn't so easy. On the way to Honduras the ship had been seized by a French pirate named Jean Hamlin and his crew of 120 particularly barbarous ruffians who used it to capture some twenty Jamaican prizes in a couple of months. Governor Lynch sent a frigate after *La Trompeuse* in October on a fruitless two-month hunt in the waters around Hispaniola and Puerto Rico. Another frigate was sent out in December when word arrived that the pirates were careening the ship at Isle la Vache, but by the time it arrived the pirates were long gone.

The same frigate, the *Guernsey* was ordered to stand off Hispaniola until Hamlin who was a veteran of many pirate campaigns in West Africa as well as the West Indies was captured. Coxon, the former buccaneer, was used as a go between for the Council, which was greatly embarrassed by the whole incident, to ask a privateer named Yankey to hunt *La Trom-peuse* for £200 prize money. The pirates inflicted such real and psychological damage on Jamaican shipping that the Council was desperate. They offered Yankey all the provisions, arms and men he would need as well as a pardon for his past crimes. Coxon was promised £200 to accompany him.

Meanwhile Hamlin was hanging out at Danish St. Thomas near Puerto Rico which had an excellent harbor and commanded the Anegada Passage, one of the principal routes between the Caribbean and the Atlantic. He took a number of ships and then sailed across to Sierra Leone where, in a matter of weeks he took seventeen prizes. Camouflaged as an English merchant ship *La Trompeuse* which carried thirty-two cannon, lured one Dutch and English ship after another into her trap amassing great amounts of gold dust and "black gold" or slaves. As often happened there was a falling-out among the crew over the spoils and one group split off to go on its own under an English captain named Morgan. Hamlin sailed back to the Caribbean. Forty of his crew deserted at Dominica so that by the time he anchored in St. Thomas harbor he had only sixteen white and twenty-two black pirates aboard.

The population of the island was a mere 350 people, mostly English flotsam including escaped servants, debtors and deserting seamen. The governor, Adolf Esmit, was an arch pirate-protector who had ousted his brother Nicholas and proceeded to turn the island into a depot for pirate prizes. The governor not only supplied outlaws of all nations with provisions and arms but also refused to hand over to their rightful owners the ships and prisoners brought into St. Thomas. Governor Stapleton of the Leeward islands ordered Captain Carlile of H.M.S. *Francis* to do whatever was necessary to put an end to *La Trompeuse's* depredations. Finding her at anchor, Carlile's men boarded in the night. They set off explosive charges burning the ship and ending a year-long pirate odyssey. Hamlin and his crew managed to escape. Governor Esmit protested the British action and aided Hamlin and the other pirates to escape to Hispaniola. Less than a year later Hamlin was raiding along the Main in a thirty-six gun frigate he named *Trompeuse* with over a hundred pirates including sixty of his former crew.

Morgan hadn't converted all the buccaneers by any means although he moved against those he caught with vigor, destroying their ships, bringing them to trial and once he even sent some English pirates to Cartagena for trial. These moves hardly endeared him to his former mates. "I have put to death, imprisoned and transported to the Spaniard for execution all English and Spanish pirates I could get" he boasted. Yet, his detractors, including the Governor, Lord Vaughn, who had little love for the buccaneer turned knight, complained that at the same time he was secretly operating a private employment agency for former Port Royal buccaneers, collecting ten percent of the prizes taken under these clandestine commissions.

The fastidious Vaughn had a violent temper and a noble's distaste for the rough-edged lieutenant-governor. He and Morgan clashed repeatedly. Vaughn brought Morgan before the Council on various charges which Sir Henry's popularity repeatedly overcame. The old sea rover, allegiance torn, spent more and more time in Port Royal's taverns and in 1683 Vaughn succeeded in having him suspended from office for disloyalty and drunken disorder. In 1688 Sir Hans Sloane, whose West Indian journals form the foundation of the British Museum library, was a young physician at Port Royal. He examined the debauched Morgan describing him as "lean, sallow colored, his eyes a little yellowish and belly jutting out or prominent."

Morgan rejected Sloane's prescription of various purges and diuretics including scorpion oil in favor of treatment by a black obeah man who gave him "clysters of urine, and plastered him all over with clay and water, and by it augmented his cough." He died soon after and was buried in the churchyard at Port Royal. On June 7, 1692 the earth quaked and the sea rushed in claiming the most dazzling buccaneer of them all and the city to which he brought immortal fame.

A contemporary verse mourned the passing of the man and the era:

> You was a flyer, Morgan,
> You was the lad to crowd
> When you was in your flagship,
> But now you're in your shroud.

NOTES

1. Francis Hansen re: Port Royal, Edwards, Bryan, *The History, Civil and Commercial of the British Colonies in the West Indies*, London, 1793, p.216.

2. Letter from Sir Thomas Modyford, Calendar of State Papers, Colonial Series, America and the West Indies, 1661–68.

3. Council of Jamaica meeting minutes, Calendar Series of State Papers, Colonial Series, America and the West Indies, 1661–68.

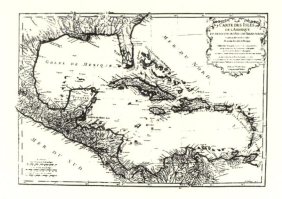

6

To the South Seas

In the sunset days of the buccaneer era, when Spanish shipping had been reduced to formidably chaperoned flotas, and opportunities for Caribbean land raids were curtailed by a flip-flop in government policies, many buccaneers were lured to the Pacific. They prowled the Pacific coasts of Central and South America sailing what were called the South Seas. They endured isolation and hardships unknown in the familiar, tropical Caribbean. "That which often spurs men on to the undertaking of the most difficult adventure is the sacred hunger of gold," explained one who accompanied Bartholomew Sharp to Panama in 1680. "Twas gold was the bait that tempted a pack of merry boys of us, near 300, being soldiers of fortune."

In particular the accounts of Drake's capture of the *Cacafuego* off Ecuador more than a century before and Cavendish's million dollar haul from the *Santa Ana* in 1587 spurred the Pacific adventurers with visions of American gold, silver, emeralds and pearls and Asian treasures of ivory, gold, jewelry, gems, sandalwood, silks, satins, perfumes and spices. They had heard the streets of Pacific towns were literally paved with gold. They went, too, because pickings were slim in their old cruising grounds and because the South Seas coast was relatively undisturbed and poorly protected.

The "merry boys" who slogged across the rain-sodden Isthmus of Panama or battled their way around Cape Horn through the punishing Strait of Magellan to plunder the remote reaches of the Spanish Empire met with mixed success. Their expeditions, approximately twenty-five of them between 1675 and 1742, were frequently marred by poor organization and dissension which was intensified by the vast distances and great obstacles they had to cope with. Some expeditions came back empty-handed, some never made it back. Others plundered cities and towns or seized prizes ranging from modest merchantmen to galleons from the Spanish treasure fleet crammed with silver. The total take, however, never equaled the magnitude of Drake's and Cavendish's nor of the booty stolen from the Spanish Indies.

Perhaps the greatest treasures from this last spark of buccaneering were the journals written by adventurers who produced some of the very best travel writing ever. Not surprisingly, the majority of the buccaneer authors were surgeons, generally the most literate of the Brethren of the Coast, many of whom couldn't even sign their own names. Surgeons, along with navigators, gunners, sailing masters, and carpenters were collectively known as "sea artists," and received a larger share of booty than ordinary buccaneers.

Copious volumes of these buccaneer accounts were devoured by the late seventeenth-century public in Europe. The best known French account was written by Sieur Ravenneau de Lussan, another in the line of ruined noblemen who raided Spanish America to repair their fortunes. "It is no very uncommon thing," wrote de Lussan whose inheritance had evaporated at the dice box, "for a child, that is a native of Paris, to go and seek his fortune abroad, and to entertain a fixed design of becoming a man engaged in hazardous adventure." His *Journal du Voyage fait à la Mer du Sud avec les Filibustiers en 1684,* recounts the saga of a year-long odyssey which took him with a peripatetic band of international maurauders across the Isthmus to Granada on the Pacific side of Nicaragua, and back across to Nicaragua battling Spanish ambushes and hostile Indians all the way until they reached the Caribbean and were rescued by an English ship.

De Lussan and the remnant with him were let off at Petit-Goâve, overjoyed to hear French spoken again, only half-believing they had survived the elements, savage Spaniards and Indians, jungle rot, starvation, and plagues like the "bloody flux" which claimed so many of their number. "I had so little hopes of ever returning, that I could not, for the space of fifteen days, take my return for anything other than an illusion, and it proceeded so far with me, that I shunned sleep for fear when I awakened I should find myself again in those countries out of which I was now safely delivered."

Even more fascinating are accounts by English buccaneers whose keen observations of the world and its peoples contributed greatly to the study of New World anthropology, geography, zoology and oceanography. Foremost among these were William Dampier and Lionel Wafer. Dampier made three voyages around the world studying flora, fauna, winds and currents. His published journals furnished Jonathan Swift with much of the background material for *Gulliver's Travels* and the character of Captain Pocock, whom Gulliver meets on his last voyage to the land of the Houyhnhnms, is based on the moody Dampier himself. Wafer, a buccaneer surgeon, published the story of his 1681 sojourn among the Cuna Indians in Panama's Darien region. He lived among the gentle Indians as one of them. Arrayed only in vegetable-dye body designs, a gold lip plate and a silver penis holder, he made notations of their language and culture which have proved extremely valuable to modern anthropologists.

Leaving the buccaneer life behind, Dampier and Wafer became the darlings of the newly formed Royal Society and were received in the best London society. Their works along with those of Basil Ringrose, a runaway apprentice, and Captain Bartholomew Sharp, on whose 1680 expedition the other three had been, were among the first in the British Museum's library. Dampier even achieved the signal honor of having his portrait hung in the National Gallery. Under it is the label "Pirate and Hydrographer."

The famed Manila galleons which drew the sea rovers to the Pacific were inaugurated in 1565 in Spain's effort to reap part of the rich Asian harvest which Portugal had monopolized. The first Manila galleon, carrying a modest cargo of cinnamon, was dispatched by Miguel Lopez de Legaspi who had taken four hundred men from Mexico across the Pacific to colonize the Philippine Islands for Spain. From 1565 to 1815 these huge galleons, at times carrying as much as two million pieces of eight each on the west bound leg, made the long, perilous voyage to Acapulco and back. The galleons and the Pacific coastal settlements basked in tranquillity until John Oxenham appeared in 1575 and seized two unarmed ships of the plate fleet conveying gold and silver bullion and bars to Panama from Peru. That time the Spaniards made good their loss when the English sea dogs were captured as they tried to carry the treasure back across the Isthmus.

The Spanish weren't too alarmed until Drake and Cavendish began nipping at their heels. Dutch raiders followed the English into the Pacific, mounting seven expeditions between 1599 and 1643 to capture treasure galleons, ravage coastal settlements, and carve out a pirate base in Chile. The most significant outcome of these efforts was the stimulus they gave the Spanish Crown to finally heed colonial pleas for the fortification of Acapulco.

There was a lull in Pacific plundering during the heyday of Caribbean buccaneering. Then in 1673, two years after Morgan's sack of Panama, a buccaneer named Thomas Peche sailed round Cape Horn and cruised north. He reportedly took his men as far as the Aleutians, but there is scant information about the expedition. A couple of years later Spanish documents begin to complain of English predators hovering off the Chilean coast. The complaints became howls of anger when Bartholomew Sharp led a buccaneer band across the Isthmus in 1680 launching a plague of piracy.

Sharp's exploit is the first described in detail and was the earliest large-scale venture to the seas around South America. In 1679 Sharp raided towns along the Gulf of Honduras along with John Coxon, who held a questionable commission granted by Captain-General Robert Clarke, the compliant Governor of the Bahamas, who turned the islands into "a nest of robbers" in the words of Jamaica's Governor Lynch. Sharp and his men took their booty consisting of five hundred chests of indigo, (a thousand according to Spanish documents), cocoa, tortoiseshell, bullion and coins to Port Royal where they were at first refused entrance. When they threatened to take their precious cargoes to Rhode Island, a new pirate refuge and contraband center, they were permitted to land and pay customs duties. Jamaica's planters and merchants loudly protested the governor's treatment of the buccaneers as legitimate traders because the surfeit of indigo they dumped on the market temporarily lowered prices and depressed production. In fact, for a brief time the contraband indigo actually replaced native indigo and sugar as a medium of exchange.

The enterprising freebooters didn't stay long in port, however. A few months later, in December, Sharp and Coxon joined forces with four other buccaneer captains, Maggott, Allison, Row, and Essex in an even more ambitious venture. They sailed from Port Morant with Governor Carlisle's permission, despite the fact that these men were all notorious buccaneers. Their declared intention of heading for the coast of Panama to cut logwood was an obvious sham. The piratical fleet strengthened by the addition of Captain Cooke, an English seaman and Captain Lessone, a French buccaneer, headed straight for Portobelo.

The master plan called for a landing near Portobelo, the capture of the Spanish settlement there, a march across the Isthmus and then a surprise attack on Panama City, the crossroad of two continents. But they had an ambitious ulterior motive. The buccaneer force expected to capture enough ships in the port of Panama to form a South Seas Buccaneer Navy and launch a brilliant era of plundering along the coasts and attacking Pacific shipping.

The vision of Manila galleons, ablaze with treasures crammed in the hold and piled high on the decks, shimmered before them as they slogged sixty miles through rough country toward Portobelo from their anchorage. For three days they had no food and many of the men had their "feet cut with rocks for want of shoes," but on the fourth day spirits soared as the church spires of Portobelo appeared ahead of them. Once again, the Spanish were caught with their guard down. The town was taken, sacked and abandoned in haste since the buccaneers feared the arrival of reinforcements. Each looter received a measly share of one hundred pieces of eight; disappointing but not depressing since greater prizes lay ahead.

The buccaneers marched back to their ships and sailed north to Boca del Toro, where they careened their ships, caught turtles and bartered with friendly Indians for other provisions. Basil Ringrose described the Indians in his account mentioning the half moon plates of gold or silver the men wore in their noses, which "when they drink they hold up with one hand, while they lift the cup with the other." He also made one of the earliest observations of albinos among native Americans, writing of women "fairer than the fairest in Europe, with hair like the finest flax." He noted that they were said to see far better in the dark than in daylight.

Captain Sawkins and Captain Harris joined the buccaneers as they began their trek across the Isthmus with a contingent of Indian guides. Two captains and a number of men were left to guard the buccaneer fleet and the 331 who were to march each received several "doughboys" or large loaves of bread and orders to drink from the rivers. Each buccaneer was armed with "fuzee (rifle), pistol and hanger (sword)" and they marched in military formation, each company falling in behind its captain and standard. The first of the seven was led by Captain Sharp whose flag was red with white and green streamers.

The Indians had told them of a town called Santa Maria, inland on a river which emptied into the Pacific at the Gulf of San Miguel. It was, according to their informants, a place where gold gathered in the surrounding mountains was stored by the Spaniards for transport to Panama. Along the way there they cracked open river rocks and found the sparkle of gold. At Santa Maria they found abundant provisions and some river boats but very little of the gold they were so hungry for. They cursed the luck that made them miss three hundred pounds of refined gold which had been shipped down to Panama three days before they arrived. They earned the gratitude of the Indian king of Darien by freeing his pregnant daughter who had been abducted and raped by a Spanish soldier.

The buccaneers elected Coxon as their chief and pressed on for Panama in thirty-six captured boats and rowed or sailed to the Pacific, guided by the Spaniard who had dishonored the Darien princess who offered to lead the pirates to the very bedchamber of the governor of Panama.

Panama turned out to be farther than the adventurers had imagined, and the way was paved with mishaps. Torrential rains turned the river into a violent adversary, booby trapped with logs and shoals. Ringrose wrecked, was captured, and escaped slaughter when the soldier from Santa María who had been in his canoe when it wrecked told his countrymen how kind the English pirates had been in saving him from the wrath of the Indians. Ringrose caught up with the rest of the buccaneers and eventually they came within sight of the city. They spied eight ships riding at anchor off the little island of Períco near Panama. Five were great treasure galleons from Peru and the others were *Barcos de la Armadilla*, guard ships.

Unfortunately for the buccaneers, the element of surprise was lost. The Spaniards, hearing of the buccaneer march, had concentrated their entire force of 228 men on the convoy ships, leaving the galleons unmanned. The three warships made straight for the buccaneer fleet of puny canoes and two larger but sluggish hollowed-out craft which they had seized a couple of days earlier. The odds were all with the Spanish, for not only did they have superior ships and arms, but the majority of the buccaneers were missing, having gone in search of fresh water. Yet once again the amazing fearlessness and drive, characteristic of sea rovers down through the ages, spurred the buccaneers on to victory in a gory battle. They took the warships, slaying two thirds of the Spanish, black, and mestizo crews. "Their blood ran down the decks in whole streams, and scarce one place in the ship was found that was free from blood," wrote Ringrose of the warship on which seventy-seven blacks had fought under the command of Don Francisco de Peralta, an old Spaniard from Andalusia. Next, the buccaneers boarded the empty galleons, making the largest one, the *Santissima Trinidad*, their flagship.

The buccaneers were at their best in battle and were undaunted by overwhelming enemy forces, however, they were often undone by internal bickering. There was quibbling over the division of labor and the sharing of booty. Within a few days of the battle Captain Coxon, who had been called a coward by some, left with his men and returned to the Caribbean the way they had come. He was an envious, bad-tempered man who had crossed swords with several of the other buccaneer leaders and no one was sorry to see him leave. A warrant for the arrest of Coxon, Sharp and the others who had sacked Portobelo had been issued in Jamaica by Lord Carlisle, who was no doubt embarrassed by what the "logwood cutting" expedition he sanctioned had turned into. Three of Coxon's men were apprehended and imprisoned. But Coxon had such influential friends on the council that when he returned to Port Royal, after pirating a bit around the San Blas Islands of Panama, he wasn't punished but instead sent by the council to hunt a troublesome French pirate named Jean Hamlin.

The buccaneers who remained behind elected the young and popular Sawkins as their leader. They cruised along Panama's Pacific coast, taking a number of ships including one laden with 2,000 jars of wine, 50 jars of gunpowder and 51,000 pieces of eight being sent from Trujillo to pay the garrison at Panama. They took merchant ships, too, selling the Africans they found aboard to Spanish merchants, ever willing to deal in contraband. Those prisoners they thought of no value were put on captured ships whose masts and sails had been destroyed and set adrift.

The buccaneers made their base for awhile on the island of Taboga off Panama. When the Governor of Panama sent a message inquiring why they had come to his part of the world, Sawkins answered "we came to assist the King of Darien, who was the true Lord of Panama and all the country thereabouts." If the governor would send fifty pieces of eight for each buccaneer, a thousand for each commander and desist from annoying the Indians, allowing them the power and freedom that were their due, then the English would be happy to leave. Otherwise, warned Sawkins, they would stay and inflict all the damage they could. To a query from the governor as to whose commission they carried, the brash buccaneer replied that "we would come and visit him at Panama and bring our commissions on the muzzles of our guns, at which time he should read them as plain as the flame of gunpowder could make them."

All this blustering came to little, for provisions ran so low that Sawkins was forced by his men to sail on even though leaving Taboga meant forfeiting the capture of a ship carrying 100,000 pieces of eight which was due into Panama momentarily from Peru. On the way to the pearl fishery island of Cayboa, which today is the penal colony known as Coiba, the buccaneers attacked the town of Pueblo Nuevo. For once the Spanish were defensively prepared and Sawkins, "a man as valiant and courageous as any could be, and likewise next to Captain Sharp, the best beloved . . . " was killed as he ran up a breastwork thrown up before the town.

Bartholomew Sharp was chosen as his replacement to lead the band to Ecuador for an attack on Guayaquil where an informant had reported they "might lay down our silver and lode our vessels with gold." They changed their objective to Arica on the Chilean coast when they were told that it was the collecting point for inland silver on its way to Panama and that they could each expect two thousand pounds worth of treasure out of the enterprise. They sailed down toward Chile, taking occasional ships that fell into their hands, although the entire Pacific coast was forewarned and shipping was drastically reduced. It was a long voyage, relieved by amusing anecdotes related by none other than Captain Peralta, the old Andalusian whom they had taken prisoner in the battle with the *Barcos de la Armadilla*. He and other prisoners of note sailed on the *Santissima Trinidad* and were treated with kindness by the buccaneers.

More frustration awaited them at Aríca where they found the beach lined with a phalanx of armed Spanish soldiers. Avoiding confrontation, they sailed further south and attacked the town of La Serena where they found little booty. The inhabitants had received warning and taken to the hills with their valuables, so there was little for the thwarted pirates to do but burn the place down. In the following months the pirate band encountered one frustration after another as they harried the Pacific coast. Sometimes ransoms were agreed upon and then ignored by the townspeople who preferred to stay in hiding until the pirates sailed away.

At La Serena a ransom of 95,000 pieces of eight had been agreed upon in exchange for not firing the town. The Spanish, however, delayed in producing the amount and the town was consequently burned. The buccaneers took what plunder they had back to their ships in the bay where they learned from those left aboard that they had very nearly lost their flagship. During the night a Spaniard, using an inflated horsehide float had swum out to the *Santissima Trinidad* and stuffed oakum and brimstone between the rudder and the stem-post and set the combustible matter afire. The blaze was discovered just in time to save the ship.

The rigors of the long cruise down the near-deserted coast and the isolation they felt in an unfamiliar world took its toll on the buccaneers. They encountered fewer ships than anticipated, missing valuable prizes when cargoes were unloaded at unknown locations along the unfamiliar coast. Rations were chronically short, and water was often scarce. Their small ships were pest-infested and stinking. Hopes dimmed as their numbers dwindled due to battle casualties and disease. The "merry boys" who had set out with such high hopes divided into two squabbling factions. Those buccaneers who had lost all their booty at dice and cards wanted to carry on with their piratical cruise in hopes of taking a Manila galleon or a plate ship. On the other hand, those who had hung onto their shares or who were sick of the lonely Pacific, urged Sharp to sail around the tip of South America and back to the Caribbean.

The gamblers succeeded in ousting Sharp, who was a skilled "sea artist" but an indifferent leader, and elected as their commander a crusty old sea rover named John Watling, who combined a piratical career with religious fervor. He recommended another try on Arica. During the shore attack Watling was one of the many killed while others were wounded and barely managed to get aboard without being taken prisoner. Three of the expedition's surgeons were taken by the Spanish because they were too drunk to escape, having sat out the battle with bottles of brandy. Captain Sharp, who had been deposed, was restored to command with the understanding that they would all head home. Some chose to go their own way but the *Santissima Trinidad* was prepared for the passage around Cape Horn by having her top deck removed, the rigging and sails repaired, and the masts and bowsprit lowered. Of the 301 who had crossed the Isthmus, 73 sailed with Sharp.

On the way south they gave chase to a ship which turned out to be the *San Pedro* which they had seized and then released the year before. This time they pillaged 21,000 pieces of eight in eight oak chests, 16,000 more in canvas sacks, and some bullion. About a week later they encountered a large merchantman. The first buccaneer volley killed the captain, and the ship, which they had feared was a warship sent after them, surrendered meekly. Her name was the *Santo Rosario* and she carried "much plate, and some money ready coined, besides 620 jars of wine and brandy, and other things." The "other things" included what appeared to be hundreds of bars of tin lying in the hold. Sharp ordered them heaved overboard thus losing the greatest treasure of all. For they were not tin but pure silver as one crew member who had kept one to cast into bullets discovered when he gave it to a metalsmith back in England. For the time being the buccaneers were delighted with the haul, "being very merry all the while with the wine and brandy" and it seems Captain Sharp was quite taken with a woman prisoner whom Ringrose called "the most beautiful woman that I ever saw in all the South Sea."

The woman and other Spanish prisoners were left aboard their ship, one mast of which was sawed off to ensure that it would not reach port too soon and give alarm. The buccaneers headed for the horn, eager to reach home and much cheered by their recent luck. The passage was a terrible one, fraught with howling snow storms, hunger, disease and other hardships. Finally, at the end of January 1682 their two-year epic cruise ended when they were given permission to land at Nevis, having been refused at Antigua and discouraged at Barbados by the presence of a British frigate on the lookout for privateers.

One man had kept a little dog he had taken from a Spanish ship as a pet and auctioned him off before the mast for forty-eight pieces of silver two days before Barbados was sighted. Captain Sharp bought the dog, "with intention to eat him, in case we did not see land very soon." The proceeds went into a fund for a last drinking bout once they were safe in port. After the farewell party, the buccaneer band which had gone through so much together broke up. Four of the buccaneers who went to Jamaica were tried for piracy. One turned state's evidence and was given immunity. Two plead not guilty and were acquitted for lack of evidence. The other, much to his regret, plead guilty and was promptly hanged. Sharp and several others were put on trial in England at the insistence of the Spanish ambassador. It proved so difficult to support the Spanish charges of piracy in the far off South Seas that they all escaped conviction. The determining factor in Sharp's acquittal was, in his own words, "a Spanish manuscript of prodigious value . . . it describes all the ports, roads, harbors, bays, sands, rocks, and rising of the land, and instructions how to work a ship into any port or harbor." This remarkable item was a collection of Spanish charts of the Pacific coasts of the New World taken from the *Rosario*.

Sharp, in his journal, noted that the Spaniards attempted to throw it overboard and cried aloud when he got hold of it. The magnificent set of maps and instructions, elaborately embellished, was indeed a treasure for it gave the English access to the most closely guarded information. Charles II showed his gratitude by appointing the veteran buccaneer to command of a warship with a commission to "apprehend Indians and Pyrates" in the Caribbean. Sharp led a charmed life. He was twice more tried for piracy and acquitted in the Vice-Admiralty Court. He was indicted at Nevis for plundering a Spanish ship off Campeche and capturing twenty Spaniards and Mayan Indians whom he sold into slavery in Bermuda. The following year Sharp faced charges of seizing the *Josiah*, a New England vessel and beat the charges with the connivance of the corrupt Governor of Nevis who cursed the witnesses for the prosecution, declaring that "the evidence of a pack of dogs should not take away the life of an Englishman." He continued his outrageous career from Anguilla, a flat, sandy island off St. Martin, where he set himself up as "Governor," selling bogus commissions and lighting his clay pipe with warrants for his arrest.

Basil Ringrose was less fortunate. After publishing his book in 1683 he returned to sea with Captain Swan on the *Cygnet* which sailed from England around Cape Horn to cash in on clandestine trade with Spanish settlements. At Plate Island, named for the division of Drake's spoil made there, Ringrose joined Captain Edward Davis, a well-known buccaneer commander who had once commanded a fleet of ten ships and more than a thousand men. They sailed north landing on the Mexican coast. Ringrose was among one hundred buccaneers who attacked the town of Santiago. They made off with a good haul but were ambushed on the way back to their ship, and Ringrose was among those killed.

Lionel Wafer also sailed with Captain Davis. The buccaneer surgeon had been among those, including Dampier, who had wearied of Pacific plundering and had turned back across the Isthmus. The crossing, undertaken in the rainy season, was a brutal one. The trail was deep mud. Clothing and provisions rotted and gunpowder became sodden. Wafer was accidentally wounded when gunpowder a buccaneer was attempting to dry out in a silver plate exploded ripping his knee and thigh open. Unable to go on, he stayed for three months with the Cuna Indians, whose initial hostility turned to admiration for his medical skills.

He returned to buccaneering in the South Sea, the Caribbean, and the Atlantic with Captain Davis and his comrade John Hingson. With Captain John Cook they took two French ships, one laden with fine wine and one armed with eighteen cannon. They retreated hastily to Virginia where officials who fancied French wine agreed to let the buccaneers refit the gun ship as a pirate vessel. They sailed out of the Chesapeake in August of 1683, on what was to be a lucrative four and a half year expedition. On his second round of Pacific cruising, Wafer ran across his old mate Dampier who was back to try his luck once more before pressing on with his epic circumnavigation, which combined oceanography and a bit of circumspect pirating. Dampier sailed west toward the amazing adventures and exotic landfalls that furnished the material for his best selling book, leaving Wafer, Davis, and Hingson to stalk Manila galleons and harass the coastal settlements. They amassed so much booty that at one share-out on the buccaneer island base of Juan Fernández each man received an estimated 5,000 pieces of eight. Their prolonged cruise was unusual in that Captain Davis remained in command the entire time and was able to prevent the formation of cliques which usually sundered buccaneer expeditions.

In 1688 the trio returned to the Caribbean to find that the king had just offered clemency to all reformed buccaneers and pirates. Instead of surrendering they sailed to the North American colonies, planning to find a refuge in Virginia. When they found that the coast was patrolled by a cordon of English Navy ships they transferred to a little row boat but were caught by H.M.S. *Quaker*. They swore they were West Indian traders come honestly by the sacks and chests they had in their possession. The men's oaths of innocence were contradicted by a slave belonging to Captain Davis and by the sheer volume of loot in their rowboat. The navy inventory, dry as it is, affords a glimpse into the buccaneers' world. Wafer had "In one bagg, 37 silver plates, two scollops; seaven dishes, silver Lace, some cupps broken. Plate weighing bagg, string and all, 74 lb." and "Three bags of Spanish money marked L. W., containing 1100 dollars or thereabouts. In a chest marked L. W., a peece of cloth and some old things, with old broken plate and some little basons, weighing in all 84 lb." The others had similar shares, including some small sacks of gold coins of all nations and silver bullets. Davis also had some "fowle lynnen" in one of his chests and "two paper books very materiall to ye matter" which were probably his ship's logs.

The buccaneers continued to plead innocence from the Jamestown jail and before the court. Wafer said he and Hingson had been traders dealing with Spanish clients and privateers, which explained the Spanish money and goods. He stated that he had inherited a lot of what he had been found with from a friend. Furthermore he claimed never to have met Captain Davis until they found themselves in the row boat. The slave turned state's evidence relating the whole South Sea saga. Consequently, Wafer, Davis and Hingson changed their plea and confessed that they were indeed former buccaneers but insisted they had surrendered to the Crown and been pardoned. They petitioned the court for the return of their effects, which the listed as being even greater than accounted for by the navy.

They were imprisoned for three years while their case turned into a bitter wrangle between the navy and the colonial court which resented the arrogance of the naval lawyers. The key naval witness against them drowned, and by a further stroke of luck the Spanish ambassador who had been prodding the case also died. In 1690 the men were permitted to return to England. A year later the buccaneers were told the case was being dropped much to the consternation of the navy's Admiral Holmes who claimed a share of the prize money for seizing them and thought "the gallows too good a reward" for them. Wafer and Davis brashly petitioned for the return of their booty, and in 1691 the Treasury was ordered to restore it all save £300. William and Mary College at Williamsburg indirectly owes its existence to the buccaneers for this sum was to be "applied to the building of a college in Virginia. . . . "

William Dampier, a farmer's son, had a checkered career. In 1671 he had sailed to the East Indies, and in 1674 he was on the way to Jamaica to manage a plantation. The next year Dampier, aged twenty-three, went to Campeche in Yucatán to cut logwood and soon enlisted as a buccaneer. His restlessness was typical of the men who became sea rovers, but it took him further than most. He had more sense of purpose and more intellectual curiosity than his peers and made the most of every opportunity. In 1691 when he returned to England after sailing around the world, he had with him a tattooed native from Mindanao in the Philippines. Dampier planned to make a fortune by exhibiting "The Painted Prince" whose "Back Parts afford us a lively Representation of one quarter of the World" and whose whole body "is curiously and most exquisitely painted and stain'd full of variety of Invention with prodigious Art and Skill perform'd." But Dampier never profited from his scheme since a shortage of cash forced him to sell his share in the curiosity, whom he had bought with a shipmate. The poor South Seas wretch was exhibited around London and environs until stricken with fatal smallpox at Oxford.

Dampier, for all his brilliance as an observer and recorder, was neither a simpatico character nor a good leader. His bestseller which thrust him into high society also brought him to the attention of the Royal Navy. He seemed to be just the man they were looking for to lead a voyage of exploration to the South Seas and Australia. He was given command of H.M.S. *Roebuck* and set sail with great expectations. But before the ship had lost sight of South America, his crew was near mutiny. The other officers and seamen loathed Dampier who was arrogant, paranoid, and morose. He beat his lieutenant, a regular naval officer, with a cane, had him thrown into jail at the Brazilian port of Bahia and then proceeded onward. The voyage was not a success. Off Ascension he lost the *Roebuck* and when he returned to England the lieutenant who had struggled back from Brazil brought charges against him. He was court-martialed, convicted and ordered to forfeit all his pay.

In spite of this record Dampier was soon given command of another expedition. Two ships sailed for the South Seas on an announced voyage of exploration. In fact, it was to be a privateering cruise with a commission from Prince George of Denmark. Moody and given to strong drink, Dampier again alienated his crew who quarreled with him and among themselves. A clumsy attack on a Manila galleon ended in failure, in fact, the entire cruise was a fiasco. In addition, the quartermaster of the *Cinque Ports,* Alexander Selkirk, had a dispute with Stradling, the captain, and chose to be marooned on the desolate little island of Juan Fernández, occasionally used as a buccaneering base. Selkirk, a stubborn Scot, was put ashore with his personal effects, a musket and a small supply of basic provisions. Ironically, Dampier was the pilot of Captain Woodes Rogers's privateering expedition which rescued Selkirk four years and four months later. Actually, once the wild man was cleaned up, Dampier recognized Selkirk as a former shipmate. They found him, wrote Rogers, "cloth'd in Goat-Skins who look'd wilder than the first Owners of them." Rogers's descriptions of the spectral creature with matted hair, who was at first barely able to talk after his years of solitude, inspired Defoe's *Robinson Crusoe.*

There was no question of Dampier receiving another command after his privateering cruise of 1702–1704. He had gained fame from his voyages but nothing else and was happy in 1708 to sign on as pilot with twenty-nine year old Woodes Rogers who had letters signed by the Lord High Admiral empowering him to attack both French and Spanish vessels. Rogers was excited by the report in a French merchant captain's journal that in the first year of a Franco-Spanish alliance, seventeen French ships had ferried treasure worth more than three million pieces of eight from South American ports to Europe. He persuaded prominent citizens of Bristol, where he lived, to finance a privateering expedition to get a share of all this wealth. The Franco-Spanish alliance alarmed the English. French ships were convoying the Spanish plate fleet so Queen Anne ordered parliament to pass a new privateering act, aimed at disrupting the flow of treasure. As an incentive, the act waived the Crown's claim to a fifth share of everything seized. All treasure was to go to the shipowners and crew, making it a pleasure to be patriotic.

Woodes Rogers's two-year cruise stands out as the best organized and most rewarding of the South Seas expeditions. It had less in common with the half-cocked, discordant exploits of the impulsive buccaneer era which it followed than with Elizabethan ventures. Both Rogers and Drake, for example, were responsible to shareholders of joint-stock companies, were undisputed commanders, and thought of themselves as gentlemen engaged in an honorable pursuit.

The Bristol Company paid the bill for two ships. The *Duke* with Rogers as captain was a private man-o-war of 320 tons. She was 80 feet long and 25 feet wide and carried 30 cannon and a crew of 181. The *Duchess*, a 260 ton vessel carried 26 cannon and 153 men. To avoid the dissension which had ruined many a cruise for plunder, the two ships sailed with a written constitution which called for an officers' committee on each and a joint council for both. The constitution stipulated that major decisions were to be made in consultation with Captain William Dampier, "Pilot for the South Sea."

The two ships sailed on August 2, 1708. Rogers dealt resolutely with problems ranging from frostbite off the wintery horn to murmurs of dissatisfaction among the seamen. The *Duchess's* crew mutinied six weeks out when the ships were at the Canaries, off Africa's northwest coast, preparing for the long trans-Atlantic leg and around South America's horn. Rogers noted in his journal that he had subdued the mutiny by rowing over from the *Duke*, singling out the leader and having him flogged by a fellow mutineer.

After rounding the horn in January 1709, the two ships cruised north along the South American coast for two thousand miles or so. At the beginning of February, they anchored among the uninhabited Juan Fernández islands, some six hundred miles west of what is today Santiago, Chile. It was there that they found Selkirk, the rescued "marooner." Rogers made him sailing master of the *Duke*.

Coasting northward, the expedition took several small Spanish ships and then looted the rich town of Guayaquil, in what is Ecuador today. They collected some £16,000 in gold chains and jewelry from a group of women near the town whose jewelry, much of it hidden in their bodices, was removed as "delicately as possible" as Rogers noted in his journal published as *A Cruising Voyage Round the World*. Rogers also collected 30,000 Spanish dollars ransom for not burning the town.

Months passed. Just before Christmas they were lying off Baja California when a large vessel sailed into view. She was an Acapulco bound galleon, laden with treasure collected in the Philippines. Armed with twenty cannon and twenty swivel guns, she had more than two million Spanish dollars worth of treasure crammed in her hold. The English ships engaged her and a battle raged at close quarters for over an hour. During the fighting Woodes Rogers's upper jaw was shot away. The privateers prevailed and took the ship and her French captain.

The captured crew told the privateers that an even richer Manila galleon, the *Begonia*, a huge vessel of 900 tons with 450 men and armed with 40 cannon and an equal number of swivel guns was not far behind. The privateer officers' council met to discuss attacking her. Rogers, in agony from his wound, voted against an attack but was overruled. In a seven hour battle the much smaller English ships assaulted the massive galleon, hitting her more than five hundred times without causing serious damage. The privateers, however, fared badly. The *Duke* suffered fourteen casualties including Rogers who was wounded a second time when his left heel was smashed. He had his foot bound and then continued to direct his forces with hand signals until he recognized victory was impossible. Twenty crew members of the *Duchess* were killed and her masts and rigging were badly damaged, before the *Begonia* escaped.

The expedition crossed six thousand miles of the Pacific in two months, reaching the island of Guam March 1, 1710. Rogers was a man of exceptional character and continued in command although he was fever-ridden, too weak to stand and in terrible pain. He began to recover after coughing up bits of jawbone which had been caught in his throat. In his daily journal entry for February 14, 1710 he wrote, "in Commemoration of the Antient custom in England of chusing Valentines, I drew up a list of the fair ladies in Bristol, that were any ways related to or concerned in the Ships, and sent for my officers into the Cabbin, where everyone drew, and drank the Lady's Health in a Cup of Punch, and to a happy Sight of 'em all; this I did to put 'em in mind of Home."

From Guam they sailed to Java in the Dutch East Indies where they refitted and sailed for England, joining a Dutch convoy in South Africa and reaching England on the first of October 1711. The expedition had circumnavigated the globe in a little more than three years, returning with what seemed like a considerable treasure worth more than £170,000. However, once the investors and crew had taken their shares, Rogers received about £1,600, hardly enough to compensate him for all he had been through. But, typically he didn't complain and was pleased when his published journal became a bestseller of the day and he was welcomed as a peer by the writers who frequented the London coffeehouses.

The first buccaneering foray into the Pacific stimulated a rash of expeditions, almost all of them poorly organized and ultimately disappointing, although they kept the Spanish and their minions fearful and trembling. In 1684 there were at least a thousand buccaneers swarming about the Isthmus with a principal base on Golden Island in the Gulf of Darien on the Atlantic side. They included small raggle-taggle bands of brawlers and larger bands like that of Captain Peter Harris who had 97 men under him, Captain Townley with 180 English sea rovers, and Captain Groignier who led 280 French and English buccaneers. In 1685 some 900 buccaneers seized Períco Island close to Panama with the help of local Indians. They strengthened the wooden palisades by stuffing the cracks with bags of stolen flour which rain hardened into cement.

While gold, silver, pearls, and other booty did pass through their hands, the rewards were small when measured against the cost. The South Seas adventurers faced freezing blasts from Antarctica, searing jungle heat, leeches, chiggers, reptiles, sea battles, ambushes, festering wounds, fevers, starvation, dehydration and a myriad of other hardships, not the least of them psychological.

The buccaneers who battled the fury of Cape Horn storms or who trudged through the jungles of the Isthmus in their efforts to plunder the Pacific fleets and settlements suffered tremendously. Still, no amount of hardship could temper the overwhelming lure of the gleaming riches they sought. Led by outstanding men like Dampier, de Lussan, Rogers, and Wafer, thousands of these adventurers made their way into the Pacific to live and write the buccaneer history of the New World's Pacific coast.

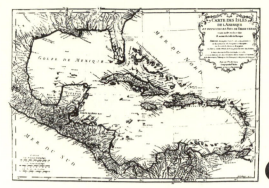

7
Piracy's
Golden Age

𝕿he Golden Age of Piracy, a brief but brilliant era between 1692 and 1725, stands as the classic period in the history of seaborne villainy. Think of pirates and what image is conjured? Most likely one engendered by the art of Howard Pyle or the tales of Robert Louis Stevenson who captured the style and spirit of early eighteenth-century piracy. The classic pirate comes into focus. His scarred hide is tanned mahogany by sun, salt and lack of soap. He swaggers about the deck in a hodge podge of crusted rags and greasy finery stolen at sword point from an international array of victims. A scraggly moustache droops about a sensual mouth. A hoop dangles from one ear, that little bit of gold he'll need to pay the entrance fee to Fiddler's Green, the mariners' paradise. Drunk or sober, his gaze seems fixed on an invisible horizon over which a richly laden prize, canvas billowing, may sail at any moment. From the top of his tricorn hat to the tip of his boots the classic pirate, with his brace of pistols, boarding axe, cutlass and saber, is the quint-essential sea rover who participated in the unparalleled burst of sea rob-bery which erupted after Port Royal, seamy pirate haunt and treasure mart *extraordinaire*, sank beneath the Caribbean.

During wars pirates carried on much as before under the flag of what-ever nation had enlisted their ungovernable talents. In times of uneasy peace they attacked indiscriminately flying the grisly jolly roger (or jack as it was also known), the pirate flag most commonly featuring a skull and crossbones on a black field. More misfits, out of step with their restrictive societies or out of hope, flocked to sign "on the account" than ever before. There were ample opportunities for adventurers of every stripe from those content to rifle West Indian inter-island shipping to the notorious deep water captains like John Every, the "Arch Pirate" who pioneered the great Pirate Round, linking New World ports to the Indian Ocean.

For some forty years pirates girdled the globe. They roamed north to New England and the Middle Atlantic colonies. Once West Indian colonial officials ceased issuing pardons New England became a favored haunt because there pirates received a free pardon. Government authorities and merchants in North Carolina, Virginia, Rhode Island, New Jersey, New York, and Massachusetts welcomed pirate ships and their plunder, choosing to believe their captains who swore they had acquired their cargoes in legitimate trade or by salvaging wrecks. Officials were easy to bribe. Many officials were happy to underwrite or otherwise participate in pirate expeditions which plundered the shipping lanes of the Indian Ocean, the Red Sea, and the Persian Gulf and brought back masses of luxurious merchandise. The pirate vessels, called plate ships for the treasure they carried, brought back so much Arabian gold to the North American colonies that Arabian gold coins called sequins were accepted as currency along the eastern seaboard. So were Spanish gold doubloons and silver pieces of eight which were legal tender in the United States until 1878. The colonists welcomed the pirate fleets too, reveling in the variety of tax-free goods they made available. In Boston an angry crowd tore down the royal proclamation outlawing the buccaneers.

In the Caribbean the dawn of this daredevil age overlapped the sunset of the buccaneer era when hard-bitten buccaneers who spurned rehabilitation were transformed by decree into outlaws. The penal codes didn't recognize degrees of wickedness and desperate men reckoned they might as well hang for a sheep as a lamb. Unlike the buccaneers, however, the pirates of the first quarter of the eighteenth century confined their depredations to the seas except during wartime. There were almost none of the amphibious operations of earlier times, little of the ransoming, sacking and burning of town and cities which had kept the inhabitants of the Caribbean islands and the Central American coast in a state of perpetual terror. In the 1690s a force of 3,000 descended on Jamaica from Petit Goâve with orders to conquer the island. French military leaders gave up hope of seizing Jamaica when they realized their irregulars, most of whom were veteran buccaneers, preferred looting and destroying to actual combat. They destroyed hundreds of homes, crops, livestock and orchards, demolished fifty sugar works and sailed back to Petit Goâve with several thousand slaves and an immense amount of booty.

A couple af years later French attacks having continued on their settlements, English and Spanish privateers and troops invaded French Hispaniola. The English privateers raced ahead and sacked several towns on the north coast, denying the Spanish troops their share of loot. The En-

glish objective was Petit Goâve which posed a continuing threat. The
Spanish general, however, declined to press on. Fighting broke out among
the allied forces and the expedition was disbanded after the division of
140 cannon which had been captured from the northern coastal settlements.

Piracy remained an endemic hazard in the Caribbean after the turn of
the century despite stepped up naval patrols and hostility from former
friends on the plantation islands. The Treaty of Utrecht signed at the end
of the Anglo-French War of Queen Anne's reign, brought a quarter century of peace to Europe but "beyond the line" hostilities continued with
the French and English pitted against each other in a struggle to fill the
power vacuum left by the erosion of Spanish supremacy in the Caribbean.

Pirate attacks were carefully choreographed. Surprise was essential.
Pirate vessels were sleek and swift, kept in top shape so they could catch
any vessel. Armed with pistols and gleaming cutlasses, pirates "clapped
aboard." With grappling hooks and boarding nets the pirates swarmed
onto a prize shouting and cursing. To the rhythm of drum and trumpet
they engaged the defenders, if they hadn't surrendered at once, in combat
amid the added din of sulphurous stink bombs and grenades.

The pedestrian nature of most seaborne cargoes made the Caribbean
far less attractive than it had been when silver rather than salted fish was
crammed in the holds. In 1692 a man was sentenced to death in the West
Indies for taking a typical cargo of 500 salt fish, 40 bushels of corn and
400 pieces of eight. In contrast, East India pirates John Ireland and
Thomas Hickman went to the gallows in 1688 for taking two ships whose
rich cargoes indicate why the eastern seas became the lodestone for first-
rate pirates like Thomas Tew, "Long Ben" Avery and Bartholomew Roberts, the most successful of them all who took 400 prizes. Ireland and
Hickman, sailing with the *Charming Mary* took a Moorish ship near
Ceylon. They plundered and sunk her, forcing the English captain to serve
as their pilot. Two weeks later, they took a Portuguese prize which carried
fourteen bales of silk "richly flowered with gold" worth 6,000 pounds,
sixty-four pounds of China gold "all in Lumps and divers other Goods
to a great Value."

Ambitious deep-water pirates lured by such plunder began to gravitate
to the Indian Ocean, the Red Sea and the west coast of Africa. At the turn
of the century as it became clear that the routes between India and the
Red Sea carried far more valuable shipping than the atrophying treasure
lanes between the New World and Europe, sea outlaws began to leave the
Caribbean for the east. Their prey was varied. The East India ships of
England, Holland, Portugal and France carrying the wealth of the East
Indies and India were tempting targets as were the ships carrying the

slaves, gold dust and ivory of Africa. But the greatest prizes in those remote waters were the Moorish treasure ships which often had European crews and commanders. Many were pilgrim ships ferrying the Moslem faithful and their offerings from India to Red Sea ports leading to Mecca. The richest of all were vessels of the Great Mogul's fleet belonging to the ruler of India. The Mogul dynasty which had ruled uninterrupted since 1526 brought India to a zenith of unity and prosperity. Mogul trading ships were laden with gold, silver, precious gems, pearls, spices, damasks and silks; treasures with no equal in Christendom. The Mogul sat on the canopied Peacock Throne—a magnificent golden affair set with diamonds, emeralds, rubies, pearls and garnets worth six million pounds, more than nine times King William III of England's personal income. A French jewel and trader who visited the opulent court of Aurangzeb, the sixth Mogul emperor, marveled at the tribute in "diamonds, rubies, emeralds, brocades of gold and silver, and other stuffs" presented by the Mogul's subjects at the annual tribute ceremony.

Aurangzeb was a brutal tyrant who had beheaded two brothers, and imprisoned his father, three of his sons and a daughter to maintain imperial power. India's Hindu majority loathed his harsh Moslem rule and onerous taxes. Hindu uprisings weakened him and for years his fleets were vulnerable. Beginning in the late 1680s the Pirate Round took advantage of the poor protection given Mogul shipping and of the insatiable hunger of the North American colonists for smuggled goods. After years of predation, Aurangzeb insisted that the European nations which profited so much by trade with India be responsible for the safe conduct of Mogul ships. The Mogul was particularly enraged at the English because most of the pirates on the Round were American colonials or English, many of them graduates of Caribbean pirate training. England responded by sending armed convoys of East Indiamen as escorts and by stepping up British Navy operations against pirates.

In the decade or so of the Round pirates fitted out in a dozen ports along the eastern seaboard including Philadelphia, Newport, New York and Boston. Adventurers begged to sign on the tall ships in such number that the commanders could pick and choose the most "seaworthy artists," those with the most experience of long range navigation and deep water pirating. It was a long dangerous voyage but the stakes were incredibly high. A pirate could make more at one stroke than a leading English financier or a great landowner earned in two or three years. Not all did, of course, but many expeditions netted their members as much as £2,000 and at one astounding share-out each pirate received £4,000 worth of loot.

Three English pirates were acquitted by a London jury when they protested that they had claimed their share of the booty from a Moorish ship only because they "durst not declare their Abhorrence of such an Undertaking" for fear of losing their lives. Included in the plunder of the "Great Mahomet" were hundreds of pounds of precious spices and dyes, "4000 ounces of silver, 8000 Rix Dollars (Dutch), 200 gold bars, 40 ounces of gold dust, 10,000 gold coins, 4000 other pieces of gold, 30,000 Dollars, 100,000 Pieces of Eight and divers other Goods to a great Value."

Pirates multiplied along with the worldwide opportunities for plunder during the Golden Age of piracy. So did the bases and the markets which they depended on. In the Caribbean the Bahamian island of New Providence became a pirate paradise where brigands and whores gathered by the thousands in the greatest concentration of lowlife the New World had ever seen. The little English colony on New Providence had been woefully neglected. The numbers of planters dwindled and by the turn of the century the majority of the population consisted of pirates. Led by a former privateer, Henry Jennings, they set up a boozy, brawling shantytown of sailcloth tents and timbers from rotting hulks on the beach by present day Nassau.

The island was beautifully situated at the edge of the Florida Channel, the route between the North American and European ports and the settlements of the West Indies and the Spanish Main. The Treaty of Utrecht in 1713 abruptly cast prodigious numbers of unemployed privateers into the ranks of the more than 2,000 pirates who made up the "Pirate Republic" of the Bahamas. The growing prosperity of the West India colonies at the war's end brought an increased volume of ships carrying far more valuable cargoes into the area making the Caribbean a more profitable cruising ground than it had been for over a century. The New Providence lair, host to such rogues as Henry Jennings, Charles Vane, Charles Bellamy, Oliver la Bouche, Calico Jack Rackham, Benjamin Hornigold and his protégé Blackbeard, became such a menace that Caribbean trade was almost at a standstill. "North and South America are infested with the Rogues," lamented the Governor of Bermuda in 1717. Naval attempts to cope with the English pirates operating out of New Providence, French pirates out of Martinique and Spanish pirates from Puerto Rico and Cuba fell far short of the mark. Finally, in 1718, Woodes Rogers was appointed governor. Almost singlehandedly this brilliant veteran of the South Seas wiped out the nest of pirates, convincing the most able of them to work for him in turning New Providence into a colony of settled planters.

The first important eastern pirate base on the Round was the scorched island of Perim, known to the pirates as Bab's Cay, at the mouth of the Red Sea. It was soon eclipsed by the large island of Madagascar 250 miles off the east coast of Africa where both English and French pirates clustered. Lying within striking distance of the Indian Ocean and the Red Sea, the fertile island had tolerant natives, abundant water, scurvy-preventing citrus fruits and fine natural harbors. In short, it was a perfect pirate center. Pirates and hangers-on by the thousands flocked to Madagascar and nearby islets, turning them into pirate kingdoms. Misson, a French captain, founded the pirate republic of Libertatia, a loose confederation of sea rovers who spoke a distinctive patois and practiced a form of communism. A Jamaican pirate named James Plantain who proclaimed himself "King" of Ranter Bay had a bevy of native Malagasy wives and female servants to whom he gave English names like Kate, Moll, Sue or Peggy and showered with gifts of European gowns and diamond necklaces.

Another self-styled "King of the Pirates" was Adam Baldridge, also a Jamaican who held sway over the tiny island of St. Mary's right off the Madagascar coast. He built a great stone castle and fort overlooking the superb harbor where pirates could careen their ships. Baldridge had dozens of warehouses filled with pirate plunder. As recognized ruler of local tribes he received tribute in the form of produce, livestock and sometimes even slaves which he traded with the pirates for booty. In addition, he sold them ammunition, naval stores and other supplies which had been brought across the Atlantic, around the tip of Africa to St. Mary's on the ships of the New England syndicate he was agent for in the 1690s.

Piracy was big business, profitable for everyone involved and indeed almost everyone was involved. American merchants shipped rum worth two shillings a gallon in New York to the pirate port where Baldridge retailed it for three pounds sterling a gallon. Wine sold in St. Mary's for fifteen times its New York price. Back in the colonies the common man was delighted to get his hands on calicoes, muslins and other pirated luxuries which, free of taxes, sold at bargain rates. Profiteering merchants bought stolen cargoes wholesale.

Pirate brokering was the foundation of several great fortunes, including that of the New York Philipse family, whose Sleepy Hollow manor is now a museum. Frederick Philipse and his son Adolph had a fleet which sailed regularly to Madagascar laden with manufactures and staples, returning with pirated booty and slaves. Wealthy merchants with an eye for a winning proposition openly bankrolled pirate expeditions. Colonial officials consorted with known pirates, inviting them to dine and accepting lavish gifts in exchange for their protection.

Very few people in the colonies were unsympathetic to the pirates. Officials sent out from England to assess the situation were outraged at what they found. Edward Randolph, Surveyor-General of the Customs in America, wrote a "Discourse About Pyrates, With Proper Remedies to Suppress Them" which indicted virtually every governor and official as "in no sort fit for Office" and almost every colony as "a Receptacle of Pyrats." Virginia alone was without stain since Governor Nicholson was a man "truly zealous to suppress Pyracy and illegal Trade."

The mother country's cavalier attitude toward her colonies, which led eventually to the American Revolution, was responsible for the North American colonies relative tolerance of the pirates for so long. In view of statements like Lord Sheffield's that "the only use for the American colonies is the monopoly of their consumption and the carriage of their produce," it was not surprising. The chief goad was the series of Navigation Acts which England enacted, despite Spain's ruinous example, to exclude all nations but England from trading with English colonies. All merchandise from Europe or the East had to be imported to the colonies through England. All goods shipped in and out of the colonies were to be carried aboard British built vessels manned by British crews. The protectionist acts which benefited England at the expense of the colonies stipulated that such produce as tobacco, sugar, raw cotton, dyes and spices could be sold in England where the market was too limited to absorb the entire production. The colonists were even prohibited from making woolen cloth and other manufactures. At the opening of the Golden Age fixed low prices for their exports, artificially high prices for imports, excessive taxes and duties made the colonists ripe for traffic with the pirates.

"We have a parcel of pyrates called the Red Sea Men in these parts," a New Yorker named Peter De La Noy wrote in 1695, "who get a great booty of Arabian gold. The Governor encourages them because they make due acknowledgements." Benjamin Fletcher to whom De La Noy was referring protected pirates, letting one ship land for an "offering" of £700. He openly accepted sums, ranging from a few dollars to over 100 per crew member and sold commissions for about 300 through Mr. Nicoll, his secretary. A pirate captain named Coates who wished to bring his plunder into New York harbor was required to give an "offering" of £700. Instead he gave Fletcher his ship which the governor sold for £800. In answer to a reprimand regarding his selling of commissions the governor wrote, "It may be my unhappiness, but not my crime if they turn pyrates." The governor's wife and daughters wore dresses of India silk and were adorned with gem-studded Mogul jewelry which the governor received from pirates such as the notorious Captain Tew who was "received and caressed" by Fletcher and invited to dine often with his family. The governor presented Tew with a gold watch and urged him to make New York his port upon the return of his next voyage.

The New England colonies, unlike the southern plantation colonies, depended on trade for their existence. Smarting under a system whereby, in the words of Lord Chatham, "The British Colonists in North America have no right to manufacture as much as a nail for a horse shoe," they wooed the pirates, welcoming the nourishment they brought to the local economy, an estimated £100,000 annually into New York alone. In Philadelphia men who had made fortunes pirating moved in the best circles and Governor Markham wed his daughter to a pirate. In Boston a mint was opened to turn pirate silver and gold into coins. In 1685 a French privateering vessel *La Trompeuse* had been welcomed into Boston harbor by Bostonians despite the fact that her captain was Michel Breha, a pirate "famous in bloodshed and robberies." When Breha was later captured by a naval expedition and executed, Boston merchants vowed to "beat out the brains" of the men who had caught him. Pirates who had been repairing to Philadelphia were invited to Massachusetts by the governor, Sir William Phipps. Phipps was a former adventurer, a sloop captain who had convinced King Charles II to fund his search for a Spanish treasure galleon which sank on Silver Shoals off the north coast of Hispaniola in 1641. Forty-four years after it wrecked, Phipps located the galleon and salvaged 300,000 pounds worth of gold, silver and other treasure from it. James II, who had become King, was so delighted at this windfall that he struck a medal commemorating the find. James got 20,000 pounds as his royal share and Phipps got a knighthood, £16,000 pounds and eventually the governorship of the huge Massachusetts Bay Colony a position that increased his wealth through pirate brokering.

Governor Markham of Pennsylvania, a Quaker, was a notorious "Steddy friend" of pirates. "These Quaker have a neat way of getting money by encouraging the pyrates when they bring in a good store of gold," wrote an observer in 1703, when William Penn had replaced Markham. Penn had heard in London that the people of Pennsylvania "not onlie wink att but imbrace pirats, Shipps and men." When his daughter Jane, married James Brown, a pirate who had sailed with Avery, he helped his son-in-law take a seat in the Assembly. A hundred pounds bought Markham's protection. For a somewhat larger amount an ex-pirate named Captain Robert Sneed was named a justice of the peace. Sneed surprised Markham by turning on him, prosecuting pirates and accusing Markham of collusion. The governor reacted by issuing warrants against him. Sneed recorded the particulars of a conversation he had with Markham "for ye Justification" of his inability to apprehend pirates named on an English warrant. Sneed accused Markham of harboring several pirates from "Long Ben" Avery's crew who were in Philadelphia and whose arrest had been ordered by the Lords Justices in England. Markham claimed not to have seen the proclamation. When Sneed said he could "prove to ye contrary" but would again show him a copy if need be, Markham said it was not directed to him "so that He was not Bound to take notice of it, nor to Examine men from whence they came; so they brought money with them."

"I being at ye time very Intimate with him, told him very plainly that there was a good understanding between him and ye Pyrates, and none so blind as those ye would not see," recorded Steed. "He said tis true the men had been civill to him, they had brought in money which was an advantage to the countrey." Sneed was reviled in the streets as an informer and lived in fear of his life while trying every avenue to bring the pirates to a "speedy tryall." He had several other encounters with the governor who ordered him to stop sending "warrants up and down whistling to scare People (meaning the Pyrates)."

Pirates on the Round fitted out at Boston, New York, Philadelphia and to a lesser degree in ports of the Middle Colonies of New Jersey, Delaware and Maryland. The "Chief Refuge for Pyrates" for half a century was Rhode Island which served as a fitting out station and a clearing house for eastern treasure. Long after the other colonies responded to royal pressure by suppressing piracy and smuggling, Rhode Island remained a mecca for pirates and a place where they were routinely acquitted if brought to trial. In fact, one man who ingenuously plead guilty was acquitted by the jury which couldn't imagine anyone doing such a thing.

Anglo-French controversy over Adam's Will; over territorial control of Spain's New World dominions and over monopoly of trade lasted throughout the eighteenth century. The War of Spanish Succession began in 1702, when England and the Netherlands declared war on France and Spain, and lasted through most of the reign of Queen Anne of England. The British and Dutch did not want France heir to the Spanish colonies. They were alarmed that the childless Spanish king, Charles II, who was mentally feeble and a chronic invalid, had left the crown of Spain to Philip of Anjou the grandson of Louis XIV. The war was essentially a naval war and brought into play more well-armed ships and crewmen than the West Indies had ever seen. During the war pirates were absorbed into the ranks of privateers although recruiting proved more difficult than in the past until the English Prize Act of 1708 was enacted to counteract the lure of eastern water. Its liberal provisions gave privateers 100 percent of their take plus a bounty. The war also greatly reduced piratical activity in the Caribbean.

In the Caribbean English, French, Dutch and Spanish privateers harassed each other's shipping and settlements. When the Treaty of Utrecht ended the war in 1713, thousands of skilled privateers were thrown out of work as they had been a century before when James I ended privateering by making peace with Spain. A Jamaican planter voiced the concern of many that the war's conclusion would "leave to the world a brood of pirates to infest it." Following the war the Spanish treasure flotas resumed sailing and trade between Britain and her colonies expanded greatly. Riffraff from all over washed up on the shores of the Caribbean which again offered outstanding piratical opportunities.

The Dutch government was the only one with enough foresight to realize that hostilities might be over but would certainly resume again before long. To keep their skilled troops available, the government paid them to work in the herring fleet so that Hollanders were conspicuous by their absence from the great flare-up of piracy which convulsed the Caribbean, the southeastern coast of North America, the Indian Ocean and the Gulf of Guinea in the years following the war.

Most of the pirates who took part in the seaborne epic have been forgotten. They were neither outstandingly successful nor otherwise remarkable. The final words of many of those who died on the gallows of "hempen fever," are all that remain of brief, violent and ultimately pathetic lives. But never before had the pirate ranks contained so many colorful characters, many of whom cultivated their notoriety. Daniel Defoe, alias Captain Charles Johnson, immortalized many of these pioneers of psychological warfare in his "History of the Robberies and Murders of the Most Notorious Pirates" first published in 1724. Even before Defoe gave them a boost the pirates enjoyed great renown. In 1713 *The Successful Pirate*, a play by Charles Johnson, not Defoe, was produced at Drury Lane in London. Based on the exciting life of John Avery, it was the first of a rash of wildly popular entertainments which had pirates as their theme. A critic thought it dreadful to make "a tarpaulin and a Swabber . . . the Hero of a Tragedy," but the public loved it.

The exploits of the pirates were printed on handbills and followed with baited breath. A pirate trial was always crowded with spectators but what everyone loved best was a good hanging. Many of the rogues went to the gallows displaying the dash which had marked their meteoric careers. Dressed in silk and velvet, a condemned man might sprinkle the mob with gold coins or pearls before he swung off. Earnest clerics worked feverishly to the last minute to wring repentance from convicted pirates. Booklets containing the final words and touching letters of penitent and not-so-penitent pirates were composed by clergymen who sometimes recorded what they would like to have heard rather than the blasphemous utterances they were subjected to.

It hardly seems likely an old reprobate would express such pious sentiments as the following which appeared in a collection of the last utterances of twenty-six pirates executed at Newport, Rhode Island on July 19, 1723. One John Browne is quoted as warning youths to fear God and obey their parents, who know what is best for them. He urges men to obey their superiors who can teach them good things. What pirate worth his salt would beseech others to "live Soberly, and not let yourselves be overcome with strong Drink. Fly all Temptations, all Opportunities, all Importunities, tending that way. Alas! It's a sad Thing, a too reigning vice . . . Beware of the abominable Sin of Uncleanliness . . . suffer not the least Spark of that Infernal Fire of Lust to hover about your Heart and Mind?"[1] In any case, these little moralistic volumes sold so well that they often went into many editions. As a thirteen-year old printer's apprentice Benjamin Franklin composed, printed and hawked through the streets a "sailor" song on the taking of Teach (Blackbeard) the Pirate. A stanza of the ballad attributed to him expresses a common pirate sentiment:

> So each man to his gun,
> For the work must be done,
> With cutlass, sword or pistol.
> And when we no longer can strike a blow,
> Then fire the magazine, boys, and up we go!
> It's better to swim in the sea below
> Than to swing in the air and feed the crow,
> Says jolly Ned Teach of Bristol.[2]

Considering their numbers, relatively few of the pirates died on the gibbet. Many, however, met a violent end or were felled by fever, venereal disease, drink or septic wounds. A few like Blackbeard died like epic heroes. Blackbeard, reputed to have survived twenty saber wounds and five bullets in his final battle, fought on even as blood gushed in great spurts from his slashed throat until he slowly crumpled to the gore covered deck. His large severed head was fixed as a grotesque figurehead to the bowsprit of the Royal naval sloop, whose captain had led the fight against him, and carried back to Virginia. It was widely believed that his headless body, which was thrown overboard, swam around the ship three times before sinking.

Blackbeard was the epitome of the self-consciously melodramatic eighteenth-century pirate. To discourage resistance he brilliantly combined a showman's flair with a genuine bizarre streak to create a terrifying persona. A great bear of a man, well over six-feet tall, Teach built his image around the copious jet black growth which Defoe described "like a frightful meteor covered his whole face, and frightened America more than any comet that has appeared in a long time." In contrast to the unkempt mat on his head and his beetling brows which grew every which way, the beard was twined with multicolored ribbons into plaits, some of which hung down his chest and some which he trained behind his ears. To highlight his horrifying appearance in battle, Blackbeard tucked lighted matches into the mane under his hat. He was in no danger of burning for the long hemp fuses dipped in saltpeter and limewater which were used to light cannon burned at the rate of a foot an hour. The hellish aura of smoke and fumes which they provided did as much to intimidate his prey as the three braces of pistols slung in a bandolier and the other guns, cutlass and daggers tucked into his broad belt. No wonder he was a living legend, the bogey man of colonial children from the Carolinas to Massachusetts.

The pirates of the Golden Age differed from their predecessors the buccaneers in method of operation as well as style. Changes at the close of the seventeenth century altered the pattern of sea robbery which had prevailed in the New World for almost two centuries. Spain had been humbled. Her monopoly had been challenged and broken, her vast colonial empire was shrinking. Treasure still poured from the mines but only one flota made the crossing each year and it was so heavily guarded by French warships that there was more of a threat from hurricanes than pirates. The cities and towns which had served as the savings banks from which generations of rovers made regular withdrawals were either out of funds or very well defended. England and France had wrested control of strategic Caribbean areas and established viable plantation colonies which depended on imported slave labor. The Netherlands, a trading nation first and forever, had its own enclaves around which most Caribbean commerce pivoted. Even Denmark and Brandenburg-Prussia had staked claims in Spain's former preserve.

One of the biggest changes was the growth in importance of the North American colonies along the Atlantic seaboard. Once Jamaica was on its feet as a viable colony the buccaneers who had been courted for their protection and prize goods became an embarrassment and were turned away. Those buccaneers who refused government offers of amnesty were forced to look to new horizons for havens, for markets and for prey. They were to find replacements for all three without difficulty. North America offered vast new markets as well as quarry. Danish St. Thomas, French Martinique and the nominally English islands of the Bahamas north of the Caribbean became hotbeds of pirate activity and for several years New Providence Island in the Bahamas functioned as a brawling, primitive pirate republic. Corrupt officials in ports from New England to the Carolinas welcomed pirates with outstretched arms—palms upward to receive their share of booty which ran the gamut from the gold of Arabia to English manufactures seized en route to the colonies.

The anti-buccaneer act enforced on Jamaica was followed by Sir Robert Holmes's sweep of the seas with a naval squadron sent to the West Indies in 1687. His commission empowered him to grant a second chance to those outlaws who had refused earlier offers of free land and a pardon in exchange for turning from their wicked ways. Very few came forward. Most scurried away like cockroaches exposed to sudden light so that although Holmes did clear the Caribbean of pirates, they returned as soon as his squadron headed home.

There were bright new prospects farther afield but the less ambitious and able of the pirates were content to confine their cruising to the familiar balmy waters where they had been trained. The Caribbean offered less in the way of glittering prizes than the Indian Ocean and the Red Sea which had become the focus of intense piratical activity. However, pirates operating among the thousands of islands and islets that stud the tropical Caribbean found compensation aplenty. They were seldom out of sight of land or far from a fresh supply of food and water. It was cheaper to outfit an expedition and the shallow water required small ships which were relatively easy to come by and maintain. They carried fewer guns than the long distance ships, relying on boarding a prize rather than destroying it with cannon fire. There was a lot to be said for sticking to an area where a man knew every shoal and reef like the back of his hand. In their small boats seldom over fifty tons the pirates could easily elude naval patrols or the *guarda-costas*, the Spanish government patrol ships, whose underpaid crews didn't hesitate to plunder any vessel they could chase down. The Caribbean, after all, had been the nursery of New World piracy and rovers who had been raised there knew a thousand and one secret coves perfect for hiding, ambush or refreshment. They knew, too, the secluded beaches best for careening their sloops and brigantines.

Surprise was everything to the pirate and speed was essential to surprise. Weeds, barnacles and the mollusks called teredo worms which flourished in the warm water, tunneling through the wooden hulls, slowed ships down drastically. Four or five times a year it was necessary to careen a ship. This was done by bringing the boat ashore at a place where there were trees to hitch blocks and tackles to. Once the craft was emptied, the topmast was lowered. Using blocks and tackles the crew turned the boat almost completely over on its side. They scraped the hull, caulked open seams, replaced rotted planking and then coated it with a protective blend of sulfur, tar and tallow.

The square riggers the Caribbean pirates favored as prizes when they needed something larger than a sloop or schooner were sailed to isolated anchorages where they were transformed into versatile pirate brigantines by a few structural changes. Ships were sometimes re-rigged for greater speed. Swivel guns and cannons might be mounted or provisions made for oars. The gunwales were raised chest high to afford more protection during an encounter. The higher gunwales could also be used to conceal armed pirates while others paraded on deck disguised as merchants or even women. All deck houses and superstructures were removed to clear the decks for action.

Even the international rovers who went after big game often wintered in the West Indies particularly at St. Thomas or in the Bahamas, taking time to careen their vessels and rest. They might sally south to strike at Spanish or Dutch cargo vessels off the Main or bear down indiscriminately on French, British and American ships. In spring they headed for Florida cruising up the coast to Charleston, Newport, Philadelphia, New York, Boston and Salem, harassing shipping as far north as Newfoundland, selling their booty to agents in ports along the way. They found recruits everywhere. The most eager were fishermen or cod splitters and dryers in Newfoundland. They were poor West Countrymen from England or Welshmen who slaved for low wages. They had to pay their own way home at the end of the season and were happy to exchange their bleak existence on the frigid Newfoundland Banks for the chance of netting a far more valuable catch.

Not that there was any shortage of enlistees in the Caribbean. Social conditions for the average white man had not improved. The importation of greater numbers of African slaves had displaced even more whites and created a growing class of landless whose prospects on the plantation islands were not bright. Piracy offered an escape from penury and the lure of great reward. In 1695 the governor of Jamaica wrote the King of England that so many men were involved in piracy that it was impossible to find crew for merchant ships throughout the West Indies. To a man bound for sea there was no comparison between serving on a merchant or naval vessel and signing on with an outlaw pirate crew. Mutinous crews killed their captains or cast them away with any officers who declined to join them in their transformation from merchantmen to prowling marauders.

It was a cruel age and life aboard ship accentuated the discrimination and brutality that reigned ashore. An ordinary swabber on a naval vessel had little to look forward to but a lifetime of grueling, repetitive work, low wages, scant benefits, stinking accommodations, foul food and the cut of the lash. Advancement up the ranks was beyond the pale for the seaman who was always subject to his officers' whims. Rations were foul and often lacking because money for them had gone into the purser's pocket. Malnutrition made seamen even more vulnerable to tropical maladies which sometimes swept through ships leaving only one or two men alive.

Some officers were notorious sadists, a few were psychopaths and virtually all meted out or condoned harsh, inhumane punishment. Sailors, including mere boys, were beaten with a rattan cane or flogged with the knotted cords of a cat o'nine tails or with a thick tarred rope, often tipped with lead. Salt or brine was rubbed into the wounds which could, depending on the severity of the sentence, flay a man's back open to the bone. It wasn't uncommon for men to receive as many as three hundred lashes or more. Nor was it uncommon for them to die soon after. A sadistic officer could do what he liked with a common seaman short of outright murder. He could force him to eat maggots, cockroaches or rats. For a graver offense a sailor might be chained to the deck in a tortuous position, forced overboard to cling on a trailing line or keel hauled—a barbarous punishment which scraped a man raw as he was pulled across the barnacled hull.

Even in the best of circumstances a lowly naval seaman was the powerless victim of a despotic system. Numerous trial proceedings record the pleas of those who claimed to have been forced to join pirate crews which had captured their ships. In fact, pirates didn't often have to press seamen, who preferred the pirate life to life in the navy. Pirates were most interested in having "sea artists," men with special skills such as pilots, shipwrights, surgeons, musicians, coopers and carpenters join them and were unlikely to let them go if they chose not to join them.

On a pirate ship the bilges still stank, the food was often rotten or riddled with weevils. The quarters were filthy, perennially wet, cramped and overrun with vermin. But a man was free of the tyranny that oppressed him aboard a naval ship or a merchant vessel. All men aboard were equal or almost equal for "sea artists" generally received a larger share than ordinary pirates. The captain chosen for his courage, ability and luck, served only as long as he enjoyed a vote of confidence. Although he was obeyed implicitly during an action, he had few special privileges beyond his extra share. His men might enter the captain's cabin and sit freely at his table. Defoe wrote that "They only permit him to be captain on condition that they may be captain over him" save in battle when his power was absolute "drubbing, cutting, or even shooting anyone who denies his command." There could be quite a turnover. One crew ran through thirteen captains within a couple of months. Another ship kept a man in command for years, even through lean times because he had been born with a caul, or membrane, enveloping his head. Pirates were a superstitious lot and believed that made him lucky and protected him from disaster at sea.

Most pirates were seasoned seamen when they first went on the account and had sampled the gross inequities of eighteenth-century life ashore. They embraced the pirate existence despite all its uncertainties and perils. One unwilling wretch who got caught in the works was a man named John Upton. He joined the crew of a merchantman in Boston after twenty-two years service in the Royal Navy. On his first voyage the *Perry Galley*, en route to Bristol via Barbados, was captured by pirates off Dominica. They released all but three of the crew whose services they needed. Upton was among the prisoners and as soon as another prize was taken, Joseph Cooper, the pirate chieftain, put him at the wheel. He tried to break out of formation in the middle of the night hoping to make for Jamaica and an encounter with an English patrol vessel but was discovered and tortured.

Thereafter he obediently followed orders until he escaped while the pirate fleet was off the Mosquito Coast of Nicaragua. With the help of an Englishman who lived in the forest he made it down to a settlement called Carpenter's River where he received permission from the Spanish governor to accompany a mule train carrying supplies to Chinandega on the Pacific. Upton hoped to take a boat up to Panama and then make it back to the Caribbean. When he reached Panama six months later he was accused of being a spy and was given the choice of going to prison or serving aboard a Spanish ship. Upton displayed more national pride than good sense and spent four months in a dark cell until he was forced to serve as a guard aboard a ship taking thirty Dutch prisoners to Portobelo. There he and the Dutch were to embark on a galleon sailing to Spain. The night before it left, Upton gave his captors the slip and found refuge aboard a New York ship headed for Jamaica and freedom. But his tribulations were not over. Upton was abducted by a Royal Navy press gang and made to work on H.M.S. *Nottingham* whose captain believed he was a pirate. He was arrested when the ship reached England and eventually stood trial and was acquitted.

The real power aboard a pirate vessel lay with the quartermaster who was also chosen by the crew. He was the chief authority save during battle. Offenses not serious enough to be tried by a pirate jury were handled by the quartermaster. He was the only officer allowed to flog a man, although he needed permission from a majority of the crew to administer such a hated punishment. In addition to acting as the ship's magistrate, he served as "the trustee for the whole ship's company" in Defoe's words, "for the captain can do nothing which the quartermaster does not approve of . . . for he speaks for and looks after the interest of the company." He was the first aboard a prize, overseeing the selection and division of the plunder, determining what might be returned to the owners "excepting gold and silver which they have voted not returnable." Like the captain he remained in office only as long as his men supported him.

English juries tended to exonerate former officers but ordinary seamen were often convicted on the premise that they had willingly taken to the "sweet trade" since it offered so much more than they had previously had.

Under the Defense of the Realm Acts it was legal for a Royal Navy ship in port and in need of men to send a gang armed with clubs to roam the seedy section of town until they had rounded up their quota of "recruits," who were taken on board and off to sea. Mariners were encouraged to defend their ship against pirates. If wounded they were admitted to Greenwich Naval Hospital, if they lived long enough to reach England, and they received a reward. Those who failed to resist attack were imprisoned and docked six months wages. Anyone found to have supplied a pirate with naval stores, provisions or ammunition, was guilty of piracy under the Piracy Act of 1721.

It took many centuries for English law to come to grips with piracy. Civil courts heard piracy cases until the fourteenth century when Edward III established Admiralty courts to try all crimes committed below the high water mark. A man was sentenced to death only if he confessed or had been seen in the act. Henry VIII in 1536 created the position of Vice-Admiral of the coast, responsible for dealing with piracies. Many of the vice-admirals including members of the notorious Killigrew clan of Cornwall were in cahoots with the pirates and little progress was made. In 1615 a temporary Vice-Admiralty Court, the first outside Britain, was established in Newfoundland to cope with the piracies and other crimes committed on the Banks during the cod fishing season.

Until Parliament under William III passed the Piracy Act at the turn of the eighteenth century, pirates apprehended in the West Indies, Bahamas, North America or anywhere outside of English waters had to be brought to London for trial, along with the necessary witnesses. The new act was aimed specifically at the "many idle and profligate persons" who were turning to the wicked life safe from prosecution "by reason of the great trouble and expense that will necessarily fall upon such as shall attempt to apprehend and persecute them." Colonial officials were reluctant to instigate proceedings. Corrupt officials in the pay of pirates accounted for a certain lack of zeal. However even diligent officials were discouraged by the expense, paper work and tedium of the lengthy process. The 1699 act, prompted by the drastic situation in the Caribbean and Atlantic, made allowance for trying pirates in the colonies before a Vice-Admiralty court. Parliament recognized the sympathy with which pirates were regarded in the colonies where evasion of the repressive Navigation Acts was a way of life and the sweet trade was something few colonists didn't benefit by to some degree. Parliament knew, too, how often colonial authorities succumbed to bribes so Vice-Admiralty courts were to include a Royal Navy commander and members appointed by the Crown in addition to the governor and lieutenant governor. Accessories to pirate crimes were still transported to England for trial for fear they would receive preferential treatment abroad.

Trying pirates on the spot was no guarantee, however, that they would be sentenced. An accused pirate named Moses Butterworth was brought to trial in Middletown, New Jersey in March 1701. He had confessed to sailing with Captain Kidd but the townsfolk led by "one Samuel Willett, Innholder" felt he ought to be released. Willett led about forty men, armed with rifles and clubs, into the courtroom. A drummer was with them and according to an eyewitness, they made such a racket "that ye court could not Examine ye Prisoner at the Barr." Several men seized the accused "by ye arms and about ye middle and forct him from ye Barr." When the Constable and under Sheriff tried to stop them they were assaulted. While the drummer kept up the beat, a general free-for-all broke out with the Justices and King's Attorney-Generall drawing their swords and entering the fracas. The crowd which had grown to a hundred carried off the prisoner and seized the sheriff and the clerk of court and held them under guard. In most colonial courts such drastic action wasn't necessary at the turn of the century as many pirates walked off scot free with the conniv- ance of their patrons. The Carolinas which were a notorious "Receptacle of Pyrats" condemned a few from time to time as a sop to the Crown. The ones who were hanged were generally poor. Rich pirates such as those who sailed into Charleston in 1693 from Jamaica with "a vaste quantity of Gold from the Red Sea" were welcomed and invited into the homes of local society.

The Crown dispatched George Larkin to the North American colonies to set up the colonial courts. He found fault with everything he saw and was incensed to find pirates in New England "entertained and caressed" by colonial officials and the leading merchants. He found "no money but Arabian gold" in circulation and lamented that the only way to organize the new courts was under judges brought over from England. Poor Larkin went on to Bermuda where he ran up against the Lieutenant Governor Benjamin Bennett who had done much to make Bermuda a favored pirate enclave. Bennett forced a slave to accuse Larkin of rape and had him imprisoned. He was released after several months by order of the Council for Trade and Plantations which heeded his complaint of ill treatment at Bennett's hand "since I was hurl'd betwixt these disconsolate walls." Ben- nett, who was very popular with the Bermudans most of whom made their living on the sea, received an official reprimand but remained in office while Larkin died soon after unmourned by the islanders.

The typical pirate ship had a motley crew. The majority of those who participated in the Pirate Round were men with roots in England's West Country and Wales, where piracy was in the genes. Nearly half of the fifty-two members of Black Bart Roberts's crew hung at Cape Coast Castle on Africa's Gold Coast in 1722 were Welsh or West Countrymen.

Catholic Irish and Scots pirates often signed on Spanish and French expeditions. Protestant Frenchmen served aboard English pirate ships. On many ships there was a sprinkling of runaway slaves and a mulatto or two. For twenty years a band of Spaniards, Portuguese, Scots, English, blacks and mulattos was headquartered in the Bahamas under the leadership of a Spaniard named Agostino Blanco. Other nationalities were represented throughout the era including Dutch, Scandinavians, Greeks and East Indians.

Most pirates were very young. The average age was twenty-five. An arrest warrant issued in December of 1699 by Governor Nicholson of Virginia, one of the few colonial authorities genuinely committed to suppressing piracy, gives a glimpse of a pirate crew. Among the outlaws at large in Virginia and wanted for plundering in the Red Sea on the *Adventure* were: "Tee Wetherlly, short, very small, blind in one eye, about eighteen; Thomas Jameson, cooper, Scot, tall, meagre, sickly look, large black eyes, twenty; William Griffith, short, well set, broad face, darkest hair, about thirty." There was another thirty-year-old, John Loyd "of ordinary stature, rawboned, very pale, dark hair, remarkably deformed in the lower eyelid" and two children, one fifteen and "Thomas Simpson, short and small, much squint-eyed, about ten of age."

Thanks to the efforts of Governor Nicholson, a French pirate, Lewis Guittar and seventy of his crew, were tried in October of 1700 in London's Old Bailey criminal court. Guittar commanded a fleet of two pinks, a sloop and *La Paix*. She was a large Dutch-built ship with twenty cannon mounted on her flush decks which he had seized in Dutch Surinam and converted into his flagship. He made a profitable cruise through the Caribbean. Like a returning robin, Guittar headed for the Virginia Capes at the first whiff of Spring. During the third week of April the pirates captured six merchantmen by flying Dutch flags until the prey was within range. Then he struck the false flag and ran up the blood red pennant favored by French rovers. The crews were treated roughly, particularly those men who refused to sign articles with Guittar and those on ships whose cargoes were disappointing. The ships were stripped of valuables and several of them burned. When the entire crew of the *Barbados Merchant* en route to Virginia from Bristol refused to sign on with them, the pirates stripped the captain and beat him almost to death. Guittar ordered the destruction of the masts, sails, bowsprit and rudder. He took all their candles and smashed the compass, leaving the broken ship and its crew adrift, minus the carpenter and one seaman who had signed articles.

Governor Nicholson had complained long and loudly about the vulnerability of ships along his coastline. Every spring the pirates stirred out of hibernation in the Bahamas and the West Indies and swarmed along the coasts of the Carolinas, Virginia, Maryland and to the north. The only real deterrent was the occasional scattered patrol vessel sent over from England. The *Essex Prize* attached to Virginia was commanded by Captain John Aldred, a hot tempered mariner somewhat lacking in courage and determination. The pirates made sport of him and his ship. His own men detested him. Many deserted so that he resorted to press gangs to bring up his complement, even seizing a bridegroom the night before his wedding and craftsmen whose skills were not even needed aboard. Nicholson and Aldred were at loggerheads. The *Essex Prize* was in deplorable condition as well as undermanned and it was rumored that Aldred extorted bribes from captains he falsely accused of bribery.

Aldred consistently refused to sail out on patrol giving one excuse after another from illness to bad weather. Finally he was recalled and the *Shoreham* was sent to the Virginia Station. The *Shoreham* under Captain Passenger sailed in pursuit of Guittar. Captain Aldred who had not yet left for England and Governor Nicholson were also aboard when they came upon Guittar who had just taken another prize. The pirates had surprised the *Nicholson* as she rode at anchor in Lynnhaven Bay, replying in English to a shouted "From whence do you come?" with "From the Sea you Dogs" at the same time the bloody colors were hoisted. Guittar had some of the *Nicholson*'s crew tortured in an effort to find out if there were any English men-o'-war in the Chesapeake Bay area. The ship's carpenter had his thumb and little finger mashed in a musket lock from which the flint was removed and then he was beaten with the flat of pirate cutlasses. At the trial he testified they told him they would cut his head off. They made him lie down and put their cutlass blades on his neck but didn't cut him much. He told how he had received some five hundred blows until one pirate said he'd had enough, although another said "tis good sport."

The *Shoreham* engaged the pirate fleet in a short range battle which lasted from before dawn to four in the afternoon. Governor Nicholson who remained on the quarterdeck of the *Shoreham* spurred on the navy men with promises of gold. Aldred redeemed himself by fighting valiantly and by mid-afternoon the *La Paix* had been pounded into smithereens. There was no hope for Guittar but he tried one last ploy in an effort to dictate the terms of his surrender. There were about fifty English prisoners locked in the hold of his ship. He laid a fuse from the hold where some fifty English prisoners were chained to kegs of powder and threatened to blow the prisoners up. Guittar gave up along with the 120 pirates who had survived the engagement. Before they could be shipped to England they were split up for security reasons among twenty-eight ships but three pirates escaped. They were caught and tried in Virginia, since they had been retaken on shore. All three hewed to the classic line of defense, pleading innocence by virtue of having been coerced into pirate service. Assuring the jury that he always shot wide of the mark in battle even though it brought curses on his head from the others, Cornelius Franc vowed he had been made to turn pirate because of his linguistic ability and asked "Must I be hanged that can speak all languages?" Franc and his cronies were sentenced to hang, their bodies to be left rotting until they fell to the ground.

Of those tried in England some pleaded they were under age or ill. Most claimed they were "forced on Board, being taken out of Ships and Barks at Rochel, Petit Goâve, Curacao and other Places, and others that they were Hunters in the Woods, and others Fisher-Men, and some of them proving their Allegations, they were Acquitted." Fifty-two were condemned to die of whom three died in Newgate prison and twenty-five were reprieved. The remaining outlaws were hanged at Execution Dock November 14th, 1700. "They being Foreigners," says an account, "and of Divers Nations, and many of them French Catholicks, made but little or no Confession; the Ordinary (chaplain) only says this of them, that several of them seemed penitent, and he hoped they were so."

In an age when a man or even a child could be hanged for stealing a loaf of bread the specter of the noose was hardly a deterrent to a hopeful rover. Black Bart Roberts summed up the pirate attitude: "In an honest service there is thin rations, low wages and hard labor; in this, plenty and satiety, pleasure and ease, liberty and power; and who would not balance creditor on this side, when all hazard that is run for it, at worst, is only a sour look or two at choking. No, a merry life and a short one shall be my motto."

The following paraphrased list of articles given in Defoe's book as those sworn to over a Bible or boarding axe by Roberts's crew are typical of the laws which regulated life aboard a pirate ship. Derived from privateering articles they varied slightly from captain to captain. Defoe's own comments are in parentheses:

> I. Every man has a vote in affairs of moment; has equal title to the fresh provisions or strong liquors at any time seized, and may use them at pleasure unless a scarcity (no uncommon thing among them) make it necessary for the good of all to vote a retrenchment.
>
> II. Every man to be called fairly in turn, by list, on board of prizes, because over and above their proper share, they are allowed a shift of clothes. But if they defrauded the Company to the value of a dollar, in plate, jewels or money, Marooning was the punishment. (This was a barbarous custom of putting the offender on shore on some desolate or uninhabited cape or island, with a gun, a few shot, a bottle of water and a bottle of powder, to

subsist with or starve.) If the robbery was only between one another they contented themselves with slitting the ears and nose of him that was guilty, and set him on shore, not in an uninhabited place, but somewhere where he was sure to encounter hardships.

III. No person to game at cards or dice for money.

IV. The lights and candles to be put out at eight o'clock at night. If any of the crew at that hour remained inclined to drinking, they were to do it on the open deck (which Roberts believed would give a check to their debauchs, for he was a sober man himself; but he found that all his endeavours to put an end to this debauch proved ineffectual).

V. To keep their piece, pistols, and cutlass clean and fit for service. (In this they were extravagantly nice, endeavouring to outdo one another in the beauty and richness of their arms, giving sometimes at an auction at the mast, thirty or forty for a pair of pistols. These were slung in time of service with different coloured ribbons over their shoulders in a way peculiar to those fellows, in which they took great delight.)

VI. No boy or woman to be allowed among men If any man be found seducing any of the latter sex, and carried her to sea disguised, he was to suffer Death. (So that when any fell into their hands, as it chanced on the *Onslow*, they put a sentinel immediately over her to prevent ill consequences from so dangerous an instrument of division and quarrel. But then here lies the roguery; they contend who shall be sentinel, which happens generally to one of the greatest bullies who, to secure the lady's virtue, will let none lie with her but himself.)

VII. To desert their ship or their quarters in battle was punished with Death or Marooning.

VIII. No striking one another on board, but every man's quarrels to be ended on shore, at sword and pistol. (Thus, the quartermaster of the ship, when the parties will not come to any reconciliation, accompanies them on shore with what assistance he thinks proper, and turns the disputants back to back at so many paces distant, At the word of command they turn and fire immediately or else the piece is knocked out of their hands. If both miss they come to their cutlasses and then he is declared victor who draws the first blood.)

IX. No man to talk of breaking up their way of living till each had a share of 1,000. If, in order to do this, any man lost a limb or became a cripple in their service, he was to have 800 dollars out of the public stock, and for lesser hurts proportionately.

X. The Captain and the Quartermaster to receive two shares of a prize; the master, boatswain and gunner, one share and a half, and the other officers one and a quarter.

XI. The musicians to have rest on the Sabbath day, but the other six days and nights none, without special favour.[3]

Defoe wrote that the original signed articles had been thrown overboard when Roberts was captured, hinting that there were clauses which contained "something too horrid to be disclosed to any except such as were willing to be sharers in the iniquity of them."

The spectacular success of Rhode Island's Thomas Tew sparked the sea fever of the Golden Age. Until "a shot carried away the rim of Tew's belly" and he died after holding "his Bowels with his Hands some small space," he was living proof of how a mariner of modest background could catapult to international fame and fortune. He had sailed in late 1692 aboard the *Amity* with a commission from Isaac Richier, the Governor of Bermuda, to assist the British Royal Africa Company take a French trading post on the Guinea Coast. The *Amity* was owned by a syndicate of Bermuda merchants and officials from whom Tew bought a share and the right to crew it with sixty seasoned privateers.

No sooner were they at sea than Tew expressed an opinion that must have been already foremost in his mens' minds. "Why sail on their stated mission," he asked, when "if they succeeded they would do no service to the public, advantaging only a private company from which they could expect no proper reward for their bravery." Defoe relates that "Tew proposed launching a course which should lead them to Ease and Plenty, in which they might pass the rest of their Days. That one bold Push would do their Business, and then might return home, not only without Danger, but even with Reputation." To a man the crew vowed: "A gold chain or a wooden leg, we'll stand by you."

With that the *Amity* headed around the Cape of Good Hope and into the Red Sea. After months of cruising they happened on an electrifying prize—a ship of the Grand Mogul's en route from India. Her three hundred-man crew surrendered without a fight giving up a cargo of £100,000 worth of gold and silver, coffers of gems, pearls, a king's ransom in "elephants teeth," spices and bales of silk fabrics. Tew quit while he was ahead, sailing to St. Mary's where he careened the *Amity* and shared out the plunder. Each pirate received one share worth £1,200. Tew received two shares and the quartermaster and surgeon a share and a half each.

Most of the pirates carried their loot back to Newport where all but a few pulpit-pounding clergymen hailed Tew as a triumphant hero. After all, the ship he had plundered belonged to "heathen Moors." The merchants of Boston descended in droves to buy up the plunder. Tew was fussed over by Newport society and invited to New York by Governor Fletcher. To complaints that he had received a known pirate, and been seen riding in public and dining with him, the governor wrote to the Lords of Trade saying that he found him a most engaging man and that "at some times when the labours of my day were over it was some divertisement as well as information to me, to hear him talk."

Tew sailed again in November 1694. His luck ran out less than a year later when he was killed boarding another Mogul merchantman. By that time scores of expeditions, fitted out in the New World had sailed in his wake. On his last expedition Tew had joined forces with Henry Every, the "Arch Pirate." Widely known as John Avery, this chubby son of a Plymouth innkeeper signed himself Henry Every and was called Long Ben by his associates. He had served in the Royal Navy and in the merchant marine before launching a piratical career under the protection of Cadwallader Jones, Governor of the Bahamas of whom it was said that "he highly caressed those Pirates that came to Providence" and "gave Commissions to pirates without and contrary to the advice of the Council." Jones, who reportedly kept the inhabitants of the proprietary colony on New Providence in "abominable slavery," was at such odds with his Council that he had his son train the guns of a ship in the harbor on the Council Chamber. He had been overthrown and imprisoned by the Council at one point but in February 1692 he was rescued from prison and restored to power by "some desperate Rogues, Pirates and others . . . a seditious rabble."

Much of Avery's life is sketchy. Pirates were often reluctant to talk much of their childhood, home or family, hoping someday to return and settle down on the proceeds of their endeavors. Avery had a varied career. He seems to have been successively the captain of a logwood freighter plying the Bay of Campeche, a slaver for the Royal Africa Company employed by the Governor of Bermuda and a pirate under "Red Hand" Nicholls in the West Indies in the early 1690s. All this led up to the exploits which were to make Long Ben the pirates' pirate, the best known and most imitated of them all and the subject of spirited conversation from the drawing rooms of London to the brothels and barracks of every colony.

Avery was sailing master aboard a Bristol privateer hired by Spain to attack French smugglers based on Martinique who were trading with Spanish colonies. Under Avery's leadership the crew which had not been paid for eight months mutinied at La Coruña, a Spanish port where they put in for passengers. The ship was rechristened the *Fancy* and set a course for the Indian Ocean. Off the Comoro Islands northwest of Madagascar Avery seized a French pirate vessel jammed with plundered Moorish treasure and signed on most of her crew.

He came upon Tew and they decided to collaborate. Soon a former mate of Tew's, Captain Want, sailing a Spanish prize and three other Rhode Island pirate vessels joined them to form a formidable fleet under Avery's command. Just north of Madagascar they captured a ship crammed with some £40,000 in gold and silver, the *Fateh Mohamed*, which belonged to the wealthiest merchant of Surat, an important seaport on the northwest coast of India. The *Ganj Suwai*, a much larger vessel owned by the Grand Mogul himself, was ahead of the *Fateh Mohamed* on its way to Surat and also fell into Avery's hands. Its name means "Exceeding Treasure" and the treasures it yielded truly surpassed anything yet seen. The ship, with eighty guns and four hundred soldiers, was transporting high ranking Moslems home from the pilgrimage to Mecca and was laden with £500,000 worth of dazzling treasures. The pirates behaved abominably toward the passengers. The East India Company confirmed Indian reports of torture, rape and pillage. Some noble ladies were so barbarously treated that they plunged daggers into their own hearts from shame. Others jumped into the sea rather than submit to the pirates who were so savage that a number of women didn't survive, including the aged wife of a relative of the Grand Mogul. When the pirates tired of abusing the women among whom were a number of Turkish concubines, they threw some of them overboard. Then they sailed to Reunion Island, a pirate base in the vicinity of Madagascar where they shared out the plunder.

They had a breathtaking array of swag to divide including half a million gold and silver coins, chests and chests of jewels and a gold trimmed saddle and bridle set with rubies, a present for the Grand Mogul. Each of the four hundred pirates who had participated, got a share of £1,000 plus some gems. A number of youngsters under eighteen received £500 each (the amount a merchant seaman might make in his whole career) and a few boys who were under fourteen were each given £100 which the pirates intended to be used "to apprentice themselves to an honest trade ashore." Avery took the customary two shares for the captain but it was felt he had cheated his associates and held back more.

The Mogul was enraged and did nothing to quell a riot in which one Englishman was stoned to death and many others were severely beaten. Sixty-seven of England's East India Company officials in Surat were imprisoned for almost a year until the Company made good the loss. The East India Company which stood to lose its foothold in the India trade was aghast at the pirate situation. Meanwhile Avery's fleet split up with ships heading for Madagascar, the Persian Gulf and Ethiopia. Fifty of the *Fancy*'s crew elected to settle on Reunion. Avery replaced them with ninety slaves before heading home to the Bahamas. At the Portuguese island of São Tomé off West Africa he bought supplies which he paid for with a phony and funny bill of exchange drawn on the fictitious Bank of Aldgate Pump with the signatures of one Timothy Tugmutton and a certain Simon Whifflepin.

Oblivious of the price on his head—£500 from the British Government and £500 from the East Indian Company—Avery made landfall at St. Thomas. The worldly Père Labat, who had sailed with the buccaneers was among the customers who had a field day buying bargain priced loot. He noted in his journal that "A roll of muslin embroidered with gold could be had for only twenty sols and the rest of the cargo in proportion." Many merchants in St. Thomas filled their stores with the sumptuous Indian fabrics and other pirated goods. Labat spent all the money he had and borrowed an additional 200 écus to buy fabrics. The Caribbean was becoming an international emporium.

Avery found himself welcomed in the Bahamas after he offered 7,000 pounds worth of goods, some ivory and 2,000 pieces of eight to Governor Trott, who had replaced the notorious pirate-protector, Jones. Trott, however, informed the pirate he could not issue the pardon Avery expected. Avery then sent a letter to the Governor of Jamaica offering him "a great gun," a bribe of £20,000, for a pardon. The Arch Pirate was refused again, most likely because the eyes of the world were upon him. The *Fancy's* crew trickled into the colonies where pardons were obtained (Governors Fletcher and Markham being most helpful) and before long many of the pirates were back on the high seas.

Some of Avery's men landed a little sloop at Westport in County Mayo in June of 1696. Local folk were amazed at the boat's unusual cargo of chests of gold and silver. When the mariners offered to buy horses worth ten shillings for as much as ten pounds at any price the local sheriff became suspicious and detained them. One who escaped, John Dann, was soon arrested in an inn at Rochester when a curious chambermaid discovered £1,045 in gold coins concealed in his quilted jacket. Goldsmiths in the large towns were alerted and eventually twenty-four of Avery's men were arrested in England.

Avery himself was never caught. He had started calling himself Bridgeman and sailed for Ireland where he vanished. Former mates gave conflicting accounts of his whereabouts. The public, inspired by the spate of plays, broadsides, ballads and pamphlets about "the Scourge of the Indies" believed he had wed a gorgeous Mogul princess from the *Ganj Sawai* and retired to Madagascar where he ruled over a native kingdom. Defoe, however, recounted that Avery holed up in a little Devon hamlet where he died a pauper in 1727. According to Defoe, unscrupulous fences in Bristol took his treasure which consisted of diamonds and gem studded gold goblets in return for a small cash down payment and then reneged on the balance. They threatened to turn him in if he asked for more and he died cursing them for "being as good Pyrates at land as he was at sea."

NOTES

1. John Browne's last words, *An Account of the Pirates with Divers of their Speeches, Letter and a Poem* (*26 executed July 19, 1723 at Newport*), pamphlet reprinted 1769.

2. Ben Franklin's youthful verse, Larabee, Leonard, W., editor, *The Autobiography of Benjamin Franklin*, New Haven, Yale University Press, 1964, p. 29.

3. Long quote from Defoe, Defoe, Daniel (under pseudonym Captain Charles Johnson), *A General History of the Pyrates*, edited by Arthur L. Hayward, Routledge and Kegan Paul, London, 1955, pp. 182–84.

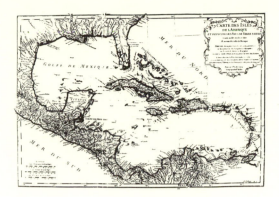

8
Global Outreach

A very led the way to the eastern seas. A host of adventurers followed him. The best remembered was William Kidd, a prominent and affluent New Yorker who was a merchant, landowner and ship captain. Born in Scotland he came to New York in 1691 and married Sarah Oort, the wealthiest widow in the city. Fortunately for him she was beautiful and young. He captained a privateer which made several successful Caribbean cruises and was highly respected. A single exploit made Kidd the best known pirate in history. Kidd gained epic stature in his own day and the accretions of legend have credited him with every sort of heinous crime and vast amounts of still-buried treasure. Scrutiny of his ill-fated piratical career reveals that he was really a rather mediocre and unlucky pirate who was done in by indecision, bad judgment and politics. What began in 1695 as an expedition with great promise turned into a nightmare and took him to Execution Dock on the Thames where he was hanged in May of 1701.

Kidd's history has little to do with the Caribbean but no history of piracy would be complete without mention of this adventurer. East India Company vessels were preyed upon by American and English pirates and in 1695 the Company pressured King William III to suppress piracy. He replaced the infamous Governor Fletcher with Richard Coote, Earl of Bellomont, as Governor of New England and charged him with putting an end to the North American pirates. Bellomont happened to meet Kidd in London and enlisted his aid. Kidd received a royal commission empowering "our trusty and well beloved Captain Kid, Commander of the *Adventure Galley* to capture Tew, Wake, John Ireland and other pirates based in the colonies who "commit many and great Piracies, robberies and depredations on the seas . . . to the great hindrance and discouragement of trade and navigation."

It looked like a fail-proof opportunity to make a legitimate fortune from French shipping and pirate plunder of all nations. Kidd organized the expedition which was a joint-stock venture whose subscribers were among the most influential men in the realm. They included the Whig leaders then in power: Somers, the Lord Chancellor; the Earl of Oxford, First Lord of the Admiralty; the two Secretaries of State, the Duke of Shrewsbury and the Earl of Romney. The king was to come in for a tenth of the profits and Kidd himself put in £600 of the £6,000 needed to outfit the expedition. It seemed insignificant in the flush of anticipation that none of the backers' names appeared publicly in connection with the venture, save that of Kidd's patron, Bellomont.

He sailed for New York on a newly built 284 tonner with thirty-four cannon, a hand-picked crew and Bellomont's commission which made him an authorized privateer. In fact he had two letters. One empowered him to capture pirates named in the document and the other gave him license to capture French ships. An ominous event occurred as the ship set sail when Kidd failed to dip his flag in deference to a Royal Navy sloop. Perhaps in retaliation for his arrogance a pressgang boarded and hustled off many of his men. He was forced to replace them with assorted scum, many of scarcely veiled piratical leanings. In New York he took on additional seamen trying to make sure none of them were "Madagascar men" because, at that point, piracy was not on his agenda.

He sailed for the Indian Ocean in September of 1696, aiming for the pirate nest of Madagascar. Things did not go well. The ship began to take on water. In the space of a week a third of the crew perished from cholera. Weakened by scurvy during the 9,000 mile voyage the remainder of the crew began to mutter about going on the account. At Johanna Island in the Comoro Gulf he took on fifty replacements, obviously veteran rovers. Kidd appears to have been tortured by indecision as he cruised the tropical waters. Months passed and no significant prey appeared. Should he adhere to the terms of his privateering commission or turn pirate? The crew became more mutinous and he allowed them to attempt culling a Moorish merchantman from its escort of Dutch and French ships. The effort failed and time wore on. An Arab vessel which they plundered for provisions spread the word to East India Company officials that English pirates were about. Near Goa two Portuguese *guarda-costas* battled the *Adventure Galley*, tearing her rigging and splintering the hull.

The ship moved sluggishly over a vacant sea, through stifling air. No prizes appeared. The rotting food crawled with maggots. The water was foul. Days became weeks. Finally, just off the tip of India a merchant ship was sighted. She turned out to be the *Loyal Captain*, an English ship and Kidd refused to take her. Another couple of weeks passed with no prize on the horizon The gunner, a feisty man named William Moore, taunted Kidd and a fierce fight ensued. In the course of it Kidd smashed a wooden bucket on Moore's head. The gunner crumpled to the deck and next day he was dead. It was this incident which eventually put the noose around Kidd's neck but at the time what concerned him was the deplorable condition of both the ship and crew. As for the death of a mutinous seaman, he assured the surgeon that he had friends in England who would take care of "that matter" should it ever be necessary.

The *Adventure Galley* was leaking so badly that hourly shifts of eight men had to work the pumps around the clock. Cables were cinched around the hull to keep her from falling apart. More than a year had passed; a tortuous year which had brought privation, illness and dwindling hopes. The mirage of a treasure laden prize continued to elude them. They did seize a number of vessels following Moore's death but they carried an assortment of cotton, candy, wax, opium, iron, butter and coffee—hardly what they'd hoped for and suffered for.

In February of 1698 the long awaited opportunity presented itself as the *Adventure Galley* cruised sluggishly along the Malabar coast. The *Quedah Merchant* sailed into view riding low in the water, weighted down with cargo. The pirates took her easily. She was owned by Indian merchants from Surat and carried a cargo valued at £710,000 belonging to Persian Armenians. The *Quedah Merchant* had an English captain, Dutch officers and a Moslem crew. But her pass was French, issued by the French East Indian Company so Kidd, with some qualms claimed her as a lawful prize. His men swarmed aboard ripping into the hold where they found gold, silks, jewels, muslins, sugar, guns, iron and other goods. They had finally hit the jackpot. The memory of the past months' privations vanished before such an array of treasure.

Poor Kidd—bad luck still dogged him. He took his ship and the *Quedah Merchant* into St. Mary's, a pirate port on Madagascar. The only other ship anchored there was an East India Company frigate, the *Mocha* which had been captured by Robert Culliford. Culliford was the same pirate who, with the connivance of some of Kidd's crew, had snatched his brigantine in the Caribbean while Kidd was ashore on Antigua. Culliford had a crew of forty and Kidd proposed to his larger contingent that they take the *Mocha*. After all, Culliford was a pirate and Kidd's commission called for the capture of such rovers and their vessels.

Kidd's crew would have none of it. They turned on their captain, jeering at his leadership and said they would rather fire guns at him than at the pirate. Kidd sold £10,000 worth of cargo and shared it out. As soon as they had their share of the *Quedah* plunder ninety-seven of Kidd's crew defected to Culliford. Kidd, thoroughly demoralized, was left with a skeleton crew of eighteen, a sinking ship and a long trip ahead. He wasn't even sure Culliford, who now had the upper hand, would let him sail. His former crew ransacked both the *Adventure Galley* and the *Quedah*, stripping them of gear, hand guns, cannon and even sails. They threatened to blow Kidd's head off if he tried to stop them. His sea chest was pillaged and the *Adventure Galley's* log was burned while Kidd remained locked in his cabin with loaded guns. When he emerged Culliford magnanimously invited him to join him aboard the *Mocha* to drink "bombo" the pirates' potent lemonade and make peace. Kidd had no choice if he wanted to get home with his share of the *Quedah* cargo.

He abandoned the derelict *Adventure Galley*, picked up a raggle taggle crew on the beach to man the *Quedah* and headed for the Caribbean after a tedious five month wait for the northeast monsoon to drive him around the Cape of Good Hope. In London, meanwhile, the political crisis that was to spell Kidd's doom was taking shape. The Tories made much of the fact that Kidd, whose exploits had appeared in exaggerated form in a report on piracies in the Indian Ocean, was backed by leading Whigs. The Whig government, attacked as "a Corporation of Pirates," had no choice but to defend itself by labeling Kidd an "obnoxious pirate" and exclude him from a royal offer of pardon to all surrendering Indian Ocean pirates. Colonial authorities from the West Indies to Massachusetts were ordered to arrest him on sight.

It was only when he anchored at the little island of Anguilla that Kidd learned he was the "Scourge of the Indies." He was alarmed to hear he was a vicious pirate with a price on his head but he was confident that with the aid of his patron, Governor Bellomont, and the French passes from the ships he had taken he would be cleared of any charges. He tried and failed to land at St. Thomas despite an offer of 45,000 pieces of eight. Not even the neutral Danes were willing to play host to such a wanted man, even though Kidd assured officials there that he only sought safe haven until he could make contact with his powerful friends.

Kidd, family man, pillar of the community, was a fugitive. He had to make it to Bellomont in New York. He realized the bulky *Quedah* could never outrun one of the men-o-war which were on the lookout for him so he ran her up a river on the isolated southeast coast of Hispaniola. A portion of the cargo, including his share of gold bars, gold dust, silver plate, jewels and silks, was transferred to his sloop. The remainder of the cargo was left under guard until he could clear himself.

In his anonymous sloop Kidd and twenty-one men made it safely to Long Island. There he learned Bellomont was in Boston. An old friend whom he contacted acted as a go-between, making a trip to Boston to explain Kidd's case and returning with a deceptive letter from the Governor. Bellomont betrayed Kidd with no evident remorse, luring him to Boston. Before he went, Kidd sent Bellomont's young wife an enameled jewel box with some gems. He also sold off some of the *Quedah* cargo which by Admiralty law should have been brought before a court before being disposed of, even under the new law which gave one hundred percent of a prize to a commissioned privateer. He acted as if he were dealing with his own property, putting gold bars in keeping with a pirate friend from Rhode Island and burying chests of gold and gems on Gardiner's Island, owned by his friend John Gardiner who gave him a receipt for the treasure.

In Boston, Kidd tried to negotiate with Bellomont. He gave his wife a further bribe of gold bars worth £1,000 presented in a green silk pouch. Her aging husband made her send them back and refused to meet with Kidd privately. Kidd was arrested and imprisoned. His parceled out treasure was recovered for evidence. Bellomont even sent a sloop to Antigua, St. Thomas, Curacao and Jamaica to search for booty he might have sold. The cache on Gardiner's Island was recovered too, although even today there is a persistent belief that Kidd's treasure is buried on the island which the Gardiner family still owns. Later, Bellomont was to write to London asking for the one-third share due him as Vice-Admiral of the American seas. Kidd's former friend, eager to disassociate himself from a project gone sour, wrote Lord Somers calling the prisoner "a monster . . . there was never a greater liar or thief in the world than Kidd." Throughout the freezing winter of 1699, Kidd was shackled in irons in a damp Boston prison. By the time he arrived in England the following April, the passions of Parliament and the public were inflamed by the "Kidd Affair."

William Kidd, the reluctant pirate, never had a chance to acquit himself. Too many politicians were set on seeing him "jerked into the Devil's arms." He had handed the two French passes, which were his tickets to freedom, to Bellomont in Boston. He never saw them again. Kidd was the scapegoat for both Whigs and Tories. During his four trials he could not prove his innocence because his log had been burned and his passes turned over to Bellomont who denied having seen them. All his papers had disappeared and prosecution and defense conspired against him. He was found guilty of murder and five counts of piracy and condemned to death.

William Kidd, honored New Yorker, pew holder in Trinity Church was to hang like the vilest outlaw, not even granted a gentleman's death by firing squad. On May 23, 1701, he left Newgate Prison in a procession led by a Deputy Marshall who carried on his shoulder the silver oar, symbol of the Admiralty Court. Kidd was in an open cart draped in black, a noose already around his neck. A sea of revelers swarmed about him "swilling beer and gin, hurling impudent and ribald jests, picking pockets . . . singing ballads . . . one continual fair all the way."

A sympathetic warden had furnished him with a numbing amount of liquor so that he was reeling drunk and scarcely aware of the macabre parade that wound its way through the squalid slums to the mud flats at Wapping. Bad luck dogged him to the very end for when he was "turned off" the makeshift gibbet at the river's edge, the rope broke and he fell to the ground. The second time the noose held. His corpse was chained to a post at the water's edge until the tide washed over it three times in fulfillment of Admiralty law. Then Kidd's head was coated with tar, bound with iron bands and encased in a metal cage to hold the skull in place as the tissues rotted. The grisly corpse was displayed on a gibbet at Tilbury Point in the Thames Estuary, remaining for several years to serve as "a greater Terrour to all Persons from committing ye like Crimes for the time to come." Thus ended the brief career of the "milk and water" pirate, done in by ambition and fatal misjudgments.

Dead, even more than alive, Kidd took on mythic proportions. Tales of "Kidd's treasure" have mesmerized generations of children. Countless holes have been dug all along the Atlantic Coast and in the islands by searchers, more than a little afraid to find any treasure for fear that his restless shade, eyes glowing like coals, might appear to defend his buried gold. A New York legend reflects the melancholy character of the amateur pirate. Kidd eternally wanders the countryside in damp, salt-stiffened sea clothes, asking for a place to sleep at isolated farmhouses. In the morning, the story goes, he is gone but there are a few gold Mogul coins by his bedside. No treasure has come to light because there is none but, ironically the two French passes, the only treasure which might have turned the tide for the hapless Kidd, were found by an American researcher at London's Public Records Office in 1911.

Of the six men convicted with Kidd, only one was executed. The others were reprieved. Two bribed their Newgate jailers and embarked for America sailing past Kidd's gruesome corpse. In Pennsylvania they retrieved £2,300 worth of gold they had buried when they arrived with Kidd from Hispaniola. Three days after Kidd's execution Bradenham, a surgeon, and Palmer, two men who had turned Crown witness, were fully pardoned. A pirate named Theophilus Turner who testified for the Crown was reprieved at the last minute and demanded the return of his sea chest which contained, according to an inventory, "1,600 heavy "Peeces of eight, 249 ounces of plate 20 peeces of Chickines (gold sequin coins), a gold box, 200 pieces of eight ryalls quarter, amber, woods, muslins, floured satin, some plain and four striped with silk thread, 2 dozen pair fine worsted stockings, spices, cloves, nutmegs, broadcloth and Scarlett and Green cloth, books, navigation instruments." He also demanded restitution of a small Negro boy aged ten or eleven. Kidd's share of the *Quedah Merchant* plunder was forfeited to the Crown. The gold, silver, gems and rich fabrics were auctioned off for almost £6,500. Part of the profit was used to purchase one of the buildings of England's National Maritime Museum at Greenwich.

Kidd's foray came at the end of the heyday of the Pirate Round. The various East India companies and their governments beefed up defensive and offensive measures against the pirates. On the Atlantic side, it became apparent that the profitable collusion between the freebooters and American colonials was under Crown scrutiny and couldn't continue forever. The pirates, deserters and beach bums who had found sanctuary on Madagascar and adjacent islands mourned the passing of piracy's most lucrative phase. In 1699 a Royal Navy squadron appeared off St. Mary's Island sending some fifteen hundred pirates into the woods or over to Madagascar. A couple of years later the threat from pirates was considered so minute that the patrols were recalled for European duty. The pirates who had settled on Madagascar were reduced to poverty and despised by the natives and by 1726 there were reportedly fewer than twenty of them left who were hiding in the woods to escape the vengeance of the natives whom they had abused for so long.

The rewards of pursuing the sweet trade in the eastern seas remained tempting and piracy didn't die out completely in spite of the increased dangers and the decreasing volume of rich cargo shipments from the waning Mogul Empire. After a lull of twenty years Madagascar once again bloomed as a pirate haunt and the eastern seas boasted the boldest and best of the sea's outlaw rovers. Men like Christopher Condent, Edward England, Howell Davis and John Taylor led the way from the New World after 1718 when the pirate stronghold on New Providence had been wiped out by Woodes Rogers.

Condent was one of the first to sail east on the old Round route. Off Bombay he took an Arab ship carrying £150,000 in gold and silver, the richest prize since the end of the Round. At the share-out held on the beach at St. Mary's each man received close to £3000. There was such a plethora of goods that packets of spices, bolts of silks and gold-embellished muslins were left strewn on the sand. Condent and forty of his crew showed uncommon good sense in retiring on the strength of their phenomenal haul. They were granted French pardons by the Governor of Reunion (formerly Bourbon) Island. Condent married the Governor's sister-in-law and became a wealthy shipowner in St. Malo, the former corsair base on the northern coast of France.

Others followed him, clearing out of American waters which had become too dangerous. They plundered the Indian Ocean, the Red Sea, the Persian Gulf and all around the coast of Africa until there was such an outcry from European trading companies that the leading trading nations cooperated to eradicate piracy from the eastern seas. The British Admiralty dispatched a squadron of warships to the south Indian Ocean. Mauritius and Reunion which had become favored pirate settlements were destroyed in 1721. The French navy concentrated on pirates in the Persian Gulf and the Dutch supplied three ships to protect the Mocha fleet in the Red Sea. By the end of that year most of the new surge of English and American pirates had vanished into retirement, sailed back to the West Indies or drifted around the Cape of Good Hope to the 3,000 mile long Guinea Coast where the Golden Age rovers had their final fling preying on trading ships laden with gold, slaves and ivory.

One of the pirates who went back to the West Indies was John Taylor, a ruthless veteran of New Providence. In the Indian Ocean his company had joined forces with that led by another New Providence pirate, Edward England, an Irishman whom Defoe characterized as "having a great deal of good nature . . . courageous, not over-avaricious, humane, but too often over-ruled." Taylor commanding the *Victory* and England in the *Fancy* engaged the *Cassandra*, an English East Indiaman they encountered at the island of Johanna near Madagascar in one of piracy's most famous battles. In August 1720 the pirate ships, having seized a number of prizes, repaired to Johanna, a watering place frequented by both pirates and merchantmen. They found two East Indiamen there. One, the *Greenwich* slipped out of the bay but the *Cassandra* under James Macrae, son of a poor English cottager who had made a rare upward climb to a naval command, fought bitterly for several hours. The other East Indiaman, whose captain had deserted Macrae despite a vow to face any pirate attack together, watched from a safe distance. Thirteen crewmen were killed and twenty-four wounded on the *Cassandra*. Casualties were even greater on the pirate ships. But Macrae had little hope in the face of such great odds. The pirates with their black and bloody flags flying forced Macrae to run his ship aground. Those who didn't escape ashore in time were slaughtered when the pirates swarmed aboard.

Macrae negotiated with the pirate captains although he had a severe head wound. Against Taylor's will, England insisted Macrae be given the all-but-sinking *Fancy*, half his original cargo and a skeleton crew. During the seven weeks it took them to reach Bombay, most of Macrae's men died of thirst. He was greeted as a hero by the East Indian Company and promoted a number of times, becoming Governor of Madras within a year and a half—a position paying £500 per annum which offered such opportunities for further gain that Macrae was able to retire after six years in office with a fortune of well over £100,000.

England, the humane pirate, fared less well. His own company deposed him for "softness" toward Macrae. He and a few others who were also expelled made a gruelling passage to Madagascar in an open boat, where he was reduced to begging and died soon afterward. One of those banished for standing by Macrae was a pirate who swore he had once sailed with the valiant captain. Described by Defoe as "a man with a terrible pair of whiskers and a wooden leg, being stuck round with pistols" he became Robert Louis Stevenson's inspiration for Long John Silver in *Treasure Island*.

According to Defoe no part of the *Cassandra* booty was so highly valued as the surgeon's chest "for they were all poxed to a great degree." After they had treated their venereal sores with mercury compound the pirates set off under Taylor on a rampage which scored the single greatest hit of the Golden Age. Sailing in the *Cassandra* and the *Victory* they took prize after prize from Arab dhows to an Indiaman, torturing and murdering the crews. In April of 1721 Taylor on the *Cassandra* and Oliver La Bouche (yet another refugee from the Bahamas) commanding the *Victory* sailed into the harbor at St. Denis on the island of Bourbon with two hundred ferocious cutthroats.

What they found there exceeded all expectations. Anchored in the harbor was the *Nossa Senhora do Cabo*, a Portuguese carrack which had been dismasted in a storm while en route from Goa, the Portuguese enclave on the southwest coast of India. In addition to the usual eastern luxuries the *Cabo* was laden with a stunningly large and precious shipment of sparkling diamonds. A large share of the consignment belonged to the retiring Viceroy of Goa, Luis de Meneses, Count of Ericeira and Marquis of Lourical. The gems were the fruit of his private dealings and were earmarked for replenishing his family's depleted fortune. The unlucky Count not only lost his entire stock but also royal favor. Some of the diamonds were being sent to the king of Portugal who was so put out at the loss that he banished Ericeira from court for ten years.

The Count had gallantly defended his poorly armed vessel, stopping only when his sword snapped in hand-to-hand combat on the quarterdeck. The pirates admired the viceroy's courage. Taylor returned his diamond studded gold sword hilt to him and wanted to give him back his personal belongings but the count proudly spurned the offer, stating he wished no distinction to be made between himself and the other captives. As a consequence, the boorish pirates, who were ignorant of their value, shredded unique oriental manuscripts to make wadding for their guns.

The island's governor paid a ransom for the Viceroy who was set free.

The pirates transferred to the prize with the armaments and cargo from their weather-beaten vessels and sailed off to St. Mary's for the share-out. All told the cruise yielded more than a million pounds worth of plunder. The *Cabo* cargo, exclusive of the diamonds, was worth some £375,000. The gems alone were worth more than half a million. Each of the rovers received more than £4,000 and a handful of gems. Defoe wrote that each man got forty-two small diamonds or less if the gems were larger. "An ignorant or merry fellow, who had only one in this division, as being adjudged equal to forty-two small, muttered very much at the lot and went and broke it in a mortar, swearing afterwards he had a better share than any of them, for he had beat it, he said, into forty-three sparks."

Despite the outstanding amount each pirate received, most of them continued on the account with Taylor and la Bouche. Plans for another cruise and a voyage to Cochin on the south Indochina coast to sell the diamonds were scuttled by advance warning of a British naval squadron on its way to purge the Indian Ocean. Taylor and his men repaired to the West Indies expecting to buy a pardon from the Governor of Jamaica. The political climate, however, had changed by 1723 and he refused them, so they sought refuge at Portobelo. The authorities there welcomed the well-heeled English and American pirates, granting them all royal pardons. Taylor bought a Spanish commission and in 1723 was captain of a ship which attacked the English logwood cutters in the Bay of Campeche, seizing eleven of their vessels and killing their crews in cold blood. A pirate ship captained by Edward Low, credited with taking 140 prizes in twenty months, appeared as the slaughter was ending and slew every Spaniard in sight. Somehow Taylor eluded him for there is evidence that in 1744 he was living in Cuba with a wife and three children.

Edward Low and George Lowther with whom he sailed early in his career represent the acme of senseless pirate cruelty which reached a peak around 1720 as the number of pirates was diminishing. Lowther began as a second mate on a Royal Africa Company ship carrying slaves. He led a mutiny off the coast of Gambia and was elected captain of the ship which appeared in the Caribbean in search of plunder. The Cayman Islands where the buccaneers had gone for turtles had become something of a pirate sanctuary and it was there that Lowther met up with Low, whom he made his lieutenant.

Low was a bad seed from his childhood in Westminster where he was the neighborhood bully, beating smaller children and stealing. After a stint as a merchant seaman he found employment in a Boston shipyard which ended before long, thanks to his antisocial behavior. Like so many others who couldn't make a go of it elsewhere, Low found his way to the Bay of Honduras to cut logwood. After shooting a bystander during a violent argument with his boss, Low fled the camp. He and a dozen companions seized a small vessel and set out to "make a black Flag and declare War against all the World."

Lowther and Low were two of a kind and together they cruised the West Indies and the Virginia Capes, plundering one ship after another and barbarously torturing their captives. Lowther's specialty was putting slow burning matches between a man's fingers, letting them burn through to the bone if his victim didn't divulge where his valuables were hidden. In May of 1722 Low split off with forty-four pirates to form his own company. Lowther's luck took a turn for the worse. His ship was all but destroyed when the *Amy*, an English merchantman put up a surprisingly strong defense when attacked off South Carolina. Lowther was forced to hole up for the winter in a remote North Carolina inlet, living off the land while the ship was repaired.

In the spring he headed north and spent the summer plundering vessels with modest cargoes on the Newfoundland Banks. Following the traditional pattern of wintering in a more hospitable climate, Lowther headed for the West Indies in August of 1723. He seized a few prizes among the islands but most of the time his men were on half rations for lack of provisions. When it was time for the periodic careening of his sloop Lowther headed for the small island of Blanquilla, northeast of Tortuga. It was popular with pirates because of the number of turtles and iguanas there. As their ship lay careened on its side, masts and rigging on the beach, Lowther and his company were surprised by the *Eagle*, a sloop out of Barbados which belonged to the South Sea Company.

In one of the few cases where pirates were attacked while careening, the *Eagle*'s crew engaged the outlaws, killing several of them and capturing all the rest save Lowther, three others and a small drummer boy. Lowther was found dead on the beach next to his gun after the *Eagle* had sailed away with his ship and captive men, most of whom were condemned by a Vice-Admiralty Court at St. Kitts and executed. He appears to have committed suicide, an act exceedingly rare among pirates.

The psychopathic Low fared better leading his company of sadists on many daring attacks, sometimes cutting rich prizes right out of guarded harbors. He swept over the seas, from the West Indies to Newfoundland and across to the Azores, the Canaries and Cape Verde. Sailors' blood turned cold at the sight of his ensign which was originally plain blue. Once he had a fleet he flew a black flag with a red skeleton. Low's appearance was equally bloodcurdling. His face had been disfigured when one of his drunken men missed a prisoner with his cutlass and slashed the side of Low's face open. The surgeon who sewed it up was none too sober and when Low criticized his technique, he hit Low full force in the face, ripping out the stitches and then told him to "sew up his Chops himself and be damned."

Low and his barbaric gang lopped heads off with abandon. They cut off a New England whaling captain's ears and made him eat them seasoned with pepper and salt. They ripped men open for sport and strung two Portuguese friars to a yardarm and left them dangling. Defoe wrote that they "almost as often murdered a man from the excess of good humor as out of passion and resentment . . . for danger lurked in their very smiles." Low offered the captain of a Virginia prize a bowl of punch and when the trembling prisoner declined saying he was much too shaken up, Low put his pistol to the poor man's head with one hand, held the tankard in the other and told him to choose one or the other. Overcoming his nerves, the captain downed about a quart.

The pirates took a Portuguese ship they knew to be carrying rich cargo and tortured several men to find where the treasure was hidden. The Portuguese said that the captain had put 11,000 gold moidores in a bag and hung it out his cabin window as the pirates approached, cutting it when they attacked so that the coins fell into the sea. This news sent Low into an apoplectic rage. He had the captain's lips cut off and broiled in front of him and then, according to some accounts, forced the Portuguese mate to eat them before slaughtering the entire crew.

Whether the diabolic Low ever got his just desserts is unclear. Accounts vary. Some say he perished with all hands when his ship, the bizarrely named *Merry Christmas*, went down. He may have sailed to Brazil and many believed he killed his quartermaster during one of his violent rages and was cast adrift in an open unprovisioned boat with three companions. According to this version a French warship picked the men up and took them to Martinique where they were hanged.

Low and Lowther came at the close of piracy's Golden Age. The reign of terror which slowed Caribbean traffic to a trickle in the early 1720s was over by 1730. After 1728 pirates, whose depredations had been one of the chief subjects of official colonial correspondence, were seldom mentioned. The surge in piratical activity following the Peace of Utrecht in 1713 prompted Jamaica's Governor Lawes to write in 1718 that "There is hardly any ship or vessel coming or going out of this island that is not plundered."

The pirates of this extraordinary period could not have operated without their bases. None was as important as the Bahamas, particularly New Providence which by 1716 had become the "Nest of Pyrates" Virginia's Governor Spotswood was so concerned about. In 1706 John Graves, collector of Customs for the Bahamas, noted that "War is no sooner ended but the West Indies always swarm with pirates." He cannot have imagined the mushrooming of piracy that took place a few years later with the sparsely settled Bahamas as its pivot point. There had never been so many pirates as there were in the years immediately after 1713. They numbered in the thousands, drawn to the Caribbean because of the relatively richer prizes there. The Spanish treasure fleets had not sailed during the war years so there was a backlog of gold, silver, emerald and pearls to tempt them but the pirates fell on ships of all nations, forcing most vessels to sail in convoys for protection.

The Bahamas had been a pirate rendezvous since the 1680s when the obliging Governor, Robert Clarke, issued commissions giving them a veneer of legality. Succeeding governors continued to welcome the pirates for the revenue they brought to the area which was neglected by its owners, the same Lords Proprietors who held the Carolinas. The early pirates had preyed on Spanish and French shipping. When the Spaniards captured a privateer they showed what they thought of his English commission by pinning it to his chest when he was hanged. In 1684 a Spanish force of 250 raided the principal settlement (which wasn't called Nassau until 1695) in retaliation for the plundering of their ships. They murdered the governor, burned all the houses and took many men, women, children and slaves to Havana. The survivors decamped to Jamaica and for two years the island was left to the birds and lizards.

Its location, the abundance of provisions and the fact that it had the perfect pirate harbor, spacious enough for five hundred pirate craft yet too shallow for pursuing warships, made New Providence too attractive to be left alone for long. During the Pirate Round the long distance rovers mingled with Caribbean lesser groups in the rude taverns that sprang up along the glistening beach. Merchants and traders were drawn to the settlement. They catered to the outlaws needs and purchased their plunder, much of which was then smuggled to the colonies for resale. Whores and outcasts, mangy dogs and multiplying rats added to the fluctuating population. The pirates no longer restricted themselves to attacking enemy ships. By 1700 it was reported from Virginia that "all the news of America is the swarming of pirates not only on these coasts but all the West Indies over, which doth ruin trade ten times worse than a war."

The War of the Spanish Succession affected all the West Indian settlements as their security and supplies varied with the shifting control of the Caribbean routes. Martinique and Guadeloupe were reservoirs of privateering crews. French planters from other islands who had taken refuge on Martinique were faced with the prospect of starving if they didn't take to the sea. Despite their inexperience French privateers captured 163 English and colonial ships in 1704. English merchants of Barbados financed several privateering expeditions which took a number of French ships and made land raids on vulnerable French settlements but they couldn't touch Martinique. A naval fleet was sent out from England to cooperate with local forces in an attack on Martinique which was the principal French privateer base. The fleet anchored first at Barbados, dallying there until it was too late to take action.

Governor Codrington of the Leeward Islands attributed the missed opportunity to the hospitality of Barbados, where "the planters think the best way of making their strangers welcome is to murther them with drinking; the tenth part of that strong liquor which will scarce warme the blood of our West Indians, who have bodies like Egyptian mummys must certainly despatch a newcomer to the other world." Eventually the combined forces attacked less strong Guadeloupe. The ubiquitous Père Labat was on the island and wrote an account of the raid which ended with the British, many of whom were sick, retreating with considerable booty including many guns.

In 1703 a joint Franco-Spanish force plundered New Providence. A second attack the next year wiped out what was left of Nassau and drove most of the inhabitants to outer islands including Cat Island, Eleuthera, Exuma and Harbour Island. For several years there was no organized government. French privateers choked seaborne commerce and ravaged St. Kitts and Nevis. Many of England's Caribbean colonies, the Leewards and Barbados in particular, suffered doubly through the war years because of singularly inept governors. Colonel Daniel Parke, Governor of the Leeward Islands, who was appointed on the basis of looks rather than ability is a case in point.

Parke was born in Virginia, son of a wealthy landowner whose steps he followed on the Council until, for unclear reasons, he went to England leaving behind his wife, children and many relieved Virginians. He enlisted in the army, becoming the Duke of Marlborough's aide-de-camp. Queen Anne was captivated by Parke's good looks and overlooked whispers of his arrogance and savage temper to bestow upon him £1,000, a miniature jeweled portrait of herself and the governorship of the Leewards.

Parke was disappointed because he had hoped for Virginia. There was strong mutual antipathy between him and the "ill-natured and troublesome people" he was sent to govern. His most pressing task was to deal with the French enemy. He thought of using Scottish troops to take Martinique or Puerto Rico. A proposal written in January 1707 to the home government reveals his contempt for the Scots and his lack of diplomacy; "Send me over tenn thousand Scotch with otemeal enough to keep them for three or four months . . . if we take it, we will have the plunder, the Scotch will have the land, in time the warm sun will exhale all those crudeties that makes them so troublesom and . . . if I gett them all knock'd on the head, I am off the opinion the English Nation will be no great losers by it." Needless to say, not even Queen Anne could find this proposal by her favorite worthy of anything but rebuke.

Parke incurred the hatred of almost everyone he came in contact with. Any reforms he wished to effect were undone by his intransigence and immorality. He seduced the daughters and wives of numerous colonists including the wife of Edward Chester, respected Speaker of the Antigua House of Assembly and agent for the Royal Africa Company. When a man Chester had injured in a fight died, Parke pressed to have him charged with murder but the jury balked and ruled the man expired of natural causes. Parke sometimes disguised himself and wandered through the streets eavesdropping which scarcely enhanced his image, especially since he was easily recognizable in his various disguises. He was wounded in one assassination attempt and then brutally beaten to death after being shot during a rebellion on Antigua. No one mourned. An official inquiry reported that almost all Her Majesty's subjects on the island had participated in the uprising, including all but one of the members of the Assembly.

Parke's successor, Walter Douglas was little better. He covered up for the rebellion's ringleaders, accepted bribes including £5,000 and twenty slaves and purloined the church plate from the Governor's chapel. Eventually he was recalled, tried and imprisoned for five years. Until the end of the war, the Leewards were subjected to the ravages of invading privateers who repeatedly looted, burned and carried off slaves, sugar machinery and other booty.

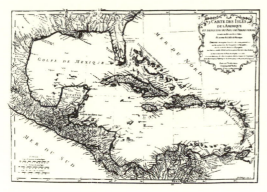

9

New
Providence
Pirate Paradise

irates replaced the privateers after 1713, bringing land raids to an end but aggravating disruption of the maritime commerce so vital to the West Indian colonies. Spanish pirates operated out of Cuba, Puerto Rico and St. Augustine. The French continued to use Martinique as their main base. The Virgin Islands harbored outlaws of all nationalities. New Providence rose again from the ashes to become the chief base for English and American pirates. At war's end some two hundred families engaged in desultory piracy and subsistence farming were sprinkled among the Bahamas. According to frequent reports from the Council of Trade and Plantations they existed "without any face or form of Government every man doing onely what's right in his own eyes." For twenty years they had been slighted, receiving no arms, ammunition or other supplies. The Council recommended that the Crown remove control of the Bahamas from the Lords Proprietors who had not fulfilled their obligation to establish a functioning administration.

During the war the settlers had been brutally victimized by roving bands of Spanish pirates. Once it was over a number of them began to gravitate from outlying cays to New Providence where pirates held sway. Belatedly a number of administrators were sent to New Providence but the burgeoning pirate forces sent them packing. One official, Thomas Walker, a former judge in the Vice Admiralty Court, had been on the island before. He returned in 1715 intending to eradicate the outlaw community but was chased off the island and fled to South Carolina.

The leadership vacuum was immediately filled by Thomas Barrow and Benjamin Hornigold, two English pirate chieftains who proclaimed a pirate republic with themselves as Governors of New Providence. They were joined by leading captains such as Charles Vane, Thomas Burgess, Calico Jack Rackham and Blackbeard. Ex-privateers, and outlaws from all over the New World swelled the population of the pirate sanctuary. Escaped servants, male and female, also found their way to the tent city that grew up around Nassau Harbor. The West Indies were still considered a dumping ground for undesirables by England and after the abortive Jacobite rebellion in 1715 some of the participants were transported to St. Kitts and Jamaica and sold as indentured servants. Their lot was grim; no better than that of the first white indentured servants. Worse actually, since vast numbers of slaves filled almost every occupational slot, including those of artisans so that after their terms expired they had little chance of earning a living in a society where the cost of living was much higher than in England.

The man responsible for the postwar boom on New Providence was Henry Jennings, the first of the pirates to recognize the island's many advantages. He was an ex-privateer, expelled from Jamaica for his part in precipitating an international incident. In 1715 the annual Spanish Plate Fleet sailing from Havana ran into a mighty hurricane and all twelve sunk off the coast of Florida, south of Cape Canaveral, with more than fourteen million pesos worth of treasure. The Viceroy of Havana immediately dispatched salvage ships with divers and soldiers. Camping along the shore the divers worked the shallows where the ships had been dashed to pieces, bringing up much of the sunken treasure. At least four million pesos worth were shipped to Havana.

Before long every would-be treasure hunter in the Caribbean heard of the disaster. Jennings, out of work since the end of the war, raised a contingent of three hundred men from Jamaica, Barbados and other islands. The pirates sailed in a little squadron right to the salvage camp where their numbers panicked the Spanish guards who fled into the bush, abandoning 350,000 pieces of eight plus assorted other treasure. On the way back they seized a Spanish cargo ship, plundering her rich cargo of cash, cochineal and indigo. The Governor of Havana sent a ship to Jamaica demanding the return of all treasure and goods Jennings's fleet had taken but the men had already disposed of the booty and gone off to plunder not only Spanish ships but French and English as well, cruising south along the Main.

The Spanish retaliated by striking at the camps of the English logwood cutters on the Bay of Campeche and the Bay of Honduras. Some of the crew members of the ships they seized in the two areas turned pirate themselves, having lost their vessels. They joined Jennings and his men on New Providence, making it in Defoe's words "their retreat and general receptacle." From there they sailed in all directions finding ample rewards for their efforts. Word spread and even greater numbers of ruffians flocked to New Providence until it was bulging. The crews of merchant ships and some naval ships mutinied at sea and turned their vessels toward the Bahamas. The pirates fattened on the postwar shipping boom. The holds of merchantmen were crammed with record cargoes of sugar, rice, indigo and tobacco which were exchanged in Europe for a large volume of tempting goods. Commodities and manufactured articles furnished the latter day pirates with their booty rather than the gold, silver, gems and pearls of earlier times.

After a cruise the pirates took shore leave on New Providence where they found buyers for plunder and balm for all their needs. As many as five hundred of their sloops, brigantines and smaller barks could lie at anchor, protected by the two narrow entrances which kept deeper-draught naval vessels at bay. The beaches were dotted with vessels being careened or modified. The men lazed in hammocks beneath the palms, swinging gently in the fanning breezes. Feral cattle and hogs on nearby islands provided fresh meat. Turtles, fish and shellfish abounded. They enjoyed a variety of vegetables and fruits including citrus so vital in combatting scurvy. Although the island has no streams or rivers there was plenty of fresh well water. The aroma wafting from cookfires blended on the tropical air with the stench of rotting garbage and human waste. Pirates liked their victuals hearty and spicy. The number one dish, which had infinite variations, was "solomon grundy" or salamagundi a sort of spicy chef's salad which included whatever was handy. At sea it might be a basic mixture of uncooked herbs, palm hearts, salt beef or pork or fish, turtle flesh (turtles, flipped on their backs, could be kept alive for relatively long periods to provide fresh meat on long cruises) highly seasoned with oil, garlic, pungent mustard seed, vinegar, salt and pepper. The shanty taverns of New Providence could offer palate-pleasing variations with hard boiled eggs, chunks of meat or fowl marinated in spiced wine and pickles of onions, cabbage, grapes and olives.

Pirate recreation was generally limited to drinking, gaming and wenching. On New Providence there were whores and camp followers galore, continuous gambling opportunities and plenty to drink. The favored libations were bumboo, rumfustian and a rousing mixture of rum and gunpowder popularized by Blackbeard. Bumboo or bombo, a concoction of rum, water, sugar and nutmeg was the most common pirate beverage. A slightly more complex compound was a rum-free blend of raw eggs, sugar, sherry, gin and beer drunk hot and confusingly called rumfustian. New Providence was so congenial that it was said a pirate didn't dream of Heaven at life's end but prayed to return to the island paradise.

Pirates at sea generally wore rude trousers and jerkins made of drab sailcloth. In combat a few wore colorful, formal outfits but most wore clothes coated with a layer of pitch which could deflect some sword thrusts or doublets of thick leather which served the same purpose. Ashore they liked to ape the dress of gentlemen, if not gentlemanly hygiene, donning colorful combinations of garments of embroidered silks and satins, velvets and lace which often verged on the ludicrous. Pirates loved jewelry, wearing elaborate earrings, pearls, ornate gold chains and diamond and emerald crosses stolen from Catholic ships. Like London dandies certain of the pirates powdered their faces and minced along in silver-buckled high heeled shoes, tricorn hats under their arms.

They may have looked tame or even silly in their greasy finery. But there was not a man, woman or child in the New World who didn't know that beneath the silks and satins beat the blackest of hearts. The pirates took pride in their personal flags designed to strike terror in their prey. They also kept a supply of naval ensigns of various nations to fly as decoys. The Betsy Ross of the brawling community was an alcoholic, sailmaker's widow who kept herself in spirits by sewing pirate flags to order. She made it a point to never sew while drunk. The first flags had been the blood red "jolie rouge" pennants of the buccaneers. In 1700 a French pirate named Emanuel Wynne introduced the first Black Jack with a skull and crossbones in the Caribbean. Beneath the grisly motif he placed an hourglass to indicate time was running out for his victims. Avery embellished his skull with a turban and gold earring while Christopher Condent emphasized his message by flying a pennant sporting not one but three skull and crossbone motifs. Calico Jack Rackham flew a skull with two crossed swords beneath it and Stede Bonnet settled for one bone beneath the skull, a dagger to the right and a heart to the left. Edward Low displayed a blood red skeleton on a black background while Blackbeard designed a typically eccentric standard showing a horned devil's skeleton with an hourglass in one upraised hand and a spear pointing to a bleeding heart in the other. Walter Kennedy, an illiterate Irishman who began life as a pickpocket, carried his design a step further, featuring the skull and cross bones and himself above with sword and raised tankard drinking a toast to death.

Whether on shore leave or a long monotonous cruise pirates loved to gamble, although dice and cards were forbidden by some articles since the combination of confined quarters on a tedious sea voyage, rum and gambling among volatile men led to explosive quarrels. Defoe writes of a singular pirate pastime, the mock trial, a kind of amateur theatrical satire. Many of the rovers having had their day in court were familiar with judicial proceedings and every pirate lived with the specter of a bewigged judge intoning a death sentence as he stood before the court. The burlesque trial was a way to take the sting off.

The following mock trial quoted in Defoe's book allegedly came from a participant in a trial held by Captain Thomas Anstis and his crew on a cay off the coast of Cuba in 1721 where they had put in for repairs and a few days relaxation. The pirates were assigned roles from judge to hangman. George Bradley the pirate-judge sat in a tree robed in a piece of dirty tarpaulin, with a yarn cap for a wig and a pair of spectacles set on his nose. The court officials assembled beneath him bearing crowbars and handspikes in lieu of wands and tipstaffs. The criminals were led out "making a thousand sour Faces" as the pirate-Attorney General opened the charges against them:

> Attorney General: An't please your Lordship, and your Gentlemen of the Jury, here is a Fellow before you that is a sad Dog, a sad, sad Dog; and I humbly hope your Lordship will order him to be hang'd out of the Way immediately. He has committed Pyracy upon the High Seas, and we shall prove, an't please your Lordship, that this Fellow, this sad Dog before you, has escaped a thousand storms, nay, has got safe ashore when the Ship has been cast away, which is a certain Sign he was not born to be drown'd; yet not having the Fear of Hanging before his Eyes, he went on robbing and ravishing Man, Woman and Child, plundering ships' Cargoes fore and aft, burning and sinking Ship, Bark and Boat, as if the Devil had been in him. But this is not all, my Lord, he had committed worse Villanies than all these, for we shall prove that he has been guilty of drinking small beer (a barely alcoholic brew which pirates contemptuously called "belly vengeance") and your Lordship knows there never was a sober Fellow but was a Rogue . . .
>
> Judge: Hark'ee me Sirrah' You lousy, pittiful, ill-look'd Dog, what have you to say that you should not be tucked up immediately and set a sundrying like a Scare crow? Are you guilty or not guilty.
>
> Prisoner: Not guilty, an't please your Worship."
>
> Judge: Not guilty' Say so again, Sirrah, and I'll have you hang'd without any Tryal.
>
> Prisoner: An't please your Worship's Honour, my Lord, I am as honest a poor Fellow as ever went between Stem and Stern of a Ship, and can hand, reef, steer and clap two Ends of a Rope together as well as e'er a He that ever crossed salt Water; but I was taken by one George Bradley, a notorious Pyrate, a sad Rogue as ever was unhang'd and he forc'd me, an't please your Honour.
>
> (The players toss insults at one another until the judge asks if dinner is ready.)
>
> Attorney General: Yes, my Lord.
>
> Judge: Then Hark'ee, you Raskal at the Bar. Hear me, Sirrah, hear me. You must suffer for three Reasons. First, because it is not fit that I should sit here a Judge and Nobody be hang'd. Secondly, you must be hang'd

because you have a damn hanging look. And thirdly, you must be hang'd
because I am hungry; for know, Sirrah that 'tis a Custom that whenever the
Judge's Dinner is ready before the Tryal is over, the Prisoner is to be hang'd,
of Course. There's the Law for you, ye Dog. So take him away, Gaoler.[1]

The spoofs sometimes stirred such passion in piratical breasts that play
turned into tragedy. A pirate who had been a starving young actor in
England before embarking on a career of highway crime was transported
as a felon and sold to work on a Jamaican sugar plantation. He escaped
and joined the sweet trade, amusing his shipmates with recitations. In
1717 he wrote and directed a neoclassical verse play *The Royal Pyrate*
which was staged on the ship's quarterdeck. A drunken gunner who had
been in the after cabin emerged just in time to hear the character of Alexander the Great sentence the accused pirate to hang in the morning. The
gunner was so far gone in his cups that he believed it was a real court and
roused his three drinking companions to action shouting "They're a-going
to hang honest Jack Spinckes. If we suffer that we'll all hang. By God and
they shan't hang honest Jack. We'll clear the decks of 'em." The four men
burst onto the quarter deck, tossing a lighted grenade at the jury which
brought the play and its author's career to an explosive finale. Jack
Spinckes's leg was shattered. Alexander's left arm was severed with a
cutlass but with his right he killed his drunken opponent while the other
three were locked up for the night. Next morning a court martial was
held which acquitted the zealots and even praised their spirit.

By 1716 the "Flying Gang" as the New Providence exponents of sea
robbery called themselves had such a stranglehold on the sea lanes from
Nova Scotia to the Spanish Main that the Governor of Antigua wrote, "I
do not think it advisable to go from hence except upon an extraordinary
occasion, not knowing but that I may be intercepted by the pirates."
Merchant ships traveled in convoys protected by Navy warships which
charged as much as twelve and a half percent of a cargo's value for their
services. Navy ships also accepted cargoes for shipment at a lower rate
which was against the law but much done since it was mutually profitable
and the best insurance for safe delivery. The outlaws at New Providence
anticipated trouble and constructed a battery by the harbor which was
manned by watches of fifty men who scanned the horizon while the rest
of the roistering community refreshed themselves, transacted business or
worked on their vessels, careening, repairing or modifying them.

The 1715 treasure wrecks attracted further pirate attention after Jennings's initial raid. The Spanish erected shore batteries at the site but the
pirates managed on several occasions to overwhelm them and fish the
wrecks themselves. A prominent lawyer named Harry Beverley received

permission from Virginia's Governor Spotswood to sail his newly outfitted sloop with a crew of about fifty armed men to the wreck site. His aim was to help the Spanish recover treasure for a percentage. If they refused his offer he planned to "fish" the wrecks on the sly or locate and salvage wrecks in British waters. To ensure that the *Virgin of Virginia* wouldn't lose money on the voyage, he stocked her hold with provisions he could sell in the islands. The Governor asked him to investigate the disturbing developments in the Bahamas.

When Beverley sailed in the summer of 1716 Spain and England were at peace: Spanish authorities, however, were furious at a recent pirate salvaging expedition which had lifted at least 20,000 pieces of eight from the 1715 wrecks. A Spanish warship Beverley encountered fired over his bow. The Spanish captain came alongside and ordered Beverley aboard so his papers could be examined. The Virginian stated he was on a trading voyage but some of his crew—Indian slaves and indentured servants whom he had pressed—offered the information that their captain was on his way to join the pirates. The ship was seized, the cargo looted and eventually sold in Puerto Rico. His men were forced to work naked aboard the warship while Beverley was held without trial in Veracruz. By the time he escaped and returned to Virginia in August of 1717, he had learned enough to tell the governor that desperadoes were flocking to the Bahamas in record numbers. Spotswood was already aware of this for since the spring their ships had hovered about the Virginia capes preying on inbound ships laden with European goods. Spotswood noted in a report that pirates were also seizing ships to add to their fleets. He complained that the Virginians had little defence against the freebooters. The old *Shoreham* which had taken *La Paix* with its French pirate crew in 1700 was back in Virginia but with a bottom so fouled she couldn't begin to chase down a fleet pirate craft. She was reduced to sitting like a stone sentinel at the mouth of the Chesapeake Bay.

Among the New Providence sea vultures who cruised off the Capes at this period was the "Orator," Captain Bellamy, an English pirate who left a wife and children near Canterbury. He had cut his teeth in the West Indies as a "wracker," one of the peculiar breed of men and women who set out false beacons to lure unwary vessels to their shores and plundered their cargoes. Bermuda and the Bahamas were especially notorious for their "wracker" families some of whom became quite rich. Bellamy, who also fished on the 1715 galleons, made a name for himself as a pirate captain in the islands before turning to the east coast in 1717. He had two hundred men aboard his flagship the *Whidaw Galley* which mounted twenty-eight guns. His motley crew was predominantly English and Irish with a sprinkling of other nationalities, two Indians and twenty-five slaves stolen from a Guinea ship. He was accompanied on his North American cruise by a twelve-gun sloop with a crew of forty, captained by Paul Williams, a mulatto in a periwig. They took prize after prize. One of his crew later testified they had taken fifty vessels.

Some ships they scuttled and burned, others were plundered and let go after a certain number of their men had signed articles. Bellamy was dubbed "the Orator" because he enjoyed delivering impassioned speeches. In a speech credited to him by Defoe he harangued the captain of a Boston merchant ship taken off South Carolina: "I am a free prince and I have as much authority to make war on the whole World as he who has a hundred sail of ships a sea and 100,000 men in the field." Bellamy epitomized the anarchic spirit of the classic pirate who was at odds with restrictive society. When a Captain Beer declined to join his crew Bellamy spat at him:

> Damn ye, you are a sneaking puppy, and so are all those who will submit to be governed by laws which rich men have made for their own security, for the cowardly whelps have not the courage otherwise to defend what they get by their knavery. But damn ye altogether. Damn them for a pack of crafty rascals, and you, who serve them, for a parcel of hen-hearted numbskulls. They villify us, the scoundrels do, then there is only this difference, they rob the poor under the cover of law, forsooth, and we plunder the rich under the protection of our own courage; had ye not better make one of us, than sneak after the arses of those villains for employment?

Bellamy's voice was soon stilled, however, for during a pitch black night of drunken reveling aboard the *Whidaw* the pilot, who was the pressed master of a prize whaler, deliberately drove the ship aground on Cape Cod. Bellamy was one of seven pirates who survived. He was arrested, tried and executed in Boston. The location of the shipwreck near Wellfleet was well known, appearing on charts from 1707 on. Locals salvaged a lot of treasure at the time of the wreck. Over the centuries coins have been found on the beach after storms. In 1984 Barry Clifford, a Cape Cod sportsdiver discovered the remains of the pirate ship in about twenty feet of water. He began salvaging her and has brought up a couple of thousand gold and silver coins, a few small gold bars and the ship's bell inscribed with her name.

Each time a pirate expedition set out on a venture it was with high hopes of success and a quick return. Many of the pirates never saw New Providence again. Some were killed in battle and others were slain by their own mates. Some drowned in shipwrecks which were a constant danger in the reef strewn waters they frequented. Like seamen throughout history many pirates couldn't swim. Many pirates were captured and either hanged or reprieved according to how moving a story they could unfold before the court. Sickness killed untold numbers and a few were cast away or marooned on uninhabited cays.

Blackbeard, "whose name was a Terror," lives on as the best known of the New Providence alumni, thanks to the vivid account of his exploits in Johnson's book. The prototypic pirate whose career lasted a mere two years, Blackbeard's myth is so powerful that it has sowed legends from New England to Honduras. But fact is more compelling than fiction particularly in regard to the "Spawn of the Devil." Like so many of his kind, his origins are obscure. His name has been rendered a dozen ways from Teach to Tash to Thatch. Some scholars assert his real name was Hyde or Drummond and that he was born in Jamaica "of very creditable parents" or in Virginia. He signed himself Edward Teach when he signed articles with Captain Hornigold but in official colonial correspondence he is referred to as Thatch, and occasionally Tach. Blackbeard who excelled at creating a terrifying image was a native of Bristol, England and came to Jamaica as a deckhand aboard a privateer during the war. He was one of those who helped themselves to the sunken 1715 treasure. He served his pirate apprenticeship on Hornigold's brigantine *Ranger*, a large ship with thirty-six guns and more than 145 men. He proved so capable and fearless that his mentor put him in charge of a six gun sloop with a crew of seventy. They cruised together taking prizes off Cuba and elsewhere along the way to the American coast where they careened their ships on the Virginia shore. After the vessels had been scraped, sealed with tallow and repaired they set out again along the coast before heading to the West Indies with their holds brimming with prize goods.

Off St. Vincent they seized a French guineaman from St. Malo en route from the African coast to Martinique with a cargo of slaves, gold dust, bullion, plate, jewels and other choice goods. The cargo was the richest they had encountered and shows the West Indies was getting more valuable imports as the colonies prospered. Hornigold rewarded Teach's ability by giving him command of the prize. She was a big Dutch-built ship, strong and well-armed. Blackbeard converted her to his use and patriotically renamed her the *Queen Anne's Revenge*. Hornigold had done well by the sweet trade, and the capture of the French merchantman clinched his decision to retire to New Providence as a landlubbing planter. So he gave Teach his blessing and the two men shook hands and parted not knowing they were never to meet again.

Hornigold's conversion to the straight and narrow came at a fortuitous moment for on a sultry July morning in 1718 Woodes Rogers arrived at Nassau with a royal commission as "Captain-General and Governor-in-Chief in and over Our Bahama Islands." He also had with him King

George I's promise of pardon for all pirates who turned themselves in before September 5, 1718 and were willing to swear an oath to abstain from further piracies. After that date all pirates were to be hunted down and hanged. After Woodes Rogers returned from his celebrated circumnavigation of the world, the ex-privateer commander had formed a joint stock company with six of Bristol's leading merchants to colonize the Bahamas and rout the freebooters. The Lords Proprietors whose neglect had led to the Bahamas becoming the world's foremost pirate haunt were only too delighted to accept Woode Rogers's proposal to turn over the civil and military administration of the islands to the Crown and lease the royalties and quitrents to Rogers's company for twenty-one years.

He was committed to succeed since the post paid only fifty pounds sterling a year for the first seven years, one hundred for the next seven and two hundred annually for the remainder of the lease, and the islands had no industry but piracy. Only by turning the sea rovers into productive farmers could he hope to make a profit. He left England with supplies, tools, stores and a thousand moralizing tracts from the Society for Promoting Christian Knowledge. A naval vessel from Bermuda had preceded him with a copy of the royal amnesty proclamation which had been issued in 1717. The captain had been booed when he read it and very few pirates chose to return to Bermuda with him. A new offer of pardon was always greeted with skepticism and apprehension about forfeiting plunder. By the time Woodes Rogers appeared, however, the majority of the pirates had agreed with Captain Jennings's suggestion that they follow his example and take the king's pardon. A few men decamped rather than forswear their seaborne profession and a small dissenting group swore to resist the Governor's authority.

When Woodes Rogers anchored at the bar of Nassau harbor there were more than two hundred ships riding at anchor within and an estimated thousand pirates were ashore. Under cover of darkness two of the Navy ships glided into the port entrance to reconnoiter, uncertain of their reception. Charles Vane, ringleader of the resisters, had prepared a very warm welcome for them indeed. He turned a French prize into a fireship loaded with ignited explosives. Cut adrift, it bore down on the English vessels. The fire's heat set off round after round of cannon balls, musket balls and bits and pieces of assorted metal scrap. As the powder magazines ignited the French ship went up like a dazzling, deafening firework display, lighting the tropic night for miles around.

In the general confusion Vane with a number of his men slipped out to the open sea in a sloop piled high with booty. Woodes Rogers sent his two sloops after them but Vane knew the adjacent waters intimately and vanished into the night. For the next three years he remained at large, poaching for silver bullion on the 1715 wrecks off Florida and cruising up the American coast where he terrorized shipping off the Carolinas. He met Blackbeard offshore one time and the two crews repaired to a quiet inlet for a drunken orgy. His luck ran out on the Spanish Main when his ship broke up in a hurricane and he was cast ashore on a little island off Honduras. Local Mosquito Indians there fed him. When an English ship appeared, Vane begged Holford, her captain, to take him to Jamaica where she was bound. The captain refused, recognizing a scoundrel when he saw one, but agreed that if Vane were still there when he returned the following month he would take him to Port Royal to be hanged. Soon after another English vessel out of Jamaica hove to and Vane managed to cajole her captain into taking him onboard. Less than two days later the ship was stopped at a signal by the first ship which was on its way back to the little island. When Captain Holford saw Vane sweating away with the deckhands he identified him as a first class seagoing brigand. Vane was clapped in irons, taken to Port Royal, tried and hanged.

The morning following Vane's dramatic escape, Governor Rogers stepped ashore, taking formal possession of New Providence. Hundreds of rough-edged pirates were formed into an honor guard of two lines stretching from the water's edge to the crumbling fort. The governor and his men passed between them as the pirates fired volley after volley of musket fire. He was a mariner, a man the pirates respected and they gave him a singular welcome. A reception committee greeted him, its members introducing themselves by name and title. One Thomas Taylor, for example, presented himself as the President of the Council and a pirate named Thomas Walker who had been appointed head of the committee introduced himself as the island's Chief Justice. Rogers diplomatically didn't quibble over their questionable credentials but took them in the spirit they were offered. In fact, he even consented to have the "Chief Justice" swear him in amid ringing cheers for King George from the ragged crowd.

Rogers faced a tough challenge, however. He had no choice but to enlist the six hundred pirates who accepted the Act of Grace in his campaign to make a go of the colony which had no really permanent buildings, a ruined fort, no passable roads and precious little agriculture. He offered free building materials and a plot of land to any man who would cultivate it and construct a permanent house on it in a year's time. But many felt the land was theirs anyway and working hard held no appeal. Rogers noted that "work they mortally hate, for when they have cleared a patch that will supply them with potatoes and yams, fish being so plentiful they thus live, poorly and indolently, and pray for wrecks or pirates."

The governor pressed on, firm in his purpose. He took up pick and shovel himself to work alongside the men restoring the fort which guarded the harbor's western entrance. He oversaw construction of a small battery overlooking the harbor's eastern entrance and assigned squads of ex-pirates to clear the impenetrable undergrowth that choked the trails and encroached on the town providing potential cover for ambushes. He used the threat of Spanish and French invasion to further his projects, organizing a militia and appointing men who had not been pirates to administrative posts and to the council.

Four days a week every man, save the officers, had to work for the colony. Rogers had brought 250 farmers and craftsmen with him to colonize the island. Most were German Protestant refugees from the Palatinate, Huguenots and Swiss Protestants. They took more willingly to the regimen of hard work than the ex-rovers who preferred the old days when being ashore meant lolling with some blowsy wench and a pot of rum in the shade of a palm. The Europeans however, had little resistance to the muggy climate and when an epidemic broke out in the late summer many of them died. Sailors aboard the warships were stricken, too, and before long all the vessels sailed off.

After the honeymoon some of the pirates left as well, finding life under the new regime far too disciplined and dull for "men o'spirit" who preferred bumboo to Bible tracts. Rogers commissioned Hornigold, his most trusted agent, and Captain Burgess another pioneer New Providence pirate, to go after the backsliders. Hornigold lost Vane without capturing him, although he did bring in the master of a trading sloop which had received stolen goods from the elusive Vane. As part of his plan to establish trade ties with the Spanish colony on Hispaniola, Rogers had sent three ships to Port-au-Prince. Two days out of Nassau they took up their old ways, "returned to their vomit" in Defoe's phrase, and it was months before Hornigold was able to round up thirteen of the mutineers, bringing back all but three who died of wounds.

One New Providence graduate who never for a moment considered accepting anyone's pardon was Blackbeard. After parting with Hornigold he sailed for the West Indies with a devoted crew of three hundred, many of whom had sailed with Hornigold. His first prize was the *Great Allen* a mighty merchant ship carrying valuable cargo from Barbados to Jamaica. She was well armed but Blackbeard prevailed in a lengthy battle off St. Vincent and the merchantman struck her colors and surrendered. A British warship mounting thirty guns went after his *Queen Anne's Revenge*. Blackbeard saw her approach and chose to stand and fight rather than flee which he could easily have done with his fleet vessel. The two ships engaged in a brutal battle which ended when the man-o-war limped away toward Barbados in the face of the pirates' superior skills.

Engagements like this made Blackbeard the most talked about man in the Caribbean. Even the reformed Hornigold boasted of his role as the great pirate's tutor and former rovers talked wistfully in the taverns of New Providence of their former comrade's raw courage in taking on and beating a Royal Navy battle ship. Even in absentia, Blackbeard made life difficult for Rogers whose hold on his pirates was tenuous at best.

"In the commonwealth of pirates he who goes the greatest length of wickedness," Defoe wrote, "is looked upon with a kind of envy amongst them as a person of extraordinary gallantry." Although Blackbeard was neither as savage nor as successful as some other pirates none surpassed him at self-promotion. He was a master at cultivating the image of a bloodthirsty demon which encouraged a speedy surrender. He was a very tall man of imposing stature. He had a naturally ferocious mien which he enhanced by plaiting his exceedingly thick, black hair and long beard into pig tails twined with colored ribbons. They stood out all over his head. In battle armed with three braces of pistols slung in bandoliers he appeared to be a fury from hell with wild eyes and smoldering gunners matches sticking out from under his hat. These matches which burned about an inch every five minutes were made of lengths of twisted hemp impregnated with salt-peter and lime-water.

Blackbeard's awesome figure was matched by his extravagant and impetuous temperament. No one drank more or cursed more profanely. If he committed even a fraction of the wicked and wanton acts he is credited with he would still seem almost a caricature of an eighteenth-century pirate. Not only his victims but even his own men were subjected to terrifying displays calculated to cow the observers. Defoe describes how one time at sea when he was drinking with his men he shouted that they should all make a hell of their own and see what it was like. He took two or three obliging crewmen into the hold where they sat on ballast rocks. Blackbeard had lighted pots of brimstone handed down. Then the hatches were closed and they sat in the pitch black breathing the suffocating fumes until one by one the crewmen begged for release from the sulphurous prison. Blackbeard finally opened the hatches, delighted that he had held out the longest.

One of his crew on the deck jokingly said "Why Captain, you look as if you were coming straight from the gallows." Breaking into an infernal grin Blackbeard roared, "My lad, that's a brilliant idea. The next time we shall play the game of gallows and see who can swing the longest on the rope without being throttled." There is no record, however, that the slightly crazed captain ever indulged in this game. One game of gratuitous violence took place just before his fatal encounter at Ocracoke Inlet off Virginia with Lieutenant Maynard. One night he was drinking with his gunner, Israel Hands, the prototype for Stevenson's Israel Hands in *Treasure Island*, and another pirate in his cabin. Suddenly without a word of warning he drew and cocked a pair of his pistols under the table. One man, wary of his captain's unpredictable temper, went on deck while Hands stayed to drink. Blackbeard snuffed the candle and fired both pistols. One slug ripped through the gunner's knee crippling him for life. When his crew asked why he had done such a thing, Blackbeard cursed them and replied that if he didn't kill one of his men now and then they would forget who he was.

Pirates stayed with him because he was incredibly, almost magically, successful. During an eighteen month rampage Blackbeard ranged from Virginia to Honduras, terrorizing shipping and taking at least twenty prizes. He burned some ships but added others to his growing fleet. Most of the American colonies had turned their backs on the pirates but struggling North Carolina lacking the lucrative trade in rice and indigo that made neighboring colonies strong enough to shun traffic with smugglers and pirates still welcomed them. In January 1718 Blackbeard and his crew surrendered to Governor Charles Eden at the town of Bath under the latest Act of Grace. Eden took a percentage of Blackbeard's booty and made no move to stop him from brazenly careening in the vicinity while he prepared for another cruise. Tobias Knight, the colony's Secretary and Collector of Customs openly aided Blackbeard before he sailed off for another foray to the Bay on Honduras.

On his first voyage to Honduras Blackbeard had met up with one of the Golden Age's least likely pirate captains, Major Stede Bonnet from Barbados. Bonnet was a middle aged gentleman planter and man of letters. He was an upperclass Englishman who had retired from the army to run a large sugar plantation near Bridgetown. It came as a shock to Barbados society when the Major deserted his comfortable life for an outlaw career at sea. Discord with his shrewish wife may have spurred him on. In any case he outfitted his sloop the *Revenge* with ten guns, breaking pirate precedent by buying the ship instead of seizing it. He crewed her with seventy men, only some of them seasoned rovers, and took off.

By the time he met up with Blackbeard's vessel and was invited aboard for a drink, Bonnet had managed to capture a few prizes without being very capable or inspiring confidence in his crew. An odder couple would be hard to imagine: the flamboyant Blackbeard, larger than life with his wild mane and blazing eyes and the pudgy little dandy with his satin waistcoat, snow white breeches and powdered wig. Despite their differences the electrifying arch pirate and the smooth-shaven Bonnet got on famously and decided to cruise together. It took only a few days, however, for Blackbeard to recognize Bonnet as a bungling amateur. The crew of the *Revenge* was pleased when Blackbeard put his second-in-command, Lieutenant Richards, in charge of Bonnet's ship. He showed uncharacteristic tact in suggesting to Bonnet that "as he had not been used to the fatigues and care of such a post, it would be better for him to decline it and live easy, at his pleasure, in such a ship as his, where he should not be obliged to perform duty, but follow his own inclinations." In effect, Bonnet was Blackbeard's prisoner.

Bonnet didn't argue, but boarded the *Queen Anne's Revenge*. His crew was dead set against him and he had begun to wonder if he wouldn't rather settle ashore in a Spanish colony. He mumbled that he could never go back to Barbados because he couldn't look an Englishman in the eye after what he had done. There was no getting away, however, as Blackbeard's fleet, increased by the *Adventure* a sloop out of Jamaica whose captain and crew signed articles when captured, beat the seas between the Carolinas and the West Indies, taking at least a dozen prizes. The sight of the black flags was enough to make four ships in the Bay of Honduras surrender without a fight. They took a turtler off Grand Cayman and sloops off Cuba where they put in for provisions and to sell booty. They even spent several days fishing for Spanish treasure on the wrecked galleons off Florida.

When the pirate fleet put in at Topsail Inlet, North Carolina, after a final haul which netted two sloops and an English brigantine en route to South Carolina from West Africa, Bonnet planned to seek a royal pardon. He left his ship, which Blackbeard had turned back to him, at the inlet and went to see Governor Eden at Bath. War had broken out between Spain and the Triple Alliance so the Governor pardoned Bonnet and gave him permission to sail for St. Thomas where he could get a privateer's commission. He went back to the inlet for his sloop. He found that Blackbeard had stripped her clean and had marooned twenty-five of her crew on a sand spit where there was "neither Bird, Beast nor Herb." Then he had sailed off with Bonnet's share of the plunder and the rest of his crew.

Bonnet fitted out and started after the treacherous Blackbeard. When he realized he couldn't catch up with him, he cruised up the coast of Virginia into Delaware Bay. He had become more adept during his sojourn with Blackbeard and seized several prizes including a large ship which he took ashore near the Cape Fear River for modifications. It was there that he was captured by Colonel William Rhett of South Carolina. A bribe of gold bought him escape from the Charleston jail but Rhett caught the portly pirate again and he was brought to trial with thirty-three other pirates in November 1718.

The presiding judge was Nicholas Trot, cousin of the pirate-broker who governed the Bahamas. The judge held no love for outlaws of any kind and pirates in particular inspired him with Bible thumping invective. The attorney-general spoke eloquently of the ravages of the sea wolves. They were worse than beasts of prey he said, "for wild beasts only devour others to satisfy their hunger, and were never observed to prey upon their own species; but Pyrates preyed on all mankind . . . and if a stop is not put to their depredations . . . all the English plantations in America will be totally ruin'd in a short time," as Jamaica had already been ruined. He pointed out that the great increase in the numbers of these Enemies of Mankind in the past few years was due to the Spaniards having broken up the logwood camps in the Bay of Campeche so that nine out of ten of the profligates who worked there turned pirate. In addition, he said, "the great expectations from wrecks on the Bahamas Islands . . . had greatly increased the number of pirates of late years."

Major Stede mistakenly thought his privileged origins would save his neck. Quite the contrary; the prosecutor was dismayed that some people seemed sympathetic to the accused because he was "a gentleman, a man of honour, a man of fortune, and one that had a liberal education." These accomplishments were "but so many Aggravations of his Crime: And how could a person be esteem'd a man of honour, who had lost all sense of humanity . . . ". South Carolina had had its fill of pirates. Bonnet was found guilty despite his pleas that he had never taken a ship save in the company of Captain Thatch (Blackbeard). He wrote a groveling letter begging for mercy from the Governor. If reprieved he would separate all his limbs from his body, he promised, "only reserving the Use of my Tongue to call continually on, and pray to the Lord." He was hanged on December 10 at White Point near Charleston, the traditional bouquet clutched in his chained hands. In his brief career as an indifferent sea wolf Bonnet achieved two firsts—he was the first pirate known to have bought his own ship and the only one who, having read too many tall tales, may have made a prisoner or two walk the plank.

The month before Bonnet's execution Blackbeard's reign of terror ended when Governor Spotswood sent H.M.S. *Lyme* and H.M.S. *Pearl* under Lieutenant Robert Maynard to beard the pirate in his den. Unhindered maritime commerce was vital to Virginia and Blackbeard's continued haunting of the sea-lanes between the West Indies and the mainland was intolerable. The pirates' sloop *Adventure* and a merchantman prize were at anchor up the Ocracoke Inlet, where word had it Blackbeard planned to carve out a pirate stronghold. He had been smitten to an unusual degree by a winsome sixteen-year old in Bath, a planter's daughter. The fearsome aspect that made men tremble in their breeches seems to have had an aphrodisiacal effect on women. He had a wench in every port and is credited with fourteen wives, although the first thirteen were probably amours of the moment who went through mock weddings conducted by one of the pirate officers. The fourteenth marriage was the real thing performed by Governor Eden himself.

The honeymoon was soon over. According to Defoe, who almost certainly exaggerated, Blackbeard was said to have preferred living aboard his ship only occasionally going ashore "where his Wife lived, with whom after he had lain all night, it was his custom to invite four or five of his brutal Companions to come ashore, and he would force her to prostitute herself to them all, one after another before his Face." Left to their own devices his rowdy crew of four hundred bullies annoyed the townspeople. Blackbeard chafed at the restrictions of local society and the expenses of a planter's life. Finally he rounded up his crew and took to plundering trading sloops in the coastal waters offering an insulting token payment for the goods he robbed.

No one was sorry to see him fit out and sail off on a cruise with his rowdies. It was to be his last. Near Bermuda he seized three English and two French ships. One was a French merchantman brimming with sugar and spices which he hid in a cove in Pamlico Sound to the west of Cape Hatteras. Blackbeard told Eden he had found the ship adrift with neither crew nor papers aboard. His old ally Governor Tobias Knight condemned the prize as a wreck making it open to salvage, although he never saw it. In case the French actually identified the ship as one of theirs Blackbeard, with Knight's connivance, unloaded it and then burned it to the waterline so that it sank. For their assistance Blackbeard gave the governor sixty hogshead of sugar and the Customs Inspector twenty.

When Governor Eden took no action against Blackbeard, the traders and plantation owners of Virginia implored Governor Spotswood, implacable pirate foe, to do something. When the Virginia legislature quibbled over how the funds for a naval expedition were to be appropriated, Spotswood lost his patience and paid the cost himself. The two sloops he dispatched to the Carolinas were shallow draft vessels, able to navigate the area's notorious shoals and channels. The *Pearl* and *Lyme* found Blackbeard's ships at dusk of November 21, 1718. Blackbeard and the eighteen men who were with him spent the night getting drunk instead of preparing for battle. Next morning, heads buzzing with hangovers that only more rum could quiet, the pirates met the Royal Navy in one of history's great pirate engagements.

The battle wasn't without its almost farcical moments. The two navy ships got stuck fast on sandbars at the outset when they tried to close in on the *Adventure* at low tide. They pulled free after jettisoning ballast and water casks and the battle commenced.

Blackbeard's colossal courage rose to new heights with every swig of rum. He ran up his death's head ensign urging his men on. The pirates gave as good as they got from the sixty-two man naval force. The pirates killed the commander of the *Lyme* early in the battle and dismasted the sloop so it could do little but observe the action. A pirate broadside smashed into Maynard's sloop, splintering the deck and wounding twenty-one of his thirty-five man crew. Maynard's shots seemed to make no dent in the pirates. Maynard had only three men on deck. Blackbeard roared alongside heaving bottle grenades filled with scrap iron, small shot and powder. Then in a mad frenzy he led his men aboard the *Pearl* vowing to cut the enemy all to pieces. Maynard valiantly commanded his men, those who could stand, to rush on deck and fight. The pirates and the seamen met in hand to hand combat with pistol and cutlass. It seemed inevitable that Blackbeard would vanquish the weakened naval force.

Then miraculously the British were victorious. Blackbeard shot at Maynard from almost point-blank range and missed. The Lieutenant's answering shot found its mark. But the wounded Blackbeard fought on like a zombie amidst the smoke and stench. The howling pirate attacked Maynard with his cutlass. Their blades clanged and flashed on the blood-slick deck until Maynard's broke off near the hilt. Just as Blackbeard went to finish Maynard a navy man slashed his throat open so that Blackbeard's thrust was deflected, barely grazing Maynard's hand. The dying giant fought on like a cornered wild beast. Drenched in blood which bubbled out of his neck Blackbeard fired his pistols until the repeated sword thrusts of the British who closed in on him finally took their toll.

Ten minutes later nine more of his men were dead and nine captured. The rest jumped overboard and drowned then or perished later, their decomposing bodies attracting circling vultures. Blackbeard's hideous head (proof the British had earned the £100 pounds sterling reward Spotswood offered) was taken to Bath and then back to Virginia on Maynard's bowsprit, a voyage of several weeks, where it was stripped of flesh and hung from a pole at the mouth of the Hampton River. After many years someone made the outsize skull into a ghoulish silver-lined punch bowl used at Williamsburg's Raleigh Tavern.

So ended the man Defoe called "that courageous Brute, who might have passed in the World for a Hero had he been Employed in a good Cause." The importance of drink and the relentless pressures on a pirate captain are evident in fragments of a journal found aboard the *Adventure Galley* and thought to be his: "Such a Day—Rum all out—Our Company somewhat sober—Rogues a plotting—great Talk of Separation—So I look'd sharp for a Prize." After plundering a merchant ship and stocking up again he wrote: "Such a Day took one, with a great deal of Liquor on board, so kept the Company hot, damn'd hot, when all Things went well again."

Fifteen of Blackbeard's men, five of them plucked off the streets of Bath, were tried at Williamsburg. Five were blacks and Spotswood sought the advice of his Council as to whether they should be tried with the others. Four of them and Israel Hands, the crippled gunner testified for the prosecution in hope of clemency. Fourteen of the pirates were convicted and sentenced to hang. Only Samuel Odell who proved he had gone aboard the "Adventure" the night before the battle to drink with the pirates was acquitted. Hands was reprieved at the last minute and shipped to London where he limped about the streets begging for food and drink.

A spate of executions in Virginia and South Carolina, where forty-four pirates were hanged in one month, broke the pirates' stranglehold on the American coast, but ships in the West Indies were still not safe as rebellious New Providencers defected from Rogers's colony and took to the seas. Although he had no legal powers to do so, Rogers held a swift trial for the ten malefactors Hornigold brought back to Nassau. Their mutiny threatened to undermine the fragile structure of his authority. The pirates must serve as an example to others who were tempted. The trial was exceedingly fair by the standards of the day. Nine were sentenced to hang and one was spared because he proved he had been forced.

On December 12, 1718, two days after they were sentenced a single gallows was erected with nine nooses dangling over a scaffold resting on three barrels. The pirates were led out, unshackled, and after their hands were tied before them they mounted the gallows. Each of the condemned men was allowed to address the crowd of about three hundred former and potential pirates. The militia of a hundred soldiers and irregulars was present to maintain order because feeling ran high in favor of the pirates who met their end with the courage that had been the hallmark of their careers. John Augur, one of Jennings's original company, asked for a glass of wine and solemnly toasted the prosperity of the colony and the health of the Governor. Twenty-two year old Thomas Morris festooned in scarlet ribbons shouted defiantly that he was sorry he hadn't been a greater plague. Dennis Macarty faced death stripped to the waist like a prize-fighter with blue silk ribbons about his neck. He smiled broadly as he kicked off his silver-buckled shoes into the crowd, saying "There was a time when there were brave fellows here who would not suffer such a sight as this. I promised once I'd never die with my shoes on, and damme, I won't." A couple repented of their evil deeds but William Dowling, a scowling young Irishman boasted he had killed his own mother, and eighteen-year old George Bendell said that although he'd never been a pirate before he'd have become "the most villainous of them all given the time."

Rogers took a risk executing the pirates but it paid off. When one member of the sullen mob jumped on a barrel to exhort the others to riot, Rogers calmly shot him dead. After that although there were mutters of rebellion, Rogers never again had a mutiny. In fact, he had the colonists staunchly behind him when thirteen hundred Spanish troops poured off four warships to attack the colony in late February of 1720. One British infantry division and five hundred rum soaked ex-rovers beat off the Spanish.

Rogers was an intelligent, courageous and resourceful leader yet his extraordinary accomplishments brought no reward. He had been ignored after his great circumnavigation and the government once again let him down, sending no reinforcements, supplies or funds. The £11,000 remaining from his share of privateer plunder went for feeding the colony and paying the garrison. His pleas to the Crown went unanswered.

He warned the Crown that the 2,000 pirates still at large in the West Indies threatened to take New Providence over. Spaniards had raided Cat Island, slaughtered the men and sailed off with the women, children and slaves. He complained about the caliber of men he had to work with noting that although the Spanish had attacked thirty-four times in the past fifteen years "these wretches can't be kept to watch at night and when they do they come very seldom sober."

Rogers's Bristol partners betrayed him, selling out the partnership without warning him. Sick in body and heart he sailed for Charleston in February of 1721 and then home to England. In fact Rogers left New Providence in 1721 exhausted by the scope of the task he had undertaken. He declared bankruptcy and for a time was sent to debtor's prison. He was replaced by George Phenney, whose wife stirred up a hornet's nest on the island. She was the instigator of a deliberate campaign to exploit the governor's position. Mrs. Phenney forced traders to sell their cargoes to her at cut-rates and then grossly inflated retail prices. She meddled in everything, insulting judges, bullying juries and scrapping with "other ladies of ye Island." She allegedly even had the fort taken apart and sold the materials. The Council for Trade and Plantations removed Phenney because of his wife's "extravagant and oppressive" conduct but thought enough of him to later appoint him Surveyor-General of Customs "in the southern part of the Continent of America."

Rogers was a hard man to knock down. When he learned Phenney was to be replaced he applied for the position. In August of 1729 he returned to Nassau as the salaried Governor of the Bahamas. In a portrait painted during his tenure by William Hogarth he appears as an affluent gentleman whose circumnavigation is symbolized by a globe. He governed the Bahamas with long overdue support from the Crown until he died in 1732 at the age of fifty-four, exhausted by the struggle to turn the islands from a nest of pirates into a flourishing colony of cotton and sugar plantations. The Englishman who was a close associate of pirates and a privateer in his youth and the scourge of Caribbean sea robbers in his maturity was buried in Nassau's coral sands where pirate feet no longer trod.

There has been only one reported find of buried treasure on New Providence. A couple of years after his death a hog rooting under an orange tree uncovered a clay jug filled with a thousand pieces of eight. A former pirate, Benjamin Sims, claimed it. He said it was booty he had given his brother to safeguard for him many years ago. The governor gave Sims the money with the proviso that half of it be left in his will for the building of a new church.

Surely the most unusual pirates ever to have set foot on the pirates' island were Anne Bonny and Mary Read. These fearless amazons sailed with Vane's former quartermaster John Rackham, whose striped pants earned him the nickname of "Calico Jack." Rackham had been voted to command Vane's ship when Vane was deposed by a vote for cowardice at not boarding a French man-o-war. Rackham had Vane and those who had voted for him cast off on a small sloop while he cruised through the Caribbean with a crew that included the only known female pirates in the New World.

The eighteenth-century press had a field day when the two were brought to trial in Port Royal. They were the subject of numerous stories and several ballads. Defoe did more than anyone to popularize and embellish their adventures. Whether Anne and Mary were in fact the passionate but faithful mates of two of their fellow pirates or whether they were whores is beside the point. No one disputes the facts of their dramatic careers which equalled those of the most dashing male pirates. Bonny and Read were the exceptions to the rule that women were not allowed aboard pirate vessels because of their disruptive influence. Captives, of course, were sometimes taken aboard but didn't participate in any action. Typically, pirate articles forbade "meddling" with a woman without her consent and female captives were aboard English pirate ships were usually sequestered and guarded to keep would-be attackers from them. Sometimes, however, discipline was lax in which case a woman might attached herself to one man in the hope of avoiding the unwelcome attention of a number of pirates.

Anne Bonny was the bastard daughter of William Cormac, a prominent Cork attorney and a housemaid. The birth was not discreetly managed so the attorney, his paramour and the baby fled Ireland and settled in Charleston, South Carolina. Cormac prospered as a businessman and planter. Anne grew up a volatile and violent child whom local folk said had stabbed a servant girl in the belly with a table knife when she was only thirteen. When her mother died she took on the duties of housekeeper for her father whose wealth made her an attractive catch despite her temper. She spurned all her suitors, however and allegedly drubbed one ardent buck who tried to seduce her so soundly that he nearly died.

When Anne eloped with a feckless sailor named James Bonny, Cormac disinherited her and the couple found their way to New Providence. When Rogers arrived he acted as an informer on the pirates. Anne's passion cooled for her husband. She fell for the dashing Jack Rackham who courted her with sweet words and stolen trinkets. He offered to buy her from her husband—divorce by sale was still practiced at that time among the lower English classes. Bonny who was detested by Anne and the community whined to the governor who threatened to publicly strip and flog Anne if she didn't behave herself properly.

Anne paid no attention to the reprimand. She was a spirited girl and plotted with Rackham to seize a sloop at anchor in the harbor which was reputed to be the swiftest in the West Indies. One midnight dressed in seamen's clothes, with her tresses tucked into a cap, Anne joined Rackham and some of his cronies in slipping aboard the sloop as the watch changed. They took it over and set off on the account. They did well, operating between Cuba and Jamaica. Allegedly, the rest of the crew had no idea of Anne's sex, even when Rackham put her ashore on Cuba for a spell while she delivered and then abandoned their child. She was as able as the men at working about the ship or in battle. It seems unlikely, however, that her sex would have gone unnoticed on a fifty-ton sloop where the crew relieved themselves in the open, squatting among the chains in the bow.

Rackham captured a Dutch prize and pressed a number of its crew to sign articles with him. One of the new pirates was a delicately handsome young boy whom Anne took a fancy to. Disappointment may have equaled shock when she discovered her favorite to be a young Englishwoman named Mary Read. Unlike Anne, Mary had spent most of her life in men's clothing. She was born to a London woman whose husband had been at sea for more than a year when she delivered a daughter. After four years her husband still had not returned so Mary's mother dressed her as a boy to replace a legitimate male child who had died, hoping in this way to eventually receive an inheritance from her husband's family.

Mary was apprenticed as a footboy to a French lady but her nature demanded more excitement and she ran away to sea signing on as a cabin boy on a warship. Later she served as an infantryman and then a mounted dragoon in Flanders where the English and French were fighting the War of the Spanish Succession. Her bravery and skill won commendations from her officers who never suspected she was a woman. She finally revealed herself to a young Dutchman in her company with whom she had fallen in love. At the close of the campaign she donned female clothing and married her former messmate to the delight of the company. The officers took up a contribution which enabled the couple to open a tavern near Breda in Holland.

Happiness slipped away when her husband died prematurely and the Utrecht Peace ruined business. Mary's wanderlust led her to sign on the Dutch merchantman bound for the West Indies which Rackham took. Anne told her lover Mary's secret which was also shared by a crew member she fell in love with and claimed to have married in "the eyes of God." So deeply did she care for this "husband" that she insisted on taking his place in a duel with another pirate since she was a better warrior. In accordance with the ship's articles, the two opponents were set on a sand-spit and as the crew watched they had it out in a bloody contest which left her lover's enemy dead of cutlass wounds. At her trial in Jamaica this incident was brought into testimony in her favor but when asked to reveal the lover's name she refused. According to Defoe he was a "forced man" and was acquitted but never had the courage to speak up and claim Mary or his unborn child.

The two women were first rate pirates never shirking battle. None among the crew "were more resolute, or ready to Board or undertake any Thing that was hazardous" Defoe asserts. Rackham's ship was anchored off Jamaica's north coast in late October 1720 and his crew was getting drunk when a British war sloop surprised them. The captain and his male shipmates were paralyzed with drink. Lieutenant Barnett, the sloop's commander, testified in court at Spanishtown that indeed only two of the pirates had put up any fight and they had fought like wildcats using pistols, cutlasses and boarding axes to fell or wound several of his men before being overpowered. One of the two he said had shot into the hold where the men were hiding, screaming like a banshee that they should come up and fight like men. It was clear that Barnett respected the raw courage of the two heavily shackled pirates who stood before the judge with unbowed heads, their sex still a secret.

Anne and Mary were sentenced to hang along with Rackham and the rest of those who had been convicted. The courtroom was astounded at the pirates' answer to the judges routine inquiry as to whether any of the condemned had anything further to say. "Milord," came the reply, "we plead our bellies." By law the court could not take the life on an unborn child by executing the mother. Surely this was some kind of bawdy joke. The courtroom erupted with laughter which turned to incredulity when a surgeon examined the two pirates and announced that they were indeed women and both were with child. Mary died of fever in prison before her baby was born, abandoned by her beloved "husband." Anne delivered safely but disappeared, perhaps paroled through her father's influence. She fades from history in a fury for as Jack Rackham was going to be hanged (near Port Royal still known as Rackham's Cay) he asked to see her. She looked at him scornfully and spat out that "Had you fought like a Man, you need not have been Hang'd like a Dog."

The loss of New Providence as an outlaw lair didn't spell an end to Caribbean piracy. In addition to those who took the pledge and those who sailed on the revival Round to the eastern seas, there were hundreds of pirates who continued to prey on West Indian shipping. They were attracted by the increased value of cargoes coming into the area. Outbound Spanish treasure flotas, infrequent as they were still exerted a powerful lure. The planting aristocracy in the West Indies grew enormously wealthy. Its members replicated European elegance in the tropics, ordering luxuries of every sort to adorn their mansions and themselves. At the same time the majority of the white population in the Indies was getting poorer and poorer and piracy was still a popular outlet for a young man without land or education.

In September 1720 pirates sailed boldly into the roadstead of Basseterre on St. Kitts, snatched several ships and sent the lieutenant-governor a contemptuous message. In October pirates, most of them British, seized more than sixteen French trading sloops off Martinique and Dominica. They tortured and maimed their prisoners and hung the Governor of Martinique who was aboard one of the prizes. Two months later the Governor of Jamaica reported that "we are dayly robb'd and plundered by vessells fitted out from Trinidado on Cuba."

Cuba with its long serrated coastline had become a favored base for pirates of all nationalities. French and Spanish pirates operating out of St. Augustine, Florida infested the American coast and the islands. The Turks and Caicos Islands southeast of the Bahamas was another pirate refuge. The Governor of Bermuda noted that his seafarers went there to trade with pirates or even have a fling at sea robbery although their declared intent was to rake salt. The lawless Virgin Islands and Anguilla remained pirate redoubts into the 1730s. A 1728 report to the British Crown stated each of the Virgins had its own lieutenant-governor "but if his cudgell happen to be one whit less strong than a sturdy subject's, Goodnight, Governour."

Official colonial correspondence of the period is filled with pleas for help in suppressing piracy. Intensified naval patrols did have some effect. A year after Calico Jack was executed a pirate ship with a crew of fifty-eight was brought into Jamaica. Forty-one of the pirates were hanged. Antigua was another island whose commerce was pirate bait and there was great rejoicing in 1723 when the notorious Captain Finn and five others were hung and displayed in chains at the water's edge. Yet the depredations continued because of the inadequate naval protection England, France and Spain provided for their colonies. Historically naval protection of the New World had always been low on the list of government priorities. Traders and authorities in the British colonies who repeatedly petitioned George I to send pirate-chasers and convoy vessels received little satisfaction. The King considered protection of his Electorate of Hanover more important and kept the British fleet concentrated in the Baltic.

In 1719 the Governor of Jamaica, Sir Nicholas Lawes who had complained to the Crown frequently wrote "I am sorry I have it to say, that his Majesty's ships of war attending this Island have either been so stationed as not to have been in the way of the pirates and Spaniards, or else had the misfortune not to meet with them." Succeeding governors continued to complain that naval commanders were derelict in their duty, leaving their ships to gather barnacles at anchor while they made money carrying merchandise among the islands. For a time private cargoes had illegally been carried, for a hefty price on naval ships, leaving those merchants who didn't participate to take their chances with unconvoyed vessels. When this practice was stopped the Navy captains simply left their official ships at anchor and bought or leased fast shallow-draft sloops using navy crews and provisions to carry on their lucrative convoy services.

A number of factors brought the golden age of piracy to a gradual conclusion. By the end of the 1720s the naval abuses mentioned above had ceased. The passage of the expanded piracy act of 1721 stated that anyone who "shall trade with, by truck, barter, or exchange" with a pirate would also be guilty of piracy. This legislation aided officials like Governor Spotswood who had been frustrated by the extent to which the community was involved with pirates. With time local economies were strong enough to shun trafficking with pirated goods. Piracy waned as the quality of government officials improved. Corrupt officials were replaced with better men when the Crown ceased issuing proprietary charters. The threat of revocation encouraged administrators to suppress piracy in those colonies which retained their charters.

In addition, the barbarous behavior of so many of the sea outlaws sickened people, outweighing their romantic appeal. Lowther and Low were the epitome of pirate savagery but atrocities were commonplace, escalating as suppression and hanging of pirates increased. The New England based John Roberts, for example, invariably tortured captives, urging his men on it the most sadistic acts. They whipped men to death, used them as target practice avoiding a fatal shot until it pleased them, or cut off ears and noses. The governor of Martinique had the misfortune to be taken by Roberts. Despite his pleas and promise of ransom, Roberts strung the governor from the yardarm as his ship crossed the Tropic of Cancer.

After 1724 the majority of pirate ships operating in the West Indies and along the American coast were Spanish. The Spanish were ships of the *Guardia de la Costa*, nominally privateers with commissions from Spanish colonial governors but committing piratical acts outside their jurisdiction. Their crews, however, included Spanish, French, Irish, and occasionally English, some of whom had been pressed into service. Stepped up patrols, the West Indies Squadron and the growing economic strength of the major island colonies greatly reduced piratical opportunities. Up until 1728 piracy was one of the primary subjects dealt with in official colonial correspondence. After that year it is seldom mentioned although a rash of mutinies occurred in the 1730s when crews mutinied, taking over their vessels for piratical cruises. Seamen turned pirate from the Long Island merchantman *Revovery* were hanged in Barbados after being caught less than a week into their new careers. They had slit the captain's throat and killed the chief mate with an axe when he refused to join them.

Bartholomew Roberts, the last of the Golden Age captains of note, was also the greatest. He has been overshadowed by Kidd and Blackbeard but in his own day he was the "Great Pyrate Roberts," undisputed king of rovers and he still stands as one of history's most brilliant pirates. A Welshman, he also holds the distinction of being piracy's only recorded teetotaler, preferring tea to rum. He kept a tight reign on his crew, forbidding gambling for money and encouraging prayer. Pirates who signed his articles agreed to put candles out by eight o'clock and not to drink below decks after that hour. All disputes between crew members were to be settled ashore.

Roberts criss-crossed the globe with a fleet so formidable that naval squadrons in the West Indies sent out to capture him, turned away at the sight of his flag rather than risk confrontation. He flew the standard jack, the skeleton with crossbones in one hand and an hourglass in the other. But his most famous flag depicted him standing on two skulls with a flaming sword in his grasp. The skulls represented his vendetta against Martinique and Barbados.

In June of 1720 Roberts appeared in Trepassey Bay at the southeastern tip of Newfoundland with a single ten-gun sloop and a crew of sixty. More than twelve hundred men were aboard the twenty-two ships at anchor. Roberts's pirates took them all. Drums were beating and trumpets blaring as the terror stricken crews of the anchored ships scurried into launches and pulled for shore. The Great Pirate Roberts, whose amazing boldness inspired his men to the most daring acts, plundered each ship and then sank all but a brigantine to carry the booty. He wasn't fazed a bit by a large French flotilla he encountered not far from the harbor. He attacked and destroyed it save for a large brigantine which he renamed the *Royal Fortune* and made his flagship. In the waning days of the golden era he was the pirates' advocate. In 1721 he threatened to invade Virginia and kill every man, woman and child in revenge for recent pirate executions there. Roberts was fearless, original and a superlative seaman. He embarked on a piratical career not because he had no other way of making a living but "to get rid of the disagreeable Superiority of some Masters he was acquainted with . . . and the Love of Novelty and Change."

Roberts was from Pembrokshire, a handsome, commanding figure according to Defoe, with the dark complexion common among Welshman. He was a dandy who dressed for battle and he died wearing a rich crimson damask waistcoat and breeches, a scarlet plume in his hat and a massive gold chain attached to a diamond cross, for he was a pious man outlawing fighting on the Sabbath. He carried two braces of pistols in a silk sling over his shoulder and a razor sharp cutlass which was his preferred weapon. He became a pirate at the advanced age of thirty-six. Born in 1682 he began his career in the merchant service. In 1719 he shipped as second mate on the *Princess* bound from London to the Guinea Coast to load slaves. Off the West African coast the ship was seized by the famed Welsh pirate, Captain Howell Davis.

Davis himself had launched his pirate career after serving as mate on a slaver which was captured by Edward England the Irish pirate who was en route from Nassau to Madagascar. Davis had accepted the King's pardon on New Providence and sailed on the *Buck*, a sloop crewed by former pirates, which Rogers sent to trade with Spanish and French colonies. At Martinique Davis led a mutiny and was proclaimed captain of thirty five men delighted to be on the account once again. Their first prize was a French ship which Davis used as a decoy to take a second French ship by pretending the captives were captured pirates. After prowling the West Indies Davis headed for the eastern seas like so many of the West Indies rovers.

In Gambia he presented himself to the Governor of Gambia Castle as a Liverpool trader on the way to Senegal for resin and elephant's teeth.

He was invited to dinner along with the ship's surgeon and master. They presented the governor with a gift of wine and then held him prisoner until they were given gold bars and ivory. By the time Davis met Roberts he had taken many prizes loaded with gold dust, bar gold, coins, ivory and slaves. Davis prided himself on never having to force a man and was delighted when his compatriot Roberts was willing to sail with him. They took a richly laden Holland bound ship with the Governor of Accra aboard.

When the pirate crew raided the Portuguese settlement on Prince's Island in the Guinea Gulf, Davis was killed in an ambush. He had come to Prince's Island flying the English flag and convinced the authorities his fleet was a naval squadron on a pirate hunting mission. The Portuguese officials wined and dined him until he put their credulity to the test by plundering a French ship that came into the harbor to refit. He asserted she had been trading with pirates and invited the Portuguese governor and other high ranking officials to come aboard and accept a gift of a dozen slaves taken from the French vessel. Davis plotted to kidnap the men and hold them for £40,000 ransom. But the plan failed when one of the slaves escaped and swam to shore during the night. Davis was killed in an ambush the next morning when the pseudo naval officers went ashore. In the mere six weeks he had been a pirate Roberts had so impressed his shipmates with his valor and intelligence that he was elected captain to replace Davis with only one dissenting vote.

Roberts was a vengeful man and led his men on a frenzied raid on the island where Davis had been slain, leveling the Portuguese settlement. Then he set his course for Bahia, the Bay of All Saints in Brazil, where he found forty-two Portuguese ships at anchor. They were riding low in the water deeply loaded for the voyage to Lisbon. He picked out the biggest, the vice-admiral's forty gun vessel, and sailed up to her so brazenly that he was able to board before the Portuguese realized what was afoot. Some of his men kept the crew engaged in hand to hand combat while others rifled the holds. The rest of the merchant fleet fired at him and raised their topgallants as a distress signal to the two warships assigned to guard the Portuguese convoy. Before they could reach him, Roberts had sailed off with his prize containing sugar, hides, tobacco and 40,000 gold moidores valued at about £80,000, gold trinkets and plate and the diamond studded cross which afterwards reposed on his chest rather than the King of Portugal's for whom it had been designed. Eventually he presented it to the Governor of Guinea in return for a favor.

The pirates then sailed north to the dreary little Spanish colony at Devil's Island off Guiana where they found female colonists especially eager to trade for the Portuguese loot. There is a legend on Little Cayman Island that the golden treasure taken at Bahia is buried deep inside a cave there but after a couple of weeks at Devil's Island, carousing, gambling and wenching, it is unlikely the pirates left with anything jingling in their pockets.

Roberts took his men into the Caribbean in the Spring of 1720. They took a few ships and then moved north to Newfoundland and Trepassey Bay when it became apparent that patrols by the Royal Navy and island auxiliaries were more vigilant than usual. Roberts found no shortage of recruits among cod-splitters eager to escape the harsh conditions of labor and climate on Newfoundland. After a summer of rampaging around the New England coast with a complement of about a hundred men, he came back to the Caribbean. They set out from Deseada in the Lesser Antilles near Guadeloupe heading for West Africa via Brava, the southernmost of the Cape Verde Islands. But once across the Atlantic the prevailing southerly wind forced them so far north they couldn't reach the Cape Verdes. They had to come back across and then head south into the Caribbean taking advantage of the western Atlantic's prevailing northeasterly trade winds.

It was a nightmarish voyage. Not having touched land for two thousand miles, only one sixty-three gallon barrel of water from Deseada was left for a crew of 124. Roberts doled it out—one mouthful per day and many men were so crazed with thirst they drank sea water or their own urine. Dysentery and fevers flashed through the crew, killing quite a few. The days became weeks, the barrel became emptier until one day there was no water at all. Roberts with his rock-ribbed faith in the Almighty was the only man who had any hope. Most of the men were beyond caring whether they lived or died when they found themselves suddenly in shallower water, indicating land was not far off. The following day they sighted land and by evening were toasting one another with fresh water from the Maroni River in Surinam on the coast of South America.

Naval patrols be damned declared Roberts after this frustrating and almost fatal episode. He unleashed his lethal forces on the Caribbean in a desperate and dazzlingly successful campaign. The governor of the French Leewards reported that in a four-day period at the end of October, 1720 the pirates had "seized, burned or sunk fifteen French and English vessels and one Dutch interloper of forty-two guns at Dominica." Sailing right under shore batteries at the Basseterre Road on St. Kitts, he plundered and burned a number of vessels at anchor. According to the Governor of Bermuda the pirates were slicing off the ears of prisoners, lashing them to the mast or yardarm and using them for target practice, whipping them to death and committing other atrocities. Roberts based his fleet off St. Lucia and concentrated his fury on French shipping. The Governor of

Martinique was so desperate that he made an unprecedented plea for help to the British Governor of Barbados and another to the Governor of the Leewards. The Leeward Islands' Governor ordered H.M.S. *Rose,* one of the four vessels that had accompanied Woodes Rogers to New Providence and then abandoned him, to hunt Roberts down. The captain impudently refused remarking that the governor had no power to issue him orders. This was technically true and had long been a bone of contention between the Admiralty and the British governors who petitioned the Crown for authority.

Once again bureaucratic bungling abetted piracy and Roberts, un-impeded by patrols, did so well in the vulnerable sea lanes that by the spring of 1721 there was little left to plunder. The holds of his ships were solidly packed with booty which could be traded at a premium for Guinea gold. So in April he made for Africa, landing on the coast of Senegal and then proceeding to Sierra Leone where his men careened their ships and relaxed in the company of English traders who operated in defiance of the Royal Africa Company's monopoly. One of the free-lancers was Benjamin Gunn, immortalized as Benn Gunn in *Treasure Island.* Another was an ex-buccaneer known as Old Crackers who fired a salute to the pirates whenever they sailed into his port.

During the summer and early fall Roberts plundered along the Guinea Coast, sometimes attempting to trade with local tribes and battling them when they refused. As late as 1920s tribal people around Old Calabar still spoke of a pirate attack which was an important event in their orally transmitted history. At Whydah Roads where Defoe wrote there was "commonly the best booty," the arch pirate took eleven French, English and Portuguese ships in a single day releasing them when each made over a ransom of eight pounds of gold dust worth about £600. One of the receipts he wrote for the gold refers to the pirates as "we Gentlemen of Fortune."

No pirate captain ever had complete command of his crew and when one of the ships refused to pay it was set afire, against Roberts's orders with its cargo of chained slaves still aboard. A Church of England priest on his way to a missionary post was captured on one ship and Roberts offered him the position of chaplain on his flagship. All he would have to do, said Roberts, was say prayers and make punch. The priest declined and Roberts let him go, keeping three prayer books and a corkscrew.

As his squadron lay at anchor in the lee of Parrot Island off Cape Lopez on the Guinea coast, Roberts's Nemesis appeared in the form of the *Swallow,* a Royal Navy sixty-gun frigate, commanded by Captain Chaloner Ogle. The *Swallow* and the H.M.S. *Weymouth* had been hunting for Roberts for six months, frustrated by the maze of rain-forested, rivers and swampy lagoons which formed the interminable coastline. When the *Swallow* finally caught sight of Roberts's squadron, the pirates thought she was a potential prize, a Portuguese merchantman and Roberts dispatched the *Great Ranger* after her. Ogle lured the *Ranger* away, out of sight and then turned on her, killing ten pirates. More than a hundred others were taken prisoner, many of them hideously wounded from gunshot and an explosion.

Five days later on February 10, 1722 Ogle returned to Parrot Island where the pirates' ships were still anchored. Captain Roberts was at a breakfast of spicy salamagundi and tea. Most of his men were sleeping off monumental hangovers following the capture of a liquor laden prize the day before. As the *Swallow* hove into view flying a French flag no one was alarmed but as it made straight for the *Royal Fortune* one of Roberts's crew, a navy deserter, recognized her as his old ship and gave a cry of alarm.

Roberts cooly appraised the situation, aware that his rum-fuddled men were in no condition to put up a good fight. He determined to cut cables and run. Then for some reason he changed his mind and gave the helmsman a foolhardy change of course—right at the big warship. Perhaps he wanted to test the *Swallow*'s firing range. As the two ships drew closer, the pirate captain jumped onto a gun carriage to direct his ship's fire. The *Swallow* set off a broadside which toppled the pirate ship's mizzen topmast. At their captain's command the pirates returned fire. When the smoke cleared they saw Roberts's great body slumped on the deck, his throat ripped open by a blast of grapeshot. His men, many of them sobbing, respected his last wishes and heaved his still bleeding corpse overboard in all its finery, jewels, weapons and all. Thus ended the stunning career of the seemingly invincible Great Pirate Roberts, who took over four hundred sail in less than four years. His men fought on but without their charismatic captain they lost their will. At two in the afternoon 152 survivors, many of them too drunk to stand, surrendered to a navy boarding party. To the amusement of Ogle's men, one dazed pirate who had spent the entire engagement in a drunken stupor came to suddenly and seeing the *Swallow* near by yelled: "A prize! A prize!" and pressed the others to take her. A large quantity of plunder was found aboard the pirate ship and Captain Ogle, who was the only naval officer ever knighted for capturing pirates, eventually became Admiral of the Navy and built a vast fortune based on gold dust he had stolen from Roberts's ship.

The 254 pirates taken from the *Great Ranger* and the *Royal Fortune* were carried to Cape Coast Castle for the largest pirate trial ever held. Fifteen died on the trip and four more in the castle dungeon before the remainder were brought to trial. Some were able to prove they had been forced and when the trial began 169 men were charged. Only eight of them were grizzled veterans—two had previously sailed with Blackbeard and six were with Davis when he died, but the rest were recruits. After a fair trial 74 men including the musicians were acquitted. Most of the 54 who were sentenced to death, 2 of whom were reprieved, were natives of London or the west of England. Another 17 were sentenced to prison in London of whom all but 4 died en route to England. Not one of the 20 sentenced to seven years' hard labor in the Gold Coast mines of the Royal Africa Company survived their sentence.

The fifty-two unrepentant pirates were hanged "like dogs" in batches over a two-week period in April of 1722 and strung up to "sun-dry". As he was led to the gallows erected outside the castle ramparts, one of Roberts's original crew known as Lord Sympson saw a woman he knew in the crowd that had gathered to watch the show. She was Elizabeth Trengrove, an Englishwoman who had been a passenger on a ship Roberts captured. "I have lain with that bitch three times," he shouted, "and now she has come to see me hanged."

The mass hangings on the African Coast, celebrated around the globe by merchants, planters and bureaucrats, marked the sunset of the Golden Age. Piracy in the Caribbean continued in sporadic outbursts of varying intensity but never again did such dashing rovers capture the attention and grudging admiration that had been the lot of the anarchic antiheroes of the early eighteenth century. Their legacy was to furnish us with the classic image of the pirate. Howard Pyle's romantic illustrations of the rum-guzzling scourges of the Spanish Main appearing in mass circulation magazines at the turn of the twentieth century fixed in the public's mind the image of the pirate as Caribbean swashbuckler: swarthy and swaggering, with salt-encrusted beard, golden earring and a brace of pistols tucked into his belt.

Hollywood pirates from Douglas Fairbanks in *The Black Pirate* of 1926 to Errol Flynn's 1940 *The Sea Hawk* swept moviegoers into a world of "thrilling adventure on the Mighty Main." An outcast who refuses to play by society's rules, the pirate has always exerted a fascination, a perverse glamor. Even today, perhaps especially now in this age of galloping technology and entangling bureaucracy, the pirate life, as portrayed in fiction and films, arouses a pang of envy. The Caribbean pirate symbolizes freedom from the constraints that harness most of us to routine lives. In spite of his crudeness, he appeals to something buried in our psyches—the fantasy of sailing for distant horizons in quest of gold and glory, heedless of the rules and ever hopeful.

In the eighteenth century when piracy was commonplace and pirate trials were widely followed by an avid public, the pirate emerged as a sinister figure, a villain. After the suppression of the Caribbean pirate chieftains a kind of nostalgia softened the writers' focus. Sir Walter Scott established the pirate as a romantic figure with *The Pirate*. The public loved it and craved more. In 1822 three versions of Scott's book were staged in London. Throughout the nineteenth century some fifty English pirate dramas were produced including *Ocean Born, or the Pirate Father* (1852) and *The Devil's Ship and the Pirates of the Charmed Life*.

Before American movies realized the box-office draw of pirate romances, American writers contributed to pirate literature with special emphasis on pirate treasure. Edgar Allan Poe's "The Gold Bug" was one of the first of these tales which often surrounded a germ of fact with accretions of wild fantasy so dear to nineteenth-century readers. Writers of the stature of Washington Irving, Harriet Beecher Stowe and John Steinbeck wrote tales of pirate treasure and of course, the greatest of all buried treasure stories is Robert Louis Stevenson's *Treasure Island*, several of whose characters were drawn from actual pirates of the Golden Age.

NOTES

1. Defoe quoting Thomas Anstis trial, Defoe, Daniel (under the pseudonym Captain Charles Johnson), *A General History of the Pyrates*, edited by Arthur L. Hayward, Routledge and Kegan Paul, London, 1955, pp. 259–60.

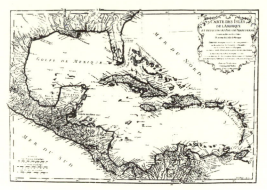

10

A Fading Frontier

The rovers who followed the Golden Age of piracy had no Esquemelin or Defoe to immortalize them. As New World piracy waned there were no more of the brilliant rover-cum-scientists like Dampier or Wafer who had adorned the buccaneer era and very few, if any, men with vision or power equal to that of Morgan or Roberts. Times had changed. The world no longer tolerated sea outlaws, no matter how colorful. Few of the latter-day pirates wrote of their adventures. When they did it was usually to defend themselves. In 1824 a British officer named Aaron Smith captured the public's attention with *The Atrocities of the Pirates*, a self-serving account of his stint as a pirate. Smith had been master mariner on a ship seized by Spanish pirates off the south coast of Cuba. He participated in several attacks on British and American ships in the West Indies and was eventually captured and taken back to trial in England. Smith persuaded the court of his innocence but public opinion and that of his peers weighed against his reputation, inspiring the book in which he pictures himself as a victim of circumstance, and coincidentally, utterly irresistible to women.

He describes a dalliance with a lively señorita named Serafina, whose father was a Cuban magistrate. He accepted her amorous advances readily enough. But he describes fighting off the proffered charms of a Spanish matron who had been taken prisoner with her husband when the pirates seized their ship. Quarters were cramped and the couple was assigned to share a cabin with Smith. "One night, after we had retired to our respective mattresses," he wrote, "I woke about midnight, to find the lady by my side and her arms thrown round my neck fast asleep." He woke her up and shooed her back to her husband's side, sure there had been some misunderstanding. The next night, however, when he was roused by the Señora's caresses her husband also awoke and bellowed so loudly that the captain rushed to the scene. Smith prudently pretended to be asleep through the whole incident leaving his ardent admirer to explain how she must have wandered in her sleep. Fortunately for our hero, after a few more close calls the couple was given their freedom and left for Havana. Smith impresses on the reader his desire to escape. He professes amazement that when the pirates were captured and he was arrested by the Spanish and thrown into a Cuban jail, he was not aided by his government but handed over to Admiral Sir Charles Rowley who had him clapped in irons and taken to England like a common felon. The appearance at his trial of his tearful fiancee moved the jury to acquit Smith, who published his account, probably with the help of a ghost writer, the following year.

One West Indian pirate whose exploits have been remembered is Captain Henry Johnson, a one-armed Irishman who was known as "Henriques, el Inglés," by his predominantly Spanish crew. This alliance was unusual but not unheard of for Irish Catholics had far more in common with Spaniards than with their hated English oppressors. Johnson lost an arm in a pirate battle but managed to cock his musket with his remaining hand and then brace it on the stump to shoot with remarkable accuracy. On March 20, 1730 off Swan Island his *Two Brothers* engaged the *John and Jane* out of Jamaica. The pirates had ninety men and eighteen big cannons, the defenders only twenty-five men, eight carriage guns and twelve swivel guns yet they fought bravely for almost six hours before surrendering.

The pirate crew swarmed aboard the *John and Jane*, stepping over bodies on the bloody deck. The few men who had survived were stripped naked in preparation for hanging but Johnson and another English pirate ordered a halt to the sport. Pedro Poleas, the pirates' first mate found a woman hidden in the hold. She identified herself as a Mrs. Groves whose husband had been killed in the battle. Poleas was on the point of raping her when Johnson intervened, ordering the Spaniard to restore the lady's clothing. When she finally returned to Jamaica she praised the gentleman pirate who had guarded her from his lustful crew for the remainder of the voyage.

There were fewer pirates operating in the West Indies than in the past but a record number of privateers whose depredations had a crippling effect on the West Indian economy for almost a century. The British moved against French and Dutch islands used as privateering bases; Deseada and Marie Galante in 1808 and St. Eustatius twenty-seven years earlier. When Admiral Rodney took St. Eustatius, a thriving market for prize goods, in January of 1781, he captured 150 merchant ships in the harbor and impounded warehouses crammed with booty worth in excess of three million pounds sterling.

The century following the mass hangings at Cape Coast Castle was punctuated with a series of wars involving the old European powers and the western Atlantic. England's commercial conflict with Spain, The War of Jenkins's Ear, was followed by the struggle over the Austrian Succession. Known in the American colonies as "King George's War," it was settled in 1748 by the Treaty of Aix-la-Chapelle. The Seven Years War erupted eight years later and in 1775 the American Revolution began. The American side was bolstered by the participation of France in 1778, Spain in 1779 and Holland in 1780. In 1789 The French Revolution began, convulsing Europe in a conflict that didn't end until 1815 when Napoleon was defeated at Waterloo.

Thus, for close to a century naval operations absorbed seamen who would otherwise have been prime candidates for piracy. As privateers they operated in that twilight zone where patently immoral acts were cloaked in quasi-legality. There were always scattered flare-ups of piracy but it wasn't until thousands of ex-privateers who had been engaged in the War of 1812, the Napoleonic conflicts and the Latin American wars of Liberation were out of commissions that piracy had its last and most savage outburst.

It matters little that there were no talented chroniclers of that final era for few of its participants merit immortality. Most of them would have been scorned by their predecessors as a scurvy lot. Gone were the days when a pirate crew was a band of brothers united by a compelling dream of infinite riches and equally precious freedom. The subsistence-pirates may have dreamed of shimmering heaps of gold and silver, emeralds and pearls but most often they were scavengers, barely eking out a living. When the U.S. brig *Washington* was boarded by Spanish pirates near Cuba in 1822 the booty consisted of $16 from the captain's sea chest, the ship's compass, a hailing trumpet, some lines, the cook's utensils and all the potatoes on board.

Without a land base such as New Providence, without the receptive ports that had served as clearing houses for plundered goods, without the protection of powerful political authorities, the pirates couldn't hope to organize on any scale. The many decades of naval warfare were a major factor in the decline of piracy in the New World. Changing times also played a role. Piracy thrives on the instability which characterizes a frontier situation. As the frontier moved from the West Indies and the Atlantic coast to the interior of the vast North American continent piracy was doomed. The islands and the Spanish Main had developed viable economies which depended as much on eradicating the pirates as they had once depended on their contraband goods for survival.

The sea-lanes were better patrolled and ships were organized into convoys for protection. St. Kitts was the rendezvous for English ships sailing home from the eastern Caribbean in the eighteenth century. The convoys could be very large. Three hundred merchant vessels escorted by six ships-of-the-line left St. Kitts in a single convoy in June 1759. In 1757 a convoy from England arrived with cargo valued at two million pounds sterling—a tempting but unobtainable prize. In the face of such might there was little the poorly organized ruffians in their single ships could do. In addition, local administrations became more vigorous in the application of justice and less corrupt. Except for the Spanish refuges of Cuba, the Isle of Pines, Puerto Rico, parts of Hispaniola, Cozumel, Isla Mujeres, Isla Margarita, and a few scattered out of the way hiding holes, there was no place a pirate could seek sanctuary.

The pool of pirate recruits continued to dry up throughout the eighteenth century. With the development of the North American colonies, there were new opportunities for white men who found no place in West Indian society. The indenture system had been replaced by slavery reducing the flow of white immigrants to a relative trickle and fewer felons were transported to the colonies, in part because they had been such a disruptive influence. The Royal Navy and merchant service became somewhat, if not a great deal, more humane.

A century of naval warfare offered thousands of restless souls the prospect of making a good living as legitimate privateers, although the navy still had to press men to fill their berths. A letter from St. Kitts in 1744, published in *Gentleman's Magazine* stated that "A Man of War coming down from Antigua sent her Barge ashore to press some of the Privateers' Men, which amount to about 1,000 in Number." The privateers made sport of the navy by seizing the barge "as soon as she came ashore and having with infinite labour got her into the middle of the Town, made her full of Punch, and were merry on the occasion." The same letter reported that in 1744 when France declared war on England at the behest of her ally Spain which had been engaged against the British since 1739 in the so-called War of Jenkins's Ear, St. Kitts already had ten privateers at sea and was outfitting four more. "We flow in money," the correspondent wrote, "a Division being lately made between one or more Privateers each man had 200 pounds sterling."

Jenkins of the eponymous war was an Englishman, a master mariner who dabbled in a bit of piracy. In 1731 he relieved a Spanish salvage party of treasure they were bringing up from a wrecked galleon. The ship he commanded was boarded by a Spanish *guarda costa*, one of the patrol ships which frequently stopped British vessels in contravention of the Peace of Utrecht. The trade laws of Spain outlawed British commerce with Spanish colonies and the zealous Spanish coast guard patrols were the bane of West Indian and American shipping lanes, plundering cargoes and mistreating crews of vessels they considered smugglers. The captain who boarded Jenkins's vessel allegedly sliced off his ear then handed it back to him to take to England to show what the Spaniard would do to the King if he had the chance.

Spanish outrages against British shipping in the West Indies continued until in 1738 Jenkins appeared before a Committee of the House of Commons with a shriveled bit of flesh he claimed was his missing ear and pleaded for reprisals. The war which was aimed at ridding the Caribbean of the piratical *guarda-costas*, many of which were fitted out at Portobelo, settled nothing and soon blurred into the War of the Austrian Succession which entangled most of Europe. In the Caribbean the French and English waged a bitter war against one another involving the Spanish and the Dutch and Danish whose island possessions were used as smuggling bases where merchants were happy to do business, regardless of the current political situation.

Privateers figured prominently in the hostilities. Distribution centers like St. Eustatius were ravaged again and again by both France and England. The numbers of captured vessels indicate the heavy volume of seagoing traffic during the period. All told the British took 2,185 Spanish ships and 1,249 French vessels which amounted to only 196 more than they lost. The French had seized 1,878 of their ships and the Spanish captured 1,360. However, in terms of value, the British did well for a number of their prizes carried cargoes of great value. Privateers from both sides sometimes behaved badly, raiding islands and carrying off slaves and other valuables. When the French on St. Bartholomew surrendered, there was no controlling a British privateer mob out of St. Kitts that swarmed over the island like locusts.

The young United States fought the world's mightiest sea power in both the Revolution and the War of 1812 using virtually all-privateer navies. American families, particularly from the New England colonies which had profiteered during the Pirate Round, outfitted privateering vessels and participated in clandestine trade with the West Indies, making great fortunes. The Derby family of Salem owned or had shares in more than fifty ships. Shipyards along the coast developed sleek topsail schooners which could carry a fair load of merchandise or prize goods and yet outrun a larger man-o-war. These shallow-draft ships carried about seventy-five to a hundred men.

Rhode Island, Tew's old hangout, led the way in privateering in the mid-eighteenth century. Until the American Revolution the privateers preyed chiefly on French shipping although Spanish prizes were not scorned. The *Bethel* of Boston seized the hundred-man Spanish merchantman *Jesus, Mary and Joseph* in 1748 and got twenty-six large cannons and $300,000 worth of cargo, including $171,000 in cash. Despite the almost constant tremors which shook the Caribbean there were attractive prizes plying the sea. In 1744 a squadron of four privateers from New York seized a convoy of six prizes, none smaller than 180 tons.

No ships were safe regardless of nationality or alliances. Privateering was a license to steal and even when there was a respite from declared warfare, sea robbers connived to carry out their marauding. Neutral French ships were prowling the Caribbean with Spanish letters of marque before becoming officially involved in the war against England. Throughout the eighteenth century privateers routinely carried multiple papers made out to ships of different nationalities so that whichever papers satisfied the questioner of the moment could be produced and the others concealed or thrown overboard.

One American captain was done in by a bizarre turn of events. As the H.M.S. *Sparrow* bore down on his Baltimore brig, the *Nancy*, he heaved incriminating papers over the side. Much to his amazement they reappeared at his trial before Port Royal's Vice Admiralty Court in 1779. A Royal Navy Lieutenant fishing from a nearby ship caught a shark soon after the American's capture and found the sodden but still legible bundle of documents in its bulging stomach.

At the beginning of the Revolution the rebellious colonies pitted thirteen worm-riddled frigates against 100 well-armed British warships already in American waters, which were backed up by many others ready to head west at a command. During the entire war the British only commissioned 120 vessels. By 1782 although the official American Navy only had seven ships left, the British quailed before the onslaught of civilian privateers commissioned by Congress. In an effort to beat the odds the Americans issued letters of marque to merchantmen, pilot boats, whalers, longboats—anything short of a raft. Some of the 2,500 vessels commissioned by the states and Congress were pathetically small but the determined men who crewed them ranged far and wide. A Chesapeake cockleshell which crossed the Atlantic to take several prizes in the Irish Sea was so minute that the captain of one prize assumed it was a pinnace and asked the crew where their mother ship was.

During the Revolution seventy thousand men participated in history's greatest privateering venture. They brought back to American ports a total of $50 million worth of prizes from 2,980 British merchantmen and 16 warships. The West Indies suffered terribly. The prices of sugar and rum plummeted while insurance rates soared. The privateers paralyzed the economy. As vital supplies dwindled, the price of corn rose by 400 percent and many slaves starved to death. Privateers took 700 ships worth some two million pounds sterling in one six-month period alone.

Once the French who had been tacitly aiding the Americans declared their allegiance in 1778, American privateers sailed with international crews out of French ports, on French-owned ships, flying French flags. Not surprisingly there were some ugly incidents and neutral ships were not necessarily safe. The *Eclipse* an American privateer under the weak command of Captain Nathaniel Fanning of Connecticut intercepted the merchantman *Emiliard* in the English Channel as it was returning from the West Indies under the neutral Danish flag. The privateers boarded her, robbed the passengers and stripped off their clothes. France, Denmark and England, who considered all American privateers to be pirates since they didn't recognize their rebel government, complained. It came out at an inquiry that the captain was under the influence of Thomas Potter, the strong willed first mate who directed the action. Testimony revealed that Potter had enticed Fanning into donning some of the elegant apparel taken from the passengers and parading about before his crew. Fanning was also found to have two logs, one for official consumption and one in code.

One feature of West Indian shipping during the eighteenth century was the abuse of flags of truce. The English and French had a mutual agreement whereby their prisoners could be exchanged. The Americans had no such system, although Benjamin Franklin tried to institute one when he was Minister at the French court. He proposed setting up privateering expeditions aimed not at getting prize goods but at capturing seamen who could then be exchanged for American prisoners. During the Seven Years War which began in 1756 American ships were deeply involved in illicit trading with the French under the guise of participating in exchanges of British and French prisoners. The colonial governors of North America, Bermuda and the Bahamas freely granted flags to whomever made it worth their while. Governor Popple of Bermuda even supplied a French prisoner with one of each flag.

Government reports noted that the American colonies, especially Rhode Island, carried on a brisk trade with the French this way, prolonging the war by supplying the enemy with provisions. Admiral Knowles wrote that the northern colonies "used to buy French prisoners at a great price one of another for a pretence to go to the French islands." The port of Monte Cristi on the north coast of Spanish Hispaniola was the chief depot for this trade which so enraged the English. As many as 130 ships were anchored there at a time, each with a false flag of truce and a token prisoner.

Britain had a hard time of it. France, the new American republic, Spain and the Netherlands all had a go at British shipping during the wars of the eighteenth century. The English took many ships, of course, but during the upheavals which rocked the Caribbean in the wake of the French Revolution filibustiers sailing out of Haiti and Martinique or directly from the old corsair ports on the coast of France swooped down and seized 2,266 ships. The English captured a mere 375. An American named Moultson sailing for France struck the sharpest blow when he smashed the Jamaica fleet in 1795. American ships suspected of trading with British ports were also set upon by the French filibustiers who achieved phenomenal success in remarkably small boats. So many American traders complained that Congress made it legal to seize any French ship in American waters. Subsequently, the two countries agreed to let one another's ships pass unmolested unless they carried war contraband.

The son of a Marseille banker named Victor Hugues was the outstanding figure in this epoch when privateering frequently degenerated into piracy. Hugues was a ruthless revolutionary, a former innkeeper in Haiti. He was forced out of Port-au-Prince by Toussaint l'Overture's slave rebellion and moved to Guadeloupe where he established a clearinghouse for privateers at Point-a-Pitre. His captains brought in so much loot that for a brief span the sleepy, tropical town was one of the richest ports in the New World. He issued "commissions" to ruthless corsair bands which preyed on American and British ships, treating their passengers and crew with casual cruelty.

Hugues accused the Americans of furnishing England with war materials and ships. Captains detained by the corsairs were coerced into signing documents stating they carried British cargoes. "To remind this treacherous nation," he said, "that but for us, who squandered our blood and money to give them their independence, George Washington would have been hanged as a traitor," Hugues declared war on the United States. He also declared war on the ruling Paris Directory which he labeled "antirevolutionary." It was because of his bloodthirsty campaign that Congress declared war on France in American waters. His captains were a frightening lot of thugs, a cosmopolitan group which included Pierre Gros, Joseph Murphy, Peg-leg Langlois, Petréas the Mulatto and the brothers Modesto and Antonio Fuët of Narbonne. Antonio was dubbed Captain Moëda (Moidore) for his flamboyant gesture of bombarding a Portuguese prize with gold coins when he had exhausted his supply of shot. According to the story, after he took the ship, his surgeons dug out embedded coins from the Portuguese dead and wounded.

During the War of 1812 American privateers once again proved their worth, virtually winning the war despite what on paper at least looked like vastly superior British naval power. The war had been provoked by U.S. resentment of trade restrictions and the continued stopping at sea and searching of American vessels by British warships looking for British deserters. Little American boats armed with a couple of guns set out to make their fortunes and harass the mighty enemy. *The Times* of London reported that American privateers in the West Indies were "so daring as even to cut vessels out of harbours and send raiding parties to carry cattle off from the plantations."

In 1813 privateers landed on Harbour Island in the Bahamas and set the town on fire in retaliation for the partial burning of Washington by British Army troops. Other British settlements were also burned and the coast of Jamaica was almost completely blockaded.

The single most effective weapon the Americans had was a new ship design, the Baltimore clippers. They were ideally suited to the two leading industries of the period: privateering and slaving. Graceful, lean craft, riding low in the water, they were unbeatable and beautiful. With all canvas on her tall rakish masts, a Baltimore clipper could swoop down on a merchantman or British ship of the line with lightning swiftness. With equal agility she could snatch a merchant ship out of a convoy and when pursued she could escape with ease.

These sleek beautiful machines developed out of the Bermuda sloops which pirates had favored and were the forerunners of the nineteenth-century China clippers, the swiftest and most elegant ships ever built. If the American privateering vessels of this period had a weakness it was the relatively unseasoned pine they were built of which was softer and less durable than the oak used for British and European ships.

Privateering had been the mainspring of Rhode Island's prosperity since the 1740s. The industry supported thousands of people: shipowners, bankers, lawyers, crew, shipyard workers, provisioners, not to mention those employed in the hospitality industry who catered to privateers on shore leave.

Before the war was over in 1814 the Americans lost 900 ships but seized 1,300. The government paid a bounty of half the estimated value of any armed enemy ship which was sunk. New York had 120 privateers cruising as far away as the Irish coast. They brought home 275 prizes and sunk many more. One vessel eluded 17 British warships to carry back $300,000 worth of booty. On a sixteen-month cruise the *America* out of Salem took 41 prizes for a net profit of over one million dollars. The *True-Blooded Yankee* was the greatest prize winner, bagging 27 ships in 37 days for a total of three million dollars in prize money.

Insurance rates went through the ceiling, reaching 35.5 percent at Halifax. The English merchants reacted as Thomas Jefferson had predicted they would in a letter to Monroe: "Encourage these privateers to burn their prizes and let the public pay for them. They will cheat us enormously. No matter, they will make the Merchants of England feel and squeal and cry out for peace." The pain inflicted by the Americans who had "the blood of Drake" in their veins, led to Ghent where a peace treaty was signed in December of 1814. Privateers weren't universally popular, even among their countrymen. Benjamin Franklin complained of "this odious usage of privateers, ancient relic of piracy," and encouraged a deputy to the French National Assembly in 1792 to introduce a proposal outlawing privateering.

The proposal failed to pass. Maritime nations couldn't yet manage without privateers notwithstanding their frequent degeneration into piracy. Privateering wasn't outlawed on an international scale until the Paris Peace Conference in 1856 at the conclusion of the Crimean War. But it never again played a significant military role after the War of 1812, except for a brief period during the United States Civil War when the Confederacy relied on secessionist privateers who were treated as pirates by the Union. However, privateering as a profitable venture was intertwined with slaving well beyond the end of the War of 1812. Since 1794 American citizens had been prohibited from selling slaves to foreign countries. In 1808 a British act abolished all trade in African slaves and the U.S. Constitution outlawed the importation of slaves into the country. But the demand for slaves was greater than ever. There was no shortage of privateers to supply them despite British and American naval patrols that hunted slavers and harsh penalties including transportation for British subjects and hanging for Americans. Privateers dealing in slaves sometimes pirated them from ships returning from the African coast rather than sail that far. It wasn't until 1862 that the last convicted slaver in the United States was executed.

Two nineteenth-century slavers, Jean and Pierre Lafitte, are the most intriguing of the latter-day pirates. Over the years claims have been made that Jean Lafitte, one of history's most colorful sea outlaws, was a cousin of Napoleon and the nephew of John Paul Jones. He has mistakenly been credited with inventing the breech loading gun, which he introduced during the famous battle between Jones's *Bonhomme Richard* and the British frigate *Serapis*. He is alleged to have buried millions in treasure including a horde on Pecan Island in Louisiana's Vermillion Bay, another cache near Houston at the mouth of the Trinity River and an enormous chest filled with gold and jewels at a spot marked with a brass surveyor's rod up a channel off Lavaca Bay in Texas.

Jean Lafitte claimed to be a native of Bordeaux who had been brought as an infant to Santo Domingo. Others said he came from St. Malo, the ancient corsair port. In fact, he was probably a Creole, born in Port-au-Prince, Haiti in 1782 of a Spanish Jewess and a French father. At eighteen he married a girl who died giving birth while the couple was at sea. In 1804 the brothers were in New Orleans which had become an American port as part of the Louisiana Purchase of 1803. They were, they said, sailing against English ships with valid letters of marque. Local authorities had suspicions that Pierre was an arms smuggler. They had no idea, until it was too late, that the brazen brothers were outright pirates. Two of their three ships were actually American merchantmen they had seized and modified.

In 1805 they set up a blacksmith shop which served as a cover for their contraband dealing in slaves. In 1806 they received a slaving license but operating within the law was too tame. Jean became the chief of a growing band of smuggler-pirates. In 1807 they established a base on Grande Terre island in Barataria Bay which is separated from New Orleans by a low lying labyrinth of bayous and lakes. Pierre lived in the city, managing legitimate business interests and married the daughter of a prominent miniature-painter. Both brothers moved easily in New Orleans society.

Jean and his cronies ignored the distinction between privateering and piracy. They plundered slavers en route to the Caribbean plantations and sold their human cargoes to Louisiana planters for a dollar a pound. With a commission from the anti-Spanish authorities at Cartagena, they preyed on Spanish shipping as well. They were so outrageously bold in their piratical activities that in 1812 the Governor of Louisiana had no choice but to arrest them for contraband activity. They were released on bond after two weeks in jail and vanished into their Barataria lair which was organized as a commune. Before long they were carrying on as before. The governor offered a reward of five thousand dollars for Jean Lafitte, dead or alive. Lafitte's retort was his offer of fifty thousand for the governor's capture. By 1814 the pirate stronghold had about a thousand members and during one six-month period in 1814 booty worth at least a million dollars came into the community, most of it in slaves. The business that was so good for the Lafittes was also profitable for an estimated 10 percent of the population of New Orleans who were peripherally involved.

In 1814, in spite of their impressive New Orleans connections Jean was impeached by a grand jury for piracy. Pierre was thrown in prison when he ventured out of the island stronghold but shortly escaped.

The British sent emissaries to Barataria to ask Jean Lafitte for aid in an attack on New Orleans. Lafitte graciously entertained the envoys while he secretly dispatched a message to the Governor of Louisiana offering to help the United States instead. He made good on his offer to help

General Jackson repel the British attack even though the Louisiana government had meanwhile launched a naval attack on the pirate community, seizing the island, half a million dollars worth of booty and some of Lafitte's pirate lieutenants.

After the war the brothers were pardoned by President Madison and embarked on further piratical exploits sailing new clippers built in Baltimore. Jean established a new base on Galveston Island off the Texas coast after expelling the French privateer Louis d'Avry and his 500 men. He convinced d'Avry who sailed with letters from Mexico's rebel republican government to assist the republicans in their struggle against the Spanish government of Mexico. Spain was concerned about a postwar resurgence of piracy in the Gulf of Mexico. Père Antoine, a Spanish spy who was a priest in New Orleans at the cathedral of St. Louis had recruited Jean to help solve the problem. Jean was on the payroll of the Spanish authorities in Havana as an agent for $18,000 a year at the same time that he fortified Galveston Island and enrolled the forty or so remaining inhabitants into his ranks forcing them to swear allegiance to the free republic of Mexico.

Lafitte ignored both the Spanish and American governments once he had taken Galveston and accepted the position of Governor of the island from the Mexicans. Bachelors lived in separate barracks from the married pirates in the island commune which Lafitte ruled with an iron hand leading his men out to indiscriminately pirate the ships of all nations. In 1818 nature answered Spanish and American prayers by devastating the pirate settlement in a hurricane. Lafitte sold the island's slaves to finance reconstruction but the community faltered and continued harassment by U.S. navy patrols led Lafitte to abandon Galveston in the spring of 1821. An American naval officer who saw him then described him as "a stout, rather gentlemanly personage, some five feet ten in height, dressed very simply in a foraging cap and blue frock-coat of villainous fit; his complexion, like most Creoles, olive . . . " He had a mild manner but flashing black eyes which gave the officer the feeling that when provoked the "*Capitano* might be . . . a very ugly customer."

For over a century Jean's fate remained a mystery. He was reported to have slipped away in his lean clipper-built schooner to meet an early death in southern Mexico. Other reports placed him in Paris. Recent research indicates that far from perishing he changed his name to John Lafflin and became a respected merchant and shipowner in Charleston, South Carolina. In 1832 he married the daughter of his business partner, Edward Mortimore and moved with her and their infant son to St. Louis. Lafitte-Lafflin was still a man of surprises for in 1847 he went to Europe where he attended various secret revolutionary conclaves. He returned to the States with copies of some of the writings of Marx and Engels, whom he had met. At his request, Lafitte's father-in-law sent the works to a young congressman, Abraham Lincoln. Lafitte may have helped financed publication of the *Communist Manifesto* which brought to international attention an alternative method of organizing society which pirates had been practicing since antiquity.

None of the estimated 10,000 privateers who found themselves out of work at the conclusion of the European wars were as complex as Jean Lafitte. But like him they were propelled onto the seas again. Lacking his talent and direction they either set out on their own, plundering maritime commerce which was booming thanks to the Industrial Revolution or joined the piratical rebel navies of the Spanish colonies. The pirate pestilence reached its peak in the Caribbean during the 1820s and early 1830s. The waters around Cuba, Puerto Rico, the Virgin Islands and off the coast of Central America were especially dangerous. In 1824 the U.S. Government despatched naval ships to Cuba to attack nests of pirates; a mission which was recalled on the floor of the U.S. Senate in January of 1991 during debate on the war in the Persian Gulf. During the same period former privateers attacked shipping in the Atlantic, the Guinea Coast and the Arabian Sea.

Privateering commissions were easily available from the Spanish government whose *guarda-costas* inflicted so much damage on British and American ships. The new Hispanic republics which Simón Bolívar led to freedom also offered letters of marque such as those Lafitte procured from Colombia. The Spanish Indies had been in decline since the sixteenth century. Generations of corrupt officials, long-distance administration and neglect of anything peripheral to the production of treasure took their toll. There had been a brief period of economic revival in the late 1700s but it was cut short by Spanish entanglements in the Napoleonic Wars. With her energies otherwise employed, Spain could do little to suppress the revolutionary movements which flared first in Mexico in 1810 and then burst into flame throughout Central and South America.

By 1821, when Mexico declared her independence, all of Central America had thrown off the Spanish yoke. That was also the year that Spain ceded Florida to the United States. Spain could not police Florida's extensive coast and innumerable keys which were perfect pirate hideouts. In 1817 Sir Gregor MacGregor, a veteran of the European Napoleonic campaigns, who had served as a general with Bolívar in the Venezuelan revolution, went on a pirate binge and seized Amelia Island, off the northeast coast of Florida. Other pirates joined him there, including Louis d'Avry formerly of Galveston. The sea outlaws flew the new republican flags of Venezuela, Nueva Granada, Mexico and Rio de la Plata over Spanish Florida and made Amelia Island and nearby Fernandina a bustling pirate and smuggling port where slaves and other goods were exchanged. Many slaves were smuggled up the Saint Mary's River and into Georgia. A U.S. naval squadron drove the pirates out and held the island for Spain until she ceded all of Florida to the United States. MacGregor sailed off to Jamaica where he organized a company of rovers which sailed south to plunder Spanish ships. They took and briefly held Portobelo, by then a sleepy, decaying town which retained little of its former glory.

Spain's long tenure in the Indies was over by 1825 although she didn't recognize the independence of her former colonies until 1845. With no organized navies the struggling republics had to rely on privateers of many nations. Privateering became synonymous with violent piracy as seaborne scum cashed in on the struggle between moribund Spain and her mutinous colonies devastating shipping worldwide. Men of all nationalities and races enlisted under the new flags, signing on the small, swift schooners, sloops and brigantines that terrorized the Caribbean from 1815 on. The majority of the ships and their crews were American. They sailed out of Buenos Aires and Cartagena in ever widening sorties. In 1819 forty-four American ships were plundered in the West Indies, many of them by American privateers who blatantly abused their commissions which limited attacks to Spanish ships. Privateering vessels crisscrossed the Atlantic to plunder ships off Portugal, in the Mediterranean and even in the distant Black Sea.

The most notorious of these wretches were Cofrecina, Benito De Soto, Diabolito and an Irishman named Guillermo Brown who sailed from Buenos Aires, which from 1815 was headquarters for particularly vicious pirates who infested the Caribbean. Cofrecina was a nasty character who slaughtered every man aboard a Spanish vessel captured off St. Thomas and marooned all the female passengers on Sail Rock, a deserted cay. He then sailed off to dispose of the ship's considerable booty and when he came back for them they were gone. Apparently they had thrown themselves into the sea rather than fall into the hands of the pirates. Cofrecina had his comeuppance in 1825 when a U.S. armed schooner commanded by Hull Foote, a young midshipman chased him down and defeated him in a raging battle. The pirate and his crew were tried and convicted in Puerto Rico by Spanish authorities and garroted to death. Foote who went on to attack slaving ships off the African coast, was an ardent teetotaller and deserves mention as commander of the first temperance ship in the U.S. Navy.

The bold career of Rhode Island born Charles Gibbs, "notorious adept in piracy and blood," sent many a shudder down nineteenth-century spines. An 1831 book *The Great Events of Our Past Century* by R. M. Devens devoted a chapter to the pirate which included the following verse:

> Leading a pirate's crew,
> O'er the dark sea we flew,
> Wild was the life we led,
> Many the souls that sped,
> Many the hearts that bled,
> By our stem orders.[1]

The author outlined "His bold, Enterprising, Desperate, And Successful War for Many Years, Against the Commerce of all Nations—Terror Inspired by His Name as the Scourge of the Ocean and the Enemy of Mankind.—Scores of Vessels Taken, Plundered, and Destroyed.—Their Crews and Passengers, Male and Female, Instantly Butchered . . . Booty Sold in Havana.—No Lives Spared.—One Beautiful Girl Excepted.—Atrocious Use Made of Her" and chronicled his "Black Record of Crime and Blood"[2] which was brought to an end in 1831 when he was hanged at New York.

Gibbs served with distinction as a seaman aboard the *Chesapeake* during the War of 1812. He was captured when the British frigate *Shannon* bested the *Chesapeake* in the famous battle and spent the remainder of the war in England's bleak Dartmoor Prison. Gibbs returned to Boston where he borrowed money to open a grocery on Ann Street. A contemporary record describes the shop which also sold liquor as being near "what was then called the 'Tin Pot', a place full of abandoned women and dissolute fellows." His best customers were "loose girls who paid him in their coin, which though it answered his purposes, would neither buy him goods or pay his rent. . . . "

So Gibbs soon found himself out of business and compelled to sign on an Argentinean privateer. A dispute among the officers and crew over prize money turned into a mutiny and Gibbs emerged in command of the ship, setting those who refused to follow him ashore on the wild coast of Florida. Using Cuba as a base he racketed around the Caribbean with a squadron of schooners plundering and raising hell. His men, declaring "dead men tell no tales," killed those who refused to join when their ship was taken. On at least one occasion he burned a merchantman crew alive and once hacked off a captain's arms and legs. A beautiful young woman taken from a Dutch ship and "made atrocious use of" by the pirates for two months at their fortified stronghold on Cuba's western tip was poisoned when they tired of her.

In 1821 the situation was so alarming that the United States sent six warships and three gunboats to patrol the Caribbean and the Gulf of Mexico. Gibbs and his crew of a hundred were surprised by the brigantine *Enterprise* off Cape Antonio, Cuba while attacking three merchantmen.

Gibbs escaped to shore and plunged into the jungle with sixty of his villains but forty were apprehended. Gibbs surfaced in New York City some time later. A woman who was a cleverer thief than he stole Gibbs's heart and cleaned him out of his plundered gold or so the story goes and he was forced to return to a life of crime on the high seas. In 1831 he was finally caught, tried and convicted and hanged, dressed in "a blue round-about jacket and trousers, with a foul anchor on his right arm." His body was given to New York's College of Physicians and Surgeons for dissection.

Privateers were boldly using such American ports as Philadelphia, New Orleans and Baltimore. They preyed on ships of all nations with fine impartiality. In 1821 Captain Lincoln's *Exertion* was seized off Florida's Key Largo by a fairly representative bunch of pirates. He reported: "It is impossible to give an account of the filthiness of this crew . . . In their appearance they were terrific, wearing black whiskers and long beards, the receptacles of dirt and vermin. They used continually the most profane language; had frequent quarrels, and so great was their love of gambling that the captain would play cards with the meanest man on board."[3] Captain Lincoln was lucky to survive his ordeal. A less fortunate merchantman captain was forced to lie on a pile of turpentine soaked oakum (hemp fibers) which was also stuffed into his mouth and then set on fire after his arms had been severed at the elbows.

In 1823 one Josef Perez was tried in New York City on charges stemming from the piracy of the American merchant ship *Bee*. A transcript of the proceedings reveals the scavenging nature of the thugs who practiced during piracy's waning days. The *Bee* was en route from Charleston to Cuba with a cargo earlier rovers would have scorned: soap, flour, rice, butter and tin wares. Captain Edward Johnson, her owner and captain, testified that on August 14, 1822 what appeared to be a Baltimore-built schooner of about thirty tons "came from under the land of Cuba Shore, and hailed us with Buenos Ayres' colors flying and directed us to heave to." About twenty Spanish speaking pirates swarmed aboard the *Bee*. They beat the crew with cutlasses and ropes, broke open the hatches and rifled the ship of everything aboard.

Captain Johnson and his men were made to pitch the pirate vessel's ballast rocks overboard to make room for stowing prize goods. The *Bee* was taken in closer to shore. The crew was locked in the cabin at night and allowed on deck during the day to watch as small Cuban boats came out from the beach to buy the pirated cargo.

The pirates were angry at having found no more than seven dollars on board and periodically threatened to hang the cook from the yardarm. Captain Johnson testified he kept mum about the thirty-seven doubloons he had hidden in the keelson. The pirates detained their victims for a week, transferring them to a prize British schooner which stayed farther offshore. The *Bee* was beached and then burned. Before casting their captives adrift in a leaky skiff with a tattered sail and broken oars, the pirates made a final search for gold. Captain Johnson testified that Josef Perez, the prisoner at the bar, pulled off the captain's clothes, inspected his shoes and cut the lining out of his hat searching for gold. The crew drifted into Matanzas after five grueling days.

The man on trial spoke not a word of English but many spoke on his behalf, including Don Thomas Staughton, the Spanish Consul in New York, who helped convince the jury that the prisoner before them was "a destitute foreigner, an unfortunate and helpless stranger," and a scapegoat. Perez who had been arrested on the streets of New York when a former crewman of the *Bee* spotted him was acquitted. The court was aware that hanging Perez might very well lead to reprisals from Havana "that very center of piratical ground."

The Buenos Aires government was alarmed at the excesses of the "patriots" sailing under their flag and outlawed privateering in October 1821. The magnitude of piratical activities and the pirate penchant for slaughtering everyone on captured ships so as to leave no witnesses forced the hand of the United States Government. In 1822 Congress passed an appropriation of half a million dollars, an amazing amount for the time, to establish a squadron of pirate chasers for the Caribbean. The man chosen to head the so-called "Mosquito Fleet" was Commodore David Porter. Under his brilliant direction a fleet was organized that was perfectly suited to the mission of exterminating the pirates from the reef-strewn West Indian waters. Porter selected eight shallow draft, swift schooners of the type the pirates themselves used, a Connecticut steamship which was the first of its kind ever used in naval engagements, a merchantman with six camouflaged cannon to act as a decoy and five-oared barges to use as landing craft.

He enlisted 1,150 sailors and marines and set to work. In April 1823 the "Mosquito Fleet" attacked the dread Cuban pirate Diabolito and killed 70 of his crew. Within the next two years American forces captured 1,300 pirates and seized or destroyed 79 pirate vessels in the Caribbean and South Atlantic. By 1830 piracy had all but vanished from the seas where men had sailed in fear for hundreds of years.

A few villains remained at large. The most savage was Benito De Soto, who is sometimes confused with Benito Bonito or Bernardo De Soto (mate on the pirate ship *Panda*). He was a born to Portuguese parents in La Coruña, Spain. In 1827 he sailed as mate on a slaver out of Buenos Aires bound for Africa. While the captain of the ship, a large brigantine named the *Defensor de Pedro* was ashore, De Soto seized the ship's command. De Soto cast off those who refused to mutiny and slit the first mate's throat. Renaming the ship the *Black Joke* De Soto embarked on a pirate cruise in the South Atlantic.

He attacked the *Morning Star*, an unarmed Indiaman off Ascension Island on February 21, 1832. The captain of the badly damaged ship was ordered to report at once to De Soto. The pirate captain felt the Englishman was dawdling and when he arrived he shouted, "Thus does Benito De Soto reward those who disobey him" and raising his cutlass split the captain's head in two. He allowed his crew to rape the women passengers who were the wives and daughters of English officials and soldiers on their way home. When they had finished their insane orgy, the pirates threw all the survivors into the hold, locked the hatches and bored holes in the hull before sailing off to further pillage, rape and slaughter around the Azores. The *Morning Star* survivors whom he had left to drown managed to open the hatches, plug the leaks and sail into port.

De Soto wrecked the *Black Joke* on the Spanish coast near Cádiz where he was heading to sell accumulated plunder. He and the crew posing as legitimate merchantmen proceeded to Cádiz where some of the crew were arrested in a tavern when drink had loosened their tongues. De Soto thought himself safe in Gibraltar but one of the *Morning Star* survivors recognized him in a tavern and he was arrested and tried. Found guilty De Soto was hanged.

On September 20, 1832 the American brig *Mexican* en route from Salem to Rio de Janeiro with 20,000 dollars in silver hidden aboard was seized by the *Panda* flying the "patriotic colors" of Colombia. John Battis of Salem, of the *Mexican*, provided a vivid description of the Spanish pirate schooner. The *Panda* was typical of pirate ships of the late period which were dual purpose slavers and pirate ships. "She was a long low straight topsail schooner of about 150 tons burthen, painted black with a narrow white streak, a large figure-head with a horn of plenty painted white; masts raked aft, and a large main topsail, a regular Baltimore clipper. We could not see her name. She carried thirty or more men, with a long thirty-two pound swivel amidships, with four brass guns, two on each side." The *Mexican* couldn't outrun the pirate ship and her two guns, short carronades, were worthless since there was no shot to fit.

The pirates, pistols in hand and long knives up their sleeves, teemed aboard and asked the captain for his papers and the cargo manifest which listed one hundred bags of saltpeter and one hundred chests of tea but not the silver stored in ten boxes under the cabin floor. Pedro Gibert, the pirate captain, told his men to search the *Mexican* thoroughly. When they asked what to do with the crew he shrugged and said "Dead cats don't mew. . . . " The pirates found the $20,000 and some small caches be-longing to crew members but they failed to find $700 the captain had in the false bottom of his sea chest. Fortunately, they also overlooked the ship's compass, quadrant and sextant which the captain had hidden in the steerage at the first sight of the *Panda*.

The prisoners were locked in the pitch-black forecastle while the pirates looted the ship and then destroyed her rigging and sails. They filled the galley with combustible tar and oakum and then set it on fire before sailing away from the smouldering pyre. The crew broke out of the fo-recastle but were clever enough to only partially extinguish the blaze, leaving plumes of smoke ascending into the air which the pirates took to be the end of the affair. Once the *Panda* was over the horizon, the Ameri-cans managed to repair enough of the damage to set a homeward course, reaching Salem after five weeks at sea.

Gibert and some of his men were taken when their ship ran aground on the coast of West Africa. The H.M.S. *Curlew* attacked the *Panda* but most of the pirates escaped to shore and fled into the jungle. Twelve were captured by a native chief who turned them over to the British. They were sent in irons to England and then in 1834 were extradited to Boston for trial. Ruiz, the ship's carpenter was judged insane and spared. Another man, the mate De Soto, was pardoned by President Jackson because of an incident that had occurred three years earlier when De Soto rescued seventy victims from the *Minerva* which shipwrecked on the Bahamas reefs.

The hanging of five of the *Panda* crew brought the curtain down on three hundred years of systematic plundering in American waters. Twenty-four years later privateering was officially declared unlawful by the seven signatories of the Declaration of Paris thus ending three cen-turies of nationally sanctioned pirating. In scattered incidents, notably during the rum-running Prohibition era, pirates continued to annoy ships but they were gadflies compared to the masterful rovers who put a men-acing sea curse on the Caribbean for so long. Pirates and privateers were major players in the history of the New World. The Caribbean was their nursery, the training ground for a fraternity that ranged round the globe. Pirates and privateers were indispensable to European expansion over-seas, to nations vying for power and maritime supremacy.

Pioneers on a treasure filled frontier, the pirates of the Caribbean were misfits of the civilizations for which they were the vanguard. The world has seen the last of the classic pirates who ranged from gentlemen adven-turers to freedom-seekers to mercurial psychopaths. Today men who are socially, politically or economically at odds with society have many other outlets. The men who had been innovators in marine technology became its victims. The change from sail to steam and the development of electronic inventions from radio to radar to satellite observation from space dealt piracy, already wounded by international governmental cooperation, a near mortal blow.

But pirates, like cockroaches, will always be with us. In fact, in the past twenty years they have multiplied like cockroaches. After almost a century and a half of relative tranquillity, there has been a truly frightening resurgence of piracy on a global scale. Pirates infest the sea-lanes from the west coast of Africa to the eastern Mediterranean, from the west coast of South America to the South China Sea and prowl among the islands of the Caribbean and along the old Spanish Main. Coastal travel is risky around India and Sri Lanka. It is dangerous off Ethiopia and Somalia on Africa's northeast coast and off Mauritania, the Western Sahara and especially hazardous off the West African nations of Nigeria, Liberia and Senegal, a zone pirates have haunted for centuries. There are so many pirates around Lagos, Nigeria that ships remain in motion, tying up for only as long as it takes to load and unload.

The problem with harbor pirates in Lagos illustrates the situation in much of the developing world where ports are not equipped to handle the volume of incoming vessels unloading manufactured goods and picking up oil, raw materials and agricultural products. Endemic corruption going back to the African chieftains who made deals with the slavers pervades every transaction. Bribes are necessary for everything, but even when paid, there is such a dearth of capacity that ships back up and if they are berthed they are ransacked. One tanker's crew was so terrorized by a pirate attack that at the next port every single man aboard gave notice. The government has been slow to ameliorate the situation and international shippers have had to take their own, sometimes unusual, measures. In 1983 the Norwegian Karlander Line took advantage of the Hausa tribe's reputation as fierce warriors by posting Hausa guards armed with traditional bows and arrows aboard ships at anchor.

Today's pirates are faceless, nameless and routinely violent, adhering to the credo that dead men tell no tales. There is no aura of romance about their exploits. Thousands of sailors, fishermen, yachtsmen and boat-borne refugees have been murdered in the past decade by maritime outlaws, or cast adrift and are presumed dead. No group has suffered more than the hapless refugees from Vietnam and Cambodia. For years the "boat people" packed on rickety craft have gone from one nightmare to another, easy prey for pirates who know they carry their life savings in the form of small ingots of gold.

Men are frequently killed or forced overboard, women and children are raped repeatedly and often clubbed or thrown into the sea. It has been estimated that 50 percent of refugee craft are attacked at least once. One ill-fated boat which set out with 380 Vietnamese from 66 families was boarded by Thai fishermen turned pirates. who robbed the passengers and raped the women and children for hours in what was the first of twenty-three attacks. In the 1970s as many as sixty five thousand refugees a month embarked across the Gulf of Siam on a quest for sanctuary. Today the numbers are way down. Malaysia and Thailand no longer welcome refugees. But many still flee and, in spite of a ten-year joint Thai-United Nations anti-piracy program, the number of dead and missing from boats reaching Thailand and Malaysia increased from 92 in 1987 to 750 in 1989.

The toll is high in economic terms too. According to Eric Ellen, director of the International Maritime Bureau in London, annual losses due to maritime crime, including piracy, amount to a staggering $13 billion. The pirate menace threatens oceangoing vessels as well as small boats. Ironically, technological advances have made even giant tankers vulnerable to attack. A fraction of the men once needed to crew a merchant ship can handle a modem cargo ship. At night only one or two men may be on watch and pirates can slip up to a giant vessel in small wooden speedboats or motorized outriggers which are undetected by radar systems. Statistics compiled by The U.S. Maritime Administration show that since 1986 more than seventy oceangoing vessels around the world have been attacked. Kevin Takarski, one of the analysts who compiled the list admits the list probably reflects only 40 percent of the total pirate attacks.

Shippers are wary of reporting crimes at sea because of spiraling insurance premiums. Reported annual losses in the Philippines are currently $100 million according to Lloyd's List International. Some ships are recovered. The oil tanker *Patrick G.* was found emptied of its cargo after it had been seized by brash pirates right in Manila's harbor. The crew had been thrown overboard but fishermen rescued the captain and one seaman.

Ellen emphasizes that ships can and do vanish. On October 15, 1990, for example, the 17,000 ton *Zilwena*, a very big ship laden with cement simply disappeared from Manila Bay. In August of 1989, pirates off Iligan, a port on Mindanao in the southern Philippines, took a ship loaded with 4,500 tons of steel. They kept three crewmen as hostages, cast twenty-seven others adrift in a rubber raft and vanished. Word had it the ship went to China. The majority of "phantom ships" in the Philippines have been singled out as targets by pirates who capture ships to order. The going rate ranges from $50,000 to $300,000. Airports everywhere are notified when an aircraft is stolen but no corresponding system exists in the maritime world to track missing vessels. Harbor and coast guard officials around the globe are bribed to furnish bogus papers and new call signs. The Law of the Sea treaty defines piracy as an act that takes place on the high seas for private gain. Since most pirate attacks occurs in coastal waters or disputed zones they are not subject to the jurisdiction of international law. There is growing concern that the surge in piracy increases the likelihood of a major environmental disaster. Michael Gray, a writer for Lloyd's List International, the daily shipping newspaper published in London, worries that a tanker carrying oil or chemicals might wreck and spill its contents during a pirate attack.

The figures for pirated yachts, fishing boats and refugee boats run into the thousands. In the past two years some fifty ships were seized by armed pirates off the Mediterranean coast along Lebanon. The pirate plague is particularly virulent in Southeast Asia. The most perilous areas for navigation are the Phillip Channel and the narrow Strait of Malacca between Indonesia and Singapore, the South China Sea, the Sulu Sea and the Celebes Sea. In the eighteen months prior to mid-1986 an estimated 560 fishing boats and motor launches were taken by pirates, many of whom were Moslem rebels from the southern Philippines. In 1988 the Singapore Shipping Association reported ten pirate attacks on oceangoing vessels. In 1989 there were three but in 1990 at least twenty-five oil tankers and freighters were taken by pirates near Singapore.

On September 21, 1990 four vessels were attacked. In one instance pirates in a speedboat came alongside the 20,000-ton Australian-registered *TNT Express* about twenty miles south of Singapore and boarded her, using the pirate's traditional grappling hook. The pirates, one with a *ninja*-type mask, ransacked the ship while holding the captain at knifepoint. A few days later the *Brussel*, her sister ship, was attacked as she left Singapore harbor.

The Philippines with more than 7,000 coral-girt islands is a pirate's dream. The beautiful archipelago was once a yachtsman's paradise too but few venture there these days. Vicious pirates prey on vessels of all sizes. More than a dozen oceangoing ships have been stolen in Philippine waters since 1982 and some two hundred people have been killed. At least five freighters were seized in the past two years and turned into "phantom ships" which steam from port to port plundering cargoes and changing names. One Philippine vessel underwent five changes of identification. On September 15, 1988 a gang of disaffected officers from the country's miniscule navy seized the *Silver Med*, a 5,350-ton cargo ship in Manila harbor. Two weeks later the ship now called the *Lambamba* was sighted in Singapore waters. Subsequently she eluded an Indonesian patrol off Sabah. According to shipping reports the vessel, now called the *Searex*, took on a cargo of plywood, in Borneo. She became the *Star Ace* and, finally, the *Sanford* which ran aground in January of 1989 off western Luzon.

A world away in waters around South America, latter-day pirates menace shipping approaching Ecuador, Brazil, Colombia and Panama. In December of 1989, for example, pirates seized a Liberian-flagged container ship, the *Asian Senator* from anchorage in Port Colón, at the Caribbean entrance to the Panama Canal. Guayaquil, Ecuador's chief port, has been the focus of a score of major pirate attacks. On Brazil's east coast at Aratu six pirates brandishing knives, machine guns and pistols boarded a large chemical tanker, the *Solt Eagle* in December of 1989. They wounded three of the crew, ransacked the ship, stealing more than $15,000 and then rowed away from the giant ship in a small boat.

In the past several years yachtsmen and fishermen in the Caribbean and Gulf of Mexico have enjoyed relative calm, although there are still instances of piracy and hijacking. But it is nothing like the 1970s and 1980s when sailors in the Caribbean had more to fear from pirates than at any time since the 1830s. Marijuana, cocaine and arms have replaced gold and silver as booty. Until 1970 cocaine was as rare as frankincense in the United States; its use restricted to high altitude farmers in Peru and Bolivia. Marijuana had been around for decades but until the 1970s the supply was small and Colombia barely figured as an exporter. Then came the drug explosion. Massive amounts of marijuana and cocaine and smaller amounts of heroin have poured into North America, much of it through the southeastern coast, especially Florida, where drugs have had a major impact on the economies of Key West and Miami.

U.S. Customs figures of confiscated drugs reflect a steady increase in volume through the mid-1980's. In 1975 Customs seized 728.5 pounds of cocaine. In 1979 the number almost doubled to 1,438.1 pounds. A year later the figure was 4,742.9 pounds and in 1982 Customs confiscated 11,149.5 pounds of cocaine. These amounts represented a very small fraction of the cocaine headed for American markets. Seizures of marijuana, again representing only a tiny portion of shipments from Caribbean ports show a dramatic increase in volume between 1975 when Customs seized almost 500,000 pounds nationwide to 1978 when they confiscated 4.5 million pounds of the aromatic leaf. In 1982 the newly created South Florida Task Force alone seized 500,000 pounds.

Eighty-five percent of all the cocaine and marijuana that flooded North America in the 1970s and 1980s passed through Caribbean ports once favored by the pirates of yore including Cartagena, Baranquilla, and Santa Marta in Colombia and Kingston in Jamaica. Vast amounts of drugs were transhipped in the waters around the islands of the Caribbean which provided ideal transfer points for drugs destined for the United States.

The Bahamas by virtue of geography played the starring role in drug smuggling and twentieth century-Caribbean piracy. Tiny Norman's Cay was turned into a smuggler's base by Carlos Lehder, the Colombian cartel kingpin who bought some land there. In 1978 Lehder's goons ran residents and owners of vacation houses off the cay, bulldozed extensively with heavy machinery brought in by landing craft and constructed an airfield with two runways. Planes landed around the clock with cargoes of drugs which were transferred to fast boats for the short run to the Florida coast. Bimini, the island closest to Florida was also a haven where drug smugglers openly pursued their business with planes and boats.

Typically marijuana which is bulky and less valuable per pound is loaded on mother ships in Columbian ports; small freighters, trawlers, or yachts which may have been modified for drug-smuggling to provide concealment in false compartments. Then it is transfered to speedboats or small planes which carry it to the U.S. coast. Cocaine enters the country in a thousand guises, hidden in sea or air cargo; amid fresh flowers, concealed in terra cotta statues or inside human carriers called "mules." A great deal of both marijuana and cocaine enters the country in slower craft from catamarans to shrimpers or has been dumped from small aircraft flying low and at night to avoid radar detection. Pilots have made as much as $300,000 for a single mission. Some of them never had the chance to try again. Many planes crashed.

The majority of drugs come in by sea. In 1978 Customs seized 334 vessels involved in smuggling operations. Two years later they seized 1,319 vessels, almost four times as many. These were the tip of the iceberg. With the explosion of marijuana and cocaine smuggling piracy reappeared because smugglers require a never ending supply of craft to bring in the contraband. A 1974 report issued by the U.S. House of Representatives Merchant Marine and Fisheries committee concluded that, "Hundreds of crew members, passengers and boats have disappeared in the southeastern Atlantic and the Gulf of Mexico . . . A great percentage of the victims were actual or suspected targets of drug smugglers who have found hijacking can be accomplished easily and the owners of the vessels disposed of without much fear of apprehension." In 1972 and 1973 at least 496 private yachts, cabin cruisers and motor vessels vanished in the Caribbean with no distress signal and no sign of shipwreck. Congressman John M. Murphy, noted in a 1984 hearing before the U.S. House Subcommittee on Merchant Marine and Fisheries that "countless yachts were disgorging their cargoes of marijuana, hashish, cocaine, and heroin." He asked "Where did these boats come from? . . . "

They came from a variety of sources during the two decades of rampant smuggling. Boats were stolen from marinas and back yard anchorages.

Stealing boats is laughably easy. In the 1970s the United Boat Owners of America reported that 90,000 boats of all sizes were stolen each year. They were also "borrowed" or rented from owners not averse to making a huge amount tax-free by winking an eye at the obvious intended use of their vessels. Anomalies multiplied. Motor cruisers were seen moving through night without lights. Fishing boats were seen with no nets, shrimp boats with impossibly rusted gear. The names of vessels were crudely painted over. Wooden plaques with unregistered names were hung on the transom to conceal a boat's real identity. In the early years of the drug boom before the organized syndicates controlled the business there were thousands of amateurs playing the game. It seemed glamorous and exciting and it was hard to resist such easy money for so little work.

Increasingly smuggling craft were bought with cash. In the mid-1970s It wasn't unusual for a shaggy-haired buyer, a "grasshopper" as they are called in south Florida, to pull two hundred thousand dollars or more out of a paper bag to purchase a Donzi, Scarab or Cigarette, the sleek speedboats favored by smugglers for taking drugs from a mother ship to shore. Not surprisingly they didn't mind that insurance brokers wouldn't underwrite policies for them. They seldom used the vessels more than once or twice. Boats were scuttled or abandoned when danger threatens. Beachgoers frequently found "square groupers," water-logged bales of marijuana, on the beach or bobbing close to shore from a delivery gone wrong. The number of these incidents increased as the U.S. Coast Guard stepped up its intervention program. Many boats have shipwrecked in the dark of unfamiliar shallows. Many yachts were hijacked by crew members taken on by unwary owners or were hijacked from drug runners by others of the same stripe.

Piracy motivated by drug smuggling accounts for many disappearances on the high seas. Pirates have attacked vessels they wished to use as drug runners and they have attacked vessels loaded with drugs. Sometimes intended victims overcame their attackers. In 1982, at Joulter's Cay, off the northern tip of Andros, three pirates boarded a thirty-seven-foot cruiser belonging to Lawrence Halloway, a retired Pan-Am pilot. As one of them held a knife at Halloway's throat, Mrs. Halloway came up the companionway with a .45 caliber pistol. The pirate was distracted for a second and Halloway grabbed the gun and shot the man weilding the knife and then fatally wounded the other two when they tried to overpower him. Halloway was cleared by Bahamian authorities, but not without an outcry from the local villagers. In an unusual incident in the Bahamas a boat carrying bales of marijuana was buzzed by a plane with bogus U.S. Coast Guard markings. The alarmed crew threw the entire cargo overboard, only to see it retrieved by accomplices of the plane's crew who arrived on the scene almost at once. Drugs are not the goal in all Caribbean pirate attacks. A German national spent two and a half years in jail on the island of Martinique for hijacking four yachts for resale.

In the mid 1970s leading yachting publications including the *Yachtsman's Guide to the Bahamas* and *Yachting World* warned of the danger of pirate attack on boats sailing in the Caribbean, especially around the Bahamas, and in the Gulf of Mexico. In 1977 the Coast Guard issued an unprecedented warning to Caribbean-bound recreational vessels, urging special caution in the Bahamas where piracy and hijacking (internal take-over of a vessel) were rampant. The Caribbean is safer and quieter now than during the "wild-west" days of the mid 1970s. Pirate incidents diminished significantly after 1981. The concentration of the drug business in the hands of the Columbian cartel families and, to a much lesser extent, organized Jamaican organizations, changed the nature of drug smuggling. The insatiable appetite for boats to carry drugs disappeared as the cartel streamlined shipments on larger vessels and by air. The U.S. Government's declared war on drugs while not wildly successful has made the Caribbean relatively safe for pleasure cruising, although the Spanish Main is still hazardous and sporadic pirate attacks are reported around the Bahamas. Anyone sailing in the drug smuggling zone is still highly vigilant and often armed.

For years the the multiagency Blue Lightning Strike Force relied on a system of "condo radars" along the South Florida oceanfront to help intercept boats ferrying drugs from mother ships lying off the coast. The chain of twenty-five drug-tracking radar units located atop tall buildings, many of them condominiums, became obsolete as smugglers perfected counterdetection methods and more sophisticated methods. In January, 1991 the Customs Service announced the costly system would be dismantled. The radar's range is twelve miles but airdrops are now commonly made 150 to 250 miles offshore to boats with elaborate hidden compartments, which mingle with the thousands of pleasure boats that daily go in and out of southeastern ports.

Piracy will never disappear. Economic incentive which propelled the earliest pirates on ancient seas remains strong today. Piracy has flourished in times marked by social and economic inequity, political unrest, restrictive trade and a corrupt establishment. Above all piracy takes advantage of jurisdictional confusion and pirates plunder with impunity when the law and its enforcers are weak. In the past national rivalries have abetted pirates but in many areas of concern the world appears to be moving toward an era of global cooperation.

Nearly three thousand years ago on the Mediterranean island of Rhodes, Greek thinkers and merchants formulated the concept that the seas should be governed by one law. The exact origins are cloudy, but portions of the law were subsequently incorporated into the Roman code. Through the ages there were countless conventions and intermittent efforts to establish international maritime law but it wasn't until December, 1982 that delegates from around the globe gathered at Montego Bay, Jamaica to sign the Law of the Sea Treaty. One of the areas this immensely significant document deals with is crime on the seas, although it will be years before the desired goal is realized.

The sea is no longer the frontier. Even as we grapple with the rule of law on the oceans a new element beckons pirates of the future. Mankind looks to the skies beyond our watery planet for new worlds to conquer. Earthbound governments have yet to address the inevitable questions that will arise just as they did during the centuries when European exploration of the Americas made the Caribbean an international arena for piracy and privateering. We are on the threshold of interplanetary travel and commerce. Who knows? As tempting cargoes hurtle through oceanic space, pirates and privateers may once again play a pioneer role in mankind's expansion.

NOTES

1. Verse on Gibbs, Devons, R. M., *Our First Century: being a popular descriptive portraiture of one hundred great and memorable events . . . in the history of our country*, C. A. Nicholas, Chicago, 1880, p. 314, (first published in 1831).

2. More on Gibbs, op. sit., p. 318.

3. Captain Lincoln of the *Exertion*, Lincoln, Captain Branabas, *Narrative of the Capture, Suffering and Escape of Captain Branabas Lincoln and his Crew . . .*, Boston: Ezra Lincoln, 1822, p. 11.

Select Bibliography

Allen, Gardner W., *A Naval History of the American Revolution*, 2 vols., New York: Corner House, 1913.

Andrews, K. R., ed. *English Privateering Voyages to the West Indies*, London: Hakluyt Society (Second Series Vol. 111), 1959.

Elizabethan Privateering, Cambridge: Cambridge University Press, 1964.

The Spanish Caribbean, Trade and Plunder 1530–1630, New Haven and London: Yale University, 1978.

Arber, E., editor, *The True Travels and Adventures of Captaine John Smith 1608–1631*, Birmingham (England) 1884.

Arciniegas, German, *The Caribbean*, translated by Harriet de Onis, New York: Knopf, 1954.

Acts of the Privy Council of England, Colonial Series, six volumes covering the years 1916–1783. London.

Ayres, P., *Voyages and Adventures of Captain B. Sharp*, London, 1684. Gainsville: Microfilms of the University of Florida.

Bell, H. C. and D. W. Parker, *Guide to British West Indian Archive Materials*, Washington: Library of Congress, 1926.

Blond, Georges *Grands Corsaires*, Paris: Presses de la Cité, 1969.

Botting, Douglas and the editors of Time-Life Books, *The Pirates*, Alexandria, Virginia, 1978.

Boxer, C. R., *The Dutch Seaborne Empire 1600–1800*, New York: Knopf, 1965. *The Portuguese Seaborne Empire 1415–1825*, New York: Knopf, 1969.

Bradleee, Francis B.C., *Piracy in the West Indies and Its Suppression*, Salem, Mass., The Essex Institute, 1923.

Braudel, Fernand, *The Structures of Everyday Life*, New York, Harper & Row, 1982.

Bridges, G. W., *The Annals of Jamaica*, London: J. Murray, 1837.

Brock, R. A., editor, *The Official Letters of Alexander Spotswood, Lieutentant Governor of the Colony of Virginia, 1710–22, 2 vols.* Richmond: Virginia Historical Society, 1882–5.

Burns, Sir Alan Cuthbert, *History of the British West Indies*, London: Allen & Unwin, 1954.

Calendar of State Papers, Colonial Series, American and West Indies 1574–1733, 27 volumes, London: Public Records Office, 1862–1939.

Calendar of State Papers, Venetian Series 1201–1652, London: Public Records Office, 1879–1916.

Cambridge History of the British Empire, Volume I, Cambridge: Cambridge University Press, 1960.

Carse, Robert, *The Age of Piracy*, New York: Rhinehart & Company, 1957.

Casson, Lionel, *The Ancient Mariners*, New York: Macmillan, 1959.

Castro y Bravo, Frederico de, *Las Naos Españolas en la carrera de las Indias*, Madrid: Editorial Volventad, 1927.

Chaunu, H. and P., *Seville et l'Atlantique*, 1504–1660, 6 vols., Paris, S.E.V.P.E.N., 1956.

Crouse, Nellie M., *French Pioneers in the West Indies 1624–1664*, New York: Columbia University Press, 1940.

   The French Struggle for the West Indies 1665–1713, New York: Columbia University Press, 1943.

Cuddy, Don, *A License For Piracy Down South*, Sea Magazine, March, 1979.

Dampier, William, *Voyages Round the World*, London: J. J. Knapton, 1729.

Defoe, Daniel (under pseudonym Captain Charles Johnson), *A General History of the Pyrates*, edited by Arthur L. Hayward, London: Routledge and Kegan Paul, 1955. (first published in 1724).

de Laet, Joannes, *Le Linschoten Vereeniging 1624–36*, 13 volumes, Amsterdam: A. Eymery, 1638.

Devens, R. M. *Our First Century: being a popular descriptive portraiture of one hundred great and memorable events . . . in the history of our country.*, C. A. Nicholas, Chicago, 1881. (first published 1831).

Drogin, Bob, "Pirates Setting Sail for New Plunder," *Los Angeles Times*, (November 27, 1990), p. H1 and H5.

Drury, Robert, *Madagascar; Or, Robert Drury's Journal.* Westport, Conn., Negro Universities Press, 1960 (reprint of 1890 edition).

Duro, Fernández Cesareo de, *La Armada Española*, nine volumes, Madrid: Museo Naval, 1895–1903.

Dutertre, Jean Baptiste, *Histoire Générale des Antilles*, Paris 1667–71.

Edwards, Bryan, *The History, Civil and Commercial, of the British Colonies in the West Indies.* London: J. Stockdale, 1801.

Ellms, Charles, *The Pirates Own Book*, Philadelphia: Thomas Copperthwaite, 1844.

Esquemelin, (Exquemelin), A. O., *The Buccaneers of America*, London: George Rutledge & Sons, 1893. (first published in 1678).

Fisher, Sir Godfrey *Barbary Legend: War, Trade and Piracy in North Africa, 1415–1830*, Oxford and New York: Oxford University Press, 1957.

Gebhardt, Victor, *Historia General de España y sus Indias*, Madrid, 1864.

Goslinga, Cornelis Ch., *The Dutch in the Caribbean*, Gainsville: University of Florida Press, 1971.

Gosse, Philip, *The History of Piracy*, London: Longmans Green, 1932.

Hakluyt, Richard, *Hakluyt's Voyages*, (selected), Boston: Hakluyt Society, 1929.

Hanson, Earl P., editor, *South From the Spanish Main*, New York: Delacorte Press, 1967.

Haring, C. H., *Trade and Navigation between Spain and the Indies*, Cambridge: Harvard University Press, 1918.

The Buccaneers in the West Indies in the Seventeenth Century, New York: E. P. Dutton, 1910.

Jameson, J. G., *Privateering and Piracy in the Colonial Period: Illustrative Documents*, New York, 1923.

Johnson, Charles Capt. (pseudonym of Daniel Defoe), *A General History of the Pirates*, London: Routledge & Kegan, 1955, (first published in 1724).

Juarez, Juan, *Piratas y Corsarios en Veracruz y Campeche*, Seville: Escuela de estudios Hispano-Americanos de Sevilla, 1972.

Kidd, William, *A Full Account of the Proceedings in relation to Capt. Kidd* (pamphlet), London: printed and sold by the booksellers of London and Westminster, 1701.

Labat, Père Jean-Baptiste, *Memoirs 1693–1705*, London: F. Cass, 1970.

Larabee, Leonard, W., editor, *The Autobiography of Benjamin Franklin*, New Haven: Yale University Press, 1964.

Le Golif, Louis, *Memoirs of a Buccaneer*, New York: Simon & Schuster, 1954. Linage, Joseph de Vieta, *Norte de la Contratacion de las Indias Occidentales*, two volumes, Seville: Talleres Bartolomé, 1671.

Lindsay, Philip, *The Great Buccaneer*, New York: Wilfrid & Funk, 1951.

Lucie-Smith, Edward, *Outcasts of the Seas*, New York and London: Paddington Press, 1978.

Lee, Robert E., *Blackbeard the Pirate*, Winston-Salem, N.C.: J. F. Blair, 1974.

Lucas, C. P. *A Historical Geography of the British Colonies*, four volumes, Oxford: Oxford University Press, 1905.

Mahan, Alfred Thayer, *The Influence of Sea Power Upon History* 1660–1783. New York, Hill & Wang, 1968.

Mannix, Daniel P., and Crowley, Malcom, *Black Cargoes: A History of the Atlantic Slave Trade*, 1518–1865. New York, Viking Press, 1962.

Martin-Nieto, Antonio, *Pirates del Pacifico*, Bilbao: Moreton, 1968.

Marx, Robert F., *The Treasure Fleets of the Spanish Main*, Cleveland and New York: World, 1968.

The Capture of the Treasure Fleet, New York, 1977. *Pirate Port*, Cleveland and New York: World, 1967.

Port Royal Rediscovered, New York: Doubleday, 1973.

Masefield, John, *On the Spanish Main*, London, Methuen, 1906.

Masía De Ros, Angeles, *Historia General de la Pirateria*, Barcelona: Editorial Mateu, 1959.

Mitchell, David, *Pirates, an Illustrated History*, London and New York: Dial Press, 1976.

Mueller, G. O. W. and Adler, Freda, *Outlaws of the Ocean*, New York: William Morrow, 1985.

Murphy, John M., Chairman, Committee on Merchant Marine and Fisheries, in cosponsoring H.R. 2538 in hearings before the Subcommittee on Coast Guard and Navigation. U.S. House of Representatives, Ninety-sixth Congress, First Session, S.N. 96-20, p. 3. Washington D.C., U.S.: Government Printing Office, 1982.

National Maritime Museum, *Piracy and Priovateering: catalogue of the library, vol. IV*, London: Her Majesty's Stationery Office, 1972.

Newton, A. P., *European Nations in the West Indies*, 1493–1688, London: A. C. Black, 1933.

Oldmixon, John, *The British Empire in America*, two volumes, London: J. Brotherton and J. Clarke, 1741.

Ormerod, Henry, *Piracy in the Ancient World*, London: Hodder and Stoughton, 1924.

Parry, J. H., *The Spanish Seaborne Empire*, London: Hutchinson, 1966. *Trade and Dominion*, London: Weidenfeld & Nicolson, 1971.

Philips, J., printer "*A Compleat Coll. of Remarkable Tryals of the Most Notorious Malefactors etc.*, two vols., London: J. Philips, 1718.

Rankin, Hugh F., *The Golden Age of Piracy*, New York: Holt, Rinehart & Winston, 1969.

Rediker, Marcus, *Between the Devil & the Deep Blue Sea*, London & New York: Cambridge University Press, 1987.

Rhode Island Pirates, *An Account of the Pirates with Divers of their Speeches, Letter and a Poem (26 executed July 19, 1723 at Newport)*, pamphlet reprinted 1769.

Roberts, W. A., *The French in the West Indies*, Indianapolis and New York: Bobbs-Merrill, 1942.

Rogers, Woodes, *A Cruising Voyage Round the World*, Magnolia, Mass., Peter Smith (reprint of 1712 edition).

Severin, Timothy, *The Golden Antilles*, London, Hamilton, 1970.

Shepard, A. M., *Sea Power in Ancient History*, Boston, Little Brown & Co., 1924.

Sloane, Sir Hans, *A Voyage to the Islands*, London, vol. I, London: printed by British Museum for the author, 1707; vol. II, London: printed by the author, 1725.

Smith, Aaron, *The Atrocities of the Pirates*, London, 1824.

Smith, John, *True Travels and Adventures*, London, 1630.

State Trials and Proceedings etc. (trials of Major Stede Bonnet and 33 others), Vol. VIII, London: Public Records Office, 1731.

Snelgrave, Captain Wiliam, *A New Account of Some Parts of Guinea and the Slave-Trade*, Portland, Ore., International Scholarly Book Service, 1972 (reprint of 1734 edition).

Thomas, Dalby, *An Historical Account of the Rise and Growth of the West India Colonies, and the Great Advantage They are to England in respect to Trade*, London, 1690.

Thrower, Rayner, *The Pirate Picture*, London: Phillimore, 1980.

Tryals of Captain John Rackham and other Pyrates, pamphlet, London, 1721.

Unwin, Rayner, *The Defeat of Sir John Hawkins*, London: Allen & Unwin, 1960.

Westergaard, W., *The Danish West Indies under Company Rule*, 1671–1754, New York, 1917.

Williams, Eric, *From Columbus to Castro*, New York: Harper & Row, 1971.

Williams, Neville, *Captains Outrageous*, New York: Weidenfeld & Nicolson, 1962.

The Sea Dogs, New York: Weidenfeld & Nicolson, 1975.

Winston, Alexander, *No Purchase, No Pay*, London: Eyre & Spottiswoode, 1970.

Woodbury, George, *The Great Days of Piracy in the West Indies*, New York: Norton, 1951.

Wright, Irene A., ed. *Spanish Documents concerning English Voyages to the Caribbean* 1527–68 (Hakluyt Society, 2nd series, vol. 62), London, 1928.

ed. *Documents Concerning English Voyages to the Spanish Main, 1569–1580* (Hakluyt Society, 2nd series, vol. 71), London, 1932.

ed. *Further English Voyages to Spanish America* (Hakluyt Society, 2nd series, vol. 99), London, 1951.

Index

Bartolome Portugues

Francis Lolonois

Roche Brasillano